Lecture Notes in Computer Scien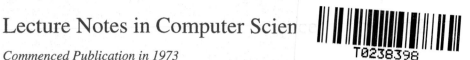

Commenced Publication in 1973
Founding and Former Series Editors:
Gerhard Goos, Juris Hartmanis, and Jan van Leeuwen

Patrick McDaniel   Shyam K. Gupta (Eds.)

Information Systems Security

Third International Conference, ICISS 2007
Delhi, India, December 16-20, 2007
Proceedings

 Springer

Volume Editors

Patrick McDaniel
The Pennsylvania State University
360A IST/CSE Building, University Park, PA 16802, USA
E-mail: mcdaniel@cse.psu.edu

Shyam K. Gupta
Indian Institute of Technology Hauz Khas
Department of Computer Science and Engineering
New Delhi, 11016, India
E-mail: skg@cse.iitd.ernet.in

Library of Congress Control Number: 2007940398

CR Subject Classification (1998): C.2.0, D.4.6, E.3, H.2.0, K.4.4, K.6.5

LNCS Sublibrary: SL 4 – Security and Cryptology

ISSN   0302-9743
ISBN-10   3-540-77085-2 Springer Berlin Heidelberg New York
ISBN-13   978-3-540-77085-5 Springer Berlin Heidelberg New York

Springer is a part of Springer Science+Business Media

springer.com

© Springer-Verlag Berlin Heidelberg 2007
Printed in Germany

Typesetting: Camera-ready by author, data conversion by Scientific Publishing Services, Chennai, India
Printed on acid-free paper   SPIN: 12199075   06/3180   5 4 3 2 1 0

Preface

The 3rd International Conference on Information System Security (ICISS 2007) was held from December 16–20, 2007 at the University of Delhi in Delhi, India. The conference was the third in the successful series of technical meetings of peer-reviewed research in information security hosted by Indian institutions. While held in India, the conference had a decidedly international flavor. This year's conference garnered submissions from all corners of the globe–the final program contains papers from the United States, India, China, Korea, Germany, France, Japan, Iran, and Italy. Support within the Indian academic community was also quite visible. The program included talks from a broad range of institutions spanning nearly the entirety of the Indian subcontinent. The broad demographic illustrated the truly exceptional growth of this relatively young conference.

This year's program contains 18 full papers, 5 short papers, and 4 keynote talk papers. The 78 papers submitted to the conference were as diverse as their authors. The submitted topics in cryptography, intrusion detection, network security, information flow systems, Web security, and many others offered a detailed view of the state of the art in information security. There were many more scientifically strong papers than could reasonably be accepted. This left the committee with a number of tough choices, but ultimately led to the technically strong and engaging program presented within these pages.

We are particularly grateful to Atul Prakash, Yves Deswarte, Sabrina de Capitani di Vimercati, and Kotagiri Rao for accepting our invitation to deliver invited talks at this year's conference. The conference was preceded by four tutorials held over the two days preceding the peer-reviewed technical content. We wish to thank the University of Delhi for providing the space to hold the conference.

We would like to acknowledge the exceptional effort by Kevin Butler in maintaining the website, marshaling the papers, and working with local organizers. He was essential to the success of this conference.

Lastly, we wish to express our deepest thanks to the members of the Program Committee, who gave their personal free time to perform the often thankless job of reviewing many papers under extremely short deadlines, and to the volunteers and local assistants who made this program a success.

December 2007

Patrick McDaniel
Shyam K. Gupta
Program Chairs

Organization

Patron   Deepak Pental
                                   Vice-Chancellor, University of Delhi, India

General Chair   N. Vijayaditya
                                   Controller of Certifying Authorities, India

Advisory Committee Chair   N. Vijayaditya
                                   Controller of Certifying Authorities, India

Program Co-chairs   Shyam K. Gupta
                                   IIT Delhi, India
                                   Patrick McDaniel
                                   Pennsylvania State University, USA

Submissions and Website Chair   Kevin Butler
                                   Pennsylvania State University, USA

Invited Talks Chair   Indrakshi Ray
                                   Colorado State University, USA

Tutorial Co-chairs   Vijay Atluri
                                   Rutgers University, USA
                                   Arun K. Pujari
                                   University of Hyderabad, India

Panel Chair   Rattan K. Datta
                                   SBBSIET, Jallandhar, India

Organizing Chair   Punam Bedi
                                   University of Delhi, India

Publicity Chairs   Chandan Majumdar
                                   Jadavpur University, India
                                   Marina Blanton
                                   University of Notre Dame, USA

Finance Chair   Shri Kant
                                   DRDO, India

Sponsorship Chair   Anuj Khare
                                   Appin Systems, India

Registration Co-chairs   Neelima Gupta
                                   University of Delhi, India
                                   Sameep Mehta
                                   IBM IRL, India
                                   D.V.L.N. Somayajulu
                                   NIT Warangal, India

Steering Committee

Sushil Jajodia	George Mason University, USA, Chair
Vijay Atluri	Rutgers University, USA
Aditya Bagchi	Indian Statistical Institute, India
A.K. Chakrabarti	Dept. of IT, Govt. of India
Prem Chand	Mahindra British Telecom, India
Shyam K. Gupta	IIT Delhi, India
Arun K. Majumdar	IIT Kharagpur, India
Chandan Mazumdar	Jadavpur University, Kolkata, India
Patrick McDaniel	Pennsylvania State University, USA
Arun K. Pujari	LNMITT Jaipur, India
Pierangela Samarati	University of Milan, Italy
R. Sekar	SUNY Stony Brook, USA
N. Sitaram	CAIR, India
Vijay Varadharajan	Macquarie University, Australia
N. Vijayaditya	Controller of Certifying Authorities, India

Program Committee

R.K. Agrawal	Jawaharlal University, India
Raj Bhatnagar	University of Cincinnati, USA
Vasudha Bhatnagar	University of Delhi, India
Joachim Biskup	University of Dortmund, Germany
Kevin Butler	Pennsylvania State University, USA
William Enck	Pennsylvania State University, USA
Deborah Frincke	Pacific Northwest National Laboratory, USA
Somnath Ghosh	University of Latrobe, Australia
Jonathan Giffin	Georgia Tech University, USA
Shantanu Godbole	IBM IRL, India
Qijun Gu	Texas State University, USA
Patrick C.K. Hung	University of Ontario Institute of Technology, Canada
Sushil Jajodia	George Mason University, USA
Karin Kalling	IBM Almaden Research Center, USA
Shri Kant	DRDO Delhi, India
Kamal Karlapalem	IIIT Hyderabad, India
Jun Li	University of Oregon, USA
Arun K. Majumdar	IIT Kharagpur, India
Chandan Mazumdar	University of Jadhavpur, India
Nasir Memon	Polytechnic University, USA
Ravi Mukkamala	Old Dominion University, USA
Lukasz Opyrchal	Miami University of Ohio, USA
Brajendra Panda	University of Arkansas, USA
Arun Pujari	University of Hyderabad, India

P. Radha Krishna	IDRBT Hyderabad, India
Indrajit Ray	Colorado State University, USA
Indrakshi Ray	Colorado State University, USA
R. Sekar	SUNY Stony Brook, USA
Sumit Sarkar	University of Texas-Dallas, USA
S. Sudarshan	IIT Bombay, India
Jaideep Vaidya	Rutgers University, USA
Alec Yasinsac	Florida State University, USA

Advisory Committee

R.K. Arora	Ex-Professor, IIT Delhi, India
Rattan K. Datta	SBBSIET, Jallandhar, India
B.N. Jain	IIT Delhi, India
J.P. Gupta	JPIT, Noida, India
M.L. Goyal	CMC, New Delhi, India
Mukesh Mohania	IBM IRL, India
Y.K. Sharma	NIC, India
S.W. Wason	Jamia Milia University, India

Local Arrangments Committee

R.K. Agrawal	JNU Delhi, India
Abhay Bansal	ITS Gaziabad, India
M.P.S. Bhatia	NSIT Delhi, India
Vasudha Bhatnagar	University of Delhi, India
Anjana Choudhary	NIC, India
Sanjay Goel	JIIT, Noida, India
Anand Gupta	NSIT, Delhi, India
Neelima Gupta	University of Delhi, India
Rakesh Gupta	NIC, India
P.K. Hazra	University of Delhi, India
M.N. Hoda	Bharti Vidyapeeth, Delhi, India
Anil K. Kaushik	MCIT, Delhi, India
Rajeev Kumar	DCE, Delhi, India
Shobhit Mahajan	University of Delhi, India
Manohar Lal	IGNOU, Delhi, India
V. Kulkarni	University of Delhi, India
Rajeev Kumar	DCE, Delhi, India
S.K. Muttoo	University of Delhi, India
B.G. Prasad	EPCET, Bangalore, India
Sangeeta Sabharwal	NSIT, Delhi, India
Gaurav Saxena	Hans Raj College, Delhi, India
Neeraj Sharma	RLA College, Delhi, India

V.K. Singh   MSIT, Delhi, India
D.V.L.N. Somayajulu   NIT, Warangal, India
R.K. Vyas   University of Delhi, India

Sponsoring Institutions

University of Delhi, India
Center for Secure Information Systems, George Mason University, USA
Systems and Information Infrastructure Security Laboratory, Pennsylvania State
    University, USA

Table of Contents

Cryptanalysis

Keynote Talk

Protocols

Keynote Talk

Short Papers

Detection and Recognition

Security in Practice – Security-Usability Chasm

Atul Prakash

Computer Science and Engineering Division,
University of Michigan, Ann Arbor, MI 48109, USA

Abstract. Computer systems security area has received increased attention from both academics and in industry. However, recent work indicates that substantial security gaps emerge when systems are deployed, even with the use of state-of-the-art security protocols. Our findings suggest that wide-spread security problems exist even when protocols such as SSL and SSH are deployed because systems today do not give security warnings properly or make it trivial for users to bypass them. Even when these protocols are deployed correctly, systems often leave themselves vulnerable to social-engineering attacks as an artifact of their design. In one of our studies, we examined the web sites of 706 financial institutions and found over 90% of them to have made poor design choices when it comes to security, even though all deployed SSL for communicating passwords and doing transactions. In another study, we examined the usage of SSH within our own department and found that most users would be susceptible to a man-in-the-middle attack. Based on our studies, we postulate that some of the most interesting challenges for security researchers and practitioners lie at the intersection of security theory, their application to practice, and user behavior. We point out some of those challenges and hope that the research community can help address them.

1 Introduction

Online activities become an integral part of our day to day life. For example, in the financial world, many people have given up conventional check writing in favor of online banking. Brokerage sites are available for people to buy and trade stock online. Financial institutions have a substantial stake in securing their customer accounts. In order to protect customer accounts, financial institutions deploy latest security technology, such as SSL/TLS [1] (originally developed by Netscape), and employ security specialists to design their systems. Organizations are also increasing deploying security protocols, such as SSH [2], to prove remote secure access to their servers, in place of insecure protocols such as telnet.

A question that arises is whether the current practices for deployment of security solutions are adequate. We have done some preliminary studies that suggest most systems today continue to be vulnerable to network and spoofing attacks, even when they deploy secure communication protocols. This is true for both systems in academia as well as in the commercial world. Most of the problems that we identified are at the intersection of usability and security, but some appear to be due to insufficient appreciation of security risks beyond

P. McDaniel and S.K. Gupta (Eds.): ICISS 2007, LNCS 4812, pp. 1–9, 2007.

eavesdropping of passwords or sensitive network communication. We therefore submit that research needs to take place at the intersection of security principles and its practice at the end-user level to address security gaps that arise at the end-user level. In my talk, I plan to present some of our findings and hope that the research community as well as the commercial world will explore solutions to addressing those gaps.

We carried out two studies. The first study [3] examined the usage of SSH within our department and the second study [4] analyzed the design of web sites of financial institutions in the United States from a security perspective. We will not go into the details of the studies in this paper, but just highlight some of the security gaps that were identified by these studies. Besides our studies, other studies [5,6] also identified gaps in security in real-world systems due to inadequate interface design. Our studies highlight gaps even for sophisticated users who understand security.

In the next section, we discuss the results from two of our studies. In Section 3, we present some challenges in IT security in developing countries such as India that will be increasingly pushing information technology use to people in rural areas. In Section 4, we discuss some of the lessons learned and some open challenges. Finally, we conclude the paper.

2   Results from Studies

We briefly describe preliminary results from two on-going studies of vulnerabilities at the user level. The first study examined the vulnerability of users to man-in-the-middle attacks on SSH on our department's machines. The users in this study can be considered to be fairly sophisticated users since they mostly consist of computer science graduate students and some faculty. The second study analyzed over 700 web sites of banks for a range of vulnerabilities that resulted from poor web-site design decisions from a security perspective, as opposed to vulnerabilities that result from poor coding practices (which lead to vulnerability to attacks such as SQL injection or cross-side scripting) or incorrect configuration of SSL.

2.1   Vulnerability Assessment of an SSH Deployment

SSH is considered to be a well-designed protocol from a security perspective and is widely deployed. When used properly, it is designed to provide protection against both passive and active network attacks. One limitation of SSH is that a client must have the server's public key *a priori*; SSH does not provide secure support for key distribution. However, implementations of SSH do provide error messages and, if so configured, terminate the connection if the destination host is unable to present proof of possession of the server's private key.

We monitored SSH logs to analyze user behavior when our system administrators changed the SSH host key on a popular server within our department. The server's public key had remained static for over two years and thus expected to be installed at most user's machines. Over 70 users attempted to login over the server after the key change during the monitored period. We found that less than 10% of the users asked the administrators if there was a key change and none verified the actual key. Rest of the users decided to log in, ignoring the warnings from SSH. This was true for even users whose connections were terminated by SSH (this happens in SSH in "strict checking" mode). Almost all of these users logged in later – presumably after deleting the offending server's host key from their configuration file, typically /.ssh/known_hosts on non-Windows hosts, so that it could be replaced automatically on the next SSH login.

We also analyzed the SSH logs of users who had opened accounts in the last three months on the server and inquired as to if any of them had asked our administrators for the server's host key. None had. All users accepted the initial key that was provided by the server.

An interesting question is why did users in our study make poor security choices when using SSH? One could potentially say that they were ignorant of risks, but we do not believe that to be the case. Most of the users in our study were graduate students and faculty in Computer Science and were sophisticated enough to get around SSH warnings by removing the offending keys from /.ssh/known_hosts file. Furthermore, SSH gives pretty explicit warnings about the risks of establishing the connection. We do not have data to answer this question conclusively, but we did talk to a few of the users, including some we knew were aware of the risks (because they have done research related to security).

Based on our conversations, we came up with a few possible factors. Some users may simply be using the *path of least resistance*. They perceived the SSH error to be an obstacle to connecting to the server. The simplest solution to get around the problem was to delete the server's public key rather than contact an administrator to verify the key. This suggests that the simplest path to getting around a security error for a user should be carefully secured, rather than being treated as a rare anomaly that is not particularly interesting from security perspective. SSH does not do that well. SSH warnings do suggest to contact the administrator, but they do not say how or what to do if the administrator is not available (e.g., late at night). Thus, the easiest path for a user is an alternative one – delete the offending key and accept the new key.

Unfortunately, other systems, such as web sites, do not fare much better either in handling security errors. Many sites will send temporary passwords via email, for example, when users forget their password. The assumption is that the path from the server to user's email account is secure (or someone else's problem). But we security researchers know that is not necessarily the case. The last hop to the user is perhaps the most vulnerable link because a user could be connected to an insecure wireless network and accessing his email account. Most web-based email systems today (e.g., gmail, yahoo) authenticate users over SSL, but deliver email in the clear. A variety of other solutions for handling forgotten passwords are available, some better than this. But there is no clear standard or guidelines from the security community for the best way to address this problem, even though it occurs so frequently in practice, which is an astonishing gap.

Another factor could be that users get frequent security warnings from SSH when logging to different hosts around the campus that they tune out the warnings and consider them as essentially a nuisance from SSH. Lack of consistency in user experience to security-related events can really hurt system security. Unfortunately, our study shows that it does not help for administrators of one machine to provide a consistent experience. In our study, SSH host keys did not change on the server for over two years. But users do get SSH warnings from other machines, including login server pools, and when logging in from new machines. We believe that this may be diluting the impact of a security warning even from a machine that gives warnings rarely.

In our SSH user study, we found that most users bypassed SSH warnings even though the host key was changed after a period of two years. As we mentioned earlier, one problem is that standard SSH warnings tell you that there could be an active attack going on, but not how to get around the problem and accomplish the work. Not connection to the server, as the warnings suggest that the users do, is not really an option for most users because they need to get their work done. Instead, if the warnings provide clear instructions for verifying the new key (perhaps by providing a secure URL to a well-known, standardized site), more users may have followed those instructions. Of course, it is possible that the instructions themselves could be tampered with by an attacker, leading to an interesting challenge. In SSH, the key distribution problem is simply left as an assumption for security. Unfortunately, no standard ways have evolved for guiding administrators on how to best address it.

Though our study is limited to only one department and one type of population, it strongly suggests that SSH deployments fails to provide protection against man-in-the-middle attacks at the user-level, even though the protocol itself may be designed to prevent man-in-the-middle attacks when correctly used. We note that if a user uses password-based authentication in SSH, they are susceptible to a man-in-the-middle attack. It would be safer for a user to use public-key based authentication in SSH (using passphrases). In that case, an attacker could spoof a server, but not login as the user to the real server. In our study, we found that most users did not use passphrases though that is an available option. Perhaps, passwords are more convenient and provide a path of less resistance than passphrases.

It is possible that the users made, what they considered to be, a rational decision. They perceived the risk of an actual man-in-the-middle attack to be low and the possibility of a configuration change at the server higher. But that is disconcerting because it means that users will discount security risks and will use unsafe methods, if given a choice.

SSH designers made the choice to trusts the users to make the right security decisions. Most SSH clients, when seeing a bad server's key, very clearly tell a user not to connect and to verify the server's fingerprint with an administrator because they may be subject to a serious attack that will totally compromise the session's security. But it also tells them that they can get around the problem by deleting the cached server's key. Our study indicates that most users will choose the latter option, raising the question whether even sophisticated users should be trusted by implementers of security systems to make security decisions.

2.2 Vulnerability Assessment of Financial Websites

In [4], we analyzed over 700 web sites of financial institutions with presence in the United States. The main aspect we were looking for is how these institutions structured the online interaction with their customers from the perspective of security vulnerabilities. The good news is that almost sites use SSL for authenticating their web server to users and do not send passwords in the clear. The bad news is that most of them still make poor design decisions at the macro level that leave their users more vulnerable to spoofing, phishing, and social engineering attacks.

Below are two representative examples of poor design decisions that many of the financial web sites suffered from (several other vulnerabilities can be found in [4]):

1. Providing a secure login window, but on an insecure page
2. Insecure pages for customer service and instructions for password reset

Why do these decisions get made and why are they poor decisions from a security perspective? Let us consider each of the two examples in turn. Here is a plausible chain of events between an hypothetical bank's user-interface design group and its security group that lead to the first decision:

1. Providing a login window on the home page is convenient for users, as per the user-interface team. It saves users one click in going to a separate login page and we know that the number of clicks matter, when it comes to ease-of-use.
2. The security group rationalizes that the userid and password is being submitted securely over SSL. Therefore, the credentials are safe against spoofing and network attacks.

Thus, it is plausible that the software group at the bank rationalizes that the design decision of providing the login window on an insecure home page is reasonable because the Javascript code that handles the login window submits the userid and password over an SSL-protected session. SSL guarantees security (assuming that SSL is secure), therefore the login process is secure.

Unfortunately, the reasoning is faulty. From a user's perspective, they do not know if the login window form is genuine or not, since it is on an unauthenticated page. Thus, the login credentials must be entered based on blind faith that the login page is not spoofed and not tampered with, and that the financial institution has taken precautions to submit the information securely.

I recall reporting this problem to my brokerage company (which I shall leave unnamed) in United States several years ago when they used to provide a login/password window on an insecure home page (though the credentials were submitted over SSL). The response was that if I was concerned, I should just click the login button without entering the user id and password. That will take me to an SSL-protected page, where I could enter the correct user ID and password. I would argue that it it unreasonable to expect most users to be aware of such a workaround and most users will not use it anyway since it is not the path of least resistance. To that company's credit, at least they had a solution for me and eventually they modified their login procedures so that they are no longer vulnerable to that problem. Many other financial institutions, however, continue to take that risk.

Now, let's examine the second problem of providing contact information on an insecure page. One of the institutions that holds retirement accounts for faculty at my university, TIAA/CREF, was guilty of that. Why is this a poor security decision? Let us assume that part of the threat model is a man-in-the-middle attack or a site spoofing attack. That is one of the reasons why the use of SSL for protecting communication related to authentication and transactions makes sense. Suppose that an attacker redirects the user to a spoofed "Contact Us" page that contains bad phone numbers for TIAA-CREF that are actually manned by the attacker. If a user were to use those phone numbers for account queries, it is conceivable that user would be asked to provide credentials, such as social security number and birthdate, to verify their identity and would simply end up giving those to the attacker.

I initially suspected that the problem was primarily due to TIAA/CREF not being aware of the risk. They could easily have provided the information on an SSL-protected page. Not using SSL for all pages does potentially reduce the load on the web server, but I doubt that protecting the "Contact Us" page with SSL, or even the whole web site, would be a major expense for a large company that handles billions of customer dollars. I did report the problem to them but, at the time of this writing, they continue to provide contact information on a non-protected page. Hopefully, they are working on it. Hit the "Contact Us" link at their site to see if they have since fixed the problem.

A few financial web sites have addressed this problem. For example, Fidelity brokerage uses SSL to protect their entire site. However, a vast majority of sites remain vulnerable today.

3   Broader Problem of Authenticating Users

So far, we only touched on the problem of verifying identity in the context of an authentication protocol. But, there is a more general problem that has broader implications. In the United States, social security numbers serve as universal, unique identifiers for individuals and form the basis of establishing credentials for other services such as bank accounts and credit cards. But, as is well-known, the use of a single identifier also increases the risk of identity theft. In developing countries, such as India, most citizens do not have a unique ID assigned at present. Tax IDs and voter cards are being increasingly assigned to individuals, but they are not yet universal. So, there is a window of opportunity to recommend better systems if the security community can come up with them.

Another interesting problem in a country like India is that of identifying people over the phone. A large percentage of people do not speak English, the country is multi-lingual, and as a result the mapping to a bit string that represents a name in an authentication database is ambiguous. Other attributes, such as home address, are also ambiguous because many addresses, particularly in rural areas, are simply a collection of attributes that describe the place sufficiently for the local mail delivery person; a classical example given in India is an address specified by just the recipient's name and a nearby local landmark - presumably the postal carrier would know the person and how to deliver the letter). This raises the question how to do verification. For example, if a user gives an approximately matching name and address (rather than an exact match), should that be accepted for locating a record? Would it reduce the "number of bits" in the verification process? I conjecture that it does, since it is akin to doing an approximate match on passwords, rather than an exact match. But analyzing the extent of its impact on authentication systems requires further research.

4 Lessons Learned

Fortunately, the situation is not entire hopeless. Our studies suggest a few design principles that may help in securing systems as well as providing good usability, though their validation requires further work:

End-user visibility of security guarantees: System designers must not only secure the network communication channel, but also ensure that the end-user application is able to make that security visible to the end-user before the user uses that channel. Ideally, this visibility of security attributes to the end-user should be tamper-proof for the desired threat model and be presented in a way that the user is likely to understand and notice. Unfortunately, providing good user presentation of security guarantees is easier said than done. The work by Cranor et al. [7] shows that it can be a significant challenge in designing interfaces that present P3P privacy policies of web sites to users so that users are likely to notice them and be able to use them for making informed security decisions. The work in [5] highlights similar problems in web browsers for presenting SSL security context. Providing a tamper-proof way of displaying security guarantees is also a challenge. For example, Javascript could be used to control the contents of the displayed URL at the bottom of a page when a link is highlighted. Many users rely on that to see if a link should be trusted prior to clicking. Browsers are doing a better job today of preventing scripts from modifying the displayed security context, but it is still an arms race.

Secure the context: This is a well-known principle that not only communication must be secured but also its context [8,9]. For example, SSL 2.0 was vulnerable to cipher rollback attack because it did not adequately protect the key negotiation steps. SSH fails to do that for host keys. Unfortunately, most administrators do not adequately tell users how to verify the host keys in a convenient way, leaving users vulnerable to security attacks. Providing a login window (even that is submitted over SSL) on an insecure page is also an example of this problem; it would be easy for the attacker to replace the page contents so that the information is submitted insecurely. For a bank to provide contact phone numbers on an insecure page is also an example of this problem.

Secure the path of least resistance when errors occur: Security errors may be rare (most logins are successful), but the implications can be significant if those errors are not correctly handled. A careful analysis of users' likely responses to errors and the security implications of that must be done and standards evolved for handling them safely. That analysis should assume that most users will choose the simplest path to getting around the problem rather than the most secure path.

Security warnings should be rare events: In our SSH study, it is conceivable that users get SSH warnings about bad or missing host keys so frequently that they have come to accept it as "normal", rather than a possible security risk. Organizationally, system administrators should make it a high priority to not change host keys except when a key is suspected to be compromised. For example, if a server is upgraded (e.g., new computer replacing an old one), it would be better to transfer the old machine's key rather than generating new keys. It would be even better to consider standard extensions to SSH to support signed host keys (using long-term certificates of organization's authorities). That may help make the warnings rarer when machines are upgraded and new host keys are installed.

End-user verification of security-related information: If a protocol gives security warnings with information such as fingerprints, the user must be told how to verify them. SSH fails in that regard. It does print out the fingerprint of the host's key. However, most users are unlikely to be aware how to verify that fingerprint.

5 Conclusions

We presented some of the findings from two of our studies that suggest existence of wide-spread security problems at the end-user level in systems that attempt to deploy security protocols to secure user interactions. Our findings suggest that significant security gaps are introduced at the application level, even in systems where security is the primary concern and users can be considered to be sophisticated about security. This points to a significant challenge for the security community. The community must not simply ignore this issue, leaving it to application writers or user-interface designers to address. We must develop security-oriented guidelines for application developers as well as automatic security modeling and evaluation tools to assist the developers in assessing the security of their systems. The guidelines and tools should factor in results from existing studies on user behavior.

Acknowledgments

The results from studies cited in this paper would not have been possible without the help of graduate students, Brett Clippingdale and Laura Falk. Brett was instrumental in collection and analysis of results on SSH usage. Laura Falk was instrumental in writing scripts to help analyze security at bank sites. I also thank the organizers of ICISS 2007 for the opportunity to present this work.

References

1. Rescorla, E.: SSL and TLS: Designing and Building Secure Systems. Addison-Wesley, Reading (2000)
2. Ylonen, T., Lonvick, C.: The secure shell (SSH) protocol architecture, RFC 4251, IETF draft (January 2006)
3. Clippingale, B., Prakash, A.: Usability vulnerabilities in SSH: When good users go bad. Unpublished manuscript. Contact author(s) for a copy (September 2007)
4. Prakash, A., Falk, L.: Web security analysis of financial institutions. Technical Report CSE-TR-534-07, Department of EECS, University of Michigan (2007)
5. Schechter, S., Dhamija, R., Ozment, A., Fischer, I.: The emperor's new security indicators: An evaluation of website authentication and the effect of role playing on usability studies. In: IEEE Symposium on Security and Privacy (2007)
6. Whitten, A., Tygar, J.: Why Johnny can't encrypt: A usability evaluation of PGP 5.0. In: Proc. of the 8th Usenix Security Symposium (1999)
7. Cranor, L., Guduru, P., Arjula, M.: User interfaces for privacy agents. ACM Transactions on Computer Human Interaction 12(2), 135–178 (2006)
8. Wagner, D., Schneier, B.: Analysis of the SSL 3.0 protocol. In: Proc. of The 2nd Usenix Workshop on Electronic Commerce, Revised April, 2007 (November 1996)
9. McDaniel, P.: On context in authorization policy. In: SACMAT. Proc. of the 8th ACM Symposium on Access Control Models and Technologies, pp. 80–89 (June 2003)

Investigating the Impact of Real-World Factors on Internet Worm Propagation

Daniel A. Ray[1], Charles B. Ward[1], Bogdan Munteanu[1], Jonathan Blackwell[1], Xiaoyan Hong[1], and Jun Li[2]

[1] Department of Computer Science
University of Alabama, Tuscaloosa, AL 35487
[2] Department of Computer and Information Science
University of Oregon, Eugene, OR 97403
lijun@cs.uoregon.edu

Abstract. This paper reports the results of our experimentation with modeling worm behavior on a large scale, fully adaptable network simulator. Our experiments focused on areas of worm scanning methods, IP address structure, and wireless links that, to the best of our knowledge, have been mostly neglected or abstracted away in prior worm simulations. Namely, our intent was to first study by direct observation of our simulations the effects of various IP scanning techniques on the effectiveness of worm spread. Second, our intent was to research the effects that having a larger IP address space (specifically a sparsely populated IP address space like that provided by Internet Protocol Version 6) would have on the effectiveness of several worms. Third, we study how the wireless media may affect the propagation of worms. In order to perform these simulations we have made use of the Georgia Institute of Technology's network simulator, GTNetS, extending the worm classes packaged with the simulator.

1 Introduction

The propagation of Internet worms has a devastating effect on the normal operations of the Internet. Because of the cost of worm attacks, much research has recently been devoted to trying to understand, detect, and prevent the spread of Internet worms. While various analytical modeling and empirical analyses have been conducted to study the propagation nature of various Internet worms, the effects of real-world factors on the propagation of worms with various scanning methods are still not fully understood. In this work, we study two major factors on the propagation of Internet worms—IP address distribution and wireless media—while worms can choose various scanning methods.

- *IP address distribution.* While relatively dense, the current IPv4 address space still has a large portion of unallocated addresses. When a worm scans for victims, its success rate is affected by whether or not a scanned address is allocated. Studying this may potentially help design a more worm-resistant

P. McDaniel and S.K. Gupta (Eds.): ICISS 2007, LNCS 4812, pp. 10–24, 2007.

IP address allocation policy. In addition, it also warrants further study to know how worms may propagate in the much larger IPv6 address space.
– *Wireless media.* Every day many nodes are connected to the Internet through wireless media using WLAN, WiFi, upcoming Mesh networking, Bluetooth PAN or 3G cellular technologies. Little is known regarding the speed and style Internet worms may propagate through these wireless media to users. Various networking choices (e.g., a single large subnet vs. dispersed sub-networks) or access control techniques (MAC address filtering vs. password protection) may or may not affect the behavior of worm propagation. User mobility could have both a positive and negative impact on the worm spread. To the best of our knowledge, no work has been extensively performed in this area.

Internet worms can scan in many different ways. Scans can be random, local preference, hitlist-based, permutation, topological, or some combination of these. It can be based on either TCP or UDP, or even piggybacked onto other networking traffic. With the various scanning methods, we investigate the impact of IP address distribution and wireless media on Internet worms spread through a systematic, comprehensive analysis that compares the propagation speeds and trends in an Internet-like networking environment.

We use a packet-level network simulator, *GTNetS*. Our work identifies and explores parameters affecting worm-propagation which have been largely ignored, abstracted away, or overlooked in previous studies. Most previous simulation studies of worms have not simulated worm behavior at a per-packet level; instead, they rely on certain analytical models to reduce the computational complexity which could be substantial when simulating a worm outbreak on a network of non-trivial size. Even relatively small networks take an enormous amount of CPU time to simulate at a packet-level because of the massive traffic load needed to be simulated as a matter of course when analyzing worm behavior. However, with improved simulators, and the ever increasing computational power available, simulating outbreaks at a per-packet level on networks of non-trivial size has been shown to be feasible. For example, work has been done by George F. Riley and his colleagues at Georgia Tech [1,2].

The rest of this paper is organized as follows. We first describe previous work in Section 2. We then describe our GTNetS-based simulation environment in Section 3, and illustrate our approach in detail in Section 4. Our results are presented in Section 5. We conclude our paper and point out future work in Section 6.

2   Previous Work

Worms pose a substantial threat to the Internet and much work has been done to study real worm outbreaks [3,4,5,6,7,8]. The previous work is generally divided into two categories, analytical modeling and empirical simulations. In addition, researchers have studied various approaches in detecting worms, such as [15]. Theoretical analyses of worms have been performed as far back as [9], but not until Staniford et al. systematically categorized and analyzed the threats from various worm propagation techniques in [10] was the threat really well understood. Another study by Staniford et al. [21] was on flash worms, showing that using a pre-computed spread tree, an UDP worm could infect up to 1 million hosts in half a second, or in 1.3 seconds if the worm uses TCP. In [22], address space distribution is modeled far from uniform. The authors analyze the impact of unused blocks of the IP space and provide a model for implementing a distributed traffic monitor system. Further work on worm propagation models [11,12] and the potential sophistication of worms [13,14] also show that worms are an ever-increasing threat that will not be easily stamped out.

The previous work on worm simulations has not focused on the key issues of our research. Namely, these are the effects of varying worm IP block scanning methods and the effects of a larger IP address space and other changes provided by IPv6, as well as the effect of wireless media. Work in [21] focuses on one scanning strategy - hit-list, while our work analyzes multiple scanning methods as well as different topologies and IP address distributions. Also, compared to work in [22], we study the effect of a much larger IP address space while also taking into consideration multiple network topologies.

2.1 Analytical Modeling

Analytical modeling is a significant area of research. Internet worm research, in particular, has made use of analytical modeling to study worm behavior. Generally speaking, the idea of analytical modeling is to, through analysis of a problem domain, define and apply a mathematical model that fits the system being analyzed within an acceptable margin of error. Analytical models benefit from computational efficiency because calculations are largely independent of the size of the network. Generally, however, there will be some necessary uncertainty inherent in the relationship between the mathematical model and real world behavior. On top of this uncertainty, analytical models are often easily implementable and cannot interact with any proposed detection and defensive mechanism or varying network and worm parameters without altering the mathematical model on which they depend [16].

Chen, Gao, and Kwiat [12] give an analytical model for the spread of worms which they dub Analytical Active Worm Propagation (AAWP) model. Their AAWP model characterizes the propagation of worms that employ random IP-block scanning. This model is a prime example showing that analytical models are suitable for the study of Internet worms. However, the model's mathematical complexity as well as its inflexibility (especially in the method for handling IP-block scanning) shows that it still suffers from problems inherent to all analytical models.

2.2 Empirical Simulations

With the problems inherent in analytical models many researchers have begun a push to use empirical simulations to test hypotheses concerning the behavior and propagation of worms in various network models. Our research falls in this vein. To our knowledge, however, there have been no papers published that focus on the comparative effects of varying IP-block scanning techniques as well as the effects of a larger address space.

As discussed before, Riley et al. [1,2] give an interesting framework for how Internet worms might be simulated using the GTNetS simulator.

Wei, Mirkovic, and Swany [17] perform research on worm simulation on simulators that are very similar in nature to GTNetS. Their simulations exhibit high-fidelity through their use of packet level simulations. They also provide some flexibility for varying worm types, though not to the level proposed by our research. For instance, they developed classes for worms with random scanning and subnet scanning, but have not extended the classes beyond these approaches. Wei et al. also expound upon the limitations of GTNetS. Mainly, GTNetS requires a good deal of centralized computational power. The simulator from Wei, et al. is a distributed simulator that uses normal PC nodes to run their distributed simulation algorithms and treats the PC nodes as existing at the Autonomous System network level. Unfortunately, this distributed algorithm suffers from the complexity inherent in distributed computing.

Weaver, Staniford, and Paxson [18] present an algorithm for worm propagation retardation which they call the Threshold Random Walk (TRW) algorithm. They begin with this algorithm for containment of scanning worms and try to make *ad hoc* changes to general purpose system's hardware and specific choices for software implementation that work together to form an *ad hoc* simulator that is suitable to test their algorithm and various hypotheses. This approach turns our approach, in which we move from a general simulator to a specific worm implementation, on its head, and is a much less flexible approach.

3   GTNetS-Based Worm Simulation Environment

The work by Riley et al. has resulted in the development of a fully adaptable real-world network simulator that is capable of supporting the modeling of Internet worms. Some simple worm examples have already been created for use with the simulator.

GTNetS is unique amongst computer network simulators in that it is designed to allow for large-scale packet-level network simulations. There are several issues that must be solved in order to allow for simulations of these kinds due to the extreme demands on memory and computational power. We will briefly discuss how GTNetS solves these issues. For a full explanation, refer to [1,2].

3.1   Simulating Large-Scale Networks

GTNetS has been designed from the ground up to provide for large-scale network simulations. GTNetS uses several approaches to limit the computational complexity and memory use of simulating networks on a large scale, thus freeing us from these considerations. First, GTNetS addresses the memory complexity of such simulations by employing NIx-Vectors [19] for routing simulation. This approach does not maintain routing tables, but rather uses a source-based method in which routing information is stored in each packet. As such, routes are computed only as needed, and are cached at packet sources for later use. This approach is useful because normal routing tables in network simulations cause a large overhead in memory.

Also in an effort to reduce memory complexity for the simulator, special consideration is taken of leaf nodes or subnetworks of leaf nodes that are known to have a single gateway router as an access point to the rest of the network. GTNetS first attempts to route the packet within the subnetwork (this will only be possible if leaves in the subnetwork are interconnected). If this is not possible then the packet is unconditionally forwarded to the gateway router. This simple step saves a large amount of memory, and is an advance over other simulators.

Second, GTNetS addresses the complexity inherent in maintaining an "event list" by attempting to control the size of the list. The event list is the list of events (sending packet, receiving packet, etc.) that the simulator must simulate. The first method for controlling the size of this list is to use FIFO receive queues which, they explain, will limit the number of events necessary in the event list for receiving packets. Also, they note that in many cases the queuing delay for a packet in a FIFO queue (such as a basic Drop Tail queue) can be deterministically calculated. Thus, GTNetS uses "Abstract Queuing" such that information about transmitted packets is stored deterministically and packets are never queued at the transmitter. Instead, these packets are given the appropriate queuing delay and sent directly to the receiver. Finally, GTNetS uses a data structure called a "Timer Bucket" which is used to abstract out network delays such as the round-trip time (RTT) in order to model TCP timeout events in an efficient way and thus reduce the size of the event list.

Third, and finally, GTNetS reduces the computational and memory complexity of simulating large-scale networks by limiting the size of log files that are normally kept by simulators for storing the results of a simulation. It does this by providing pre-packaged statistical packages that can create the desired statistics and allow for the removal of raw fine-granularity files from the kept log files.

3.2   The Worm Simulation Environment

As we mentioned above, not only is GTNetS specifically designed for large-scale networks, it is also highly adaptable to various network environments. This turns out to be very useful, especially in the simulation of worms. A major concern of our research, as well as all research in the area, is exactly which elements of the network environment to hold constant and which elements to test against. We discuss these decisions in depth below. Here, however, we discuss exactly what options are available to us via the GTNetS simulator.

The first and foremost concern is the network itself; that is, the network topology. This is important because GTNetS is fully flexible in this regard, both in network structure, bandwidth, and IP address assignment. GTNetS provides a robust interface for creating network graphs, including limited functionality for generating random network topologies fitting certain regular patterns. These include common graph types such as star graphs, dumbbell graphs (bandwidth bottleneck graphs), and trees. However, it does not natively provide support for generating more complicated types of random networks. Fortunately, it does provide a facility whereby random graphs can be imported from random graph generation programs such as BRITE, which generates random graphs which mathematically resemble the AS structures of the existing Internet. Other graph generation tools such as iNet (another Internet-like topology generator) can also be used [20].

Second, but no less important, is the structure of the worm packets themselves which help define the worm's structure. GTNetS is capable of supporting worm packet classes of either TCP or UDP. Thus, worms with varying infection lengths, selected infection ports, and varying number of connections can be appropriately simulated. Also very important to our research is the fact that GTNetS allows for worm classes with varying IP block scanning and selection patterns via the use of a standard extensible C++ class, as well as varying scan rates.

In short, the full flexibility of GTNetS allows us to gather empirical data from simulations that are based on a great variety of simulated networks and worm types that behave as in the real world. Thus, our research results should very closely mimic empirical observations of the real world, without putting any hardware at risk or causing billions of dollars of damage.

4 Our Approach

Our approach centers around the manipulation of code provided with the GT-NetS simulator to facilitate our simulations. Our first step was to design a working model on a single processor. As described above, the GTNetS simulator is designed to provide simulations with characteristics of real networks in mind. Thus, there are several variables for both network related and worm related characteristics that needed to be addressed. Specifically, what needed to be decided was which variables would be held constant across the spectrum of our simulations. As we previously stated, the goal of our research is to discover the effects of varying IP address population density and scanning methods on the propagation of worms. With that in mind, we made decisions concerning network and worm characteristics as described below.

4.1 Constants

There are really two types of constants that we must address. We will deal with network-related characteristic constants first. Prime among these was the network topology itself. Rather than deal with the uncertainty that multiple network topologies would bring into our simulations, we decided that the best course of action was to select a suitable topology and to hold this topology constant across various simulations. GTNetS comes pre-equipped with a simple network topology generator. However, this generator only accepts the number of required nodes and arranges the nodes in patterns which are unlike real-world networks. Because we are primarily interested in Internet worms, we decided to create a network topology that would be more characteristic of the Internet. In order to do this, we created a network using the BRITE graph generation program. BRITE creates Internet-like AS and subnet structures at random. After creating a network topology we assigned IPs at random with respect to subnets such that subnets would have IPs within a given range. The network topology was held constant, but we eliminated unnecessary overhead by not holding IP addresses constant over all the simulations.

The wireless networks are treated differently. They are subnets in the Internet topology with different link bandwidth and packet loss rate. A wireless subnet can be a large address space that adheres to a higher level on the topology tree or a small one to a lower address topology tree. For example, a campus wireless network can use a campus-wide universal subnet that accommodates a large number of IP addresses, or a small subnet that builds within each department. These two types of configurations are modeled using GTNetS directly as: a *wider-tree* with a few levels in a topology tree and lowest level has large amount of fan out links for the first case, and a *deeper-tree* with more levels and less fan out links in the lowest level.

There is also the issue of network traffic that is not worm related. In dealing with this issue we simply abstracted out all other network traffic. We do so with full realization that congestion in one network subnet could affect worm propagation. However, for ease of simulation, and because congestion is partly a factor of the network topology itself (i.e. number of nodes in a subnet, speed of connections, etc.), we have chosen to focus only on "ideal" networks where congestion is uniform (or non-existent). Future endeavors may deal more directly with this issue.

Finally is the issue of individual node vulnerability. GTNetS decides worm vulnerability by assigning a vulnerable state to individual generated nodes according to some probability. In an effort to make our simulated network as Internet like as possible we held this probability constant across our simulations and assigned the probability to 90%. We arrived at this number by determining that approximately 97% of machines on the Internet run Windows operating systems of one variety or another, thus making them the main targets of most attacks. We then reduced the overall percentage marginally to account for instances where, for whatever reason, a machine may be running a Windows O.S. and not be vulnerable to attack, thus arriving at the approximated value of 90% vulnerability across our simulated network.

Next, we deal with worm related characteristic constants. Because our research focuses only on the worm scanning method all other worm characteristics were held constant with the exception of that one. Scan rate, infection length, infection port, and the number of TCP connections have all been held constant at default GTNetS settings across simulations.

4.2   Variables

Obviously, those network and worm characteristics that we have not held constant must still be dealt with. In fact such characteristics allow us to make observations as to how certain aspects affect worm propagation. We vary the IP address space population density to simulate the effects of implementing IPv6 (with its larger address space) on the Internet. Specifically, our simulations were set to use approximately one IP address in every thirty-five available IP addresses for dense (IPv4 like) networks, and one in every one hundred and thirty-four for sparsely populated (IPv6 like) networks. These numbers are best guess efforts at assigning Internet like IP addresses. For IPv4 approximately 75% of available /8 blocks have been assigned. However, there are many IP addresses within each block that are still available. Unfortunately, specifics about individual networks are not readily available, so we have made our best guess in assigning 1/35 addresses for our simulations [11]. We further noted that the full address space of IPv4 is much less than one percent of the entire address space of IPv6. However, for the sake of the computational time of our simulations, and to obtain more meaningful results, we assigned our simulations of IPv6 address space to have just less than 1% of address spaces to be occupied.

There are also two worm characteristics which varied across our simulation. First, we obviously varied the worm scanning method across our simulations. GTNetS provides simple worm scan methods including uniform random IP scanning, and local preference scanning. We have added to these hit-list scanning which assumes that worm propagation does not begin until a certain set of key nodes has been pre-infected.

Finally, in the case of hit-list scanning, unlike in the other cases, we have run simulations using both TCP connections and UDP connections. All of our other simulations have been run using UDP connections with a constant default scan rate because UDP worms are most effective. So, in order to compare high and low density address space simulations using hit-list scanning with our other simulations we have first run UDP hit-list worms. However, because we are already spending time to select certain nodes across the network to pre-infect, we wanted to test what effect a TCP hit-list worm would have. As such, we have run an additional TCP hit-list worm simulation for both high and low density address space populations.

4.3   Simulations

This subsection, in way of an overview of the previous subsection and a precursor to the next section, gives a complete account of the simulations which we have performed. For each UDP worm the scan rate has been held at a constant default value of 100, and for each TCP worm the number of connection threads has been held at a constant default of 3. Also, in the case of all simulations, the infection length and infection port, which we have not concerned ourselves with as we have abstracted out all other traffic, have been held at constant default values. Finally, each worm type simulation has been run twice, once with a densely populated (IPv4 like) IP address space and once with a sparsely populated (IPv6 like) IP address space. Densely populated networks were generated such that 1/34 of the available address space is used, and sparsely populated networks were generated such that 1/134 of the available address space is used.

Each of the following worm simulations was run as described above. First was the UDP uniform random scanning worm. Second was the UDP local preference scanning worm. Next, we generated a simulation using a UDP hit-list worm using local preference scanning after the hit-list is established. Finally, the same hit-list local preference scanning worm was simulated again, only this time TCP connections were used to propagate the worm. The results of these scans are given in the next section of this paper.

4.4   Results

The final aspect of our approach involves exactly what statistics we have chosen to acquire from our simulations. Using the data provided by GTNetS and the program gnuplot, we have plotted interval infection rates for our various simulations. This allows us to provide a graphical representation of how well a worm is able to propagate across a network at given time intervals. In each case our simulations were run until all 1000 nodes were infected. The graphs that are provided in the next section each contain at least two simulation plots for comparative purposes.

5   Analysis of Results

Our results, like our simulations, are divided into worm classes based on IP block scanning methods as described above. Below we attempt to both give an overview of results for individual worm classes as well as results from comparisons of our results.

5.1   Comparing Worm Types on Sparse and Dense Graphs

First we consider Figure 1 and Figure 2. The two worm types are the uniform random scanning and the local preference scanning. We tested each of these two methods in both dense and sparse graphs. There are several areas of interest on the curve of the infection interval. The first is the slope of the curve itself. If the slope is steep, then the worm has infected the nodes very quickly. The less steep the curve is, the longer it has taken the worm to infect the network's vulnerable nodes. This is true for each of the graphs provided.

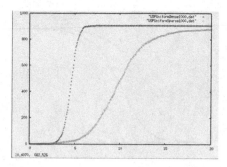

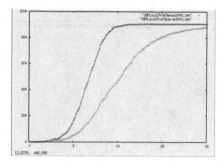

Fig. 1. Comparison of Uniform Random Worms

Fig. 2. Comparison of Local Preference Worms

The graphs of Figure 1 and Figure 2 show that the worms which are operating on dense graphs are much more successful than the worms that are operating on sparse graphs. In other words, if the network is sparsely populated then the worm has much more trouble finding and infecting vulnerable nodes quickly. This is not unexpected, but it does present a good argument for migrating the Internet to IPv6. However, it is interesting to note that it has still taken about the same amount of total time to infect all vulnerable nodes for both sparse and dense graphs in the case of these simulations.

5.2   Comparing Sparse and Dense Networks Overall

We now look at comparing the effects of sparse and dense networks overall. Figure 3 gives a side-by-side comparison of all three worm types on a dense network and Figure 4 gives a side-by-side comparison of all three worm types on a sparse network. Here we add worm type of hit-list pre-seeding for both dense and sparse networks. In this section we attempt to shed more light on exactly what the effects of dense and sparse networks are by comparing the three together.

For the case of dense networks we can examine Figure 3 to see our graphical comparison of infection intervals. What we note from this graph is that the curves of the infection intervals themselves are very similar. This is not unexpected because the worm types of hit-list and local preference scanning use the same IP block scanning method. However, more importantly, we can actually see the effect of the pre-seeding of worm infected nodes in various subnetworks from the hit-list worm. The hit-list worm infection interval is shifted to the left, indicating an overall increase in virulence.

As for the case of sparse networks we examine Figure 4. What we find is that for hit-list and local preference plots the slope of the graph is flatter. This effect is the same effect as noted before for worms working on sparse networks. However, we still see, as was hinted at above, that the hit-list worm infection interval is shifted to the left.

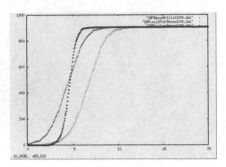

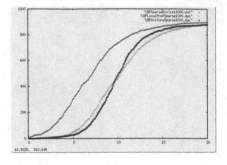

Fig. 3. Comparison of UDP worms on dense graph

Fig. 4. Comparison of UDP worms on sparse graph

These graphs highlight that the order of the effectiveness of the three worm types is not changed drastically due to the change from densely to sparsely populated graphs, though uniform random scanning worms suffer a greater flattening effect than the others. The graphs also further indicate that a sparsely populated network is going to suppress the effectiveness of worm spread, regardless of worm type.

5.3   Comparing TCP and UDP Hit-List Worms

Finally, we examine the tests we ran on hit-list worms with local preference scanning using TCP and UDP connections respectively as in Figure 5 and Figure 6. Dense and sparse networks are compared. The most obvious thing to note is that the simulation for sparse networks is unfinished for TCP hit-list worm. The reason for this is that the overhead for creating a TCP worm is exemplified in the simulation itself. As a result, the machine on which the simulation was run ran out of memory before the simulation could complete, even after a substantial memory upgrade. We discuss options for further research with more computational power in the final section. However, what we can tell from this simulation is that the overhead is substantial.

Further, what we can tell by comparing dense and sparse networks is that the hit-list worm with TCP connections is an improvement in the case of dense networks, but it has no real effect in the worm spread for sparse networks. Not surprisingly, TCP hit-list worms work better on dense networks and do not work as well with sparse networks. In short, overall TCP hit-list worms seem to add significantly to the overhead of hit-list worms, especially in sparse networks, without adding any benefit to worm spread.

5.4   Worm Propagation in Wireless Media

We simulate wireless media in two different network architectures, namely, a wired Internet backbone (or high bandwidth link) with local WLANs directly

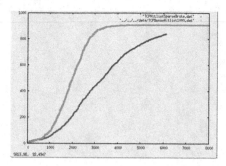

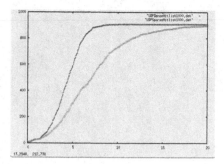

Fig. 5. Comparison of TCP Hit-list Worms

Fig. 6. Comparison of Hit-list Worms

attached to it, and a leveled organizational network tree with the WLAN subnets penetrated as smaller subnets at lower levels. A *wider-tree* topology is designed to reflect the first network architecture and a *deeper-tree* topology represents the second case. In the following Figures, curves numbered 1 are results run on *deeper-tree* topology and curves numbered 2 are results run on *wider-tree*. We compare both TCP and UDP worms with uniform scanning and local preference scanning methods.

Figure 7 shows a comparison of TCP worms using uniform scan in the two topologies. The Figure shows that worms start infection much later and propagate much slower in the deeper-tree topology than them in the wider-tree topology. Figure 8 shows a comparison of TCP works using local preference scanning. Similar trends as observed before are present here as well.

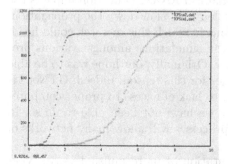

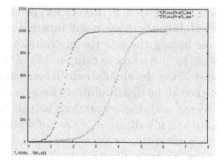

Fig. 7. Wireless TCP Uniform Worms

Fig. 8. Wireless TCP Local Preference Worms

Figure 9 and Figure 10 show a comparison of UDP worms using uniform and local preference scan in the two topologies respectively. Again, the Figures show that deeper tree topology can slow down worm propagation due to the fact that

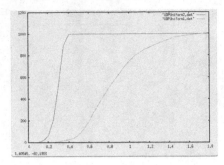 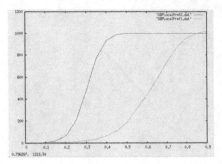

Fig. 9. Wireless UDP Uniform Worms   **Fig. 10.** Wireless UDP Local Preference Worms

more links need to be searched for the preferred addresses. These results suggest that the commonly used WLAN configuration of creating a single direct subnet for wireless access as in parallel to other organizational subnets may not be a preferred network topology in hampering worm propagation speed.

6   Conclusion and Future Directions

In this paper we investigated two major factors that impact the propagation of worms with a few major propagation methods. Especially we investigated the influence of IP address space and wireless links. We use GTNetS, a detailed network packet level simulator to conduct the evaluation. Our simulation results show that worms propagate slower in IPv6 address space due to the sparse address allocation. The results also show that WLAN configuration impacts the worm propagation. A deep tree type of topology can slow down the propagation.

Certainly, there are many future directions in which this research could head. Prime among these is the distribution of the simulations amongst various processors to give us more computational power. Originally, our hope was to be able to distribute the simulations in some manner for this reason. Indeed, GTNetS is designed to be distributable. However, due to lack of access to proper computer hardware and documentation, at this time we have not been able to do so. In the future, distribution of the simulation processes will allow many networks of much greater size to be analyzed.

Also, another direction is the implementation of more unusual worm types which we chose not to implement due to the exotic nature of the worms and the foundational nature of our initial research. Namely, these worm types are those which use permutation scanning and topological scanning to obtain a measure of synchronization among worms; this could prove to render the worms more effective in sparse networks if the overhead of such synchronization could be managed.

Finally, future research could take advantage of other scanning methods than local preference for hit-list worms. Local preference was chosen for this research because it seemed to be a best fit for a worm type that is pre-seeded in different subnets. However, this hypothesis could be tested by choosing different scanning methods.

References

1. Riley, G.F.: Large-scale network simulations with GTNetS. In: Proceedings of the 2003 Winter Simulation Conference (2003)
2. Riley, G.F., Sharif, M.I., Lee, W.: Simulating internet worms. In: Proceedings of MASCOTS (2004)
3. Spafford, E.: The Internet worm: Crisis and aftermath. Communications of the ACM 32(6), 678–687 (1989)
4. Arron, E.J.: The Nimda worm: An overview (October 2001), http://www.sans.org/rr/catindex.php?cat_id=36
5. Moore, D., Shannon, C., Claffy, kc.: Code-Red: A case study on the spread and victims of an Internet worm. In: Proc. ACM Internet Measurement Workshop, pp. 273–284 (2002)
6. Moore, D., Paxson, V., Savage, S., Shannon, C., Staniford, S., Weaver, N.: The spread of the Sapphire/Slammer SQL worm. CAIDA, La Jolla, CA, Tech. Rep. (2003), http://www.caida.org/analysis/security/sapphire/
7. Moore, D., Paxson, V., Savage, S., Shannon, C., Staniford, S., Weaver, N.: Inside the Slammer worm. IEEE Security and Privacy 1(4), 33–39 (2003)
8. Yegneswaran, V., Barford, P., Ullrich, J.: Internet intrusions: Global characteristics and prevalence. In: Proc. ACM SIGMETRICS, pp. 138–147. ACM Press, New York (2003)
9. Kephart, J.O., White, S.R.: Directed-graph epidemiological models of computer viruses. In: Proc. IEEE Symposium on Security and Privacy, pp. 343–361 (May 1991)
10. Staniford, S., Paxson, V., Weaver, N.: How to Own the Internet in your spare time. In: USENIX Security Symposium, USENIX, Berkeley, CA, pp. 149–167 (August 2002)
11. Garetto, M., Gong, W.: Modeling malware spreading dynamics. In: Proc. IEEE INFOCOM, vol. 3, pp. 1869–1879. IEEE Computer Society Press, Washington, DC (2003)
12. Chen, Z., Gao, L., Kwiat, K.: Modeling the spread of active worms. In: Proc. IEEE INFOCOM, pp. 1890–1900. IEEE Computer Society Press, Washington, DC (2003)
13. Zou, C.C., Gao, L., Gong, W., Towsley, D.: Advanced polymorphic worms: Evading IDS by blending in with normal traffic. In: Proc. Conference on Computer and Communications Security (2003)
14. Chen, Z., Ji, C.: A self-learning worm using importance scanning. In: Proc. Workshop on Rapid Malcode (2005)
15. Zou, C.C., Gao, L., Gong, W., Towsley, D.: Monitoring and early warning for Internet worms. In: Proc. Conference on Computer and Communications Security, pp. 190–199. ACM Press, New York (2003)
16. Sharif, M., Riley, G., Lee, W.: Comparative study between analytical models and packet-level worm simulations. In: PADS (2005)
17. Wei, S., Mirkovic, J., Swany, M.: Distributed worm simulations with a realistic internet model. In: PADS (2005)

18. Weaver, N., Staniford, S., Paxson, V.: Very fast containment of scanning worms. In: USENIX Security Symposium, USENIX, Berkeley, CA, pp. 29–44 (2004)
19. Riley, G.F., Fujimoto, R.M., Ammar, M.: A generic framework for parallelization of network simulations. In: MASCOTS. Proceedings of Seventh International Symposium of Modeling, Analysis and Simulation of Computer and Telecommunication Systems (1999)
20. Winick, J., Jamin, S.: Inet-3.0: Internet topology generator, http://topology.eecs.umich.edu/inet/inet-3.0.pdf
21. Staniford, S., Moore, D., Paxson, V., Weaver, N.: The top speed of flash worms. In: WORM 2004. Proceedings of the 2004 ACM workshop on Rapid malcode, pp. 33–42. ACM Press, New York (2004)
22. Rajab, M.A., Monrose, F., Terzis, A.: On the Effectiveness of Distributed Worm Monitoring. In: USENIX Security Symposium (2005)

An OS Security Protection Model for Defeating Attacks from Network

Zhiyong Shan, Qiuyue Wang, and Xiaofeng Meng

School of Information, Renmin University of China
shanzhiyong@ruc.edu.cn

Abstract. Security threats to operating systems today largely come from network. Traditional discretionary access control mechanism alone can hardly defeat them. Although traditional mandatory access control models can effectively protect the security of OS, they have problems of application incompatibility and administration complexity. In this paper, we propose a new model, Suspicious-Taint-Based Access Control (STBAC) model, for defeating network attacks while maintaining good compatibility, simplicity and system performance. STBAC regards processes using Non-Trustable-Communications as starting points of suspicious taint, traces activities of the suspiciously tainted processes by taint rules, and forbids the suspiciously tainted processes to illegally access vital resources by protection rules. Even in the cases when some privileged processes are subverted, STBAC can still protect vital resources from being compromised by the intruder. We implemented the model in the Linux kernel and evaluated it through experiments. The evaluation showed that STBAC could protect vital resources effectively without significant impact on compatibility and performance.

Keywords: Access Control, information flow.

1 Introduction

With the rapid development and increasing use of network, threats to operating systems mostly come from network, such as buffer overflows, viruses, worms, trojans, DOS, etc. On the other hand, as computers, especially PCs, become cheaper and easier to use, people prefer to use computers exclusively and share information through network. Though on a few occasions a user may permit someone else who is fully trusted to log in his/her computer from local, most of the time users share information via network. Therefore nowadays the threat to modern OSs does not come from local, but more from remote.

Traditional DAC (Discretionary Access Control) in OS alone cannot defeat network attacks well. Traditional MAC (Mandatory Access Control) is effective in maintaining security, but it has problems of application incompatibility and administration complexity [1][2][3]. From 2000 to 2003, we developed a secure OS, which implemented BLP [5], BIBA [6], RBAC [7] and ACL. However, we found the same problems with the secure OS. Thus, the STBAC model is proposed with the following goals in mind.

P. McDaniel and S.K. Gupta (Eds.): ICISS 2007, LNCS 4812, pp. 25–36, 2007.

- Protecting vital resources: Even if some privileged processes are subverted, STBAC can still protect vital resources from being compromised. Vital resources in OS include important binary files, configuration files, directories, processes, user data, system privileges and other limited resources, such as CPU time, disk space, memory, network bandwidth and important kernel data structures. Since they are the valuable user data and foundation for OS to provide services, they usually become the final target of an intrusion. Even if an intruder gets the root identity, we can say that the intrusion has failed if the intruder cannot compromise the vital resources.
- Compatibility: STBAC enhanced OS is compatible with existing application software.
- Simplicity: STBAC is easy to understand and administer.
- Performance: STBAC can be implemented with high performance.

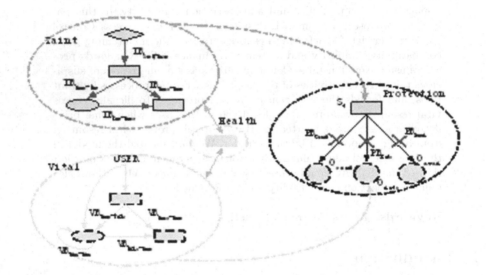

The STBAC model regards processes using Non-Trustable-Communications as starting points of suspicious taint, traces activities of the suspiciously tainted processes by taint rules, and forbids the suspiciously tainted processes to illegally access vital resources by protection rules. We implemented the STBAC model in the Linux kernel, and evaluated its protection capability, compatibility and system performance through experiments.

The paper is organized as follows. We first describe the STBAC model and its four parts in Section 2. In Section 3, the compatibility and simplicity of STBAC are analyzed. The implementation of the STBAC model in the Linux kernel is presented in Section 4. The evaluation results are shown in Section 5. In Section 6, STBAC is compared with related works. Finally, we draw the conclusion in Section 7.

2   Model Description

The STBAC model consists of four parts: Taint, Health, Vital and Protection, as shown in Figure 1, where the rectangles indicate processes; the ellipses indicate files or directories; the diamonds indicate sockets; and the balls indicate any objects in OS, such as files, directories, sockets and processes.

The Taint part, which is painted in red and enclosed by real line, is probably controlled by the intruder. It consists of suspiciously tainted subjects (S_t), suspiciously tainted objects (O_t) and taint rules (TR). TR is categorized into $TR_{sock-proc}$, $TR_{proc-proc}$, $TR_{proc-exe}$ and $TR_{exe-proc}$. The Vital part, which is painted in blue and enclosed by broken line, represents the vital resources that should be protected properly. This part consists of vital objects and vital rules (VR). The vital objects include O_{conf}, O_{inte} and O_{avai}, while VR is categorized into $VR_{proc-proc}$, $VR_{dir-dir}$, $VR_{proc-file}$ and $VR_{file-proc}$. The Protection part, which is surrounded in a black circle, consists of three protection rules (PR): PR_{conf}, PR_{inte} and PR_{avai}. PR forbids S_t to illegally access vital objects. The Health part, which is painted in gray, consists of health objects (O_h) and health subjects (S_h) that is not tainted or labeled as vital ones. We elaborate on the four parts of STBAC in the following sections.

2.1   Taint

As the Taint is probably controlled by the intruder, STBAC uses suspiciously tainted flag (F_t) to label S_t and O_t, and TR to trace S_t's activities in the kernel.

2.1.1   Taint Entities

First of all, we define remote network communications with necessary security means as **Trustable-Communications**, e.g., the secure shell, and the others as **Non-Trustable-Communications**. Security means include authentication, confidentiality protection, integrity protection, etc.

Suspiciously Tainted Subject (S_t) is a subject that may be controlled by an intruder and act for intrusion purposes. S_t is a process in general. For example, it can be a process using Non-Trustable-Communications, or a process of the executable file created by an intruder, or a process of the executable file downloaded from network, or the descendant process of the above processes. It can also be a process that communicates with the above processes, or a descendant of such a process.

Suspiciously Tainted Object (O_t) is an object that is created or modified by an intruder, and may aid in the intrusion. Generally, O_t means either the executable file created and modified by S_t, or the process created and accessed by S_t, or the file and directory accessed by S_t.

Both S_t and O_t are labeled with **Suspiciously Tainted Flag (F_t)**.

2.1.2   Taint Rules

TR includes $TR_{sock-proc}$, $TR_{proc-proc}$, $TR_{proc-exe}$ and $TR_{exe-proc}$, which can be described as follows.

Socket to Process Taint Rule ($\text{TR}_{\text{Sock-Proc}}$: $Socket \xrightarrow{F_t} Process$) depicts that the process using Non-Trustable-Communications may be breached or launched by the intruder. Thus it should be attached with F_t. In contrast, the process using Trustable-Communications should not be attached with F_t.

Process to Process Taint Rule ($\text{TR}_{\text{Proc-Proc}}$: $Process \xrightarrow{F_t} Process$) depicts that the process created by S_t or received communication message from S_t should be attached with F_t. No doubt, the process created by S_t is dangerous, so it is regarded as S_t. By means of pipe, local socket, shared memory or message queue, S_t may control other process to serve for intrusion, thus the controlled process is also regarded as S_t.

Process to Exe-file Taint Rule ($\text{TR}_{\text{Proc-Exe}}$: $Process \xrightarrow{F_t} ExecutableFile$) depicts that the executable file created or modified by S_t should be attached with F_t. Executable files created by S_t may be hostile programs, such as programs downloaded from network. On many occasions, modifying or over-writing existing executable files is a way to leave backdoor, for example, using specially modified "ls", "ps" and "netstat" to over-write existing command files.

Exe-file to Process Taint Rule ($\text{TR}_{\text{Exe-Proc}}$: $ExecutableFile \xrightarrow{F_t} Process$) depicts that the process that has executed or loaded O_t should be attached with F_t. Suspiciously tainted command file, library file, or other executable file could be an intrusion tool, so the process derived from them is dangerous.

2.2 Vital

The Vital is the target for STBAC to protect, consists of vital objects and vital rules. Vital objects include all kinds of vital resources, such as important user data, important system files or directories, limited system resources, etc. Vital rules define the conditions to spread vital flags that are used to label vital objects.

2.2.1 Vital Entities

According to the information protection targets proposed in ITSEC [14], even if OS is subverted, STBAC should still protect the following three types of objects:

Confidentiality Object (O_{conf}) is an object containing information that should be protected confidentially even if the system is breached. Generally, O_{conf} means a file or directory containing sensitive information. "/etc/passwd" and "/etc/shadow" are classical O_{conf}s. O_{conf} is labeled with **Confidentiality Flag (F_{conf})**.

Integrity Object (O_{inte}) is an object whose integrity should be protected even if the system is breached. Generally O_{inte} means binary files, important configuration files, important user data files and directories containing these files. O_{inte} is labeled with **Integrity Flag (F_{inte})**.

Availability Object (O_{avai}) is the limited resource that is necessary to run processes. Even if the system is breached, OS should guarantee that S_t could not block other vital or health processes getting O_{avai}. O_{avai} includes CPU, memory, disk space, network bandwidth and important kernel structures. O_{avai} is labeled with **Availability Flag (F_{avai})**.

In order to perfect the confidentiality protection function of STBAC, we further introduce two definitions.

Leak Object (O_{leak}) is an executable file from which a process derived may leak secrecy while writing files after reading an O_{conf}. Typical examples are "cp", "mcopy", "dd", "passwd", etc.

Leak Subject (S_{leak}) is a process derived from O_{leak} that may leak secrecy while writing files after reading an O_{conf}.

Both O_{leak} and S_{leak} are labeled with **Leak Flag (F_{leak})**.

2.2.2 Vital Rules

As presented above, STBAC identifies O_{conf}, O_{inte}, O_{avai}, O_{leak} and S_{leak} by vital flags of F_{conf}, F_{inte}, F_{avai} and F_{leak} respectively. Before running, OS configures vital flags by default or by the administrator; in running, vital flags should be spread automatically to avoid security vulnerability. Thus, four rules for spreading vital flags are designed as follows:

Directory to Directory Vital Rule ($\text{VR}_{\text{Dir-Dir}} : Directory \overset{F_{conf},F_{inte}}{\longrightarrow} Directory$) depicts that the new directory or file inherits F_{conf} and F_{inte} from the parent directory at the creation time.

Process to Process Vital Rule ($\text{VR}_{\text{Proc-Proc}} : Process \overset{F_{conf},F_{leak}}{\longrightarrow} Process$) depicts that the new process inherits F_{conf} and F_{leak} from the parent process at the creation time.

Process to File Vital Rule ($\text{VR}_{\text{Proc-File}} : Process \overset{F_{conf}}{\longrightarrow} File$) depicts that any file should inherit F_{conf} when it is created or modified by a process that has been attached with F_{conf} and F_{leak} simultaneously.

File to Process Vital Rule ($TRIALRESTRICTION$) depicts that any S_h should clean old F_{conf} and F_{leak} flags when executing a file, and then should inherit F_{leak} from the executable file. In addition, any S_h should possess F_{conf} after reading O_{conf}.

2.3 Health

The Health consists of health objects (O_h) and health subjects (S_h). A **Health Subject (S_h)** is a process that has not been tainted or labeled as vital. A **Health Object (O_h)** is an object that has not been tainted or labeled as vital. The Health can access the Taint and the Vital, and vice versa.

2.4 Protection

Corresponding to the three security protection targets, confidentiality, integrity and availability, STBAC sets up three protection rules that constitute the Protection part.

Confidentiality Protection Rule ($TRIALRESTRICTION$) forbids S_t to read O_{conf}, i.e. it forbids suspiciously tainted subjects to read sensitive files, to read or search sensitive directories, and to execute some privileged operations to destroy confidentiality, such as the "ptrace" system call.

Integrity Protection Rule ($TRIALRESTRICTION$) forbids S_t to write O_{inte}, i.e. it forbids suspiciously tainted subjects to modify, create, delete and rename a protected file or directory, and to execute some privileged operations to destroy integrity, such as the "create_module" and "setuid" system calls.

Availability Protection Rule ($TRIALRESTRICTION$) forbids an O_{avai}-allocating operation if the operation could lead to that the amount of allocated O_{avai} exceeds one of the two High Water Markers (HWM). One HWM is named HWM_{St} that represents maximum number of O_{avai} permitted to get by S_t. The other HWM is named HWM_{SYS} that represents maximum percentage of allocated O_{avai} in the whole system. (R_{St} indicates the amount of O_{avai} allocated to S_t; and R_{SYS} indicates the percentage of allocated O_{avai} in the whole system.)

3   Model Analysis

3.1   Compatibility Analysis

STBAC does not influence the actions of local users and remote users using Trustable-Communications. It also does not influence most actions of S_t, because STBAC only forbids S_t to illegally access vital resources that are merely a small part of all the resources, but does not forbid S_t to legally access vital resources, such as reading and executing O_{inte}.

Possible incompatibility can be caused by PR_{conf} and PR_{inte} since they restrict processes' actions. But they do not restrict the user who logs in by Trustable-Communications. This means that the administrator can still manage the computer and upgrade application software remotely by Trustable-Communications. PR_{avai} only restricts the resource allocation, and it'll not restrict any normal action of a process if the two High Water Markers are configured properly.

On most occasions, reading O_{conf} and modifying O_{inte} through Non-Trustable-Communications mean intrusions or network worms, and these should be forbidden by PR_{conf} and PR_{inte}. However, on special cases, we should permit processes using Non-Trustable-Communications to read O_{conf} or modify O_{inte}, which we call Shared-O_{conf} and Shared-O_{inte} respectively. And they account for incompatibility.

Shared-O_{inte} usually is a system configuration file that has to be modified by a process using Non-Trustable-Communications. Furthermore, the process cannot change to use Trustable-Communications. So the amount of Shared-O_{inte} is tiny. Shared-O_{inte} can not be a binary file, application configuration file or the majority of system configuration files, because we can use Trustable-Communications such as SSL, TSL and SSH to upgrade the system, patch software and modify configurations remotely. Only exceptional system configuration files have to be modified through Non-Trustable-Communications. In Linux, Shared-O_{inte} means /etc/resolve.conf, because dhcplient will write /etc/resolve.conf after receiving information from the remote DHCP server, whereas the communication between the DHCP client and server cannot use authentication or encryption.

Timothy Fraser successfully resolved a problem like Shared-O_{inte} by setting trusted program [3]. Here we use a similar mechanism named Trustable-Communication-List, each element of which consists of local program name, local IP and port, remote IP and port, network protocol and permitted time span. Information of remote communications that are needed when modifying Shared-O_{inte} is put in the Trustable-Communication-List. Only when a remote communication, which is ready to be launched, matches an element in the list will it be regarded as trustable. This mechanism can resolve Shared-O_{inte} problem and assure security to some degree.

Shared-O_{conf} mainly is the password files whose secrecy has to be shared by local processes and processes using Non-Trustable-Communications. Thus, the amount of Shared-O_{conf} is tiny. In Linux, Shared-O_{conf} includes /etc/passwd, /etc/shadow and /usr/local/apache/passwd/passwords.

A mechanism named Partial-Copy is designed to resolve Shared-O_{conf} problem. It generates a partial copy for each Shared-O_{conf} to save part of the Shared-O_{conf} content. The partial copy permits access by the processes using Non-Trustable-Communications. For example, we can build a partial copy of /etc/passwd to contain user information needed by process using Non-Trustable-Communications, but the information of privileged users and other important users still stay in /etc/passwd and is forbidden to be accessed by Non-Trusted-Communication processes. In order to implement the Partial-Copy mechanism, the kernel should redirect the access target of Non-Trustable-Communication processes from Shared-O_{conf} to the corresponding partial copy.

In summary, STBAC can get good compatibility because it only prevents S_t from illegally accessing vital resources. Though we have incompatibility problems from Shared-O_{conf} and Shared-O_{inte}, their amount is tiny, and can be resolved by the Trustable-Communication-List and Partial-Copy mechanisms.

3.2 Simplicity Analysis

Simplicity of STBAC derives from that it is simple to administer and easy to understand. The main work for administering STBAC is to identify those files or directories that need to be protected and set vital flags. This is straightforward and easy to understand. As the system files and directories that need protection could be set vital flags automatically by the system, the user only needs to set his/her data files and directories. Taint flag can be generated and spread automatically by the kernel, and does not need any manual operations. Partial-Copy and Trustable-Communication-List may bring some additional work, but the work is limited because of the very small amount of Shared-O_{conf} and Shared-O_{inte}.

4 Model Implementation

TRIAL RESTRICTION We have implemented a STBAC prototype in the Linux kernel 2.4.20 based on our former work. The general principle is to avoid significant reductions of simplicity, compatibility and performance of original Linux. Figure 2 shows the architecture.

Similar to the methodology of M. Abrams et al. [17], we divide the implementation into three parts: enforcement, decision and information. Separating model enforcement from model decision has the advantage of conveniently modifying and adding model rules without change of most codes, as described in [18]. The information part is not independent of the kernel, but is founded on modifying existing kernel structure.

The enforcement part intercepts accesses at related system calls or important kernel functions, and issues requests to the decision part. For the protection requests, such as confidentiality protection requests, integrity protection requests or availability protection requests, the enforcement part permits or denies the access according to the result returned by the decision part. For the spread requests, such as taint spread requests and vital flag spread requests, the enforcement part does nothing after posting the requests, and the decision part directly modifies data structures of the information part. Table 1 describes the modified system calls and kernel functions, and the corresponding model rules.

Table 1. STBAC rules and system calls

Model rules		Functions
Taint Rules	$TR_{sock-proc}$	sys_socket
	$TR_{proc-proc}$	sys_fork,sys_vfork,sys_clone,sys_pipe,sys_map,sys_shmat, sys_msgrcv,sys_mkfifo,sys_mknod
	$TR_{proc-exe}$	sys_open,sys_create,sys_chmod,sys_fchmod
	$TR_{exe-proc}$	sys_execve,sys_mmap
Vital rules	$VR_{dir-dir}$	sys_open,sys_create,sys_mkdir,sys_mknod
	$VR_{proc-proc}$	sys_fork,sys_vfork,sys_clone
	$VR_{file-proc}$	sys_execve
	$VR_{proc-file}$	Sys_open, sys_create
Protection rules	PR_{conf}	sys_open,sys_ptrace,sys_get_stbac_attr
	PR_{inte}	sys_open,sys_truncate,sys_ftruncate,sys_chmod, sys_fchmod,sys_chown,sys_fchown,sys_lchown, sys_rmdir,sys_rename,sys_unlink,sys_mount, sys_umount,sys_setrlimit,sys_reboot,sys_swapoff, sys_create_module,sys_delete_module,sys_setuid, sys_setgid,sys_setfsuid,sys_setfsgid,sys_set_stbac_attr, sys_kill
	PR_{avai}	Sys_setrlimit,sock_recvmsg,sock_sendmsg,sys_brk, schedule, ext3_alloc_block, ext2_alloc_block

The decision part is a new kernel module that is built for handling requests from the enforcement part. While making a decision, it firstly reads the STBAC flags of subject and object from the information part, and then calls corresponding module rules for deciding whether to permit the access and whether to modify the STBAC flags in the kernel data structure. In the case of denying the access, the decision part will try to redirect the access to the partial copy. If the access is from sys_socket, it will search Trustable-Communication-List to affirm whether the access opens a Trustable-Communication. The process will not be attached with F_t while the communication is trustable.

The information part saves and maintains all kinds of STBAC flags of subjects and objects. There can be two implementation options: one is to build independently STBAC data structures for saving flags, and the other is to use the existing kernel data structures for saving flags. The main advantage of the former one is that it is independent of Linux kernel codes, but the disadvantage is that it will lose performance significantly; the latter one can use kernel functions to organize and maintain data structures so that it is easy to be implemented and has little performance reduction. So the latter is adopted.

In addition, we created four commands: stbac_set_flag, stbac_get_flag, stbac_admin_trusted_comm and stbac_admin_partial_copy. The stbac_set_flag and stbac_get_flag are used to set and get all kinds of STBAC flags. They can operate on all files and directories under a directory at a time, or operate on all descendants of a process at a time. We also created a shell script named "stbac_init" to automatically initiate and check the STBAC flags for system directories and files when booting the system.

All partial copies are saved under "./stbac". The password and user management commands are modified to synchronize Shared-O_{inte} with its partial copy automatically.

5   Model Evaluation

In order to evaluate the STBAC model, we tested the STBAC prototype from three aspects: protection capability, compatibility and performance. For evaluating protection capability, we completed three tests "user-operation", "web-download" and "remote-attack", which showed that STBAC can forbid illegal accessing vital resources from remote user, downloaded program and intruder. For evaluating compatibility we have run many network applications and local applications without incompatible problems, which includes apache, vsftp, samba, telnet, sendmail, gcc, gdb, vi, etc. For evaluating performance, we compared the performance of the original Linux kernel and the STBAC-enforced Linux kernel. The result showed that performance reduction is only around 1.7% to 4.6%. Based on the above tests, we can safely say that the STBAC-enforced Linux can protect effectively important directories, files and processes without significant impact on compatibility and performance.

6   Related Works

DTE, proposed by Lee Badger et al. [8][1], is implemented in Linux by Serge Hallyn et al. [9], and is also adopted by SE-Linux [16]. It groups processes into domains, and groups files into types, and restricts access from domains to types as well as from domains to other domains. In a predefined condition, a process can switch its domain from one to another.

STBAC can be viewed as a type of dynamic DTE. It divides all processes into two domains: S_t and S_h, and divides all objects into five types: O_t, O_h, O_{inte}, O_{conf} and O_{avai}; It defines access rights of each domain: S_h can access any object; S_t can access any object except reading O_{conf}, writing O_{inte} and allocating excessive O_{avai}; S_h can switch to S_t by taint rules.

Dynamic characteristic of STBAC is reflected in that both domains and types in STBAC can change dynamically during the system execution, but in DTE only domains can change and types cannot change. Domains and types change in STBAC according to the taint rules, which are automatically triggered by the intruder's activities in the system. However, domain changing in DTE takes place when executing the entry point file that needs administrator's predefinition.

Due to this dynamic characteristic in STBAC, administration work is dramatically decreased. Users needn't predefine which subject is S_h or S_t, and which object is O_h or O_t. These definitions are automatically done by the taint rules during system execution.

Another related work is the intrusion backtracking in OS. In 2003, S.T. King and P.M. Chen built an effective intrusion backtracking and analyzing tool named Backtracker [13][10]. It can help administrator to find intrusion steps with the help of the dependency graph that is generated by logging and analyzing OS events. Zhu and Chiueh built a repairable file service named RFS [11], which supports kernel logging to allow roll-back of any file update operation, and keeps track of inter-process dependencies to quickly determine the extent of system damage after an attack/error. In 2005, Ashvin Goel and Kenneth Po built an intrusion recovery system named taser [12], which helps in selectively recovering file-system data after an attack. It determines the set of tainted file-system objects by creating dependencies among sockets, processes and files based on the entries in the system audit log. These works all focus on the intrusion analysis and recovery by logging system activities, and directly inspire the taint rules of STBAC. The most distinctive point in our work is that our objective is to build an access control mechanism that can trace and block intrusions in real time.

There are several famous Linux security enhancement projects, such as SELinux [16], LIDS [4], DTE [9], systrace [15], LOMAC [2][3], etc. SELinux is a powerful Linux security enhancement project. It can flexibly support multiple security policies. But for general users, it is difficult to bring it into play, because it requires professional knowledge on the part of the user. LOMAC has similar ideas with ours. It implements the LowWater-Mark model [6] in Linux kernel, and aims to bring simple but useful MAC integrity protection to Linux. It keeps good compatibility with existing software. But LOMAC does not consider safeguarding confidentiality and usability.

7   Conclusions

In this paper, we present a new OS access control model named STBAC. It consists of four parts: Taint, Health, Vital and Protection. The Taint might be controlled by an intruder and consists of S_t, O_t and taint rules which can trace activities of S_t. The Vital should be protected properly as it represents vital resources which are the valuable user data and the foundation for system to provide services, hence vital resources usually become the final targets of an intrusion. The Protection consists of three mandatory protection rules that forbid S_t to illegally access vital resources. The Health is not tainted or labeled as vital ones, and it can access the Taint and the Vital.

STBAC have reached its four goals: protecting vital resources, compatibility, simplicity and performance. For protecting vital resources, the three protection tests validated this experimentally. For compatibility, analysis shows that STBAC does not influence the actions of local users and remote users using Trustable-Communications. Remote administrator can still manage the computer and upgrade application software through Trustable-Communications. In addition, STBAC does not influence most actions of S_t, because it only forbids S_t to illegally access vital resources. Compatibility exceptions come from Shared-O_{conf} and Shared-O_{inte}, which are of tiny amounts, and Trustable-Communication-List and Partial-Copy mechanisms can be used to resolve them. The test on application compatibility validated this goal experimentally. For simplicity, analysis shows that the main administration work of STBAC is to set vital flags for user files and directories that need to be protected, this is straightforward and easy to understand. The vital flags of system files and directories can be automatically attached by a shell script "stbac_init" when booting the system. F_t is automatically generated and propagated by kernel and does not require any manual operation. For performance, tests showed that there is merely 1.7%~4.6% performance reduction caused by STBAC.

Therefore, the STBAC model is useful in OS to defeat network attacks while maintaining good compatibility, simplicity and system performance.

Acknowledgments. We thank the anonymous reviewers for useful feedback. This research is supported by the Natural Science Foundation of China under grant number 60703103 and 60573091, the 863 High Technology Foundation of China under grant number 2007AA01Z414, and the Research Foundation of Renmin University of China under grant number 06XNB053.

References

1. Badger, L., Sterne, D.F., Sherman, D.L., Walker, K.M., Haghighat, S.A.: A domain and type enforcement UNIX prototype. In: Proc. of the 5th USENIX UNIX Security Symposium (June 1995)
2. Fraser, T.: LOMAC: Low Water-Mark Integrity Protection for COTS Environments. In: Proceedings of the IEEE Symposium on Security and Privacy, Oakland, CA (May 2000)
3. Fraser, T.: LOMAC:MAC You Can LiveWith. In: Proceedings of the FREENIX Track, USENIX Annual Technical Conference, Boston, MA (June 2001)
4. Huagang, X.: Build a secure system with LIDS (2000), Available online at http://www.lids.org/document/build_lids-0.2.html

5. Bell, D.E., LaPadula, L.: Secure Computer Systems: Unified Exposition and Multics Interpretation, NTIS AD-A023 588, MTR 2997, ESD-TR-75-306, Mitre Corporation, Bedford MA (1976)
6. Biba, K.J.: Integrity considerations for secure computer systems. Technical Report MTR 3153, The Mitre Corporation (April 1977)
7. Sandhu, R.S., et al.: Role-Based Access Control Models. IEEE Computer 29(2), 38–47 (1996)
8. Badger, L., Sterne, D.F., Sherman, D.L., Walker, K.M., Haghighat, S.A.: Practical Domain and Type Enforcement for UNIX. In: IEEE Symposium on Security and Privacy, Oakland, CA (May 1995)
9. Hallyn, S., Kearns, P.: Domain and Type Enforcement for Linux. In: Proceedings of the 4th Annual Linux Showcase and Conference (October 2000)
10. King, S.T., Chen, P.M.: Backtracking intrusions. TOCS. ACM Transactions on Computer Systems (2005)
11. Zhu, N., Chiueh, T.: Design, implementation, and evaluation of repairable file service. In: DSN. Proceedings of the 2003 International Conference on Dependable Systems and Networks, pp. 217–226 (2003)
12. Farhadi, K., Li, Z., Goel, A., Po, K., Lara, E.: The taser intrusion recovery system. In: Proceedings of the twentieth ACM symposium on Operating systems principles (2005)
13. King, S.T., Chen, P.M.: Backtracking Intrusions. In: SOSP 2003. Proceedings of ACM Symposium on Operating Systems Principles (October 2003)
14. Information technology security evaluation criteria (ITSEC). Technical Report Version 1.2, Commission of the European Communities, Brussels, Belgium (June 1991)
15. Provos, N.: Improving Host Security with System Call Policies. In: 12th USENIX Security Symposium, Washington, DC (August 2003)
16. Loscocco, P., Smalley, S.: Integrating flexible support for security policies into the Linux operating system. In: Proc. of the 2001 USENIX, FREENIX track, pp. 29–40 (June 2001)
17. Abrams, M., LaPadula, L., Eggers, K., Olson, I.: A Generalized Framework for Access Control: an Informal Description. In: Proceedings of the 13th National Computer Security Conference, pp. 134–143 (October 1990)
18. Abrams, M.D., Joyce, M.V.: Extending the ISO Access Control Framework for Multiple Policies. In: IFIP Transactions in Computer Security A-37, Elsevier Publishers, Amsterdam (1993)

A Secure Intra-domain Routing Protocol for Wireless Mesh Networks

Ramanarayana Kandikattu and Lillykutty Jacob

Department of Electronics and Communication Engineering,
National Institute of Technology, Calicut-673601, India
k_ramnarayan@rediffmail.com, lilly@nitc.ac.in

Abstract. Wireless Mesh Networks (WMNs) is a rapidly progressing area of research, promising future broadband *anywhere and anytime* network access. WMN is anticipated to resolve the limitations of Mobile Ad hoc Networks (MANET). Secure routing in WMN still remains as an open research problem due to its special characteristics such as dedicated backbone network with static/mobile mesh clients. This paper proposes a framework that addresses: i) the application of Identity Based Cryptography (IBC) to WMN, for efficient key management and for the distribution of pair-wise shared keys among the authenticated clients; and, ii) the design of a light weight secure routing protocol for intra-domain WMN routing which protects all the fields of the routing packet against various security attacks. Security analysis shows that the proposed protocol meets the targeted security goals. Performance analysis carried out using OPNET simulation studies show that the proposed protocol adds minimal delay and communication overhead to provide security.

1 Introduction

Wireless Mesh Networks (WMNs) are anticipated to revolutionize the future broadband wireless network access. WMN consists of static or mobile mesh routers and gateways forming backbone wireless network to provide broadband Internet connectivity to mobile or static mesh clients. WMN is also anticipated to work with other wireless networks such as cellular, sensor network, wireless LAN etc. WMN can be visualized as an interconnection of several autonomous wireless network domains connected by backbone network (Fig. 1). This paper considers a typical WMN suitable for broadband Metropolitan Area Networking (MAN) applications, which comprises static backbone network with static or mobile mesh clients. For this particular scenario it is more appropriate to consider: i) 802.16 physical and MAC layer standards for interconnecting mesh routers and gateways; and, ii) 802.11 standards to provide intra-domain ad hoc connectivity among mesh clients [1,14].

Routing is a challenging issue for WMN for optimum utilization of resources such as: i) channel bandwidth; ii) battery power; iii) computational; and, iv)

P. McDaniel and S.K. Gupta (Eds.): ICISS 2007, LNCS 4812, pp. 37–50, 2007.

memory resources. Routing protocols designed for MANET cannot be applied to WMN without any modifications, because WMN comprises: i) dedicated wireless backbone comprising mesh routers and gateways with minimal mobility; and, ii) highly mobile mesh clients forming ad hoc network with other mesh clients and routers. Neither a proactive nor a reactive routing protocol is appropriate to deal with very large wireless mesh network comprising thousands of nodes forming MAN. Analogous to Internet, it is more appropriate to use hybrid protocol approach, that means a proactive inter-domain routing protocol is required for routing among static or less mobile mesh routers and a reactive intra-domain routing protocol is required for routing among mobile clients which are within an autonomous domain [2].

Security is an essential component of WMN to deal with various threats on routing as well as on data packet transmission.

This paper focuses on the framework of a Secure Intra-domain Mesh Routing Protocol (SIMRP) tailored to suit the requirements of WMN. Simulation studies have been conducted using OPNET 12.0 [13] simulator to analyze the performance of the proposed protocol.

The rest of the paper is organized as follows. Section 2 gives an overview of security issues related to WMN. Section 3 explains the concepts of IBC. Section 4 presents a detailed description of the proposed framework. Section 5 presents the simulation study and performance analysis of the proposed protocol. Finally Section 6 presents the conclusion and future work.

2   Security Issues

WMNs are prone to various active and passive attacks because of the following characteristics: i) open wireless communications; ii) dependence on neighbors; iii) resource constraints such as bandwidth and battery; iv) mobility of clients, and v) time varying intra-domain network topology etc.

This paper is restricted to security issues related to Intra-domain routing only. The intra-domain mesh network has similar characteristics as that of well studied mobile ad hoc network. Therefore, this proposal considers the well researched Ad hoc On-demand Distance Vector routing protocol (AODV) [7] as the basic protocol and novel security extensions are incorporated for intra-domain routing in WMN.

2.1   Security Requirements

The security requirements in intra-domain routing include:

- Confidentiality: It ensures that the message sent is readable only to the authorized clients
- Integrity: It ensures that the message sent is not modified by any unauthorized intermediate nodes.
- Freshness: It ensures that the message is recent and not the replay of old messages.

- Authentication: It ensures both the sender and receiver of the message that they are communicating with each other and not with the intruder.
- Availability: It ensures that the desired network services are available to the authorized party even in the presence of denial of service attacks.
- Non-repudiation: It ensures that the sender cannot deny the transmission of a message that it has previously sent. Similarly, it ensures that the receiver cannot deny the reception of previously received message.

2.2 Attacks Specific to Intra-domain Routing Protocol

The following are the common attacks on intra-domain routing:

- Impersonation Attack: Malicious node imitates a legitimate node and fabricates falsified control messages to disrupt the network.
- Modification Attack: Malicious node modifies any one or more of the fields of the routing packets for: i) creating routing loops; ii) attracting the traffic towards a selected node; iii) extending or shorting of routes; iv) partitioning of network to carryout denial of service attack; v) increasing end-to-end delay to degrade network performance, and vi) creating false route error messages etc.
- Attack on Service Availability: Denial-of-Service (DoS) attack is another attack caused by diverting the traffic towards the targeted node or network to make it overloaded.

2.3 Attack Countermeasures

To avoid impersonation attacks, every authorized client should have unique ID, bonded with its public key and private key pair. The mechanism called proactive security, wherein application of cryptography to routing protocol is used to secure the routing protocol from most of the attacks. But, this requires the efficient deployment of public, private key pairs and shared keys among the authorized participating clients. IBC provides an efficient way of key deployment. Sections 3 and 4 give more detailed discussion about IBC and key deployment. Authenticity of source and destination clients should be verified by all the nodes in the route. Authenticity of intermediate clients in the route should be verified by other clients in the route. Integrity and origin of control/ data packets should be protected with secure keyed hash algorithms or with digital signatures, to avoid modification attacks.

3 Identity-Based Cryptography(IBC)

Certificate-based Cryptography requires lengthy (typically 1K Byte) certificate to distribute the public key among the participating clients. In the ad hoc network scenario, the distribution of certificates can be done by sending the certificate piggy-backed on the routing packets. But this method incurs heavy routing overhead, consumes network bandwidth and computational resources [9].

IBC eliminates the need for certificates because public key of an authorized participating client can be extracted from the identity of that client. The concept of IBC was first introduced by Shamir in 1984 [3]. Later Boneh et al. presented Identity- based encryption scheme [4] using pairing technique in 2001 and proposed a basic Identity-based signature scheme [5]. A good survey of pairing-based cryptographic protocols is given in [6]. The following gives an overview of the basics of pairing technique.

Let G_1 be an additive group and G_2 be a multiplicative group of same order q. Let P be an arbitrary generator of G_1. Assume that the discrete logarithm problem is hard in both G_1 and G_2. A mapping $F : G_1 \rightarrow G_2$ satisfying the following properties is called a cryptographic bilinear map [6].

- Bilinearity: $F(\alpha P, \beta Q) = F(P, Q)^{\alpha\beta} = F(\alpha P, Q)^{\beta} = F(P, \beta Q)^{\alpha}$ and $\alpha, \beta \in \mathbb{Z}q^*$
- Non-degeneracy: If P is a generator of G_1, then F(P,P) is the generator of G_2. In other words $F(P, P) \neq 1$.
- Computable: There exists an efficient algorithm to compute F(P,Q) for all $P, Q \in G_1$.

Modified Weil and Tate pairings on an elliptic curve over a finite field are examples of cryptographic bilinear maps [6].

IBC consists of the following important algorithms: i) set up, ii) extract, iii) encrypt, iv) decrypt, v) sign and vi) verify. We refer to [6] and the references therein for more detailed description.

4 Proposed Protocol: Secure Intra-domain Mesh Routing Protocol (SIMRP)

This paper addresses a secure intra-mesh routing protocol, SIMRP, which is a variant of AODV [7] routing protocol with added security features. It uses IBC to simplify the key setup among the clients without using digital certificates. SIMRP is different from SAODV [8] which uses public key cryptography for protecting the routing packets. SAODV has the potential weakness in protecting hop count from any malicious intermediate node incrementing it to higher value. TRP [9] is a computationally efficient routing protocol proposed in the literature, but it also has the same weakness as that of SAODV in protecting hop count. The proposed protocol SIMRP uses some features of TRP but with a novel technique to protect the hop count.

SIMRP has the following design goals: i) To avoid digital certificates and to simplify key setup using IBC; ii) To provide security against modification, fabrication, replay, and impersonation attacks on Intra-mesh routing; iii) To achieve the routing at low computation and communication overhead, as well as with minimum latency.

There are three types of entities to be dealt with:

- Operator: The entity which operates a wireless mesh network. A wireless network may contain single domain or multiple domains of different scales, either physically adjacent or non-adjacent. Operator is responsible to setup and maintain different agents or routers. Operator is also responsible for IBC domain parameter setup, and distribution of client ID, public key, and private key among the registered clients.

- Mesh Router/Agent(A): The entity that controls a single domain. An agent is under the administrative control of an operator. An operator which has multiple domains has multiple agents,one per domain. A mesh router that can provide Internet connectivity to mesh clients is called mesh gateway router. A mesh router/agent that cannot provide Internet connectivity directly but can offer Internet connectivity through nearest gateway router is called mesh router.
- Mesh Client (MC): The entity that wants to participate either in intra-mesh routing or wants to have wireless Internet connectivity through agent. Each MC should belong to an administrative domain called its home domain.

Fig. 1 illustrates a general form of wireless mesh network. The mesh routers connected by wireless links form the backbone network. They support broadband connectivity between mesh clients and provides high speed two way Internet connectivity to any registered mesh client. Fig. 2 illustrates the logical relation between operator, agent and mesh clients.

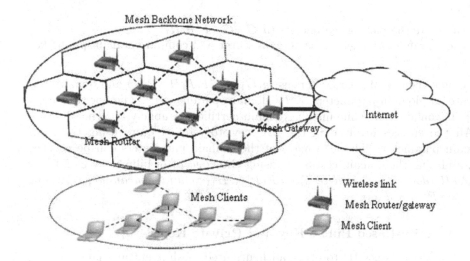

Fig. 1. A general form of Wireless Mesh Network

4.1   Notation

We use similar notation and key setup as used in [10]. Let O_i denotes i^{th} operator and $A_{i,j}$ denotes mesh agent i enrolled with operator j. Typically the standard format of $A_{i,j}$ is agent i's_IP_address@operator j's ID. Similarly, $MC_{i,j}$ denotes MC i registered with operator j. The standard format of $MC_{i,j}$ is MC i's_IP_address@operator j's ID. $ID_{A_{i,j}}$ denotes the identity of $A_{i,j}$ and $K_{A_{i,j}}^{-1}$

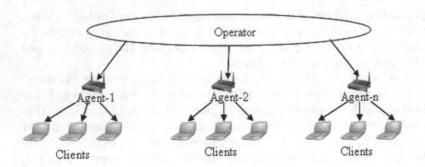

Fig. 2. Logical relation between Operator, Agent and Clients

the private key of $A_{i,j}$. Likewise, $ID_{MC_{i,j}}$ and $K^{-1}_{MC_{i,j}}$ denote the MC's ID and private key respectively. Every operator issues the ID and private key to all the agents and MCs under its administrative control.

4.2   Domain Parameter Setup

IBC requires each operator to perform the following domain-parameter initialization

- Generate the pairing parameters (q, G_1, G_2, F, P, H_1)
- Pick a random integer 's' as domain secret and compute domain-public key as $P_{pub} = sP$.

We define the domain-parameters as $(q, G_1, G_2, F, P, H_1, P_{pub})$ and domain certificate as (domain-parameters, $s.H_1($ domain-parameters)). The operator must keep 's' confidential, while making domain-certificate publicly known.

All the entities involved in the IBC cryptosystem require using the same domain parameters. The legitimacy of the domain parameters can be checked by validating the domain certificate using the concept of bilinearity as follows: $F(P, sH_1(domain-parameters)) = F(P_{pub}, H_1(domain-parameters))$ where, $P_{pub} = sP$.

4.3   Identity-Based Public Key and Private Key Setup

Every operator issues ID to every authenticated mesh agent and client who is under its administrative domain prior to the deployment. Mesh Agent i's ID issued by operator j is of the form $ID_{A_{i,j}} = (A_{i,j}, expiry - time)$, and its private key is $K^{-1}_{A_{i,j}} = s^{O_j} H_1^{O_j}(ID_{A_{i,j}})$. Similarly, MC i's ID and private key issued by operator j are $ID_{MC_{i,j}} = (MC_{i,j}, expiry - time, other - terms)$, $K^{-1}_{MC_{i,j}} = s^{O_j} H_1^{O_j}(ID_{MC_{i,j}})$ respectively. The freshness of ID is controlled by expiry time in the ID field. MC i can extract its public key $K_{MC_{i,j}}$ from its ID by applying domain hash function on it i.e. $K_{MC_{i,j}} = H_1^{O_j}(ID_{MC_{i,j}})$. Note that, the superscript O_j is used to denote operator j's domain parameters.

4.4   Identity-Based Pair-Wise Shared Key Setup

Once the registered clients $MC_{1,1}$ and $MC_{2,1}$ in an administrative domain are equipped with their ID, domain parameters, and public and private key pair then they can establish pair-wise shared key with each other using bilinearity as follows.

$$
\begin{aligned}
K_{MC_{1,1},MC_{2,1}} &= F^{O_1}(K_{MC_{1,1}}^{-1}, H^{O_1}(ID_{MC_{2,1}})) \\
&= F^{O_1}(s^{O_j} H_1^{O_j}(ID_{MC_{i,j}}), H^{O_1}(ID_{MC_{2,1}})) \\
&= F^{O_1}(H_1^{O_j}(ID_{MC_{i,j}}), s^{O_j} H^{O_1}(ID_{MC_{2,1}})) \\
&= F^{O_1}(H_1^{O_j}(ID_{MC_{i,j}}), K_{MC_{2,1}}^{-1}) \\
&= K_{MC_{2,1}MC_{1,1}}
\end{aligned}
\tag{1}
$$

4.5   Intra-mesh Communication

When any authorized client S wants to communicate with another client D within the same domain and if route to D is not known, SIMRP invokes route discovery mechanism similar to AODV. SIMRP uses similar mechanism as in [9] with modifications to protect hop count.

Route discovery. The route discovery process uses secure route request (SR-Req) and secure route reply (SRRep) packets.

SRReq packet format is similar to AODV's RReq packet except for the following modifications: i) uses ID of MC instead of IP address; ii) uses no hop count field; iii) includes Neighbor Table NT, which contain the IDs of two recently traversed clients; and, iv) includes time stamp of source client. RReq and TS are protected by the signature of source client with its private key i.e. K_s^{-1}. If client S wants to send a packet to client D and if the route to client D is not available, S initiates SRReq. The NT in SRReq is initialized with the source client's ID and the time stamp T_S is appended. The static parts of SRReq are protected with light weight identity based signature because client S cannot calculate the shared key with the client D at this moment. S broadcasts SRReq to its neighbors as in (2).

$$
S{\rightarrow}* : K_s^{-1}(RReq, T_S), NT\{S\}
\tag{2}
$$

Any 1st hop neighbor 'A' which is not the destination client, does the following in addition to the operations performed in the conventional AODV [7]: i) client A verifies the sign and authenticates S; ii) appends its ID to the NT; iii) marks its first hop neighbor in its table; and, then iv) broadcasts the message to its neighbors as in (3).

$$
A{\rightarrow}* : K_s^{-1}(RReq, T_S), NT\{S, A\}
\tag{3}
$$

Any neighbor B which is neither the first hop neighbor of S nor the destination client, records the second hop neighbor's ID in its route table as depicted in Table 1.

Table 1. Route table entries at client B in Route reply phase

Rev2ndhop	Rev1sthop	SrcMAC	DestMAC	RREQ	RREP	Token	Fwd1sthop	Fwd2ndhop
S	A	–	–	$RREQ_1$	–	–	–	–

Also, client B, removes from NT the reverse 2nd hop client's ID (i.e., S), and appends its ID as in (4), because NT holds IDs of two recently visited clients only.

$$B \to * : K_s^{-1}(RReq, T_S), NT\{A, B\} \tag{4}$$

Finally, SRReq reaches destination client 'D'. Client D makes similar entries in its route table. Client D validates the signature and authenticates client S. Client D unicasts SRRep as in (5) back to the source

$$D \to B : RRep, NT\{D\}, MIC_S, MIC_D, H_{DB}, H_{AD} \tag{5}$$

As in the case of SRReq packets, SRRep packet format is similar to AODV's RRep packet except for the following modifications: i) uses ID of MC instead of IP address; ii) uses hop count field; iii) includes Neighbor Table NT{}, which contain the IDs of two recently traversed clients; iv) includes message integrity check codes MIC_S, MIC_D; and, v) hash codes generated by two recently traversed clients to protect the hop count and other fields of SRRep.

Client D sends SRRep to B as in (5) after the following operations: i) hop count initialized to zero; ii) NT is initialized with the destination client's ID; iii) calculates $Token = H_1(T_S\|K_{SD}), MIC_S = H_1(RReq\|Token)$, and $MIC_D = H_1(RRep\|Token)$ with zero hop count; and, iv) appends keyed hash values H_{DB}, H_{DA} where B and A are the one hop and two hop neighbors respectively. Since D knows their identities from the SRReq packet and it can calculate the shared key pair with each of them with the help of bilinearity described in (1), the hash values are calculated as $H_{DB} = H_1(RRep\|K_{DB})$ and $H_{DA} = H_1(RRep\|K_{DA})$. These hash values are used to protect the hop count field from modification attack. Since, hop count value at two hop neighbor is exactly one less than the value at one hop neighbor as the packet traverses from destination to source, every intermediate client checks whether the same difference is maintained by the two hash values calculated by successive clients.

Client B verifies only H_{DB} because it has no two hop neighbor. Intermediate client B records the first hop neighbor, MIC_S, and MIC_D in its route table as shown in the Table 2.

Table 2. Route table entries at client B in Route reply phase

Rev2ndhop	Rev1sthop	SrcMAC	DestMAC	RREQ	RREP	Token	Fwd1sthop	Fwd2ndhop
S	A	MIC_S	MIC_D	$RREQ_1$	$RREP_1$	–	D	

Client B appends its hash values calculated with its reverse neighbors A and S as in (6)

$$B{\to}A : RRep, NT\{D, B\}, MIC_S, MIC_D, H_{DA}, H_{BA}, H_{BS} \qquad (6)$$

Client A does similar verification as done by client B. Finally, client A unicasts the packet to client S as in (7).

$$A{\to}S : RRep, NT\{B, A\}, MIC_S, MIC_D, H_{BS}, H_{AS} \qquad (7)$$

Clients S validates MIC_S, MIC_D and verifies H_{BS} and H_{AS}. Now S can select the lowest hop count route from the received SRRep messages as the route for its data transmission. Hop count modification is not possible because, every intermediate client checks the hop count information given by two most recently traversed clients.

After the validation of MIC_D, S authenticates D thereby completing the mutual authentication.

Now all the intermediate clients have to authenticate source and destination clients. For this purpose, source attaches a token to the data packet. Upon receiving the data packet, every intermediate client performs the following operations [13]: i) extracts the token from the data packet; ii) If token matches the one in its table then the packet will be routed according to the next hop entry in the table. If no Token found in its table, then it proceeds as follows: i) calculates $MIC_S^1 = H_1(RREQ1||token)$ and compares with the recorded MIC_S; ii) If they are same it authenticates the source. Similarly it authenticates client D by checking MIC_D. If both the verifications are satisfied intermediate client records the token in its table.

Route maintenance. Every client along the route monitors the connectivity between itself and next hop during the data packet transmission. If a client X observes link failure, it sends a Route error message (RErr) to the source client after attaching $MIC_{err} = H_1(RErr||T_x||K_{XS})$.

Secure data packet transmission. After route setup, every data packet sent along the route carries: i) Token; and, ii) $H_1(data||K_{SD})$. Every intermediate client checks the validity of token, to verify the authenticity of packet's origin. The destination client validates the token and hash code of source client before accepting the data packet. This process adds minimal communication overhead to carry token, but gives no room for attacks on the route and data.

5   Simulation Study and Performance Analysis

In order to evaluate the impact of security features on the performance of the routing protocol, we used OPNET[13] simulation tool.

5.1   Setup Parameters

A network of 50 clients randomly placed in a rectangular area of 1500m x 300m has been considered. Every client is subjected to mobility as per random way point model with a uniformly distributed speed of 0-20m/s and with a specified pause time. We varied the pause times to vary the relative speeds of the clients in order to examine its impact on the performance. We considered CBR traffic sources with a rate of 4 packets/sec. We varied the number of traffic sources to apply different loads on the network. All the sources generate 512bytes packets. At the MAC level, the 802.11 DCF protocol has been considered with a channel bandwidth of 2Mbit/s. All the Simulations run for 900 simulation seconds. Table 3 gives the different simulation parameters used for this model.

Table 3. Simulation parameters

Parameter	Value
Field Area	1500m X 300m
No.of Nodes	50
Traffic Type	CBR,4 packets/sec
No.of traffic sources	10,20,30
Packet size	512 bytes
Pause Time(sec)	0,30,60,120,300,600,900
Mobility Model	Random way point model
Node speed	uniform 0-20m/s
Field Area	1500m X 300m
Channel bandwidth	2Mbps
MAC layer	802.11g

5.2   Performance Metrics

To study the impact of added security features we compare SIMRP with AODV in terms of the following performance metrics:

Average Route discovery Time (sec): The time taken to setup the route.

Average end to end delay of data packets (sec): This includes all possible delays caused by buffering during route discovery, queuing at the interface queue, retransmission delays at the MAC, and propagation and transfer times.

Normalized byte overhead: The ratio of total routing overhead (in bytes) incurred by the network to the total number of data bytes received by the destination clients.

5.3   Performance Analysis

The computational overhead of SIMRP is very low due to the following reasons: i) Identity-based cryptography is used for the registration process and therefore avoids the certificate distribution and public key extraction from certificates; ii) Pairing based pair-wise shared key setup is used without any additional communication overhead unlike the traditional Diffie-Hellman protocol; iii) SIMRP requires minimal signature verification at intermediate clients and uses message integrity check codes and tokens extensively for hop-by-hop integrity and authentication, which are computationally cheap; and, iv) SIMRP protects hop

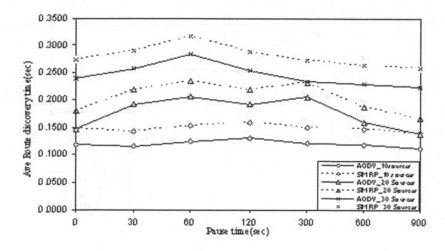

Fig. 3. Pause time Vs Route discovery time

count with the hash values of two recently traversed clients, which incurs little communication and computational overhead, where as proposals [8,9] have the weakness in protecting the hop count. Fig. 3 shows the route discovery time taken by AODV and SIMRP for different pause times. SIMRP takes additional 15% to 25% discovery time due to signature generation/ verification during request phase and hash generation and verification during reply phase. SIMRP incurs little additional end-to-end delay (Fig. 4), of the order of few micro seconds during actual data transfer because intermediate client need not do any additional computations other than comparing the token attached to the data packet with the token stored in route table. The byte overhead of SIMRP (Fig. 5) is two to three times larger than that of AODV because, SIMRP routing packets use client ID rather than IP addresses, and also carry signatures, hash values to protect the routing packets.

5.4   Security Analysis

The proposed SIMRP protocol is secure against most of the external attacks, because of the following defense mechanisms: A mesh client is permitted to participate in the routing protocol only after successful registration with its Operator. This process helps: i) To filter out external malicious clients from entering the network; and, ii) To bind a unique IP address with the ad hoc ID of the client. IP address is not only useful to uniquely identify the client in the global communication scenario but also helps to fix accountability to the participating clients. Any registered client found guilty can be fixed and such clients can be eliminated from the network. This enhances trust levels among the members of the network. Route request packet has only static fields and that is protected by signature to detect tampering by intermediate clients and to ensure that the

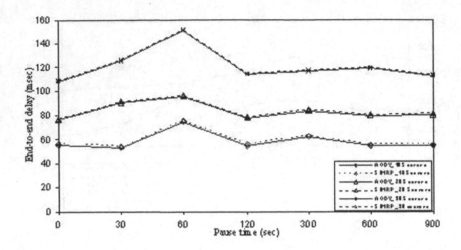

Fig. 4. Pause time Vs End-to-end delay

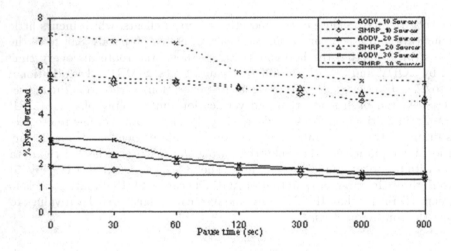

Fig. 5. Pause time Vs Byte overhead

message is originated by authorized client. Route reply carries the hop count field which is the only mutable part. It is protected by two independent message integrity check codes generated by two successive recently visited clients. This process avoids the non-colluding malicious client to carryout hop count modification attack. Token based routing avoids most of the potential modification and fabrication attacks on the source route because intermediate clients authenticate the route based on the token, which is not revealed until the exchange of route request and route reply has finished, and it is very hard to forge MIC_S and MIC_D without knowing the shared secret. End-to-end authentication in the route request phase avoids impersonation of source and destination clients.

End-to-end integrity in the route request phase avoids modification attacks by intermediate clients. Hop-by-hop authentication in the route reply phase avoids external malicious clients to participate in the routing protocol and thereby avoids the attacks caused by them.

6 Conclusion and Future Work

In this paper we proposed SIMRP, a secure intra-mesh routing protocol for WMN. Proposed protocol SIMRP uses IBC to avoid certificates, and MIC and tokens to minimize the computational overhead. SIMRP is resistant to most common security attacks such as modification, fabrication, replay attacks and it can also protect hop count. SIMRP is not resistant to collaborative, black hole, and gray hole attacks. Our future work is towards developing reactive security mechanisms to protect the network from the various colluding attacks. Secure Inter-mesh routing protocol is also a part of our future work. In addition, we would like to validate the security of SIMRP using formal security analysis techniques like BAN logic.

References

1. Akyildiz, I.F., Wang, X., Wang, W.: Wireless mesh networks: a survey Computer Networks 47, 445–487 (March 2005)
2. Waharte, S., Boutaba, R., Iraqi, Y., Ishibashi, B.: Routing Protocols in Wireless Mesh Networks: Challenges and Design Considerations Multimedia Tools and Applications (MTAP) journal. Special Issue on Advances in Consumer Communications and Networking 29(3), 285–303 (2006)
3. Shamir: Identity-based cryptosystems and Signature Schemes. In: Blakely, G.R., Chaum, D. (eds.) CRYPTO 1984. LNCS, vol. 196, pp. 47–53. Springer, Heidelberg (1985)
4. Boneh, D., Franklin, M.: Identity Based Encryption from the Weil Pairing. SIAM. J. of Computing 32, 586–615 (2003)
5. Boneh, D., Lynn, B., Shacham, H.: Short Signatures from the Weil Pairing. In: Boyd, C. (ed.) ASIACRYPT 2001. LNCS, vol. 2248, Springer, Heidelberg (2001)
6. Dutta, R., Barua, R., Sarkar, P.: Pairing-Based Cryptographic Protocols: A Survey Cryptology ePrint Archive, Report (2004)
7. Belding-Royer, E.M., Das, S.: Ad hoc on-demand distance vector (AODV) routing RFC 3561, IETF (July 2003)
8. Zapata, M.: Secure Ad hoc On-Demand Distance Vector (SAODV) Routing Internet draft (November 2004)
9. Li, L., Chigan, C.: Token Routing: A Power Efficient Method for Securing AODV Routing Protocol. In: Proceedings of the 2006 IEEE International Conference on Networking, Sensing and Control, pp. 29–34 (2006)
10. Zhang, Y., Fang, Y.: ARSA: An Attack-Resilient Security architecture for Multihop Wireless Mash Networks. IEEE Journal on Selected areas in communications 24, 1916–1928 (2006)

11. Ning, P., Sun, K.: How to misuse AODV: a case study of insider attacks against mobile ad-hoc routing protocols. In: IEEE workshop on Information Assurance, pp. 60–67 (June 2003)
12. Sanzgiri, K., Dahill, B., Levine, B.N., Belding-Royer, E.M.: A secure routing protocol for ad hoc networks. In: ICNP 2002. Proceedings of the 10th IEEE International Conference on Network protocols (2002)
13. Reference manuals from, http://www.opnet.com
14. Jianliang Zheng, L., Young-Bae, M.J., Shrestha, K.: Emerging standards for wireless mesh technology. IEEE Wireless Communications 13, 56–65 (2006)

Genetic Algorithm Based Steganography Using Wavelets

K.B. Raja, Kiran Kumar K., Satish Kumar N., Lakshmi M.S., Preeti H., Venugopal K.R.[1], and Lalit M. Patnaik[2]

[1] Department of Computer Science and Engineering
University Visvesvaraya College of Engineering
Bangalore University, Bangalore 560 001
raja_kb@yahoo.com, venugopalkr@gmail.com
[2] Microprocessor Applications Laboratory
Indian Institute of Science, Bangalore, India

Abstract. Steganography has long been a means of secure communication. Security is achieved by camouflaging the secret message. In this paper, we present a Genetic Algorithm based Steganography using Discrete Cosine Transforms(GASDCT) and Genetic Algorithm based Steganography using Discrete Wavelets Transform(GASDWT). In our approach, the Discrete Cosine Transform and Discrete Wavelet Transform are applied to the payload. Genetic Algorithm is used to generate many stego-images based on Fitness functions; one of these which give least statistical evidence of payload is selected as the best stego image to be communicated to the destination. It is observed that GASDWT has an improvement in Bit Error Rate(BER), Peak Signal to Noise Ratio(PSNR) and embedding capacity as compared to GASDCT.

1 Introduction

Steganography is the science of hiding messages in a medium called *Carrier* or the *Coverobject* in such a way that the existence of the message is concealed. The cover object could be an audio file, video file or an image file. The message to be hidden called the *Payload* could be plain text, audio, video or an image. The carrier or the cover object along with the hidden message is known as the *stego − object* or *steganogram*. Steganography is in contrast to cryptography where the existence of the hidden message is known, but the content is intentionally obscured. Steganography disguises the message to be hidden thus rendering it invisible. Hence the hidden message can be deciphered only if its existence is known. Steganography provides secure communication by embedding payload in the cover image. The development of Distributed computing, Grid computing and Computational capabilities of computers has reduced the security level in cryptography. Steganography as an alternative provides better security.

Examples of Steganography are covert channel, invisible ink, and microdot. Organic compounds such as lemon juice, milk, vinegar, fruit juices were used as

P. McDaniel and S.K. Gupta (Eds.): ICISS 2007, LNCS 4812, pp. 51–63, 2007.

invisible inks, which turned dark when held over flame revealing the hidden information. Modern invisible inks when exposed to UV light undergo fluorescence enabling retrieval of invisible message. Microdot is a high capacity miniaturized replica of the message. The message is photographed, reduced to a pre-defined size and then pasted into the cover object. Microdots also support transmission of technical drawings. Modern steganographic techniques most commonly use image as carrier, which enable secret communication for secure communications over the internet, copyright protection, and peer to peer secure communication. The main application of Steganography include that military application where military organizations use unobtrusive communications. The Steganography means in military applications include Spread Spectrum and Meteor Scatter radio which gives various combinations of resistances to detection. Other applications include the Medical safety, Indexing of voice mails e.t.c.

Steganographic methods can be classified into Spatial Domain Embedding and Frequency Domain Embedding. Spatial Domain Embedding comprises of the LSB method in which the least significant bits of the cover object are used to embed the message to be communicated secretly. As the resulting change in color is insignificant, the hidden image goes undetected by human vision. This technique enables high capacity embedding without rendering any significant changes to the cover image. The selection of LSB's could be random using a stego-key or could be confined to the noisy areas i.e., areas with large color variation of the image so as to generate least suspicion. The selection of LSB's could be done using a stego-key when security is the priority. Although the LSB method is a high capacity embedding technique, it leaves behind statistical evidences making it vulnerable to attacks.

The most popular methods under Frequency Domain Embedding are the Discrete Cosine Transformation (DCT) and Discrete Wavelet Transformation (DWT). In DCT method, the image is first transformed to frequency domain which results in spectral sub-bands. The spectral sub-bands are classified as High and Low frequency components. The Discrete Cosine coefficients of hidden image are embedded into the cover image such that the distortion is minimum and no significant changes in the statistical features of the stego image with respect to cover image occur. In DWT method, the image is decomposed based on frequency components into detailed and approximation bands, also called the sub-bands. Detailed band contains vertical, horizontal and diagonal bands. The total Information of the image is present in the approximation band. Hence the payload is normally embedded in the detailed band and rarely in the approximation band.

Contribution : In our work, the payload is converted into Discrete Cosine Transform and Discrete Wavelet Transform. There are two bands in DWT viz., Approximation band and the Detailed band. The Detailed band consists of Vertical, Horizontal and Diagonal Bands. The Discrete Cosine Transform coefficients and Discrete Wavelet Transform coefficients of the payload are embedded into the cover image by using Genetic Algorithm that have resulted in better performance and secure Steganography.

2   Related Work

Yi-Ta Wu and Frank Y. Shih [1] have developed the genetic algorithm based Steganography to generate several stego images until one of them can break the inspection of steganalytic system. The stego image is created by avoiding the change of its statistical features. Methodology based on Genetic algorithm is applied by adjusting gray values of a cover-image.

Rongrong Ji et al., [2] have presented an optimal block mapping LSB substitution method based on genetic algorithm, to minimize the degradation of the stego- image by finding global block mapping method. This minimizes MSE error between cover and the stego image. The optimal block mapping method devised confines its concern to LSB substitution which is spatial domain embedding. It does not work on frequency domain embedding methods which are more commonly used.

Sean Luke and Lee Spector [3] have presented a comparison of crossover and mutation in genetic programming. Crossover in genetic programming swaps subtrees that may be of different sizes and in different positions in their programs and mutation in genetic programming generates entire new sub-trees. This paper specifies mutation has a greater utility and crossover does not consistently have a considerable advantage over mutation. Analysis indicates that crossover is more successful than mutation overall, though mutation is often better for small population depending on domain.

Solanki et al., [4] have proposed to reserve a number of host symbols for statistical restoration. A dynamic embedding that avoids hiding in low probability regions of the host distribution is used. Security is provided by achieving zero-kulback-leiber divergence between cover and stego signal distributions. The probability density function of the stego signal exactly matches that of the original cover and it can breakthrough all the statistical steganalysis. It uses continuous statistic matching. Since random guessing is used by the detector the results obtained may not be accurate.

Amin Milani Fard et al., [5] designed genetic algorithm based process to create secure steganographic encoding of JPEG images. The encoding is based on the steganographic tool Outguess which is proved to be vulnerable. A combination of outguess and Maximum Absolute Difference (MAD) as fitness function for GA ensure image quality. The method optimizes localization in which is message to be embedded in the cover image. Experiments show that optimum solution is obtained. Although the model presented is based on JPEG images, the idea can potentially be used in other multimedia Steganography too.

LIU Tong and QUI Zheng-ding [6] have presented a paper that uses a cryptosystem for hiding payload into a color image by quantization based strategy. For computing the DWT of the host image, mallet algorithm with bi- orthogonal 9/7 basis is used. In quantization based Steganography quantization error is bounded which implies that the message embedded image is indistinguishable from the original image. Payload is hidden in every chrominance component of a color image. This method has higher hiding capacity and also free from interference from host data. Also the BER is low which adds to its strength.

Simulation results show that the proposed method is robust against commonly used processing techniques. Chin-Chen Chang et al., [7] have proposed pattern based image Steganography using wavelet transform to maximize the closeness of a stego image to its original. The cover image is transformed into wavelet co-efficient using DWT. These co-efficients are grouped together to form blocks and some blocks are selected using a key. These blocks are analyzed for their pattern types and the patterns are changed according to the secret message. The final stego image is obtained by applying inverse DWT to the coefficients. Although this method has poorer PSNR values as compared to the LSB scheme, there is no visual difference between the two images generated. An advantage of this method over the LSB scheme is that it can survive under JPEG lossy compression. Although the experimental results show that the difference between original and embedded image is visually unnoticeable it leaves behind statistical evidences for attacks.

Andrew H. Sung et al., [8] have proposed robust Steganography system in which the payload is enclosed using cryptography and the carrier is an animation or a sequence of frames using mimic functions. Encrypted payload is embedded in the individual frames of the carrier using wavelet transformation. The limitation is capacity; a huge carrier may be required to deliver a small payload. Since cryptography is employed before transmission of image, if the decoding is successful then the payload can be retrieved. Rufeng Chu et al., [9] have proposed a DCT based Steganography that can preserve image quality and also resist certain statistical attacks thereby making it secure. This method is based on the analysis of typical steganalytic algorithms, statistical distributions of DCT co-efficient and the characteristics of the typical statistical attack. Modification of DCT coefficients to hide the image can lead to noticeable changes in the Stego image.

Andreas et al., [10] proposes both visual and statistical attacks on steganographic systems. Visual attacks are based on human ability to distinguish between noise and visual patterns. The idea of visual attacks is to remove all parts of an image covering the message. The visual attacks discussed here are E-stego, s-tools, stegnos, Jsteg. The statistical attacks compare the theoretically expected frequency distributions in steganograms with some simple distribution observed in possibly changed carrier medium. When compared, statistical attacks prove superior to the visual attacks as they are less dependent on the cover used. R. Chandramouli [11] has derived lower and upper bounds on the data hiding capacity of the cover image in the presence of imperfect channel which could be due to channel estimation error, time varying adversary etc.

Phill Sallee [12] presented Steganography which uses a parametric model of the cover image in order to embed maximum length messages while avoiding a given set of statistics. Steganalysis by estimating the length of messages hidden with Jsteg in JPEG images are also discussed. Patrizio Campisi et al., [13] have proposed new application for data hiding to help improve signal compression. An unconventional two level wavelet decomposition of luminance component of a color image is considered. The perceptually irrelevant sub-bands are properly selected, zeroed and replaced with a parsimonious representation of the chrominance components. This leads to gray scale image in which color Information is piggy back without impairing the overall perceptual quality of embedded image. The compression scheme proposed is better as compared to coding schemes like JPEG and SPIHT, however it being a optimal scheme is unsupported. Ross. J et al., [14] in their paper explore the limits of Steganography. The methods of Steganography are compared and contrasted with that of cryptography and traffic security. A number of steganographic attacks are presented.

3   Model

3.1   Steganographic Model

GA based embedding using DCT: Figure 1 shows a Rugbyball considered as the cover image and Beach as the payload. Figure 2 shows the block diagram of the Genetic algorithm based Steganography using Discrete Cosine Transform (GAS-DCT). The payload is divided into 8*8 blocks and Discrete Cosine Transform (DCT) is performed on each block. Application of DCT to each block results in distribution of low frequency coefficients towards top left and the high frequency coefficients towards bottom right. The total information of the image is concentrated in low frequency coefficients. Initialize the random population from the payload and embed the same into the cover image. The best population is formed by avoiding the high frequency coefficients which do not contain significant information of the image. When DCT is performed on the payload, each coefficient is represented by utmost 11 bits. An additional 12th bit is required to represent negative DCT coefficients. Since 3 LSB's of each pixel of the cover image are allowed to be replaced, each DCT coefficient of the payload requires 4 pixel of the cover image. This constitutes the procedure of embedding. The process of generating better population by assuming fitness values and embedding is continued to obtain n stego images. The different stego images are tested for the statistical properties. The stego image which has the statistical properties close to the original cover image is a good stego image. The crossover and mutation process is performed between successive stego images to generate the optimal stego image. This optimal stego image is used as the image to be transmitted.

Fig. 1. Beach (left) and Rubgyball (right)

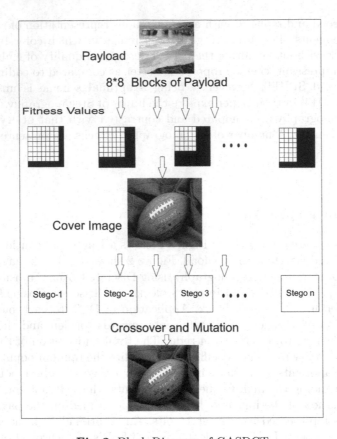

Fig. 2. Block Diagram of GASDCT

GA based embedding using DWT: Figure 3 shows James as the cover image and an image of Bird as the payload. Figure 4 shows the block diagram of GA based embedding using DWT. Figure 5 shows the Flow Chart of GASDWT. The procedure which was applied for embedding the payload using DCT transformation is applied for embedding the payload using DWT. This is achieved by converting

Fig. 3. Bird (left) and James (right)

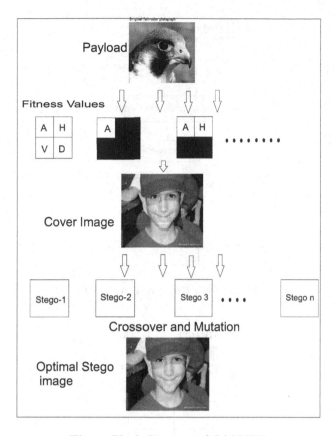

Fig. 4. Block Diagram of GASDWT

the payload into wavelet domain i.e., according to fitness function different bands of payload are selected and embedded into the cover image. This process is continued till the best stego image is obtained. DWT block performs the following process: It applies the discrete wavelet transform to the payload. This results in four different bands namely approximation band, horizontal band, vertical band and diagonal band. The next block is GA based embedding; the stego image is generated by embedding the best population from the payload depending upon fitness value. The stego image thus obtained is the combination of cover image and payload. This stego image is fed to the test statistical features block, which tests the statistical features of the cover image and the stego image. If test results satisfy the desired criteria then it will be the optimal stego image. If results do not satisfy, the loop returns to the GA based embedding block.

Figure 6 shows the flow chart of the decoder. Decoding of the stego image is done using stego key. The payload in the Stego image can be decoded only if the Stego key is known. Thus the used of Stego key increases security. In GASDWT, the payload is retrieved by taking inverse discrete wavelet transform on the decoded stego image.

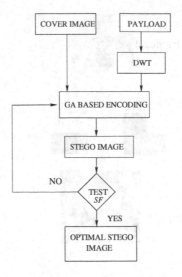

Fig. 5. Flow Chart of GASDWT

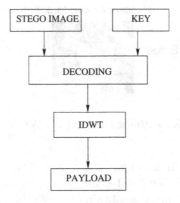

Fig. 6. Flow Chart of GASDWT Decoder

4   Algorithm

4.1   Problem Definition

Given a cover image c and payload p, the objective is to embed the payload into the cover image using Discrete Cosine and Discrete Wavelet transforms based on Genetic Algorithm.

4.2   Assumptions

(i) Cover and payload images are of any size. (ii) The communication channel is ideal.

4.3 Algorithm

(a) *DCT based embedding:* Payload in the spatial domain is converted into Discrete Cosine domain. The DCT coefficients of payload are embedded into the spatial domain of cover image to generate stego image using GA based algorithm. Statistical characteristics of stego image and cover image are compared and iterations are carried on to get optimal stego image.

Table 1.

Algorithm GASDCT: Data Embedding

1. Input: Cover image c and Payload image p.
2. Output: Stego image s.
3. Take a grayscale image of variable size as an input and paylaod of variable size.
4. Payload p is transformed into Discrete Cosine Domain.
5. The population is initialized by random selection.
6. The fitness value decides the best population.
7. The same is embedded into cover image c based on GA in spatial domain.
8. The stego-image obtained is tested on Spatial Domain Steganalytic System. If it passes, it is then considered as optimal stego-image.

Table 2.

Algorithm GASDWT: Data Embedding

1. Input: Cover image c and Payload image p.
2. Output: Stego image s.
3. Take a grayscale image of variable size as an input and the size of paylaod of variable size.
4. Payload p is transformed into Discrete Wavelet Domain.
5. The population is initialized by random selection.
6. The fitness value decides the best population.
7. The same is embedded into cover image c based on GA in spatial domain
8. The st ego-image obtained is tested on Spatial Domain Steganalytic System. If it passes, it is then considered as optimal stego-image.

(b) *DWT based embedding:* Payload in the spatial domain is converted into Wavelet domain. The DWT coefficients of payload are embedded into the spatial domain of cover image to generate stego image using GA based algorithm.

Statistical characteristics of stego image and cover image are compared and iterations are done to get optimal stego image. The Algorithm for GASDCT, GASDWT and Retrieval of Payload are presented in Table 1, Table 2 and Table 3 respectively.

Table 3.

Algorithm for Retrieval of Payload

1. Input: Cover image c and Payload image p.
2. Output: Stego image s.
3. For the retrieval of the payload, use Stego key.
4. This is followed by the Inverse Discrete Wavelet Transform.
5. The payload is obtained.

5 Performance Analysis

Simulations are carried out on images of different formats viz. JPEG, TIFF and BMP using MATLAB. Steganograms are generated using Discrete Cosine and Discrete wavelet transforms. Performance analysis of these two transforms is done based on parameters PSNR and BER.

DCT is performed on a 256*256 cover image shown in Figure 1. If three LSB's of the cover image are used for hiding the payload, the resulting capacity is 256*256*3=196608 bits i.e., approximately 196Kb of information. Thus the maximum size of payload can be 156*156 bytes.

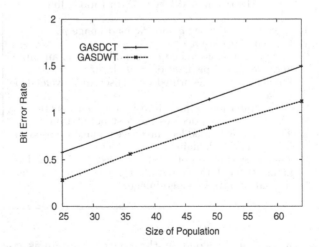

Fig. 7. Variation of Bit Error Rate with Size of Population for GASDCT and GASDWT

Table 4. Comparision of BER for GASDCT and GASDWT

	Using DCT	Using Wavelets
BER 1	1.4937	1.1214
BER 2	1.1440	0.8424
BER 3	0.8382	0.5635
BER 4	0.5794	0.2824

According to our algorithm, application of DCT to the payload instead of cover image results in high capacity embedding. Size of payload is increased by 62.8%, hence the maximum size of payload can now be 256*256. This is made possible by considering only few coefficients out of 64 in each 8*8 block of DCT transformed payload since these are sufficient for retrieval of payload. If 16 coefficients out of 64 in each 8*8 DCT transformed blocks are considered, then total number of bits to embed becomes 32*32*16*12=196608 bits. When the same algorithm using Wavelet Transform is used, the size of the payload further increases by 23% resulting in a payload size of 292*292.

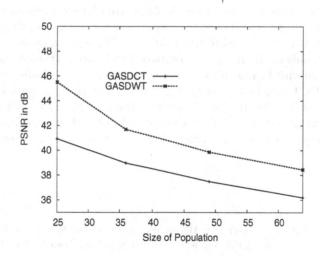

Fig. 8. Variation of Peak Signal to Noise Ratio with Size of Population for GASDCT and GASDWT

Figure 7 and Figure 8 show the Variation of Bit error rate and Peak Signal to Noise Ratio with size of population for GASDCT and GASDWT. It shows that the bit error rate is decreasing and the Peak Signal to Noise Ratio is increasing with decrease in size of the population. It also shows that there is an improvement in the Bit Error Rate and Peak Signal to Noise Ratio in case of GASDWT when compared with GASDCT. Table 4 and 5 gives the comparision of Bit Error Rate and Peak Signal to Noise Ratio for GASDCT and GASDWT for different Population size. BER1 and PSNR1 is calculated for stego-image1 derived from

Table 5. Comparision of PSNR for GASDCT and GASDWT

	Using DCT(dB)	Using Wavelet(dB)
PSNR 1	36.19	38.44
PSNR 2	37.48	39.86
PSNR 3	38.98	41.70
PSNR 4	40.92	45.5

the initial population of payload that is embedded into the cover image. The next population is generated from initial population based on Fitness function. This is now embedded into the cover image to obtain stego-image2. BER2 and PSNR2 is computed for this stego-image. Similarly BER3, PSNR3 and BER4, PSNR4 are calculated for the successive stego-images obtained.

6 Conclusion

Steganography is an art of concealing the presence of intended secret messages. In this paper, we have proposed Genetic Algorithm based Steganography using Discrete Cosine Transform (GASDCT) and Genetic Algorithm Steganography using Discrete Wavelet Transform(GASDWT). Wavelet analysis is used as it reveals finer details of the image as compared to Fourier Transforms. Here the payload is transformed from spatial domain to the Discrete Cosine and Wavelet domain. The DCT and DWT coefficients are embedded into spatial domain of cover image by using Genetic Algorithm, which has increased capacity. The proposed algorithm gives better performance viz., Bit Error Rate and Peak Signal to Noise Ratio than the earlier techniques. However, there is scope for enhancement of robustness.

References

1. Wu, Y.-T., Shih, F.Y.: Genetic Algorithm based Methodology for Breaking the Steganalytic Systems. IEEE Transactions on Systems, Man and Cybernetics 36 (Feburary 2006)
2. Ji, R., Yao, H., Liu, S., Wang, L.: Genetic Algorithm based Optimal Block Mapping Method for LSB Substitution. In: IIHP-MSP 2006. Proceedings of the International Information Hiding and Multimedia Signal Processing, pp. 215–218 (2006)
3. Luke, S., Spector, L.: A Comparison of Crossover and Mutation in Genetic Programming. In: GP 1997. Proceedings of the Second Annual Conference on Genetic Programming (1997)
4. Solanki, K., Sullivan, K., Manjunath, B.S., Chandrasekhran, S.: Provably Secure Steganography: Achieving Zero k-l Divergence using Statistical Restoration. In: Proceedings on IEEE International Conference on Image Processing, USA, pp. 125–128 (2006)
5. Amin, M.F., Mohammad, R., Akbarzadeh, T., Farshad, V.-A.: A New Genetic Algorithm Approach for Secure JPEG Steganography, pp. 22–23 (April 2006)

6. Tong, L., Zheng-ding, Q.: A DWT based Color Image Steganography Scheme. In: Proceedings of the Sixth International Conference on Signal Processing, vol. 2, pp. 1568–1571 (August 2002)
7. Chang, C.-C., Chen, T.-s., Hsia, H.-C.: An Effective Image Steganographic Scheme based on Wavelet Transformation and Pattern based Modification. In: ICCNMC 2003. Proceedings of the International Conference on Computer Networks and Mobile Computing, pp. 450–453 (October 2003)
8. Sung, A.H., Tadiparthi, G.R., Srinivas, Mukkamala: Defeating the Current Steganalysis Techniques (Robust Steganography). In: ITCC 2004. IEEE Proceedings of the International Conference on Information Technology: Coding and Computing (2004)
9. Chu, R., You, X., Kong, X., Ba, X.: A DCT-based Image Steganographic Method Resisting Statistical Attacks. In: ICASSP 2004. IEEE transaction, Acoustic, Speech and Signal Processing, vol. 5, pp. 953–956 (May 2004)
10. Westfeld, A., Pfitzmann, A.: Attacks on Steganographic Systems Breaking the Steganographic Utilities EzStego, Jsteg, Steganos, and S-Tools and Some Lessons Learned. In: Pfitzmann, A. (ed.) IH 1999. LNCS, vol. 1768, pp. 61–76. Springer, Heidelberg (2000)
11. Chandramouli, R.: Data Hiding Capacity in the Presence of an Imperfectly known Channel. In: SPIE. Proceedings of Security and Watermarking of Multimedia, vol. 2 (2001)
12. Sallee, P.: Model-Based Methods for Steganagraphy and Steganalysis. International Journal of Image and Graphics 5(1), 167–189 (2005)
13. Campisi, P., Kundur, D., Hatzinakos, D., Neri, A.: Compressive Data Hiding: An Unconventional Approach for improved Color Image Coding. Journal on Applied Signal Processing EURASIP, 152–163 (2002)
14. Anderson, R.J., Peticolas, F.A.P.: On the Limits of Steganography. IEEE journal on selected areas in Communications 16, 474–481 (1998)

Cryptanalysis of Tso et al.'s ID-Based Tripartite Authenticated Key Agreement Protocol*

Meng-Hui Lim[1], Sanggon Lee[2], and Sangjae Moon[3]

[1] Department of Ubiquitous IT, Graduate School of Design & IT,
Dongseo University, Busan 617-716, Korea
meng17121983@gmail.com
[2] Division of Internet Engineering,
Dongseo University, Busan 617-716, Korea
nok60@dongseo.ac.kr
[3] School of Electrical Engineering and Computer Science,
Kyungpook National University, Daegu 702-701, Korea
sjmoon@ee.knu.ac.kr

Abstract. A tripartite authenticated key agreement protocol is generally designed to accommodate the need of three specific entities in communicating over an open network with a shared secret key, which is used to preserve confidentiality and data integrity. Since Joux [6] initiates the development of tripartite key agreement protocol, many prominent tripartite schemes have been proposed subsequently. In 2005, Tso et al. [15] have proposed an ID-based non-interactive tripartite key agreement scheme with k-resilience. Based on this scheme, they have further proposed another one-round tripartite application scheme. Although they claimed that both schemes are efficient and secure, we discover that both schemes are in fact breakable. In this paper, we impose several impersonation attacks on Tso et al.'s schemes in order to highlight their flaws. Subsequently, we propose some applicable enhancements which will not only conquer their defects, but also preserve the security attributes of an ideal key agreement protocol.

1 Introduction

A *key agreement protocol* is the mechanism in which a shared secret key is derived by two or more protocol entities as a function of information contributed by each of these parties such that no single entity can predetermine the resulting value. Usually, this session key is established over a public network controlled by the adversaries and it would vary with every execution round (session) of the protocol. This secret key can subsequently be used to create a confidential communication channel among the entities.

The situation where three or more parties share a key is often called *conference keying*. The tripartite case is of the most practical importance, not only because it is the most common size for electronic conferences, but also because

---

* This work was supported by University IT Research Center Project of MIC, Korea.

P. McDaniel and S.K. Gupta (Eds.): ICISS 2007, LNCS 4812, pp. 64–76, 2007.

it can be used to provide a range of services for two communicating parties. For example, a third party can be added to chair, or referee a conversation for ad hoc auditing, or data recovery purposes. Besides, it can also facilitate the job of group communication.

In a tripartite key agreement protocol, authentication can be provided by employing asymmetric techniques such as certificate-based public key infrastructure [1, 5, 3, 6, 7, 8, 13] and the identity-based (ID-based) public key infrastructure [9, 10, 12, 15, 18]. In the former case, each user would be given a digital certificate issued by a mutually trusted Cerification Authority (CA) and the user is required to send this certificate together with his message to the other protocol participants in order to allow him to be authenticated. Whereas in the latter case, each entity is only required to learn the public identity of their partners such as name, social security number and email address, etc. in order to carry out a communication run while at the same time, being authenticated. Hence, ID-based protocols usually gain much popularity as it significantly simplifies the entire key agreement procedures.

Wilson and Menezes [16, 17] have defined a number of desirable security attributes which can be used to analyze a tripartite key agreement protocol. These security attributes are described as follows:

Known session key security. A protocol is considered to be *known session key secure* if it remains achieving its goal in the face of an adversary who has learned some previous session keys.

(Perfect) forward secrecy. A protocol enjoys *forward secrecy* if the secrecy of the previous session keys is not affected when the long term private keys of one or more entities are compromised. *Perfect forward secrecy* refers to the scenario when the long term private keys of all the participating entities are compromised.

Key-Compromise Impersonation Resilience. Suppose that A's long term private key has been disclosed. Obviously an adversary who knows this value can now impersonate A since it is precisely the value which identifies A. We say that a protocol is *key-compromise impersonation resilient* if this loss will not enable an adversary to masquerade as other legitimate entities to A as well or obtain other entities secret key.

Unknown Key-Share Resilience. In an unknown key-share attack, an adversary convinces a group of entities that they share a key with the adversary whereas in fact, the key is shared between the group and another party. This situation can be exploited in a number of ways by the adversary when the key is subsequently used to provide encryption or integrity.

Key Control Resilience. It should not be possible for any of the participants (or an adversary) to compel the session key to a preselected value or predict the value of the session key.

Over the years, numerous tripartite key agreement protocols have been proposed. However, most of them have been proven to be insecure [1, 4, 5, 6, 7, 9, 10, 11, 12, 13]. In 2000, Joux [6] had proposed the first one-round pairing-based tripartite Diffie-Hellman key agreement protocol. However, Shim [13] had pointed out that Joux's protocol does not authenticate the communicating entities and therefore, it is susceptible to the man-in-the-middle attack. To overcome this, Shim had proposed an improved scheme which employs the public key infrastructure to overcome the security flaw in Joux's protocol and she claimed that the improved protocol is able to withstand the man-in-the-middle attack. However, Shim's attempt has also turned out to be insecure eventually [5,7,14]. In 2005, Tso et al. [15] have proposed an *ID-based non-interactive key agreement scheme* (IDNIKS) with k-resilience for three parties. They have claimed that their protocol is the first secure non-interactive tripartite protocol which provides ID-based authenticity with no employment of hash functions. Based on this scheme, they have further proposed a tripartite application scheme which requires only one round of message transmission. Although they claimed that both schemes are efficient and secure, we discover that both schemes are in fact susceptible to various impersonation attacks.

Hence, in this paper, we highlight the weaknesses of Tso et al.'s tripartite ID-NIKS and their application scheme. In order to conquer these defects, we propose some enhancements based on their application scheme, and subsequently carry out a thorough security analysis to ensure that our enhancements have satisfied all the required security attributes of a desired key agreement protocol. The structure of this paper is organized as follows. In Section 2, we illustrate some basic properties of bilinear pairings and several Diffie-Hellman assumptions. In Section 3, we review Tso et al's tripartite IDNIKS and their subsequent application scheme. In Section 4, we present our impersonation attacks on both schemes and then in Section 5, we propose our enhancements as well as the associated security proofs. Lastly, we conclude this paper in Section 6.

2   Preliminaries

Let $\mathbf{G}_1$ be an additive group of a large prime order, q and $\mathbf{G}_2$ be a multiplicative group of the same order, q. Let $P, Q \in \mathbf{G}_1$ and $\hat{e} : \mathbf{G}_1 \times \mathbf{G}_1 \longrightarrow \mathbf{G}_2$ be a bilinear pairing with the following properties:

- **Bilinearity:** $\hat{e}(aP, bQ) = \hat{e}(P, Q)^{ab} = \hat{e}(abP, Q)$ for any $a, b \in Z_q^*$.
- **Non-degeneracy:** $\hat{e}(P, Q) \neq 1$.
- **Computability:** There exists an efficient algorithm to compute $\hat{e}(P, Q)$.

A bilinear map which satisfies all three properties above is considered as *admissible bilinear*. It is noted that the Weil and Tate pairings associated with the supersingular elliptic curves or abelian varieties, can be modified to create such bilinear maps. Now, we describe some cryptographic problems:

Bilinear Diffie-Hellman Problem (BDHP). Let $\mathbf{G}_1$, $\mathbf{G}_2$, P and $\hat{e}$ be as above with the order q being prime. Given $\langle P, aP, bP, cP \rangle$ with $a, b, c \in Z_q^*$, compute $\hat{e}(P, P)^{abc} \in \mathbf{G}_2$. An algorithm α is deemed to have an advantage ϵ in solving the BDHP in $\langle \mathbf{G}_1, \mathbf{G}_2, \hat{e} \rangle$ based on the random choices of a, b, c in Z_q^* and the internal random operation of α if

$$Pr[\alpha(\langle P, aP, bP, cP \rangle) = \hat{e}(P,P)^{abc}] \geq \epsilon.$$

Discrete Logarithm Problem (DLP). Given two groups of elements P and Q, such that $Q = nP$. Find the integer n whenever such an integer exists.

Throughout this paper, we assume that BDHP and DLP are hard such that there is no polynomial time algorithm to solve BDHP and DLP with non-negligible probability.

3 Review of Tso et al.'s Schemes

3.1 k-Resilient Tripartite IDNIKS

System Setting
As described in Sect. 2, assume that $\mathbf{G}_1$ is an additive group and $\mathbf{G}_2$ is a multiplicative group, both with prime order q. Let P be a generator of $\mathbf{G}_1$, $\hat{e} : \mathbf{G}_1 \times \mathbf{G}_1 \longrightarrow \mathbf{G}_2$ be a bilinear pairing and $k \ll q$ be the resilience parameter. These settings are assumed to be generated by the key generation center (KGC).

Key Generation
KGC picks $k + 1$ random numbers $d_0, d_1, \cdots, d_k \in Z_q^*$, and generates a polynomial $f(x)$ of degree k, where

$$f(x) = d_0 + d_1 x + \cdots + d_k x^k \in Z_q[x]. \tag{1}$$

KGC then computes

$$V_0 = d_0 P, V_1 = d_1 P, \cdots, V_k = d_k P. \tag{2}$$

The system public parameters published by KGC are $\{P, V_0, \cdots, V_k\}$ and the KGC's private keys are $\{d_0, d_1, \cdots, d_k\}$. In addition, KGC computes

$$s_i = f(ID_i) = d_0 + d_1 ID_i + \cdots + d_k (ID_i)^k \bmod q. \tag{3}$$

for the entity i with identity $ID_i \in Z_q^*$ and sends s_i to i through a private secure channel. For an IDNIKS which involves three protocol entities A, B, and C, the corresponding public / private key pairs are computed as follows:

$$A: \text{ Public key: } ID_A, \quad \text{Private key: } s_A = f(ID_A)$$
$$B: \text{ Public key: } ID_B, \quad \text{Private key: } s_B = f(ID_B)$$
$$C: \text{ Public key: } ID_C, \quad \text{Private key: } s_C = f(ID_C)$$

Key Agreement
In this non-interactive key establishment scheme, each A, B and C uses the system's public information, peer's public key as well as his own secret key to derive the shared secret with the other protocol entities.

$$\Omega_A = \sum_{i=0}^{k} (ID_A)^i V_i = s_A P. \tag{4}$$

$$\Omega_B = \sum_{i=0}^{k}(ID_B)^i V_i = s_B P. \tag{5}$$

$$\Omega_C = \sum_{i=0}^{k}(ID_C)^i V_i = s_C P. \tag{6}$$

A computes Eqs. (5) and (6), and the tripartite key

$$K_A = \hat{e}(\Omega_B, \Omega_C)^{s_A}. \tag{7}$$

B computes Eqs. (4) and (6), and the tripartite key

$$K_B = \hat{e}(\Omega_A, \Omega_C)^{s_B}. \tag{8}$$

C computes Eqs. (4) and (5), and the tripartite key

$$K_C = \hat{e}(\Omega_A, \Omega_B)^{s_C}. \tag{9}$$

Consistency

$$
\begin{aligned}
K_A &= \hat{e}(\Omega_B, \Omega_C)^{s_A} \\
&= \hat{e}(\sum_{i=0}^{k}(ID_B)^i V_i, \sum_{i=0}^{k}(ID_C)^i V_i)^{s_A} \\
&= \hat{e}(s_B P, s_C P)^{s_A} \\
&= \hat{e}(P, P)^{s_A s_B s_C} \\
&= K_B = K_C
\end{aligned}
\tag{10}
$$

3.2   One-Round IDNIKS-Based Application

Tso et al.'s application scheme has the same system setting and key generation as the previous scheme.

Key Agreement

A chooses a random number $r_A \in Z_q^*$ and computes

$$X_A = r_A P, \tag{11}$$

B chooses a random number $r_B \in Z_q^*$ and computes

$$X_B = r_B P, \tag{12}$$

C chooses a random number $r_C \in Z_q^*$ and computes

$$X_C = r_C P. \tag{13}$$

Assume that $Sig_i(\cdot)$ denotes the signature of an entity i. Then, over a public channel,

$$A \to B, C : X_A, Sig_A(X_A). \tag{14}$$

$$B \rightarrow A, C : X_B, Sig_B(X_B). \tag{15}$$

$$C \rightarrow A, B : X_C, Sig_C(X_C). \tag{16}$$

From Eqs. (5), (6), (12) and (13), A computes the tripartite key

$$K_A = \hat{e}(\Omega_B + X_B, \Omega_C + X_C)^{s_A + r_A}. \tag{17}$$

From Eqs. (4), (6), (11) and (13), B computes the tripartite key

$$K_B = \hat{e}(\Omega_A + X_A, \Omega_C + X_C)^{s_B + r_B}. \tag{18}$$

From Eqs. (4), (5), (11) and (12), C computes the tripartite key

$$K_C = \hat{e}(\Omega_A + X_A, \Omega_B + X_B)^{s_C + r_C}. \tag{19}$$

Consistency

$$\begin{aligned}
K_A &= \hat{e}(\Omega_B + X_B, \Omega_C + X_C)^{s_A + r_A} \\
&= \hat{e}(\sum_{i=0}^{k}(ID_B)^i V_i + X_B, \sum_{i=0}^{k}(ID_C)^i V_i + X_C)^{s_A + r_A} \\
&= \hat{e}(s_B P + r_B P, s_C P + r_C P)^{s_A + r_A} \\
&= \hat{e}(P, P)^{(s_A + r_A)(s_B + r_B)(s_C + r_C)} \\
&= K_B = K_C
\end{aligned} \tag{20}$$

4   Our Attacks

4.1   Impersonation Attacks on k-Resilient Tripartite IDNIKS

Key-Compromise Impersonation Attack

The Key-Compromise Impersonation (KCI) attack is deemed successful only if the adversary manages to masquerade as another protocol principal to communicate with the victim after the victim's private key has been compromised. Suppose that an adversary, E_A has the knowledge of B's private key s_B and he intends to launch the KCI attack against B by pretending to be A in a communication run. E_A then initiates a communication session with B and C. By computing Eqs. (5) and (6), E_A is then able to compute the tripartite key K_A by using Eq. (7). Similarly after compromising a legitimate entity's private key, the adversary can simply impersonate anyone from the other $(k-1)$ legitimate entities to communicate with the victim, with the aim to capture valuable information (e.g. credit card number) about him.

In this key agreement protocol, each of the protocol entities merely employs his static private key and the other entities' public keys to derive a shared secret. Since this protocol is non-interactive, no ephemeral keys are involved in computing the tripartite key. Hence, it seems difficult for IDNIKS to resist the KCI attack.

Insider Impersonation Attack

In a two-party's authentication protocol, the adversary who impersonates the communicating parties would probably be an *outsider*. However, in the k-party's case where $k \geq 3$, the adversary who impersonates the communicating parties might be a legal entity of the communicating group, known as an *insider* and this kind of impersonation attack is the *insider impersonation attack* [2]. The consequence of this attack would be disastrous if the impersonated party is a referee or an auditor.

In this tripartite IDNIKS, a malicious insider can easily impersonate any legitimate entity during a protocol run. For instance, suppose that B is the insider impersonation attacker who wishes to fool A by masquerading as C in a communication run. B initiates IDNIKS with A while at the same time, B also plays another role as B_C (B masquerading as C). By computing Eqs. (4) and (6), B can then calculate the tripartite key K_B and K_C by using Eq. (8). Since IDNIKS is non-interactive and no ephemeral values are employed, A can never find out that C is in fact absent in that communication run.

Generally, the insider impersonation attack can be launched against any legal entity in this protocol as the malicious insider can impersonate anyone from the other $(k - 2)$ entities at the same time. Hence, we argue that key agreement protocol for three or more parties' should not be designed to be non-interactive as it would be vulnerable to the insider impersonation attack under any circumstances.

4.2   Insider Impersonation Attack on One-Round IDNIKS-Based Application

In the tripartite application scheme, Tso et al. have emphasized that each protocol participant P_i must append a signature to the random parameter X_{P_i} in order to avoid the insider impersonation attack. However, we discover that their application scheme is still insecure since a malicious insider can easily replay any message together with the signature obtained from the previous session to launch the insider impersonation attack. For example, suppose that a malicious legal entity, B has obtained X_A as shown in Eq. (11) in a previous session involving A, B and C. B is now able to victimize D by replaying X_A in another communication session involving B_A (B impersonating A), B and D. The insider impersonation attack can be carried out as follows:

$$\Omega_D = \sum_{i=0}^{k} (ID_D)^i V_i \tag{21}$$

$$B_A \to B, D : X_A, Sig_A(X_A), \text{where } X_A = r_A P, \tag{22}$$

$$B \to B_A, D : X'_B, Sig_B(X'_B), \text{where } X'_B = r'_B P, \tag{23}$$

$$D \to B_A, B : X'_D, Sig_D(X'_D), \text{where } X'_D = r'_D P. \tag{24}$$

From Eqs. (4), (21), (22) and (24), B and B_A computes the tripartite key

$$K_A = K_B = \hat{e}(\Omega_A + X_A, \Omega_D + X'_D)^{s_B + r'_B}$$
$$= \hat{e}(P, P)^{(s_A + r_A)(s_B + r'_B)(s_D + r'_D)}. \tag{25}$$

From Eqs. (4), (5), (22) and (23), D computes the tripartite key

$$K_D = \hat{e}(\Omega_A + X_A, \Omega_B + X'_B)^{s_D + r'_D}$$
$$= \hat{e}(P, P)^{(s_A + r_A)(s_B + r'_B)(s_D + r'_D)}. \tag{26}$$

With this, the malicious entity B is able to cheat D by replaying A's message from a previous session and subsequently impersonating A in a particular session. As a result, B and D would agree upon a session key for the tripartite key agreement scheme without A's presence.

5 Our Enhanced Scheme

In order to protect against the insider impersonation attack, we propose two improvement methods that are applicable on the original application scheme described in Sect. 3.2. In this section, we describe informally our enhancement schemes which involves the employment of timestamps and nonces.

5.1 Protocol Improvement by Adding Timestamps

Our first improved scheme has the same system setting as the IDNIKS defined in Sect. 3.1.

Key Exchange

Assume that time synchronization is feasible. We denote $Sig_i(\cdot)$ as the signature of an entity i and $T_A, T_B, T_C \in Z_q^*$ as the timestamps generated by A, B and C respectively. Then, over a public channel,

$$A \rightarrow B, C : M_A, Sig_A(M_A), \text{where } M_A = (ID_B, ID_C, X_A, T_A). \tag{27}$$

$$B \rightarrow A, C : M_B, Sig_B(M_B), \text{where } M_B = (ID_A, ID_C, X_B, T_B). \tag{28}$$

$$C \rightarrow A, B : M_C, Sig_C(M_C), \text{where } M_C = (ID_A, ID_B, X_C, T_C). \tag{29}$$

Message Verification

Upon receiving B and C's messages, A verifies B and C's signature and subsequently checks whether T_B and T_C lie within the specific acceptable time interval.

Upon receiving A and C's messages, B verifies A and C's signature and subsequently checks whether T_A and T_C lie within the specific acceptable time interval.

Upon receiving A and B's messages, C verifies A and B's signature and subsequently checks whether T_A and T_B lie within the specific acceptable time interval.

Session key Generation

If the verification processes succeed, A, B and C compute the shared secret, Z_A, Z_B and Z_C respectively, where

$$Z_A = \hat{e}(\Omega_B + X_B, \Omega_C + X_C)^{s_A + r_A}$$
$$= \hat{e}(P, P)^{(s_A + r_A)(s_B + r_B)(s_C + r_C)}, \tag{30}$$

$$Z_B = \hat{e}(\Omega_A + X_A, \Omega_C + X_C)^{s_B + r_B}$$
$$= \hat{e}(P, P)^{(s_A + r_A)(s_B + r_B)(s_C + r_C)}, \tag{31}$$

$$Z_C = \hat{e}(\Omega_A + X_A, \Omega_B + X_B)^{s_C + r_C}$$
$$= \hat{e}(P, P)^{(s_A + r_A)(s_B + r_B)(s_C + r_C)}. \tag{32}$$

Based on this common shared secret, A, B and C then calculate the tripartite session key K_A, K_B and K_C respectively, where

$$K_A = H(Z_A \parallel ID_A \parallel ID_B \parallel ID_C \parallel X_A \parallel X_B \parallel X_C \parallel T_A \parallel T_B \parallel T_C), \tag{33}$$

$$K_B = H(Z_B \parallel ID_A \parallel ID_B \parallel ID_C \parallel X_A \parallel X_B \parallel X_C \parallel T_A \parallel T_B \parallel T_C), \tag{34}$$

$$K_C = H(Z_C \parallel ID_A \parallel ID_B \parallel ID_C \parallel X_A \parallel X_B \parallel X_C \parallel T_A \parallel T_B \parallel T_C). \tag{35}$$

5.2   Protocol Improvement by Adding Nonces

In the scenario where time synchronization is not possible, Tso et al.'s application scheme can alternatively be improved by using nonces, which requires an additional round of message broadcast from the protocol entities. Similarly in this two-round enhanced protocol, our system setting is the same as the IDNIKS defined in Sect. 3.1.

Key Exchange

Assume that $N_A, N_B, N_C \in Z_q^*$ are denoted as the nonces generated randomly by A, B and C respectively. Then, each of them performs the message transmission as follows:

First Round

$$A \to B, C : N_A. \tag{36}$$

$$B \to A, C : N_B. \tag{37}$$

$$C \to A, B : N_C. \tag{38}$$

Second Round

$$A \to B, C : M_A, Sig_A(M_A, N_B, N_C), \text{where } M_A = (ID_B, ID_C, X_A). \tag{39}$$

$$B \to A, C : M_B, Sig_B(M_B, N_A, N_C), \text{where } M_B = (ID_A, ID_C, X_B). \tag{40}$$

$$C \to A, B : M_C, Sig_C(M_C, N_A, N_B), \text{where } M_C = (ID_A, ID_B, X_C). \tag{41}$$

Message Verification and Session Key Generation

Similar to the previous improvement scheme, each A, B and C authenticates their respective partners' signature on reception of their messages in the second round of the protocol run. If the verification process succeeds, A, B and C then compute the shared secret, Z_A, Z_B and Z_C respectively, where

$$\begin{aligned} Z_A &= \hat{e}(\Omega_B + X_B, \Omega_C + X_C)^{s_A + r_A} \\ &= \hat{e}(P, P)^{(s_A + r_A)(s_B + r_B)(s_C + r_C)}, \end{aligned} \tag{42}$$

$$\begin{aligned} Z_B &= \hat{e}(\Omega_A + X_A, \Omega_C + X_C)^{s_B + r_B} \\ &= \hat{e}(P, P)^{(s_A + r_A)(s_B + r_B)(s_C + r_C)}, \end{aligned} \tag{43}$$

$$\begin{aligned} Z_C &= \hat{e}(\Omega_A + X_A, \Omega_B + X_B)^{s_C + r_C} \\ &= \hat{e}(P, P)^{(s_A + r_A)(s_B + r_B)(s_C + r_C)}. \end{aligned} \tag{44}$$

Based on this common shared secret, A, B and C then calculate the tripartite session key K_A, K_B and K_C respectively, where

$$K_A = H(Z_A \parallel ID_A \parallel ID_B \parallel ID_C \parallel X_A \parallel X_B \parallel X_C \parallel N_A \parallel N_B \parallel N_C), \tag{45}$$

$$K_B = H(Z_B \parallel ID_A \parallel ID_B \parallel ID_C \parallel X_A \parallel X_B \parallel X_C \parallel N_A \parallel N_B \parallel N_C), \tag{46}$$

$$K_C = H(Z_C \parallel ID_A \parallel ID_B \parallel ID_C \parallel X_A \parallel X_B \parallel X_C \parallel N_A \parallel N_B \parallel N_C). \tag{47}$$

5.3 Protocol Security Analysis

Known session key security. The session keys of our enhancement protocols vary with every protocol run since both session keys are established according to the values of the protocol entities' ephemeral private keys (r_A, r_B and r_C)

in a specific session. Hence, the knowledge of several previous session keys would not allow the adversary to derive any future and other previous session keys.

Perfect forward secrecy. Suppose that the entire long term private keys s_A, s_B and s_C have been disclosed to the adversary. In addition, assume that the adversary has also obtained some previous session keys established by the protocol entities. However, the adversary is unable to derive any other previously established session keys as derived in Eqs. (33), (34) and (35) for the first improved scheme as well as in Eqs. (45), (46) and (47) for the second improved scheme since the adversary does not possess any ephemeral private keys used in those particular protocol runs.

Key-Compromise Impersonation Resilience. Suppose that the long term private key s_A has been compromised and the adversary wishes to impersonate B in order to establish a session with A. However, he is unable to compute $Sig_B(M_B)$ in Eq. (28) or $Sig_B(M_B, N_A, N_C)$ in Eq. (40) since he does not know B's static private key, and thus he is unable to forge the signature on behalf of B. Suppose that the adversary then wishes to guess s_B in a random manner so as to fool A, his probability to succeed is only $\frac{1}{q}$, which is negligible as q is often chosen to be extremely large ($\geq$ 256 bits). Generally, the same situation would result when the long term key s_B or s_C is compromised as our enhanced protocols are symmetric. Hence, our enhanced protocols are able to withstand the KCI attack under any circumstances.

Insider Impersonation Resilience. Although an insider attacker, let's say A, who wishes to impersonate B, could compute the session key by using the legal method, he could not forge the signature on behalf of B with the intention of fooling C. Even if A replays any of B's previous messages, C would definitely reject the message due to the failure in verifying B's signature for both improvment schemes. This is mainly because in our first protocol, C would probably receive B's timestamp which is beyond the acceptable time interval, whereas in our second protocol, the nonce that C employs (N_C) would be different for different sessions and that is the reason why the replay of $Sig_B(M_B, N_A, N_C)$ in Eq. (40) can evidently be detected after the second message transmission . Hence, our enhancement protocols are deemed immune to the insider impersonation attack as well as replay attack.

Unknown Key-Share Resilience. In both enhancement schemes, the identities of the communicating parties have been included in the signed message of M_A, M_B and M_C as well as the session key K_A, K_B and K_C. This significantly prevents the attacker from launching the unknown key-share attack in various ways on our improved protocols. With this, a stronger sense of authentication can be achieved explicitly.

Key Control Resilience. Apparently in our protocols, no single protocol participant could force the session keys to a predetermined or predicted value since the session keys of our protocols are derived by using the long term and ephemeral private keys of all the protocol participants, as well as their corresponding timestamps or nonces employed in that particular session.

6 Conclusion

Tso et al.'s IDNIKS is impractical since a non-interactive scheme for three or more parties cannot resist the KCI attack and the insider impersonation attack under any circumstances. Furthermore, we have also pointed out the demerits of their IDNIKS-based tripartite application scheme by demonstrating an insider impersonation attack in this paper. To conquer these defects, we have proposed two improvement schemes by including the use of timestamps and nonces respectively. On top of that, we have also involved the identities of communicating entities in the broadcasted message and session key computation so as to protect further against various malicious attacks such as the unknown key share attack and the triangle attack. More significantly, we have carried out a detailed security analysis to scrutinize our enhanced scheme heuristically. In a nutshell, we have proven our enhanced ID-based tripartite authenticated key agreement protocols to be secure against various cryptographic attacks, while preserving the desired security attributes of a key agreement protocol.

References

1. Al-Riyami, S.S., Paterson, K.G.: Tripartite Authenticated Key Agreement Protocols from Pairings, Cryptology ePrint Archive: Report (035) (2002)
2. Chien, H.Y.: Comments: Insider Attack on Cheng et al.'s Pairing-based Tripartite Key Agreement Protocols, Cryptology ePrint Archive: Report (013) (2005)
3. Chien, H.Y., Lin, R.Y.: An Improved Tripartite Authenticated Key Agreement Protocol Based on Weil Pairing. Int. J. Appl. Sci. Eng. 3, 1 (2005)
4. Chou, J.S., Lin, C.H., Chiu, C.H.: Weakness of Shims New ID-based Tripartite Multiple-key Agreement Protocol, Cryptology ePrint Archive: Report (457) (2005)
5. Cheng, Z.H., Vasiu, L., Comley, R.: Pairing-based One-round Tripartite Key Agreement Protocols, Cryptology ePrint Archive: Report (079) (2004)
6. Joux, A.: A One-round Protocol for Tripartite Diffie-Hellman. In: Bosma, W. (ed.) Algorithmic Number Theory. LNCS, vol. 1838, pp. 385–394. Springer, Heidelberg (2000)
7. Lin, C.H., Li, H.H.: Secure One-Round Tripartite Authenticated Key Agreement Protocol from Weil Pairing. In: AINA 2005. Proceedings of the 19th International Conference on Advanced Information Networking and Applications, pp. 135–138 (2005)
8. Lim, M.H., Lee, S.G., Park, Y.H., Lee, H.J.: An Enhanced One-round Pairing-based Tripartite Authenticated Key Agreement Protocol, Cryptology ePrint Archive: Report (142) (2007)
9. Nalla, D.: ID-based Tripartite Key Agreement with Signatures, Cryptology ePrint Archive: Report (144) (2003)
10. Nalla, D., Reddy, K.C.: ID-based tripartite Authenticated Key Agreement Protocols from pairings, Cryptology ePrint Archive: Report (004) (2003)
11. Shim, K.: Cryptanalysis of Al-Riyami-Paterson's Authenticated Three Party Key Agreement Protocols, Cryptology ePrint Archive: Report (122) (2003)
12. Shim, K.: Efficient ID-based Authenticated Key Agreement Protocol based on Weil Pairing. Electronics Letters 39(8), 653–654 (2003)

13. Shim, K.: Efficient One-round Tripartite Authenticated Key Agreement Protocol from Weil Pairing. Electronics Letters 39(2), 208–209 (2003)
14. Sun, H.M., Hsieh, B.T.: Security Analysis of Shims Authenticated Key Agreement Protocols from Pairings, Cryptology ePrint Archive: Report (113) (2003)
15. Tso, R., Okamoto, T., Takagi, T., Okamoto, E.: An ID-based Non-Interactive Tripartite Key Agreement Protocol with K-Resilience. Communications and Computer Networks, 38–42 (2005)
16. Wilson, S.B., Menezes, A.: Authenticated Diffie-Hellman key agreement protocols. In: Tavares, S., Meijer, H. (eds.) SAC 1998. LNCS, vol. 1556, pp. 339–361. Springer, Heidelberg (1999)
17. Wilson, S.B., Johnson, D., Menezes, A.: Key Agreement Protocols and their Security Analysis. In: Darnell, M. (ed.) Cryptography and Coding. LNCS, vol. 1355, pp. 339–361. Springer, Heidelberg (1997)
18. Zhang, F.G., Liu, S.L., Kim, K.J.: ID-based One Round Authenticated Tripartite Key Agreement Protocol with Pairings, Cryptology ePrint Archive: Report (122) (2002)

A Near Optimal S-Box Design

Debojyoti Bhattacharya[1], Nitin Bansal[2], Amitava Banerjee[3],
and Dipanwita RoyChowdhury[4]

[1] IIT-Kharagpur, Kharagpur, India
debojyoti.bhattacharya@gmail.com
[2] IIT-Kharagpur, Kharagpur, India
nitin.bansal@iitkgp.ac.in
[3] IIT-Kharagpur, Kharagpur, India
amitava.ju.etce2002@gmail.com
[4] IIT-Kharagpur, Kharagpur, India
drc@iitkgp.ac.in

Abstract. In this work a cryptographically robust S-box based on non-linear Cellular Automata rules has been developed. Properties suggest that the robustness of the proposed construction is better than that proposed by Seberry et al. [1]. Though the proposed S-box is not optimal to the linear and differential attacks like Rijndael S-box, its immunity towards linear cryptanalysis and robustness against differential cryptanalysis is high and it lacks algebraic relations over finite field. Due to the presence of synchronous elements in its architecture, timing constraints can also be fulfilled efficiently if hardware masking is done on the circuit to prevent it against power attack. Also due to Cellular Automata based structure, the S-box can be efficiently implemented in hardware and in software for high speed design.

Keywords: S-box, Cellular Automata, Power Attack, Algebraic Attack.

1 Introduction

The security of symmetric key block ciphers largely depends on the cryptographic robustness of the S-boxes. Thus the construction of good S-boxes are an extremely important component of cipher design. In [2] authors first focused on the statistical properties of random, reversible S-boxes. In literature subsequently several works [3], [4], [5], [6] have been published in defining the desirable properties of S-boxes. However the drawbacks of all these proposals were pointed out in [1]. The main weakness were that the component functions of these S-boxes were quadratic and thus could be vulnerable to many classic as well as recent algebraic attacks. One of the constructions proposed in [7] is based on Maiorana-McFarland method and is built out of Linear Feedback Shift Registers (LFSRs). Apart from the above drawbacks the class of circuits built around LFSRs can be found to have the following inherent disadvantages (*i*) irregularity of the interconnection structure, (*ii*) larger delay and (*iii*) lack of modularity

P. McDaniel and S.K. Gupta (Eds.): ICISS 2007, LNCS 4812, pp. 77–90, 2007.

and cascadability. Also the resultant S-box was not balanced and had the restriction that the first half of the input that goes to the LFSRs was not zero. This restricts the usage of the generated S-Boxes. In [1] the authors describe various properties of cryptographically robust S-boxes. The various properties listed were: (i) High nonlinearity, (ii) Balanced output, (iii) Immunity against Linear Cryptanalysis, (iv) Robustness against Differential Cryptanalysis, (v) Avalanche Effect and (vi) High algebraic degree of its output boolean functions. In [4] a method was presented for $n \times n$ S-box design. However, for the S-box created by this method, its inverse S-box is almost completely linear (it has only one non-linear function) and its diffusion property cannot be ensured. In [8] the authors proposed a design methodology for $n \times n$ S-boxes. Since, the method is an exhaustive search method the complexity of the method grows as the value of n increases. In [9] a method has been described for obtaining cryptographically strong 8×8 S-boxes. However the performance of the generated S-boxes are much inferior compared to possible S-boxes that can be constructed for such dimensions.

Most of the modern day block ciphers use S-boxes. Out of the 5 AES finalists candidate algorithms, all of them except RC6 [10] use S-boxes to provide nonlinearity in the round functions. Serpent [11] uses 4×4 S-boxes which though can be implemented efficiently in hardware, is vulnerable to algebraic attacks as proposed in [12]. MARS [13] uses four 8×32 S-boxes of two kinds: $S0$ and $S1$. These large S-boxes must be implemented by SRAMs as suggested in [14], [15]. Use of lookup table to implement these S-boxes resulted in larger circuit size and long propagation delay [14]. The designer of Twofish [16] introduced a new idea of using key dependent S-boxes. Unlike the fixed S-boxes, the contents of key dependent S-boxes change for every key, making the cryptanalysis harder. But the best way of implementing these 8×8 S-boxes is to express them as memories, which could be filled with new contents every-time the keys are changed. The Rijndael algorithm uses Galois field inversion for its 8×8 S-box. Though the inversion in GF is optimally secured against Linear and Differential Cryptanalysis [17], the speed of this operation is particularly slow in software [18]. To make up for the speed look up tables must be used which can lead to cache and timing attacks [18]. Moreover Rijndael S-box is particularly algebraic over $GF(2)$. It can be characterised in several ways by algebraic relation, being true with high probability, usually 1 [19]. This may lead to algebraic attacks.

In this work the Theory of Cellular Automata (CA) has been applied to generate a cryptographically robust 8×8 S-box. The proposed CA based S-box construction is extremely efficient with respect to time, due to inherent parallelism in Cellular Automata transformations. Also as the chosen CA has a three neighbourhood cell [20] the length of interconnects would be less compared to a LFSR based S-box [7], a feature helpful for VLSI implementations. The software implementation of the proposed S-box is fast as CA rules can be efficiently implemented in software. In [21] a CA based S-box has been proposed using *Rule 30* of Cellular Automata. Results show that the robustness of the our proposed construction against Linear and Differential Cryptanalysis is better than that proposed in [21]. Cryptographic robustness of this new construction is better than that proposed in [1]. Strength of the new S-box against algebraic attack is better than that of Rijndael S-box as the proposed structure is not algebraic over finite field. Also due to presence of synchronous delay elements hardware masking can be done efficiently on our proposed S-box.

The rest of the paper is organised as follows: Section 2 discusses the preliminaries required for this work. Construction of our CA based S-box structure, CANLF has been described in Section 3. Section 4 discusses the hardware synthesis results, power analysis results and comparisons with some other well known constructions. Finally Section 5 concludes the paper and at the end of this paper we give the S-Box (Table 5) and inverse S-Box (Table 6).

2 Preliminaries

In this section we discuss some basic definitions and notations to be used in this work.

2.1 Cellular Automata Preliminaries

A Cellular Automata (CA) consists of a number of cells arranged in a regular manner, where the state transition of each cell depends on the states of its neighbours. For a three neighbourhood CA the state q of the ith cell at time $(t + 1)$ is given as $q_i^{t+1} = f(q_{i-1}^t, q_i^t, q_{i+1}^t)$ where f is the *rule* of the automata [22]. As f is a three variant function, it can have 2^8 or 256 outputs. The decimal equivalent of the output column in the truth table of f denotes the rule number. The next state function of Rule 90 and Rule 150 are given below:

Rule 90: $q_i^{t+1} = q_{i-1}^t \oplus q_{i+1}^t$ and **Rule 150:** $q_i^{t+1} = q_{i-1}^t \oplus q_i^t \oplus q_{i+1}^t$

The CA preliminaries where the CA is in $GF(2)$ are noted in [20]. For an n-cell one dimensional CA, the linear operator can be shown to be an $n \times n$ matrix [20], whose i-th row corresponds to the neighbourhood relation of the i-th cell. The next state of the CA is generated by applying the linear operator on the present state. The operation is simple matrix multiplication, but the addition involved is modulo-2 sum. The matrix is termed as the characteristics matrix of the CA and is denoted by T. If f_t represents the state of the automata at t^{th} instant of time, then the next state, i.e., the state at $(t + 1)^{th}$ instant of time, is given by $f_{t+1} = T * f_t$. If for a CA all states in a state transition graph lies in some cycle, it is called a group CA; otherwise it is a non-group CA. It has been shown in [20] that for a group CA its T matrix is non-singular, i.e., $det[T] = 1$ ($det[T]$ = determinant of T). An n-cell CA can be characterized by a $n \times n$ **characteristics matrix** T as follows:

$$T[i, j] = 1 \text{(if next state of i-th cell}$$
$$\text{depends on the present state of j-th cell)}$$
$$= 0 \text{(otherwise)}.$$

2.2 Preliminaries Related to Block Cipher Security

Definition 1. *Balancedness: The vector space of n tuples of elements from $GF(2)$ is denoted by V_n. Let g be a Boolean function from V_n to $GF(2)$. The truth table of g is defined as $(g(\alpha_0), g(\alpha_1), \ldots, g(\alpha_{n-1}))$, where α_i, $i = 0, 1, \ldots, 2^n - 1$, denote vectors in V_n. g is said to be balanced if its truth table has an equal numbers of zeroes and ones.*

Definition 2. *A boolean function $g(x)$, where x is an n variable binary string, can be uniquely written as a sum (XOR) of products (AND). This is known as Algebraic Normal Form (ANF).*

$$g(x_1, x_2, \ldots, x_n) = p_0 \oplus p_1 x_1 \oplus p_2 x_2 \oplus \ldots p_n x_n \oplus p_{1,2} x_1 x_2 \oplus p_{n-1,n} x_{n-1} x_n \oplus \ldots \oplus p_{1,2,\ldots,n} x_1 x_2 \ldots x_n.$$

The values of $(p_0, p_1, \ldots, p_{1,2,\ldots,n} \in \{0,1\})$ uniquely represent a boolean function.

Definition 3. *The algebraic degree of a boolean function is defined as the highest number of x_i that appear in a product term in the ANF.*

Definition 4. *An n variable boolean function $g(x_1, x_2, \ldots, x_n)$ is said to be an affine function if the ANF of g is of the form $g(x_1, x_2, \ldots, x_n) = \oplus_{i=0}^{n} p_i x_i \oplus q$ for $p_i, q \in \{0,1\}$. If q is 0, then the function is said to be linear.*

Definition 5. *Hamming weight of a binary string x is the number of 1's in the string and is denoted by $wt(x)$.*

Definition 6. *Hamming distance between two binary strings of equal length (say x and y) is the number of positions where x and y differ and is measured by $wt(x \oplus y)$.*

Definition 7. *Non-linearity of an n variable boolean function g is defined as the minimum Hamming distance from the set of all affine functions of n variables, i.e., $N_f = min_{a \in A_n} d_H(g, a)$, where Hamming distance is defined as, $d_H(g, a) = \{\#x | g(x) \neq a(x)\}$. A_n is the set of all n variable affine functions.*

Definition 8. *Bias of linear approximation: Let the linear approximation is of the form:*

$$< L \equiv X_{i_1} \oplus X_{i_2} \oplus \ldots X_{i_k} \oplus Y_{j_1} \oplus Y_{j_2} \oplus \ldots \oplus Y_{j_l} >= 0$$

where X_i represents the ith bit of the input $X[X_1, X_2, \ldots]$ and Y_j represents the jth bit of the output $Y[Y_1, Y_2, \ldots]$. The equation represents the XOR of k input bits and l output bits. If the bits are chosen randomly then the above linear expression will hold with a probability of $\frac{1}{2}$. If p_L is the probability with which the the expression holds, then its bias is defined as $|p_L - \frac{1}{2}|$.

Definition 9. *Robustness of S-box [1]: Let $F = (f_1, f_2, \ldots f_s)$ be an $n \times s$ S-box, where f_i is a function on V_n, $i = 1, 2, \ldots, s$, and $n \geq s$. We denote by L the largest value in the difference distribution table of F, and by R the number of non-zero entries in the first column of the table. In either case the value 2^n in* *the first row is not counted. Then we say that F is ϵ-robust against differential cryptanalysis, where ϵ is defined by*

$$\epsilon = (1 - R/2^n)(1 - L/2^n).$$

3   Construction of the CA Based S-Box: CANLF

In general an S-box takes n input bits and produces s output bits. In this work our aim was to generate a S-box where $n = s$. To generate an $n \times n$ S-box we need to work with non-linear and reversible Cellular Automata rules. For ease of VLSI implementation we concentrate upon 3-neighbourhood rules. We also used non-linear balanced rules. After several attempts we decided to use skewed version of the original rules, where the neighbourhood of a cell is shifted to its right, i.e. the next state of a cell becomes dependent on itself and on two of its right neighbours. Hence the next state of the i-th cell is written as $q_i^{t+1} = f(q_i^t, q_{i+1}^t, q_{i+2}^t)$. The construction we choose is uniform CA with null boundary conditions. We run these CAs with different number of clock cycles and checked the properties we obtained. We used the concept of cycles as used in [21]. After each cycle, the output is completely reversed, i.e. the last bit becomes first, the second last becomes second and so on. The results we obtained are as follows:

- We obtained non-linear CA rules which are reversible, balanced and give regular mapping
- Same function give different non-linearity, robustness and bias value with different number of clock cycles
- The mappings we obtained showed
  - good Avalanche Effect
  - robustness against Differential Cryptanalysis
  - immunity against Linear Cryptanalysis

In Table 1 we show different nonlinearity values and the best rules (which we tried) that obtained those nonlinearity values. All the results are shown for an 8×8 S-box. We also give the corresponding robustness against differential cryptanalysis and bias against linear cryptanalysis.

From Table 1 we choose the rule which gives optimum results in terms of robustness, bias and number of clock cycles. From Table 1, it is clear that rule 225 with 19 clocks is best compared to the other ones.

Construction of the forward transformation
Rule 225 has an update rule as follows:

$$q_i^{t+1} = 1 \oplus q_{i-1}^t \oplus (q_i^t \vee q_{i+1}^t)$$

The update rule of the skewed version is:

$$q_i^{t+1} = 1 \oplus q_i^t \oplus (q_{i+1}^t \vee q_{i+2}^t)$$

Table 1. 1st column shows the nonlinearity value and the rows are corresponding rules

	R : 30 clk : 18	R : 30 clk : 21	R : 225 clk : 18	R : 225 clk : 25
	Robustness	Robustness	Robustness	Robustness
100	.953125	.960938	.9375	.960938
	Bias :	Bias :	Bias :	Bias :
	.132812	.148438	.125	.140623
	R : 30 clk : 24	R : 30 clk : 25	**R : 225 clk : 19**	R : 225 clk : 21
	Robustness	Robustness	**Robustness**	Robustness
102	.953125	.953125	.960938	.953125
	Bias :	Bias :	**Bias :**	Bias :
	.140623	.125	.125	.125
	R : 30 clk : 23	R : 225 clk : 87		
	Robustness	Robustness		
104	.953125	.953125		
	Bias :	Bias :		
	.132812	.132812		

The $n-1$-th cell position is considered as the lsb while considering the neighbourhood. The modified rule with null boundary condition when applied to a finite field is reversible and an inverse automata exists. We configure an 8-bit CA uniformly with this rule and run it for 19 clock cycles to obtain the required transformation. In each clock cycle the bit pattern is completely reversed.

Construction of the reverse transformation

For the reverse transformation we need to find the inverse automata of the given rule. We calculate the value at instant $t-1$ given the value at instant t. To calculate the inverse, we start with the cell at $i = n - 1$(lsb). At this point

$$q_{n-1}^t = 1 \oplus q_{n-1}^{t-1}, \text{ (As it has no right neighbours)}$$
$$\therefore q_{n-1}^{t-1} = 1 \oplus q_{n-1}^t \tag{1}$$

Next we consider the cell at $i = n - 2$.

$$q_{n-2}^t = 1 \oplus q_{n-2}^{t-1} \oplus q_{n-1}^{t-1}, \text{ (It has only one right neighbour)}$$
$$\therefore q_{n-2}^t = 1 \oplus q_{n-2}^{t-1} \oplus 1 \oplus q_{n-1}^t, \text{ (from equation (1))}$$
$$\therefore q_{n-2}^{t-1} = q_{n-2}^t \oplus q_{n-1}^t \tag{2}$$

Next we consider the cell at $i = n - 3$.

$$q_{n-3}^t = 1 \oplus q_{n-3}^{t-1} \oplus (q_{n-2}^{t-1} \vee q_{n-1}^{t-1})$$
$$\therefore q_{n-3}^t = 1 \oplus q_{n-3}^{t-1} \oplus ((q_{n-2}^t \oplus q_{n-1}^t) \vee (1 \oplus q_{n-1}^t)), \text{ (Using equation (1) and (2))}$$
$$\therefore q_{n-3}^{t-1} = 1 \oplus q_{n-3}^t \oplus ((q_{n-2}^t \oplus q_{n-1}^t) \vee (1 \oplus q_{n-1}^t)) \tag{3}$$

Thus Equations 1, 2 and 3 give the inverse functions at cell positions $i = n - 1$, $n - 2$ and $n - 3$ respectively. All the other cells are like cell $n - 3$. Therefore

Equation 3 can be applied iteratively resulting in the unambiguous recovery of the entire state of the automation at the previous time step. During the forward transformation we reversed the output after each clock cycle. In order to obtain the correct inverse the same inversion is applied to the input bits of the inverse transformation. In Table 2 we list the cryptographic properties of the CA based forward and reverse transformation.

Table 2. Cryptographic Properties of CANLF

Properties	Forward Transformation	Inverse Transformation
Linear Cryptanalysis	Bias : .125	Bias : .125
Differential Cryptanalysis	Robustness : .960938	Robustness : .960938
Non-Linearity	102	100
Algebraic Degree	7	7
Avalanche Effect	4	4

4   Results and Comparisons

In this section we give the hardware synthesis results and power analysis results of our proposed S-box, CANLF. We also give comparisons with two most well known S-box constructions. The first one is based on combinatorial structure called group Hadamard matrices [1]. The authors demonstrated the method of systematic generation of cryptographically robust S-boxes. The second one being inversion over finite field, which is used in Rijndael. We show that the cryptographic strength of CANLF is better than the bijective S-box proposed in [1]. We also show that the new construction performs better than Rijndael S-box against algebraic cryptanalysis.

4.1   Hardware Synthesis Results

The Cellular Automata structure has been fully unfolded to obtain a pipelined architecture. The top level architecture is shown in Figure 1. There are two 8-bit registers at the input and the output. Different pipelining stages are possible for this architecture. We implemented a 19-stage pipelined architecture and a balanced 4-stage pipelined architecture. The 19-stage pipelined architecture achieves highest speed at the cost of extra hardware. The 4-stage pipeline implementation is optimized for speed and hardware.

The design has been synthesised on Xilinx XCV-1000 platform. The synthesis report has been summarised in Table 3.

Table 3. Synthesis Results of CANLF

Pipeline Stages	Slices	Slice FFs	4 input LUTs	Frequency
19	90	160	133	$194.89MHz$
4	69	48	136	$103.38MHz$

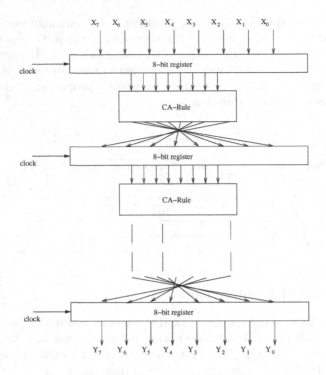

Fig. 1. Architecture of CANLF

4.2 Power Analysis Results

One of the most potential side-channel attack is Differential Power Analysis (DPA) [23]. Power consumption signals of CMOS chips are used to retrieve key values by difference of mean curves selected on defined criteria. To secure the implementations of Rijndael against DPA, researchers proposed different masking schemes where they tried to mask the intermediate values that occur during the execution of the algorithm. Different masking schemes have been studied in [24], [25], [26], [27], [28], [29]. Out of the above presented schemes, the first two are susceptible to zero-value attacks [26] and the third one is quite complex to implement in hardware. The schemes presented in [27], [28] and [29] are provably secured against DPA and can be implemented efficiently in hardware. However, several publications came out in 2005 where it was shown that even provably secure masking schemes can also be broken, if they are implemented in standard CMOS due to unintended switching activities that take place in CMOS circuits. These unintended switching activities are referred as glitches. The effect of glitches on the side-channel resistance of the masked circuits has first been analyzed in [30]. In [31] a similar analysis has been carried out. In [32] a technique to model the effect of glitches on the side-channel resistance of circuits has been proposed. In [33], the authors finally showed that glitches can indeed make circuits susceptible to DPA attacks. In [34] the authors showed that there exists

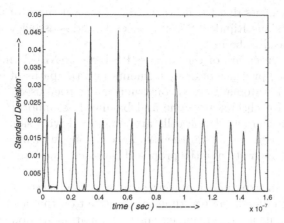

Fig. 2. Standard Deviation for input data 00011101

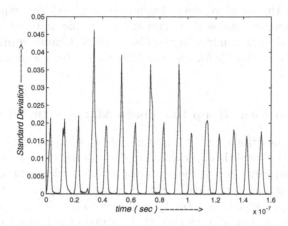

Fig. 3. Standard Deviation for input data 01010100

a family of masked gates which is theoretically secure in the presence of glitches if certain practically controllable implementation constraints are imposed.

The parts of masked Rijndael S-boxes that cause the glitches that lead to side-channel leakage has been pinpointed in [35]. The analysis in [35] reveals that glitches are caused by the switching characteristics of XOR gates in masked multipliers which are basic building blocks of masked Rijndael S-boxes. It has been shown that to prevent DPA the number of transitions at the output of an XOR gate needs to be equal to the total number of transitions occurring at the inputs, otherwise these XOR gates absorb transitions and the number of absorbed transitions is correlated to the unmasked operands of masked multiplier of Rijndael S-box. As a countermeasure, the authors proposed to insert delay elements into paths of input signals to meet timing constraints. They also pointed out that it is not always possible to efficiently fulfil the timing constraints by inserting delay elements due to the variation of arrival times of the operands. Hence efficient masking Rijndael S-boxes is costly and is associated with timing constraints that need to be fulfilled.

However the architecture of the proposed S-box, CANLF is inherently synchronous due to the presence of delay elements into the paths of its inputs and outputs as Cellular Automata based construction has been used. The path from input to output of each bits are same and balanced as uniform CA is used in the S-box construction i.e. all the cells are configured with same rule and the insertion of delay elements within the structure can be implemented efficiently. Thus masked implementation of the proposed S-box can meet timing constraints efficiently.

We performed an experiment on our proposed 'unmasked' S-box circuit to check the effect of different arrival times of the input on the power profile. Two different sets of inputs are taken and extensive simulation are done with different arrival times. We measured the leakage current and the switching power in each case. For a particular input, standard deviation of the switching power is drawn. Results show that the standard deviation is too small. All the experiments are done on the architecture proposed in Section 4.1. The simulation is done on **Cadence Spectre** using $0.5~\mu$ mixed signal library of **National Semiconductor**. The standard deviation profile for the two different inputs are shown in Figure 2 and Figure 3.

4.3   Comparison with Group Hadamard Matrices Based S-Box [1]

In [1] the authors described the systematic method of generating $n \times s$ S-box. Though it has been proved theoretically that the construction methodology generates cryptographically strong S-boxes no practical implementations has been done so far. The parameters used in this construction are k and t. The constraints on these parameters are $\lfloor n/2 \rfloor < k < n$ and $n \geq s > \lfloor n/2 \rfloor + t$. To compare with our construction we choose the value of n and s to be 8, which implies the value of $k = 5$ and $t = 3$. In Table 4 we list the comparative study.

Table 4. Comparison between CANLF and [1]

Parameters	CANLF	[1] S-box
Linear Cryptanalysis	Bias : .125	Bias : .25
Differential Cryptanalysis	Robustness : .960938	Robustness : .875
Algebraic Degree	7	4
SAC	Not Satisfied	Satisfied

From the results of Table 4, it is clear that the proposed S-box performs better against Linear and Differential Cryptanalysis than that proposed in [1]. Also as the algebraic degree of the component functions of our proposed construction is greater than that of [1], it performs better against algebraic cryptanalysis.

4.4   Comparison with Rijndael S-Box Against Algebraic Attack

CANLF has no simple algebraic description over finite field. Hence it can help to prevent algebraic attack. As the generated S-box cannot be characterized by any algebraic relations, no algebraic equations can be generated which may lead to potential algebraic attack. The Rijndael S-box can be characterized in several ways by algebraic relations, being true with high probability, usually 1 [19]. The idea of algebraic attack have been employed over stream ciphers and also block ciphers. The seminal idea of Patarin [36] and later improved

Table 5. S-Box

$f0$	$6a$	$c9$	$c0$	$c1$	69	$a1$	68	70	24	$4d$	88	62	81	$e5$	$c6$
$8f$	11	$d4$	04	eb	46	$f1$	86	ea	45	03	$e4$	65	07	51	96
$c4$	58	$0c$	59	$e0$	44	$8d$	06	36	$a4$	56	66	$b6$	ce	$5d$	$a0$
54	$d8$	$3b$	$1e$	$b1$	$6e$	50	$9d$	60	67	$6c$	dc	34	$2d$	bd	$7a$
$f4$	$c7$	$8b$	92	$b9$	48	21	$7d$	$0a$	90	$8c$	af	80	$2b$	$b2$	fd
75	$2c$	$d0$	$e2$	$a2$	$6b$	ee	$2a$	$9a$	$c3$	41	13	db	37	$a9$	fc
$a7$	09	$a3$	42	$3e$	39	cd	$e6$	$e7$	$a6$	94	78	38	$4b$	$f8$	$b0$
$3f$	10	$1f$	$a5$	$f9$	bb	$f5$	20	99	$a8$	df	16	$9e$	be	76	$6f$
ff	cb	$f3$	$8e$	$5c$	$c2$	79	$b4$	$d3$	14	49	$4c$	52	dd	47	01
$d2$	02	00	30	aa	$6d$	$c8$	$e8$	$d9$	$4f$	$1c$	$5a$	$d6$	27	$7b$	$1a$
32	$b3$	31	$4a$	18	$9b$	$0e$	19	$e1$	17	$b7$	$d7$	$f2$	77	$2f$	de
85	73	64	23	$3a$	74	ef	$e3$	$5e$	12	05	ed	$3d$	$b5$	ae	$7e$
fb	$e9$	bc	$d5$	$0d$	33	da	$1d$	95	57	89	35	15	$9c$	$0f$	91
fe	29	82	$8a$	ad	87	ec	$9f$	ab	22	$5b$	$d1$	cc	$3c$	$b8$	71
93	28	43	$f6$	ac	$1b$	63	53	$0b$	97	98	55	fa	ba	08	25
83	72	$2e$	bf	ca	26	$7c$	$4e$	$c5$	84	61	40	cf	$5f$	$7f$	$f7$

Table 6. Inverse S-Box

92	$8f$	91	$1a$	13	ba	27	$1d$	ee	61	48	$e8$	22	$c4$	$a6$	ce
71	11	$b9$	$5b$	89	cc	$7b$	$a9$	$a4$	$a7$	$9f$	$e5$	$9a$	$c7$	33	72
77	46	$d9$	$b3$	09	ef	$f5$	$9d$	$e1$	$d1$	57	$4d$	51	$3d$	$f2$	ae
93	$a2$	$a0$	$c5$	$3c$	cb	28	$5d$	$6c$	65	$b4$	32	dd	bc	64	70
fb	$5a$	63	$e2$	25	19	15	$8e$	45	$8a$	$a3$	$6d$	$8b$	$0a$	$f7$	99
36	$1e$	$8c$	$e7$	30	eb	$2a$	$c9$	21	23	$9b$	da	84	$2e$	$b8$	fd
38	fa	$0c$	$e6$	$b2$	$1c$	$2b$	39	07	05	1	55	$3a$	95	35	$7f$
08	df	$f1$	$b1$	$b5$	50	$7e$	ad	$6b$	86	$3f$	$9e$	$f6$	47	bf	fe
$4c$	$0d$	$d2$	$f0$	$f9$	$b0$	17	$d5$	$0b$	ca	$d3$	42	$4a$	26	83	10
49	cf	43	$e0$	$6a$	$c8$	$1f$	$e9$	ea	78	58	$a5$	cd	37	$7c$	$d7$
$2f$	06	54	62	29	73	69	60	79	$5e$	94	$d8$	$e4$	$d4$	be	$4b$
$6f$	34	$4e$	$a1$	87	bd	$2c$	aa	de	44	ed	75	$c2$	$3e$	$7d$	$f3$
03	04	85	59	20	$f8$	$0f$	41	96	02	$f4$	81	dc	66	$2d$	fc
52	db	90	88	12	$c3$	$9c$	ab	31	98	$c6$	$5c$	$3b$	$8d$	af	$7a$
24	$a8$	53	$b7$	$1b$	$0e$	67	68	97	$c1$	18	14	$d6$	bb	56	$b6$
00	16	ac	82	40	76	$e3$	ff	$6e$	74	ec	$c0$	$5f$	$4f$	$d0$	80

by [37], [38] has lead to the breaking of several stream ciphers [39], [40], [41], [42] and also is probing the security of Rijndael [12]. Jakobsen [43] clearly makes his point showing that to obtain secure ciphers "*... it is not enough to that round functions have high Boolean complexity. Likewise, good properties against differential and linear properties are no guarantee either. In fact, many almost perfect non-linear functions should be avoided exactly because they are too simple algebraically...*". In [19] the author makes extensive investigations on the inverse function in $GF(2^m)$ and some of its linear equivalents and uses to build them both as components of highly insecure ciphers and as the algebraic structure that can be exploited in attacks. The disadvantage of S-boxes which does not have an algebraic description is implementation. Our CA based S-box is an ideal alternative in the fact that it can be efficiently implemented and the S-box generated lacks any algebraic relation which may be exploited in attacks.

5   Conclusion

To obtain secure, realizable cipher, apart from being robust against linear and differential attack, future S-boxes should be free of algebraic weakness, they must be implemented efficiently in hardware and in software and the structure of S-boxes should help to implement hardware masking efficiently to prevent side-channel information leakage leading to power attack. In this chapter we have developed a cryptographically robust S-box, CANLF, based on non-linear Cellular Automata rules. Properties suggest that the robustness of the proposed construction is better than that proposed by Seberry et al. [1]. Though the proposed S-box is not optimal to the attacks against Linear and Differential Cryptanalysis like Rijndael S-box, its immunity towards Linear Cryptanalysis and robustness against Differential Cryptanalysis is high and it lacks simple algebraic relations over finite field. As the proposed S-box is not algebraic over finite fields it can prevent algebraic attack which is a serious weakness of Rijndael S-box. Timing constraints can also be fulfilled efficiently if hardware masking is done on the circuit to prevent it against power attack. Also due to Cellular Automata based structure, the S-box can be implemented efficiently in hardware and in software for high speed design.

References

1. Seberry, J., Zhang, X.M., Zheng, Y.: Systematic Generation of Cryptographically Robust S-Boxes. In: ACM Conference on Computer and Communications Security, pp. 171–182 (1993)
2. Gordon, J.A., Retkin, H.: Are Big S-Boxes Best? In: Beth, T. (ed.) Cryptography. LNCS, vol. 149, pp. 257–262. Springer, Heidelberg (1983)
3. Webster, A.F., Tavares, S.E.: On the Design of S-Boxes. In: Williams, H.C. (ed.) CRYPTO 1985. LNCS, vol. 218, pp. 523–534. Springer, Heidelberg (1986)
4. Pieprzyk, J., Finkelstein, G.: Towards effective nonlinear cryptosystem design. Computers and Digital Techniques, IEE Proceedings 135, 325–335 (1988)
5. Youssef, A.M., Tavares, S.E.: Resistance of balanced s-boxes to linear and differential cryptanalysis. Information Processing Letters 56(5), 249–252 (1995)

6. Youssef, A.M., Tavares, S.E.: Number of nonlinear regular s-boxes. IEE Electronic Letters 31(19), 1643–1644 (1995)
7. Nyberg, K.: Perfect Nonlinear S-Boxes. In: Davies, D.W. (ed.) EUROCRYPT 1991. LNCS, vol. 547, pp. 378–386. Springer, Heidelberg (1991)
8. Adams, C.M., Tavares, S.E.: Good S-Boxes Are Easy To Find. In: Brassard, G. (ed.) CRYPTO 1989. LNCS, vol. 435, pp. 612–615. Springer, Heidelberg (1990)
9. Yi, X., Cheng, S.X., You, X.H., Lam, K.Y.: A method for obtaining cryptographically strong 8x8 S-boxes. In: GLOBECOM 1997. Global Telecommunications Conference, vol. 2, pp. 689–693. IEEE, Los Alamitos (1997)
10. Rivest, R.L., Robshaw, M.J.B., Sidney, R., Lin, Y.L.: The rc6 block cipher, v1.1 (1998), http://www.rsalabs.com/rc6
11. Biham, E., Anderson, R.J., Knudsen, L.R.: Serpent: A new block cipher proposal. In: Fast Software Encryption, pp. 222–238 (1998)
12. Courtois, N.T., Pieprzyk, J.: Cryptanalysis of block ciphers with overdefined systems of equations. In: Zheng, Y. (ed.) ASIACRYPT 2002. LNCS, vol. 2501, pp. 267–287. Springer, Heidelberg (2002)
13. Burwick, C., Coppersmith, D., Avignon, E.D., Gennaro, R., Halevi, S., Jutla, C., Matyas, S.M., Connor, L.O., Peyravian, M., Safford, D., Zunic, N.: Mars - a candidate cipher for AES. In: First Advanced Encryption Standard (AES) Conference, Ventura, CA (1998)
14. Chodowiec, P.R.: Comparison of the hardware performance of the aes candidates using reconfigurable hardware (2002), http://ece.gmu.edu/reports/
15. Satoh, A., Ooba, N., Takano, K., D'Avignon, E.: High-speed mars hardware. In: AES Candidate Conference, pp. 305–316 (2000)
16. Schneier, B., Kelsey, J., Whiting, D., Wagner, D., Hall, C., Ferguson, N.: The Twofish encryption algorithm: a 128-bit block cipher. John Wiley & Sons, New York (1999)
17. Nyberg, K.: Differentially uniform mappings for cryptography. In: Helleseth, T. (ed.) EUROCRYPT 1993. LNCS, vol. 765, pp. 55–64. Springer, Heidelberg (1994)
18. Bernstein, D.J.: Cache-timing attacks on AES (2005), http://cr.yp.to/papers.html#cachetiming
19. Courtois, N.T.: The Inverse S-Box, Non-linear Polynomial Relations and Cryptanalysis of Block Ciphers. In: AES Conference, pp. 170–188 (2004)
20. Chaudhuri, P.P., Chowdhury, D., Nandi, S., Chattopadhyay, S.: 4. In: Additive Cellular Automata Theory and its Application, vol. 1, IEEE Computer Society Press, Los Alamitos (1997)
21. Joshi, P., Mukhopadhyay, D., RoyChowdhury, D.: Design and Analysis of a Robust and Efficient Block Cipher using Cellular Automata. In: AINA 2006. Proceedings of the 20th International Conference on Advanced Information Networking and Applications, vol. 2, pp. 67–71. IEEE Computer Society Press, Los Alamitos (2006)
22. Wolfram, S.: Statistical Mechanics of Cellular Automata. Rev. Mod. Phys. 55(3), 601–644 (1983)
23. Kocher, P., Jaffe, J., Jun, B.: Differential Power Analysis. In: Wiener, M.J. (ed.) CRYPTO 1999. LNCS, vol. 1666, pp. 388–397. Springer, Heidelberg (1999)
24. Akkar, M.L., Giraud, C.: An Implementation of DES and AES, Secure against Some Attacks. In: Koç, Ç.K., Naccache, D., Paar, C. (eds.) CHES 2001. LNCS, vol. 2162, pp. 309–318. Springer, Heidelberg (2001)
25. Trichina, E., Seta, D.D., Germani, L.: Simplified Adaptive Multiplicative Masking for AES. In: Kaliski Jr., B.S., Koç, Ç.K., Paar, C. (eds.) CHES 2002. LNCS, vol. 2523, pp. 187–197. Springer, Heidelberg (2003)

26. Golic, J.D., Tymen, C.: Multiplicative Masking and Power Analysis of AES. In: Kaliski Jr., B.S., Koç, Ç.K., Paar, C. (eds.) CHES 2002. LNCS, vol. 2523, pp. 198–212. Springer, Heidelberg (2003)
27. Morioka, S., Akishita, T.: A DPA-resistant Compact AES S-box Circuit using Additive Mask. In: CCS. Proceedings of Computer Security Composium, pp. 679–684 (2004)
28. Blömer, J., Guajardo, J., Krummel, V.: Provably Secure Masking of AES. In: Selected Areas in Cryptography, pp. 69–83. Springer, Heidelberg (2004)
29. Oswald, E., Mangard, S., Pramstaller, N., Rijmen, V.: A Side-Channel Analysis Resistant Description of the AES S-Box. In: Gilbert, H., Handschuh, H. (eds.) FSE 2005. LNCS, vol. 3557, pp. 413–423. Springer, Heidelberg (2005)
30. Mangard, S., Popp, T., Gammel, B.M.: Side-Channel Leakage of Masked CMOS Gates. In: Menezes, A.J. (ed.) CT-RSA 2005. LNCS, vol. 3376, pp. 351–365. Springer, Heidelberg (2005)
31. Suzuki, D., Saeki, M., Ichikawa, T.: Random Switching Logic: A Countermeasure against DPA based on Transition Probability. Cryptology ePrint Archive, Report 2004/346 (2004), http://eprint.iacr.org/
32. Suzuki, D., Saeki, M., Ichikawa, T.: DPA Leakage Models for CMOS Logic Circuits. In: Rao, J.R., Sunar, B. (eds.) CHES 2005. LNCS, vol. 3659, pp. 366–382. Springer, Heidelberg (2005)
33. Mangard, S., Pramstaller, N., Oswald, E.: Successfully Attacking Masked AES Hardware Implementations. In: Rao, J.R., Sunar, B. (eds.) CHES 2005. LNCS, vol. 3659, pp. 157–171. Springer, Heidelberg (2005)
34. Fischer, W., Gammel, B.M.: Masking at Gate Level in the Presence of Glitches. In: Rao, J.R., Sunar, B. (eds.) CHES 2005. LNCS, vol. 3659, pp. 187–200. Springer, Heidelberg (2005)
35. Mangard, S., Schramm, K.: Pinpointing the Side-Channel Leakage of Masked AES Hardware Implementations. In: Goubin, L., Matsui, M. (eds.) CHES 2006. LNCS, vol. 4249, pp. 76–90. Springer, Heidelberg (2006)
36. Patarin, J.: Hidden Fields Equations (HFE) and Isomorphisms of Polynomials (IP): Two New Families of Asymmetric Algorithms. In: Maurer, U.M. (ed.) EUROCRYPT 1996. LNCS, vol. 1070, pp. 33–48. Springer, Heidelberg (1996)
37. Courtois, N.: The Security of Hidden Field Equations (HFE). In: Naccache, D. (ed.) CT-RSA 2001. LNCS, vol. 2020, pp. 266–281. Springer, Heidelberg (2001)
38. Courtois, N., Daum, M., Felke, P.: On the Security of HFE, HFEv- and Quartz. In: Public Key Cryptography, pp. 337–350 (2003)
39. Courtois, N.: Higher Order Correlation Attacks, XL Algorithm and Cryptanalysis of Toyocrypt. In: Lee, P.J., Lim, C.H. (eds.) ICISC 2002. LNCS, vol. 2587, pp. 182–199. Springer, Heidelberg (2003)
40. Courtois, N., Meier, W.: Algebraic Attacks on Stream Ciphers with Linear Feedback. In: Biham, E. (ed.) EUROCRPYT 2003. LNCS, vol. 2656, pp. 345–359. Springer, Heidelberg (2003)
41. Armknecht, F., Krause, M.: Algebraic Attacks on Combiners with Memory. In: Boneh, D. (ed.) CRYPTO 2003. LNCS, vol. 2729, pp. 162–175. Springer, Heidelberg (2003)
42. Courtois, N.: Algebraic Attacks on Combiners with Memory and Several Outputs. In: Park, C.-s., Chee, S. (eds.) ICISC 2004. LNCS, vol. 3506, pp. 3–20. Springer, Heidelberg (2005)
43. Jakobsen, T.: Higher order cryptanalysis of block ciphers. Department of mathematics, University of Denmark (1999)

A Software Framework for Autonomic Security in Pervasive Environments

Anshuman Saxena[1], Marc Lacoste[2], Tahar Jarboui[2],
Ulf Lücking[3], and Bernd Steinke[3]

[1] Tata Consultancy Services
anshuman.saxena@tcs.com
[2] France Télécom R&D
{marc.lacoste, tahar.jarboui}@orange-ftgroup.com
[3] Nokia Research Center
{ulf.lucking, bernd.steinke}@nokia.com

Abstract. In Systems Beyond 3G, protection fundamentally needs to be flexible. Due to heterogeneity of access networks and mobile devices, multiple security requirements (e.g., cryptographic algorithms, network security policies) must be addressed. The security infrastructure must also be reconfigurable (e.g., system patches to defeat new attacks) to cope with extremely dynamic conditions. Autonomic security applies the idea of flexibility to the security space itself. It goes a step further than simple adaptation by automating the entire reconfiguration process, thus making the security mechanisms self-responsive. We define an autonomic security framework to build such self-protecting systems. The framework is structured around the different steps of the reconfiguration activity: sense, analyze and respond. We show how flexible access control, authentication, and cryptographic security services can be built on top of our framework, illustrating how autonomic security can be implemented in the terminal and the network.

1 Introduction

Security is usually treated as a static component in system design, with one security scheme assumed to protect the system throughout its lifetime. However, solutions based on such one-time assessment may not be adequate for systems exposed to diverse operating environments. Pervasive environments, like those addressed in Systems Beyond 3G, deal with diversely connected devices accessing a wide range of services. Heterogeneity marks every aspect of such systems, be it the user equipment (e.g., different hardware configurations), user preferences (e.g., shifting protection requirements), access networks (e.g., variable connectivity status), physical environments (e.g., different geographic locations), or the available services (e.g., sensitivity of the service accessed). In order to ensure the safety of such continuously evolving systems at all times, it is necessary to invest in mechanisms that monitor every aspect of the system and in the intelligence to carry out the necessary adaptations.

P. McDaniel and S.K. Gupta (Eds.): ICISS 2007, LNCS 4812, pp. 91–109, 2007.

The traditional approach to security takes a standalone view of each environment, developing security policies specific to the problem at hand. A possible solution to ensure the safety of a system in different settings could then be to deploy sets of such security policies, one for each environment. However, it may not always be possible to envision all the attack scenarios a system may encounter during its lifetime. Secondly, these policies remain far from being unified and may present serious composition problems, questioning their safe co-existence in the very first place. Finally, provisioning the correct security policies from the ones available would still remain an open issue.

The required flexibility can be achieved by introducing reconfigurability in the security architecture. Monitoring security-relevant inputs in the contextual space, identifying scenario-specific security requirements, developing flexible policies, and devising suitable interfaces for provisioning such solutions then become become first-class activities in system design. Security services like authentication, access control, and encryption/signature can be made adaptable to the security context. Local contextual aspects like user preferences (e.g., preferred modes, location specificities, etc.) or device characteristics (e.g., hardware configuration, battery power level, etc.) can influence the choice of an authentication method, taking into account the strength of involved cryptographic algorithms, the underlying message handshakes, or resilience to known attacks. Similarly, the choice of the authorization policy, of a trusted security gateway, or even compliance with local regulations on the usage of cryptography can depend on such contextual inputs.

For instance, consider a shopping mall where several WLANs are available (each store maintains one for its customers), each protected by mechanisms of variable strength and enforcing different security policies. When a customer goes to a different store, he/she may move from a current, high-security WLAN, to another where protection is weaker. Changing WLAN means a new security context, which may trigger a reconfiguration of the security mechanisms on the user device (e.g., access control policies, cryptographic algorithms), with possible download and installation of new security components from a remote server. The security of the network connection (e.g., an IPSec tunnel) between the access point and the security server might also be adapted. In this scenario, adaptive security solutions can greatly enhance the underlying infrastructure.

The problem requires an integrated approach: in a network setting, the elements of the security context remain distributed across geographically dispersed network entities. A complete view of end-to-end security then includes various network-related information, e.g., the neighborhood set (capabilities, availability patterns, connectivity options), the interconnecting infrastructure, the underlying trust structures, etc. The overhead involved in maintaining this information is not to be neglected, and trade-offs like performance vs. level of security are often necessary. Solutions requiring less effort to configure, manage, and administer are therefore required.

Autonomic security applies the idea of flexibility to the security space itself. It goes a step further than simple adaptation by automating the entire process of reconfiguration, thus making the security mechanisms self-responsive, running (almost) without any user intervention. From a design perspective, this introduces a control structure which oversees the different aspects of the reconfiguration activity – sense, analyze and respond. The autonomic security framework described in this paper presents a realization of this control structure and specifies the architecture of such self-protecting systems. It also provides the building blocks to realize flexible implementations of several security sub-systems, both on the terminal and the network side, e.g., access control, authentication support, cryptographic services, and network security.

The paper is organized as follows. Section 2 introduces the Sensor-Analyzer-Responder model which lays the foundation for this work. Specific challenges in realizing this model in the security space are also discussed. Section 3 details the proposed framework with precise interface definitions. Section 4 describes some implementation results, with discussion on related work in Section 5. Finally, Section 6 presents concluding remarks and future research directions.

2   General Approach

2.1   The Sensor-Analyzer-Responder Model

Unlike existing ad hoc approaches to adaptive security, we take a more general view of the problem and base our work on the well-established adaptivity model from control theory [9]. The Sensor-Analyzer-Responder model breaks the reconfiguration activity into three sub-tasks (Figure 1). Sensor modules distributed across the system monitor activities of interest and report changes to the modules qualified for analyzing these events. These analyzer modules then compute a new system configuration implied by the reported events. There can be more than one implied configuration and a difference calculation over the set of implied and existing configurations provides the cost associated in introducing each of the new configurations. The one with the lowest cost is selected for provisioning and passed on to the responder module. This cost can include domain-specific metrics like battery consumption, or even the latency to introduce the new configuration. Finally, the responder module computes the actual steps to carry out

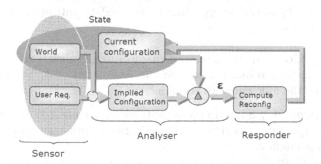

Fig. 1. Autonomic Loop for Reconfiguration

the reconfiguration process and interacts with the functional units to achieve it. The new configuration then forms the basis for future monitoring activities.

2.2 Design Considerations

Realizing this model in the security space has its own set of challenges. It not only requires a security-specific interpretation of the blocks introduced previously, but also the need to accommodate the peculiarities of the target domain.

Environment Monitoring. Ideally, one would like to have identified, at design time, all possible points in the contextual space relevant to the security of the system. To select security-relevant environment inputs, one possible approach is to look at the components of the system and to identify aspects related to each one of them. Such information can broadly be classified as: (i) *user-preferences* (e.g., mode of device operation, choice of connecting network, trust relationships with other users); (ii) *device-related* (e.g., operating environment, power levels and source, hardware availability); or (iii) *network-related* (e.g., point of attachment, network topology, connectivity options).

The context gathering mechanism should remain aware if a certain input changes with time. Static inputs can be stored in long-term profile databases, while dynamic inputs like system state, neighbor set, or trust relationships should be refreshed at regular intervals to reflect the correct state of the system. Such a diverse collection of context information presents serious inference problems.

Security Configuration. Security, as such, is hard to quantify. A metric capturing the diverse security requirements of each system component in a unified representation seems too far stretched. Yet, each component is configured to achieve some security objective. For each available security scheme, relative strength analysis should be performed in light of those security objectives. For example, at the cryptographic level, the strength of an authentication scheme can be ranked on the key size. At the protocol level, the comparison could be done on the type of handshake. A tentative solution is to adopt a tuple-based representation of the security configuration, where each attribute of a tuple captures a precise security objective, e.g., authentication, encryption, integrity, non-repudiation, etc. However, interpreting system safety entirely from such tuples still needs to be investigated.

Interpreting Cost. In the presence of multiple implied configurations, the choice of an optimal solution relies on the associated cost. Such cost can be viewed to have the following two components:

- *Provisioning Cost:* Some implementations of an algorithm may require a restart of the sub-system to initialize various data structures resulting in switch-over latency.
- *Recurring Cost:* It might also be desirable to compare solutions based on their running cost; for instance power consumption due to frequent rekeying or the duration of sleep cycles.

One can view this as an optimization problem, assigning higher weights to aspects of greater importance. The objective function can be devised accordingly.

Safe Composition. Security protocols by default may not be composable: introducing a new algorithm or a new implementation of an existing algorithm may introduce additional vulnerabilities. For instance, one security scheme may consider a nonce as a secret, while the other one might transmit it in clear. To address this critical issue, designers often advocate the principle of cryptographic separation: no security-related material should be shared between different instances of the same or different security schemes. However, such an approach to safe co-existence may cause severe performance penalties, especially on resource-constrained devices, e.g., for multiple key or random number generation.

2.3   Autonomic Security

An autonomic security loop can be instantiated using the following modules:

- *A Security Context Provider (SCP):* The SCP provides a high-level generic description of the current context. Low-level input data (e.g., a geographic location) are gathered from different sources (system/network monitoring components in the device, sensors in the environment) and aggregated into a higher-level generic representation of the current context. This can be achieved through a context management infrastructure. The SCP also provides a description of the ambient security context. A set of security-related attributes (e.g., security levels) are extracted from the generic information provided by the context management infrastructure. This can be realized through a dedicated inference engine.
- *A Decision-Making Component (DMC):* Based on the security context, the DMC decides whether or not to reconfigure the security infrastructure, for instance to relax the strength of authentication, to change cryptographic key lengths, or to select the authorization model adapted to the current network.

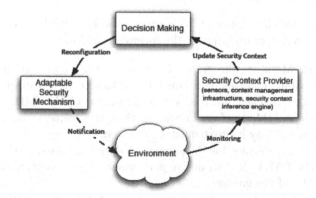

Fig. 2. Building Blocks of the Security Framework

- *Adaptable Security Mechanisms (ASMs):* The decision is then transmitted to the security mechanism which should be adapted. Reconfiguration is performed by changing the needed component. The ASMs should be flexible enough to be reconfigured, by tuning security configuration parameters, or by replacing them with other components offering similar security services. Specific support mechanisms are needed to guarantee that the reconfiguration process is safe and secure.

The autonomic loop is then set up, with monitoring, decision, and action steps: at this point, the equipment is able to negotiate the security parameters autonomously with its environment, fulfilling the vision of a self-protecting system.

2.4   Realizing the Autonomic Security Loop

To refine this view, we build on the results of the E2R (End-to-End Reconfigurability) European Research project [2] which proposed a generic architecture for management and control of a reconfigurable equipment and network. In E2R:

- *Configuration Management Modules (CMMs)* orchestrate configuration tasks in the equipment and negotiate reconfiguration decisions by entities. The CMMs manage the distributed controllers which will initiate, coordinate, and perform the different reconfiguration functions such as monitoring and discovery, download, mode selection and switching, and security.
- *Configuration Control Modules (CCM)* supervise the execution of the reconfiguration process, using specific functions of a given layer or execution environment. Three main layers are considered: application, protocol stack (L2–L4) and modem (L1).
- The *Execution Environment (ExEnv)* supplies the CMMs and CCMs with a consistent interface for the application of reconfiguration actions to the equipment. It provides the basic mechanisms for dynamic, reliable, and secure change of equipment operation.

Mapping the building blocks of the autonomic security loop to the E2R reconfigurability architecture impacts the following CMMs:

- *CMM_MD:* Monitors the state of the environment and triggers low-level events describing changes based on information retrieved from sensors.
- *CMM_Evnt:* For each received event from the CMM_MD, schedules an event to the CMM_Prof to inform it that the context has changed and hence a new security context must be derived.
- *CMM_Prof:* Aggregates low-level context data contained in the events triggered by the CMM_MD to derive a new security context, and informs the CMM_DMP of the change.
- *CMM_DMP:* Based on the new security context, takes the decision to reconfigure or not a security mechanism. If so, calls the CMM_SEC (`reconfigure()` method) to perform securely the reconfiguration operation.

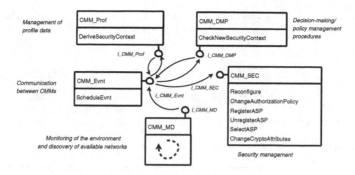

Fig. 3. Realizing the Autonomic Security Loop in E2R

- *CMM_SEC:* Reconfigures an adaptable security mechanism, e.g., installs, removes, or selects a new Authentication Service Provider (ASP), or changes the authorization policy.

Figure 3 presents the relationships between the CMMs and describes their exported interfaces.

3   A Framework for Autonomic Security

The framework aims at formalizing the interactions between the components realizing different aspects of reconfiguration (i.e., monitoring, analyzing, and responding) of a security architecture. We adopted the notion of sub-system as a guiding principle, to be generic enough to take into account the different dimensions of security which could be reconfigured. Dimensions with commonalities are grouped together and treated as one sub-system. Device, Operating Environment, Application, Communication, and Cryptography are a few example sub-systems. For instance, socket-related sensor data are more relevant to the Communication sub-system which has the necessary intelligence to respond to such events. This sub-system approach along with the event model described below forms the basis for an efficient transport mechanism for exchange of context information between different reconfiguration modules.

3.1   An Event-Based Communication Model

The monitoring, analyzing, and response modules can be located within a single system or distributed across network entities with modules added and deleted on the fly. To manage communication effectively between components in such a dynamic system, and to maintain the extensibility and generality of the solution, an event-based communication model (Figure 4) was adopted, with D-Bus [33] as the underlying message exchange mechanism.

D-Bus is an inter-process communication scheme which works both in system and network settings. Current transport mechanisms supported in D-Bus include

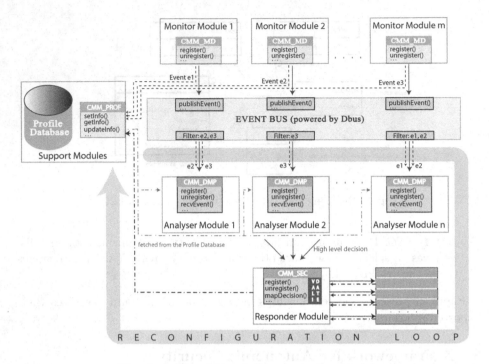

Fig. 4. An Event-Based Communication Model

Unix Domain Sockets and TCP/IP. The D-Bus 'signal' message type is closest to the notion of event, and therefore serves as the base message type in our communication model. Each message has a header and body containing the message payload. The header includes fields like the type of payload, the sender, destination, name, etc. Messages are sent to all processes, and are filtered by rules that specify the messages which may be sent to an application based on the message content. The rules are written as strings of comma-separated key/value pairs [33].

3.2 Framework Interfaces

For each event supported in the framework, there exists a module to monitor its occurrence and at least one event handler to respond to it. Each event is assigned a valid name, following the D-Bus naming convention. A representative list of security events is provided in Figure 5.

The autonomic loop is implemented as follows. After defining the security-relevant events, monitoring modules (base class: CMM_MD) are introduced in the framework to report the occurrence of these events. Analyzer modules (base class: CMM_DMP) register their interest with the framework, and receive events based on their subscription. An appropriate high-level security action to reconfigure the system is suggested, which is then mapped to an action specific

Event Name	Event Description
/ASF/Comm/SOCK_CRT	New socket created.
/ASF/Comm/TCP_CON	Reached threshold for half-open TCP connection.
/ASF/Device/AUTH_NEW	New authentication scheme available.
/ASF/Dev/BATTERY_LOW	Low battery level of the device.
/ASF/Usr/LOC_CHG	User location change.
/ASF/Usr/PREF_CHG	Change in user preference.
/ASF/Env/LOW_MEM	Low memory.

Fig. 5. A Sample List of Security-Relevant Events

Interface	Monitoring Module	Analyzer Module	Response Module
register()	Registers a well-defined event with the event bus. Registration requests from interested event handlers can now be accepted.	Registers an event handler for an existing event.	Adds a new set of security policies to the profile database. These policies may be sub-system specific.
unregister()	Unregisters an event and triggers unregistration of corresponding event handlers.	Unregisters an event handler for an event.	Removes a set of security policies from the profile database.

Fig. 6. Registering and Unregistering Modules in the Framework

to the sub-system under consideration. The configurations are validated before performing the reconfiguration process (base class: CMM_SEC).

Each module in the framework is derived from a common base class which allows to register and unregister with the framework daemon. Using the methods shown in Figure 6, a module can introduce new events to the system, add event handlers to service an event, or update the profile database with new sets of security policies. This interface may be specialized for each security sub-system, taking into account its own specificities. For example, in an access control-related sub-system, support for including multiple authorization policies, and reconfiguration between these policies might be desired. A reconfigurable security sub-system (for authentication, authorization, and cryptography) would then contain a registerASP() method to make a new authentication mechanism (Authentication Service Provider or ASP) available, with similar methods for access control and cryptography.

The events generated may need to be merged through a sub-system specific inference engine. Hence, the framework provides the addNewInferenceEngine() method to add a new inference engine to reason about the sensor data collected. The CMM_Prof module is then able to retrieve the new security context using the deriveSecurityContext() method.

When an event is reported, it can be analyzed for appropriate action using the following methods: recvEvent() to deliver the event to the associated analyzer module; and checkNewSecurityContext() to check whether a reconfiguration of the security mechanisms is needed when a new security context is computed from the environment.

The analyzer module arrives at a high-level decision which is then forwarded to the response module. Once the proposed security action is validated (checked for safe composition), it needs to be translated into domain-specific policies. This can be realized with the following methods of the CMM_SEC module: `mapDecision()` to map a high-level security action to a sub-system specific configuration, and validate the reconfiguration action, in terms of safe composition; and `reconfigure()` to issue the right operations and establish the right conditions to ensure the security of the reconfiguration process when a reconfiguration is needed.

This transformation from a high-level security action to a low-level configuration is sub-system specific. For example, the decision to increase the encryption strength can be translated into an increased key size or additional rounds of encryption based on the capability of the target functional element. To facilitate this, sub-systems can introduce specific mappings in the responder modules.

A security sub-system would then expose specialized methods like `selectASP()` to select the ASP to be used for authentication; `changeAuthorizationPolicy()` to enforce a new authorization policy; or `changeCryptoAttributes()` to change the configuration parameters of the cryptographic services, e.g., key lengths, choice of algorithms for encryption/signature, etc.

Events reported by a monitoring module might need to be stored. Similarly, specific profile information might need to be retrieved to take a decision. Thus, the CMM_Prof module provides the following methods for managing profiles: `getInfo()` to obtain profile-related information from a profile server; and `setInfo()` to update the profile server with new information.

The framework is event-based. Hence, the CMM_Evnt module is at the center of the framework by triggering all methods exported by other CMMs. The event bus exposes an interface through which the monitoring modules publish their events to the appropriate analyzer modules via the event bus, and containing the following methods: `publishEvent()` to report the occurrence of an event to the event bus; and `scheduleEvent()` to allow each CMM to register new events to be scheduled. Typically, an event corresponds to a call to another CMM. The CMM_Evnt is in charge of scheduling the calls between the CMMs.

4 Implementation

The framework was implemented on a Nokia 770 Internet tablet. This prototype implements the sample scenario sketched in the introduction, exhibiting self-protection capabilities in sub-systems like authentication and authorization, cryptographic services, and network security. However, due to space limitations, only a brief overview of each of these sub-systems is presented here.

4.1 Overall Architecture

The autonomic loop was implemented using the architecture shown above. We define a sandbox called *ThinkBox* to host security mechanisms and components which should be protected, in reference to the Think OS framework used to generate such a sandbox [18]. We specify a component-based architecture that

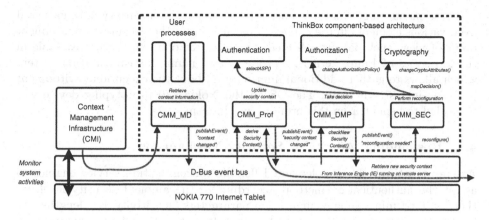

Fig. 7. Proposed Implementation Architecture: The ThinkBox

relies on its own mechanisms to reconfigure and adapt different security mechanisms depending on the security context. The user runs its processes inside the sandbox, and the security of its resources is managed inside it. We assume that the OS running on the Nokia 770 is secure enough to protect the ThinkBox.

A *Context Management Infrastructure (CMI)* monitors the state of the external environment through probes located in the system layer. It informs the CMM_MD component inside the ThinkBox of any significant changes, the CMM_MD behaving as a kind of a stub for the CMI. Context changes trigger the publication of low-level events on the D-Bus infrastructure. These events are agregated by the CMM_Prof component to derive a new security context. This operation relies on an *Inference Engine (IE)* hosted on a remote security server. If needed, the CMM_Prof publishes an event on the event-bus to notify that the security context has changed. The CMM_DMP component is then invoked to take a decision whether or not a security reconfiguration is needed. If so, the CMM_SEC component is called to perform a safe reconfiguration of the targeted security services (authentication, authorization, or cryptography).

4.2   Monitoring and Analyzing: Context Management and Inference

The CMI component is implemented in Java using the WildCAT event-based framework [16]. It provides a representation of – and primitives to compute over – the execution context of applications: raw data acquired from sensors is agregated into higher-level context information. Different forms of context can be described with dedicated ontologies.

The IE component is implemented using the Jena Java framework [3], which provides reasoning and querying facilities on the context data, notably by supporting the SPARQL query language [35]. The NRL Security Ontology [23] was selected for its comprehensive classification of types of security credentials, which can also be represented in the OWL language for automated reasoning. The IE is implemented on a remote server providing the needed processing resources.

These management and inference schemes operate on sensory data gathered from various elements in the contextual space. From the execution environment point of view, such data is collected using the Kprobe [28] facility available in the 2.6 series of Linux kernels. Kprobe is a dynamic instrumentation system which allows to gather additional information about the execution environment in a non-intrusive manner. The OS on the Nokia 770 prototyping device was upgraded to benefit from this profiling mechanism.

4.3 Responding: Adaptable Security Mechanisms

Authentication. The implemented flexible authentication service enables to adapt the authentication method according to the ambient security level, either by fine-tuning some configuration parameters (sensitivity, key lengths), or by completely replacing the authentication algorithm. We adopted an architecture of type PAM (Pluggable Authentication Modules) to allow such flexibility. *Authentication Service Providers (ASP)* implement specific authentication algorithms and manage the corresponding types of credentials: physical, electronic, biometric, etc. With the framework primitives, ASPs may be registered, unregistered, or dynamically selected. Authentication is performed transparently through an `authenticate()` method taking as parameter the security context containing the tokens to authenticate.

Authorization. We defined an architecture called CRACKER *(Component-based Reconfigurable Access Control for Kernels)* which gives the kernel developer support for policy-neutral authorization [22]. The choice of a component-oriented architecture allows enforcement of several classes of access control policies, the policy effectively enforced depending on the security context. CRACKER also supports run-time change of policies, using separate reconfiguration mechanisms implemented within the Think [10,18] component-based OS framework chosen as execution environment. Fine-grained authorization can be achieved with minimal intrusiveness, since the OS is already built from components. Evaluation results show that the performance overhead remains low.

The CRACKER architecture (Figure 8) reifies each kernel resource by a software component, described using the Fractal component model [10]. To enforce access control on a resource, a *Reference Monitor (RM)* intercepts method invocations on the interfaces provided by the corresponding protected component. For a given authorization model, policy decision-making is encapsulated in a separate *Policy Manager (PM)* component.

The Policy Manager (PM) represents the authorization policy by an efficient implementation of the access control matrix. In CRACKER, all principals are abstracted as components, both for subjects like threads, and for objects like system resources (files, IPCs, semaphores, etc.). Access decisions are based on security contexts which federate security attributes found in common authorization models, such as security levels, domains, types, roles. Customized attributes can also be defined for specific authorization models. Each newly created principal is assigned a new security context depending on the current authorization

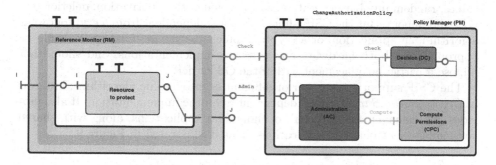

Fig. 8. The CRACKER Security Architecture

model. Then, permissions are computed, assigned according to the authorization policy, and inserted into the access matrix representation. The PM exports two interfaces, `Check` and `Admin`, for checking permissions and for policy management. The PM a composite component containing three primitive components.

The *Administration Component (AC)* stores the security contexts and the access matrix. Authorization is made at the method level. The *Decision Component (DC)* decides whether the current subject has access to the requested object. Given a pair of subjects and objects, it asks the AC for the permission corresponding to the requested operation. The *Compute Permissions Component (CPC)* defines the authorization policy. It computes permissions (`Compute` interface) and fills the access matrix. Since the AC and DC are completely independent from a security policy or model, reconfiguring the authorization policy amounts to changing only the CPC. This operation can be done statically by introducing a new CPC and recompiling the kernel, or dynamically by run-time update of the CPC.

Cryptography. The framework specifies an interface (`changeCryptoAttributes`) for flexible cryptographic services. Therefore, management functions for an adaptive cryptographic library were also designed and implemented [17]. As mandatory security requires building blocks providing authentication of identities, data-origin authentication, non-repudiation, data separation, confidentiality, and integrity. All of these properties rely on cryptographic services. To harmonize the use of cryptography in applications, a well-defined but flexible service interface, the *Cryptographic Service Interface (CSIF)* has been specified and implemented in a corresponding library. This library is encapsulated inside a Think component to deploy and execute it on the Nokia 770 platform.

Functional interfaces specify the cryptographic services (e.g., encrypt, decrypt, sign, verify), while control interfaces allow to change the length of cryptographic keys, the cryptographic algorithm used, etc.

The design requirements of the CSIF were both functional and non-functional: the CSIF should naturally provide primitives for data encryption and decryption, integrity check value generation and verification, production of irreversible hash values, random number generation, and key generation, derivation, deletion, export and import. But the CSIF should also be independent from a cryptographic algorithm, an application, or a cryptographic sub-system. That is, it should be appropriate to both hardware and software implementations, and should not impose a particular placement within the OS kernel.

The CSIF supports a number of different cryptographic algorithms, in terms of *Cryptographic Support (CS)*, dependent upon the implementation. It also provides key management on behalf of individual applications, along with shared key management between applications. This is illustrated in Figure 9.

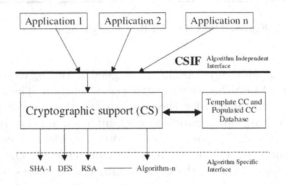

Fig. 9. The CSIF Model

The CSIF hides the details and complexities of algorithms from applications. For instance, a caller may invoke an encryption function without being aware of the algorithm used, or the specific parameters required. The CSIF also supports algorithm-specific calls for applications that require a particular set of algorithms. Implementation details as well are hidden from the callers, which cannot know if the implementation is in software, hardware, or a combination of both.

Algorithm independence is achieved due to the notion of the *Cryptographic Context (CC)*. A CC is a protected object that is opaque to callers of the CSIF, and which encapsulates all the information pertaining to the context of the cryptographic operation to be performed, including the algorithm identity, algorithm- and key-specific parameters, and optionally a key. The general method of use of a CC by a key management application is to retrieve a template CC appropriate to the functions it wishes to perform, and to populate that CC by calling on the CS to generate a key.

Network-Side Security Adaptations. The autonomic security framework was also used to adapt the security of network end-points (e.g., a wireless access point). For this purpose we focused on the use of traffic monitoring to understand application security requirements. The basic approach in the identification of network applications through traffic monitoring relies on the use of well-known ports (e.g., Cisco NetFlow [26]). However, several applications use these well-known ports as contact point and move to a different, dynamically-allocated, port once the connection is established. For example, an active FTP session can be identified based on the well-known port number 21, which is used for the control connection while the data connection is established via a new dynamically allocated port. Hence, it is important to track all the ports used during a session. Once an application is identified, it is mapped to one of the standard application groups, thus revealing its behavior. A representative list of applications and their intent is captured in Figure 10.

Application type	Representative security requirements
Bulk data transfer: FTP	Control connection: confidentiality and authentication. Data connection: message integrity for publicly available content.
P2P: Napster, Kaaza, BitTorrent	Re-authenticate periodically.
Interactive: telnet, SSH, rlogin	Non-repudiation.
Mail: POP3, SMTP, IMAP	Data confidentiality.
Streaming: RTP	Public content: authentication. Classified content: authentic and confidential.
Web: HTTP	Choice of security gateway.
System services: X11, DNS, NTP	Authenticated, but not necessarily confidential.

Fig. 10. Interpreting Security Requirements From Application Identity

To accomplish this, the socket APIs were instrumented to monitor the network association 5-tuple of source and destination addresses, port numbers, and protocol. Various events were introduced in the system to trigger network security policy reconfiguration. For instance, the creation of a new socket triggers an /ASF/Comm/SOCK_CRT event which is then communicated to interested event handlers. These event handlers were implemented as hooks to the IPSec [1] policy framework for system wide provisioning.

5   Related Work

The ever increasing diversity of access technologies in mobile communication systems – as witnessed by the growing number of standards for 3G cellular networks or wireless LANs – strongly contributed to the emergence of an intricate pervasive networking environment, where devices roam through many heterogeneous networks, and interact using a rich combination of communication protocols. The promise of Systems Beyond 3G is to overcome this complexity with an integrated information and communication infrastructure allowing diversely connected devices to transparently access services in several contexts. This objective triggered research on the design of fully reconfigurable architectures, enabling adaptation of terminal and network functionalities to the current conditions to optimize communication [20]. Yet, strong protection should also be guaranteed, networks and devices being constantly vulnerable to attacks thriving on dynamicity and complexity. Flexible security mechanisms are needed to respond to new types of attacks and to meet different network setting-specific protection requirements. The quest for the right balance between security and flexibility therefore sparked a whole line of research in the fields of reconfigurable architectures, adaptive security mechanisms, security of smart spaces and ambient intelligence, security context modelling, and security of autonomic systems.

Reconfigurability imposes specific requirements on an architecture [27], e.g., for 3G/4G networks [29]. Applying this approach to the security domain, [22] describes the design of an authorization mechanism supporting multiple classes of security policies and able to be reconfigured. But the processing of context information to trigger a reconfiguration, or the infrastructure needed to make it secure is not described. More generally, existing security solutions provide little reconfigurability, adaptation mecanisms being considered orthogonally to protection. The relationship between the physical context and the security infrastructure is usually not addressed.

Adaptive security mechanisms are found in flexible protocol stacks for wireless networks [21], context-aware access control systems [8] and security architectures [5,6,13,31,36], component-based frameworks for policy-neutral authorization [22], or architectures supporting disconnected modes [7,37]. Such schemes suffer from limited flexibility, being restricted: either to a specific application setting, such as optimising the performance of security protocols for wireless networks [21]; to a single type of network such as 3G mobile networks [5]; or to a particular security mechanism such as authorization [8,22,36]. Our solution remains independent from the network architecture, and can support several types of adaptive security mechanisms.

In the field of ambient intelligence, several systems have been developed to realize smart spaces such as intelligent homes [14,30,32,34]. Users are immersed in a well-defined region of space massively containing sensors and computing resources, integrated in an extended information system able to respond to changes in the physical context through actuators. These systems remain limited to closed pervasive environments, and generally adopt a centralized security architecture. They also rely on extended versions of RBAC (Role-Based Access Control) for authorization [15,34]. Our framework addresses open environments, allowing for instance to insert new security mechanisms, can operate in a decentralized manner, and is not tied to a particular access control model.

Security context modelling mainly tackled the formalization of relations between security attributes using ontologies [23,25]. But reconfiguration issues (decision algorithms, types of adaptable security sub-systems) remained unaddressed.

Self-protection is a key property of autonomic systems [19]: the overhead of security management is reduced by enforcing policies with minimal human intervention. Emphasis was mostly put on security of system configuration, detection and prevention of unusual events (intrusions), and appropriate recovery (self-healing), rather on contextual adaptation of security functionalities. The architecture proposed in [11] is quite similar to our framework, but does not seem to have been fully implemented, many studies remaining concentrated on theoretical foundations [4]. Autonomous adaptation of the security of network connections was explored in [24], with a similar approach to ours for IPSec security policies.

6 Conclusion

Making security truly adaptable remains a key challenge in ubiquitous environments. This paper presented an autonomic security framework to build pervasive systems which are self-protecting. The framework realizes the control structure automating the entire process of reconfiguration of security sub-systems based on contextual information. Modularity and extensibility are achieved using a component-based architecture to introduce flexibility in each step of reconfiguration: sense, analyze, and respond. The interactions between the corresponding components are event-based to be compatible with dynamic conditions of execution. The framework specifies the building blocks to realize flexible authentication, access control, and cryptographic services, and to implement autonomous security mechanisms both on the device and the network side. The framework design was validated by successfully implementing the infrastructure on Nokia 770 client devices and on a set of security servers.

Future work on the communication model concerns event scheduling algorithms and the design of event listeners. A compact representation of the security context is also left for further investigation. We plan as well to extend the infrastructure to other security services like intrusion detection and prevention.

Finally, we believe our approach to be applicable to introduce flexibility in the areas of privacy and trust management, presently not addressed, but which remain major enablers of pervasive computing [12], and where difficult trade-offs must be found. For instance, the user should control the disclosure of his personal information, and yet let the security infrastructure communicate transparently with TTPs to assess the validity of presented credentials. These issues could be handled by a specific flexible security sub-system plugged into the core framework, allowing to select the right trade-off depending on contextual security requirements. Much work still remains to be done in that area.

Acknowledgements. This work was performed in project E2R II which has received research funding from the Community's Sixth Framework programme. This paper reflects only the authors' views and the Community is not liable for any use that may be made of the information contained therein. The contributions of colleagues from the E2R II consortium are hereby acknowledged.

References

1. IP Security Working Group,
   http://www.ietf.org/html.charters/ipsp-charter.html/
2. IST E2R II Project, http://e2r.motlabs.com/
3. Jena: A Semantic Web Framework for Java, http://jena.sourceforge.net/
4. Workshop on Logical Foundations of an Adaptive Security Infrastructure (WOL-FASI). In: FCS 2004. Conjunction with Workshop on Foundations on Computer Security (2004)
5. Al-Muhtadi, J., Mickunas, D., Campbell, R.: A Lightweight Reconfigurable Security Mechanism for 3G/4G Mobile Devices. IEEE Wireless Communications 9(2), 60–65 (2002)

6. Al-Muhtadi, J., Ranganathan, A., Campbell, R., Mickunas, M.: Cerberus: A Context-Aware Security Scheme for Smart Spaces. In: PerCom 2003. International Conference on Pervasive Computing and Communications (2003)
7. Almenárez, F., Marín, A., Campo, C., García, C.: PTM: A Pervasive Trust Management Model for Dynamic Open Environments. In: PSPT. Mobiquitous Workshop on Pervasive Security, Privacy and Trust (2004)
8. Almenárez, F., Marín, A., Campo, C., García, C.: TrustAC: Trust-Based Access Control for Pervasive Devices. In: Hutter, D., Ullmann, M. (eds.) SPC 2005. LNCS, vol. 3450, Springer, Heidelberg (2005)
9. Astrom, K., Wittenmark, B.: Adaptive Control. Prentice-Hall, Englewood Cliffs (1994)
10. Bruneton, E., Coupaye, T., Leclerc, M., Quema, V., Stefani, J.B.: An Open Component Model and its Support in Java. In: Crnković, I., Stafford, J.A., Schmidt, H.W., Wallnau, K. (eds.) CBSE 2004. LNCS, vol. 3054, Springer, Heidelberg (2004)
11. Chess, D., Palmer, C., White, S.: Security in an Autonomic Computing Environment. IBM Systems Journal 42(1), 107–118 (2003)
12. Cook, D., Das, S.: Smart Environments: Technologies, Protocols, and Applications. Wiley, Chichester (2005)
13. Covington, M., Fogla, P., Zhan, Z., Ahamad, M.: A Context-Aware Security Architecture for Emerging Applications. In: ACSAC. Annual Computer Security Applications Conference (2002)
14. Covington, M., Long, W., Srinivasan, S., Dey, A., Ahamad, M., Abowd, G.: Securing Context-Aware Applications using Environment Roles. In: SACMAT 2001. Symposium on Access Control Models and Technologies (2001)
15. Covington, M., Moyer, M., Ahamad, M.: Generalized Role-Based Access control for Securing Future Applications. In: NISCC. National Information Systems Security Conference (2000)
16. David, P.C., Ledoux, T.: WildCAT: A Generic Framework for Context-Aware Applications. In: International Workshop on Middleware for Pervasive and Ad-Hoc Computing (2005)
17. E2R Deliverable D2.2. Equipment Management Framework for Reconfiguration: Architecture, Interfaces, and Functions (December 2005)
18. Fassino, J.P., Stefani, J.B., Lawall, J., Muller, G.: Think: A Software Framework for Component-Based Operating System Kernels. In: USENIX Annual Technical Conference (2002)
19. Ganek, A., Corbi, T.: The Dawning of the Autonomic Computing Era. IBM Systems Journal 42(1), 5–18 (2003)
20. Georganopoulos, N., Farnham, T., Burgess, R., Schöler, T., Sessler, J., Warr, P., Golubicic, Z., Platbrood, F., Souville, B., Buljore, S.: Terminal-Centric View of Software Reconfigurable System Architecture and Enabling Components and Technologies. IEEE Communications Magazine 42(5), 100–110 (2004)
21. Hager, C.: Context Aware and Adaptive Security for Wireless Networks. PhD thesis, Virginia Polytechnic Institute and State University (2004)
22. Jarboui, T., Lacoste, M., Wadier, P.: A Component-Based Policy-Neutral Authorization Architecture. In: CFSE 2006. French Conference on Operating Systems (2006)
23. Kim, A., Luo, J., Kang, M.: Security Ontology for Annotating Resources. In: ODBASE 2005. International Conference on Ontologies, Databases, and Application of Semantics (2005)
24. Klenk, A., Niedermayer, H., Masekowsky, M., Carle, G.: An Architecture for Autonomic Security Adaptation. Annals of Telecommunications 61(9-10) (2006)

25. Leithead, T., Nejdl, W., Oldmedilla, D., Seamons, K., Winslett, M., Yu, T., Zhang, C.: How to Exploit Ontologies in Trust Negotiation. In: Workshop on Trust, Security, and Reputation on the Semantic Web (2004)
26. Logg, C., Cottrell, L.: Characterization of the Traffic between SLAC and the Internet (2003), http://www.slac.stanford.edu/comp/net/slac-netflow/html/SLAC-netflow.html
27. MAGNET Deliverable D5.0. Impact of and Requirements on Reconfigurability (June 2004)
28. Mavinakayanahalli, A., Panchamukhi, P., Keniston, J., Keshavamurthy, A., Hiramatsu, M.: Probing the Guts of Kprobes. In: Proc. Linux Symposium, Ottawa, Canada, vol. 2, pp. 101–114 (2006)
29. Muñoz, L., Agüero, R., Choque, J., Irastorza, J., Sánchez, L., Petrova, M., Mähönen, P.: Empowering Next-Generation Wireless Personal Communication Networks. IEEE Communications Magazine 42(5), 64–70 (2004)
30. Román, M., Hess, C., Cerqueira, R., Ranganathan, A., Campbell, R., Nahrstedt, K.: Gaia: A Middleware Infrastructure to Enable Active Spaces. IEEE Pervasive Computing, 74–83 (October–December 2002)
31. Shankar, N., Balfanz, D.: Enabling Secure Ad-hoc Communication using Context-Aware Security Services. In: Borriello, G., Holmquist, L.E. (eds.) UbiComp 2002. LNCS, vol. 2498, Springer, Heidelberg (2002)
32. Stajano, F.: Security for UbiquitousComputing. Wiley, Chichester (2002)
33. Trolltech. Introduction to D-Bus, http://doc.trolltech.com/4.2/intro-to-dbus.html/
34. Undercoffer, J., Perich, F., Cedilnik, A., Kagal, L., Joshi, A.: A Secure Infrastructure for Service Discovery and Access in Pervasive Computing. ACM Mobile Networks and Applications (MONET): Special Issue on Security in Mobile Computing Environments 8(2), 113–125 (2003)
35. W3C. SPARQL Query Language for RDF, W3C Working Draft (October 2006)
36. Wullems, C., Looi, M., Clark, A.: Towards Context-aware Security: An Authorization Architecture for Intranet Environments. In: PerCom 2004. International Conference on Pervasive Computing and Communications Workshops (2004)
37. Zhang, K., Kindberg, T.: An Authorization Infrastructure for Nomadic Computing. In: SACMAT 2002. Symposium on Access Control Models and Technologies (2002)

DLPKH – Distributed Logical Public-Key Hierarchy

Rakesh Bobba and Himanshu Khurana

University of Illinois at Urbana-Champaign
{rbobba,hkhurana}@uiuc.edu

Abstract. Decentralized group key management schemes for supporting secure group communication systems have been studied in the two flavors of contributory key agreement and decentralized key distribution. However, the primary focus has been on the former because the latter have been criticized for additional overheads of establishing secure channels and for the possibility of weak keys produced by the generating entity. In this work we develop a novel decentralized key distribution that uses public-key trees to eliminate the overheads of establishing secure channels and employs a practical approach of partial contribution to minimize the possibility of weak keys. The result is a simple and secure scheme whose performance is significantly better than previous schemes that involve contribution or distribution.

Keywords: Group key management, key agreement, decentralized key distribution, logical key hierarchy, public-key trees.

1 Introduction

Distributed services spread over multiple systems and networks are becoming prevalent today. Many of these distributed systems are collaborative in nature with underlying groupware primitives such as conferencing, shared white-boards, collaborative document annotation, and distance learning. Often these services run on open networks such as the Internet and, therefore, need protection from a set of global adversaries via secure communication. Just like the transition of these services from a centralized to a decentralized nature, security mechanisms for these services also need transition to support the decentralized services. At the core of these security mechanisms are group key management techniques that enable a set of entities to share a key for exchanging secure messages as well as update the key whenever there is a group membership change to ensure secrecy. Given that users may use distributed services from a multitude of devices including resource constrained ones such as cellular phones and PDAs it is essential that the key management techniques be efficient and scalable with minimal computational and communication costs overall.

For centralized services the Logical Key Hierarchy (LKH) [15] scheme with a centralized and trusted group controller provides an efficient and scalable solution. While several optimizations to the scheme have been developed since its development (e.g., [12], [11]), the basic scheme continues to be leading example owing to its simplicity, efficiency, and scalability. Attempts to develop effective decentralized group key management schemes have taken two paths. First, *decentralized key distribution* schemes have been proposed that dynamically select group member(s) to generate and distribute

P. McDaniel and S.K. Gupta (Eds.): ICISS 2007, LNCS 4812, pp. 110–127, 2007.

keys to other members [5], [10]. Second, *decentralized group key agreement* schemes have been proposed that obtain an equal share from each member of the group towards a "contributed" common key [13], [3], [7], [8], [14], [2], [4]. Key agreement schemes are preferred over decentralized key distribution scheme because of two limitations that have been pointed out in the literature [8]. First, the distribution schemes use symmetric key trees that lack the ability to distribute key updates securely and, consequently, these schemes have high overheads for establishing secure channels. Second, distributed schemes have to rely on a single entity to generate good keys leading to the possibility of weak keys due to potential errors (or malicious acts) in random number generation.

In this work we develop a new decentralized key distribution scheme, Distributed Logical Public Key Hierarchy (DLPKH), that addresses these limitations. We address the first limitation by using public key trees to design DLPKH that enable group members to update keys without the need to setup secure channels first. We address the second limitation by combining the shares of two members for a given key update operation as well as the shares of multiple members as the key is updated over multiple membership changes – all in a simple and practical manner. By addressing these limitations we develop a scheme that is significantly more efficient and scalable than previous decentralized key distribution schemes. Furthermore, we show that DLPKH provides significant improvements, factor of $O(n)$, over contributory key agreement schemes in terms of the overall computation overhead while lagging only slightly behind, factor of $O(log(n))$, in terms of overall communication overhead, where n is group size. To demonstrate this we use metrics of total communication and computation costs that serve as an abstract measure of total energy spent in group membership events. Using these metrics we analytically and experimentally compare DLPKH with two previous decentralized key distribution schemes, Fully Distributed Logical Key Hierarchy (FDLKH) [5] and Distributed Logical Key Hierarchy (DLKH) [10], and with Tree-based Group Diffie-Hellman (TGDH) [7], [8].

The rest of this paper is organized as follows. In Section 2 we discuss related work. In Section 3 we present the DLPKH scheme with its join, leave, merge and partition protocols. We also analyze the security properties of DLPKH. In Section 4 we compare DLPKH, FDLKH, DLKH and TGDH in terms of their complexity and simulated scalability in experimental settings. We conclude in Section 5.

2 Related Work

Contributory Key Agreement. Group key management protocols that obtain a contributed share from each group member towards every new session key have been the primary focus for research in the area of decentralized group key management. Rafaili and Hutchison [9] provide an extensive survey of the vast literature in this field. Amir *et al.* [1] have conductive an extensive experiment evaluating the performance of some of the leading group key agreement protocols. Their analysis concludes that Tree-based Group Diffie-Hellman (TGDH) [7] [8] and Steer *et al.* [13] are significantly better than others. Among these TDGH has the edge with better performance for leave operations. The overall complexity of the scheme is $O(n + log n)$ for total number of bytes sent on the network and $O(n + log n)$ for total number of expensive computations undertaken for a given membership event with n group members. We show via analysis and experiments that DLPKH provides significant improvements over TGDH in computation costs by a factor of $O(n)$ while lagging only slightly behind, factor of $O(log(n))$, in communication costs.

Decentralized Key Distribution. As opposed to contributory key agreement very little focus has been devoted to decentralized key distribution protocols. Rodeh *et al.* [10] have proposed the Distributed Logical Key Hierarchy (DLKH) protocol that uses the notion of sponsors that generate and distribute updated keys to group members. These sponsors need to establish secure channels with other group members to distribute these updated keys. In addition to overheads for establishing these secure channels, DLKH does not consider backward secrecy for join operations, which can be important in many applications. Inoue and Kuroda [5] have proposed the Fully Distributed Logical Key Hierarchy (FDLKH) protocol that uses multiple sponsors to distribute the costs of setting up secure channels and also to have multiple entities contributing to the generation of the updated key. In contrast, DLPKH eliminates the expensive overheads of setting up secure channels and also provides improved "contribution" of shares for the generation of updated keys.

3   DLPKH Scheme

In this section, we describe our DLPKH: Distributed Logical Public-Key Hierarchy key management scheme. DLPKH organizes members into a logical tree-based key hierarchy similar to LKH [15]. Unlike LKH, DLPKH uses public-keys instead of symmetric keys and is distributed without the need for a centralized group manager. Group members acting as *sponsors* facilitate dynamic events like *member join* and *member leave*. These *sponsors* are determined based on the event and tree structure at the time of the event and are not fixed or privileged entities. DLPKH comprises four sub-protocols corresponding to membership events in a group, namely, *Join, Leave, Merge* and *Partition*. We only deal briefly with *Merge* and *Partition* protocols in this work due to space limitations. We describe the protocol using the ElGamal cryptosystem, however, our solution works with any suitable cryptosystem with public domain parameters such as Elliptic Curve Cryptography (ECC). Other cryptosystems like RSA would require prime number generation as an element of key generation leading to undue costs. The group parameters are assumed to be public. The notations used and the protocols are described below.

A node in a key tree is identified by the tuple $\langle l,m \rangle$, where l denotes the level to which the node belongs and m denotes the position of the node at that level. The left most node at a given level is denoted by $\langle l,0 \rangle$, i.e., $0 \leq m \leq 2^l - 1$ and the root node of the tree is at level 0 and hence is identified by $\langle 0,0 \rangle$. Members of the group occupy leaf nodes and $M_{\langle l,m \rangle}$ denotes a member occupying node $\langle l,m \rangle$. Each node $\langle l,m \rangle$ in the tree is associated with a key-pair denoted by $PK_{\langle l,m \rangle}$ and $SK_{\langle l,m \rangle}$. This key-pair is shared by all members who belong to the subtree rooted at $\langle l,m \rangle$ denoted by $T_{\langle l,m \rangle}$. In other words a member $M_{\langle l,m \rangle}$ knows every key-pair associated with set of nodes along the path, here after referred to as *key-path* and denoted by $P_{\langle l,m \rangle}$, from $\langle l,m \rangle$ to $\langle 0,0 \rangle$, i,e., the set $\{\langle (l-i), \lfloor m/2^i \rfloor \rangle | 0 \leq i \leq l\}$ of $l+1$ nodes. A member also knows all the public-keys associated with nodes that are siblings to the set of nodes on his key-path, i.e., the set $\{\langle(l-i),(\lfloor m/2^i\rfloor+(-1)^{(\lfloor m/2^i\rfloor)})\rangle|0\leq i\leq l-1\}$ of l nodes. This set of nodes is referred to as *co-path*. For example, the key-path and co-path of member $M_{\langle 3,1\rangle}$ in Figure 2(a)are the set of nodes $\{\langle 3,1\rangle,\langle 2,0\rangle,\langle 1,0\rangle,\langle 0,0\rangle\}$ and $\{\langle 3,0\rangle,\langle 2,1\rangle,\langle 1,1\rangle\}$ respectively. The key-pair associated with the root node, $(SK_{\langle 0,0\rangle},PK_{\langle 0,0\rangle})$ is shared by all the group members. The rightmost shallowest leaf node of a subtree $T_{\langle l,m\rangle}$ is the sponsor for that subtree and is denoted by $S_{\langle l,m\rangle}$. With that notation, $S_{\langle 0,0\rangle}$ denotes the sponsor for the entire group. n is the number of members in the group, d is the level of the sponsoring member before the event and h is the level of parent of a leaving member. p and g are ElGamal group parameters, where g is the group generator and p is the prime modulus. These group parameters are shared by all the group members and are assumed to be public.

3.1 Notations

n	Number of group members
G	represents the group
$\langle l,m\rangle$	m-th node at level l in a tree, where $0\leq m\leq 2^l-1$ and root node is at level 0
$M_{\langle l,m\rangle}$	Member associated with node $\langle l,m\rangle$
M_i	ith member of the group
$PK_{\langle l,m\rangle}$	Public-key associated with node $\langle l,m\rangle$
$SK_{\langle l,m\rangle}$	Private-Key associated with node $\langle l,m\rangle$
$PK'_{\langle l,m\rangle}$	New public-key to be associated with node $\langle l,m\rangle$
$SK'_{\langle l,m\rangle}$	New secret-Key to be associated with node $\langle l,m\rangle$
$E(PK,X)$	Encryption of data X using public-key PK
$T_{\langle l,m\rangle}$	Subtree rooted at node $\langle l,m\rangle$
$S_{\langle l,m\rangle}$	Sponsor for subtree rooted at node $\langle l,m\rangle$
$P_{\langle l,m\rangle}$	Key-path of node $\langle l,m\rangle$
$CP_{\langle l,m\rangle}$	Co-path of node $\langle l,m\rangle$
$M\rightarrow N:X$	M sends data X to N
d	level of the sponsoring node before the event
h	level of parent of a leaving node
p,g	ElGamal group parameters

3.2 Join Protocol

A Join protocol is executed when a new member is added to the group. The following protocol is applicable to groups of size greater than one. For a group size of one the group member and joining member perform a Diffie-Hellman key-exchange. As shown in Figure 1 the protocol involves four steps where the joining member initiates the protocol by broadcasting a join request to the group that contains her public key in Step 1.

In Step 2, all the group members receive the join request and determine independently the insertion point in the tree, the sponsor and the co-sponsor. Insertion point and the sponsor are denoted by $S_{\langle 0,0\rangle}$; i.e., rightmost shallowest leaf node of the tree. If the sibling node of sponsor is a leaf node then it acts as the co-sponsor. Otherwise

Step 1: The joining member broadcasts a request for join

$$M_{n+1} \quad \longrightarrow \quad G: \quad g^{r_{n+1}}$$

Step 2: Every Member

- determines the insertion point, sponsor and co-sponsor and updates the key-tree
- Sponsor and Co-sponsor say, $M_{\langle d+1,m \rangle}$ and $M_{\langle l,j \rangle}$ broadcast their DH public-keys (in parallel)

$$M_{\langle d+1,m \rangle} \quad \longrightarrow \quad G: \quad g^s$$
$$M_{\langle l,j \rangle} \quad \longrightarrow \quad G: \quad g^c$$

Step 3: The Sponsor

- computes new keys on its key-path by generating new keys for itself and its parent and by adding r_{dh}, agreed through DH exchange above, to the private-keys of rest of the nodes on its key path
- broadcasts 1) r_{dh} encrypted under the old group public-key, 2) new key-path keys for the joining member under joining members public-key and 3) the new public-keys of its key-path and co-path nodes

$$M_{\langle d+1,m \rangle} \longrightarrow G: \begin{cases} E\left(PK_{\langle d+1,(m+(-1)^m) \rangle}, \{SK'_{\langle (d+1), \lfloor m/2^i \rfloor \rangle} | \forall i \in [1,d+1]\} \right) \\ E(PK_{\langle 0,0 \rangle}, r_{dh}) \\ \left\{ PK'_{\langle (d+1-i), \lfloor m/2^i \rfloor \rangle} | 0 \le i \le d+1 \right\} \\ \left\{ PK_{\langle (d+1-i),(\lfloor m/2^i \rfloor + (-1)^{(\lfloor m/2^i \rfloor)}) \rangle} | 1 \le i \le d \right\} \end{cases}$$

Step 4: All group members update their key-path keys that have changed including the group key

Fig. 1. Join Protocol

the sponsor for subtree rooted at the sibling node acts as the co-sponsor. All the current members 1) create two new nodes and make them the children of the insertion point, 2) associate the sponsoring member currently associated with the insertion point to the right child node of the insertion point and 3) associate the new member and her public-key with the left child node of the insertion point. In Figure 2(a), node $\langle 2,1 \rangle$ is the insertion point, M_3, is the sponsor, and M_1 is the co-sponsor. Figure 2(b) shows the updated tree with the sponsor M_3 associated with node $\langle 3,2 \rangle$ and the joining member M_6 associated with node $\langle 3,3 \rangle$. The sponsor and co-sponsor perform a Diffie-Hellman key exchange and agree on a secret r_{dh}.

In Step 3, the sponsor picks 2 random private-keys from the underlying group, namely r_0 and r_1. The new key-pairs associated with the nodes on key-path of the sponsoring member, say $M_{\langle (d+1),m \rangle}$, are then calculated as follows:

$$SK'_{\langle (d+1-i), \lfloor m/2^i \rfloor \rangle} \leftarrow \begin{cases} r_i & \text{for} \quad i = 0,1 \\ SK_{\langle (d+1-i), \lfloor m/2^i \rfloor \rangle} + r_{dh} \quad mod \quad p & \forall i \in [2,d+1] \end{cases} \tag{1}$$

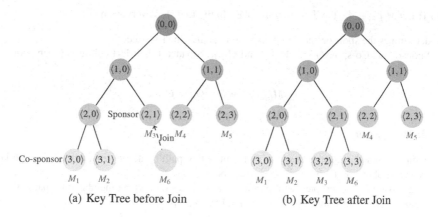

(a) Key Tree before Join   (b) Key Tree after Join

Fig. 2. Example of a Join Operation

$$PK'_{\langle(d+1-i),\lfloor m/2^i\rfloor\rangle} \leftarrow \begin{cases} g^{r_i} & \text{for } i=0,1 \\ PK_{\langle(d+1-i),\lfloor m/2^i\rfloor\rangle} \times g^{r_{dh}} \quad mod \quad p & \forall i \in [2,d+1] \end{cases} \quad (2)$$

That is, the sponsor 1) associates the private-key r_0 with its current node and private-key r_1 with its parent, and 3) for all other nodes on its key-path the sponsor updates the old private-key associated with the node by adding r_{dh}. The sponsor then broadcasts: 1) r_{dh} encrypted with old group key $PK_{\langle 0,0\rangle}$ and 2) new public-keys of each node on its key-path to the existing members of the group, The sponsor also sends to the joining member: 1) the new key-pairs associated with the nodes on its new key-path, except for the key-pair associated its own node is, encrypted with the joining members public-key, 2) the public-keys associated with the nodes on its co-path and 3) the tree structure. These two messages can be combined into a single broadcast message.

In Step 4, existing group members obtain the r_{dh} value and update the private-keys associated with the nodes on the sponsor node's key-path according to Equation 1. The joining member obtains 1) tree structure, 2) the key-pairs associated with nodes on his key-path, 3) the public-keys associated with nodes on his co-path. She associates the public-key she broadcasted in the join request and the corresponding private-key with the node she occupies in the tree. In the example shown in Figure 2, sponsor M_3 generates values r_0 and r_1, and associates them with key-path nodes $\langle 3,2\rangle$ and $\langle 2,1\rangle$ respectively. Sponsor M_3 and co-sponsor M_1 agree on the secret r_{dh} and update $\{\langle 1,0\rangle$ and $\langle 0,0\rangle\}$ by adding r_{dh}. M_3 then broadcasts a message comprising the following information. The tree structure is omitted for brevity.

$M_3 \rightarrow G: E(PK_{\langle 0,0\rangle}, r_{dh}),$	*new key-path keys for existing members*
$E\left(PK_{\langle 3,3\rangle}, \left(SK'_{\langle 0,0\rangle}, SK'_{\langle 1,0\rangle}, SK'_{\langle 2,1\rangle}\right)\right),$	*new key-path keys for the joining member*
$PK'_{\langle 2,1\rangle}, PK'_{\langle 1,0\rangle}, PK1'_{\langle 0,0\rangle}$	*new key-path public-keys for other members*
$PK'_{\langle 3,2\rangle}, PK'_{\langle 2,0\rangle}, PK'_{\langle 1,1\rangle}.$	*new co-path public-keys for joining member*

Step 1: Let $M_{\langle h+1,m \rangle}$ be the departing member. In the first step every Member

- determines the sponsor and co-sponsor and updates the key-tree
- Sponsor and Co-sponsor say, $M_{\langle d,e \rangle}$ and $M_{\langle l,j \rangle}$, broadcast their DH public-keys (in parallel)

$$M_{\langle d,e \rangle} \quad \longrightarrow \quad G: \quad g^s$$
$$M_{\langle l,j \rangle} \quad \longrightarrow \quad G: \quad g^c$$

Step 2: The Sponsor

- computes new keys for nodes leaving member key-path by adding r_{dh}, agreed through DH exchange above, to their old private-keys nodes
- broadcasts 1) r_{dh} encrypted with public-keys of nodes on leaving member's co-path, and 2) the new public-keys nodes on leaving member's key-path

$$M_{\langle d,e \rangle} \longrightarrow G: \begin{cases} E\left(PK_{\langle (h+1-i),(\lfloor m/2^i \rfloor + (-1)^{(\lfloor m/2^i \rfloor)})\rangle}, r_{dh}\right) | 1 \leq i \leq h \\ PK'_{\langle (h+1-i),\lfloor m/2^i \rfloor \rangle} | 2 \leq i \leq h+1 \end{cases}$$

Step 3: All group members compute and update their key-path keys that have changed including the group key

Fig. 3. Leave Protocol

3.3 Leave Protocol

A Leave protocol is initiated when the group members receive a leave event from the underlying group communication service. Let $M_{\langle h+1,m \rangle}$ be the leaving member. As shown in Figure 3, in Step 1, group members determine the sponsor and co-sponsor. The sponsor in this case is that for the subtree rooted at sibling of the leaving node denoted by $S_{\langle (h+1),(m+(-1)^m)\rangle}$. The co-sponsor is the sponsor of the subtree rooted at the sibling node of leaving node's parent, i.e., $S_{\langle h,(\lfloor m/2 \rfloor + (-1)^{\lfloor m/2 \rfloor})\rangle}$. Members update the tree by removing the leaving node and promoting the subtree rooted at leaving node's sibling node to be rooted at the leaving node's parent node. In the example in Figure 4(a), $M_{\langle 3,5 \rangle}$ is the leaving member and $M_{\langle 4,8 \rangle}$ is the sponsor and $M_{\langle 3,6 \rangle}$ is the co-sponsor. Figure 4(b), shows the key tree after tree update where the subtree that was rooted at $\langle 3,4 \rangle$ is promoted to be rooted at $\langle 2,2 \rangle$. The group needs to update all keys that the leaving member had access to for forward secrecy. To do so the sponsor and co-sponsor perform a Diffie-Hellman key-exchange and agree on a secret r_{dh}.

In Step 2, for each node $\langle (h+1-i), \lfloor m/2^i \rfloor \rangle$ in the key-path of the leaving member (where $2 \leq i \leq h+1$) the sponsor calculates new key-pairs associated the nodes according to Equations 1 and 2. That is, the sponsor adds r_{dh} to the private-key of each of those nodes and updates the public-key accordingly. Note that we are leaving out two nodes on the leaving member's key-path, i.e., the leaving member and its parent node, as they are no longer part of the new tree. The sponsor then broadcasts 1) r_{dh} encrypted with the public-keys of nodes on the co-path of the leaving member, and 2) the new public-keys of the key-path nodes. Note that the sponsor cannot use the old public-key of the group to encrypt r_{dh} (which was done in the join protocol) as the old key is

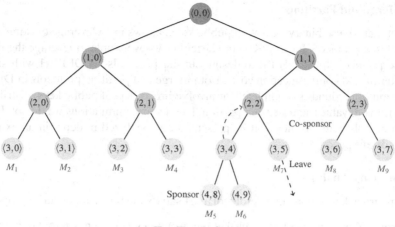

(a) Key Tree before leave

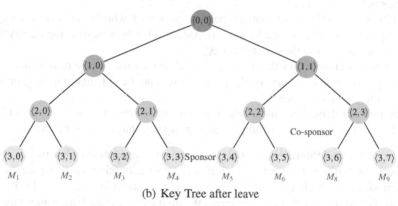

(b) Key Tree after leave

Fig. 4. Example of a Leave Operation

available to the leaving member. Instead, the sponsor has public-keys of all nodes on his co-path, which is a super set of the co-path of the leaving member, so he knows all the keys needed for this operation.

In Step 3, other group members obtain r_{dh} from the message and update the private-key associated with those key-path nodes for which they have access to the old private-key. In the example shown in Figure 4, sponsor M_5 and co-sponsor M_8 agree on r_{dh}. The sponsor calculates the new key-pairs associated with nodes $\{\langle 1,1 \rangle, \langle 0,0 \rangle\}$ according to Equations 1 and 2. The sponsor M_5 then broadcasts a message comprising the following information.

$$M_5 \rightarrow G : E(PK_{\langle 2,3 \rangle}, r_{dh}), E(PK_{\langle 1,0 \rangle}, h_{dh}), PK'_{\langle 1,1 \rangle}$$

All other members decrypt this message to obtain r_{dh} and update the key-path keys that have changed by adding r_{dh} to them, including the group key.

3.4   Merge and Partition

The fact that we use binary trees with public keys, allows us to leverage existing merge and partition protocols for DLPKH. In particular, we were able to leverage the design of these protocols in TGDH [8] to design similar protocols for DLPKH with similar computation and communication costs. Both merge and partition protocols in DLPKH require multiple rounds to complete that involve broadcasts of public keys, distribution of new random values, and tree compaction. Due to space limitations we do not discuss these protocols here but they will be presented and analyzed in-depth in an extended version of this paper.

3.5   Security Analysis

A secure group key management protocol must satisfy the following security properties:

- **Group-Key Secrecy** guarantees that the group key is not known to passive adversaries outside the group.
- **Backward Secrecy** states that any passive adversary who has access to a set $\mathcal{K}$ of contiguous group keys used by the group should not be able to compute any group key used prior to the those in the set $\mathcal{K}$.
- **Forward Secrecy** states that any passive adversary who has access to a set $\mathcal{K}$ of contiguous group keys used by the group should not be able to compute group keys used after those in the set $\mathcal{K}$.
- **Key Independence** guarantees that any passive adversary who has access to a set of $\mathcal{K}$ of group keys cannot compute any group key that is not in the set $\mathcal{K}$.

Note that above definitions deal only with passive adversaries. That is, adversaries can observe all traffic but cannot inject or modify traffic. In other words we assume that all channels are public but authentic. We can achieve authentic channels by integrity protecting messages with digital signatures. We also assume that all messages have type identifiers and sequence numbers. Compilers [6] exist that can be used to construct a group key management scheme secure against an active adversary given a scheme secure against a passive adversary by adding on additional round and digital signatures. We also assume that all group members are honest, in other words we do not consider insider attacks.

We now give a proof for the security of our scheme. We assume that all keys are generated fresh and cryptographic primitives are ideal. We use the following invariants that we show are preserved by our protocols:

- **Invariant 1 or Key-Tree Secrecy.** *An outside adversary cannot determine any secret-key associated with nodes on the key-tree.*
- **Invariant 2.** *No group member can determine private-keys other than those associated with nodes on his key-path.*

Note that Key-Tree Secrecy implies Group-Key Secrecy. Also note that Forward Secrecy together with Backward secrecy imply Key Independence and Key Independence implies all the previous three. We will show that Join and Leave protocols satisfy the security properties 1) Group-Key secrecy, 2) Backward Secrecy and 3) Forward Secrecy and 4) Key-Independence. We first prove the following claims needed for the proof.

Claim 1. *Join protocol preserves the invariants and security properties, i.e., if the invariants and security properties hold for a k member group they will hold for the k + 1 member after the join protocol.*

Case n = k. Let us now consider the join protocol between a k member group and a new member. Let us assume that the k member group satisfies the above invariants and the security properties. The sponsor generates new random keys r_0 and r_1 and associates them with its node and its parent node in the new key-tree. The keys of all other nodes on the key-path of the joining member are updated by adding r_{dh}, which is generated through a DH key-exchange with a co-sponsor. The new keys of nodes on the key-path of the joining member are broadcast on the public channel encrypted with the joining member's public-key (note that this is not long term key). r_{dh} is broadcast after being encrypted with the group's old public-key.

Invariant 1. Since Invariant 1 is true for the k member group a passive outside adversary cannot get access to r_{dh}. Assuming that the secret-key of the joining member is not compromised the adversary cannot get access to the new key-path keys. Thus, Invariant 1 holds for the $k + 1$ member group.

Invariant 2. We can see that the joining member gets access to only those keys that are on his key-path. Existing group members can compute the updated key for a node only if they had access to the node's old private-key. Hence they will not have access to any more private-keys than they had before. Thus if Invariant 2 is true for the k member it will also be true for the new $k + 1$ member group.

Group-Key Secrecy. Invariant 1 implies Group-Key Secrecy.

Backward Secrecy. Since both the invariants and the four security properties are satisfied by the k member group, and the keys generated during the join protocol, namely, r_0, r_1 and r_{dh} are fresh and random, i.e., unrelated to any old keys, the only backward secrecy violation we need to worry about is that of the joining member computing the old group key used by the k member group. Since Invariant 1 holds for the k member group and Invariant 2 holds for the $k + 1$ member group, the joining member cannot get access to r_{dh} and thus backward secrecy is also satisfied for the $k + 1$ member group.

Forward Secrecy. Forward secrecy is satisfied by the $k + 1$ group given that (1) both the invariants and security properties hold for the k member group, (2) Invariant 1 holds for the $k + 1$ group, and (3) keys generated in the protocol are independent.

Key Independence. Given that Backward and Forward secrecy are preserved, key independence is preserved.

It is trivial to see that the join protocol between a 1 member group and a new member preserves the above invariants and satisfies the above four security properties as the protocol is a DH key-exchange. It is also easy to see that a join protocol between a 2 member group and a new member also preserves the above invariants and satisfies the four security properties.

Claim 2. *Leave protocol preserves the invariants and security properties, i.e., if the invariants and security properties hold for a k member group they will hold for the k − 1 member after the leave protocol.*

Similar to the above argument we argue that the invariants, group key secrecy, forward secrecy, backward secrecy and key independence are preserved by the leave protocol.

Case n=k. The keys of all the nodes on the key-path of the leaving node that are part of the new tree are updated by adding the value r_{dh} agreed upon by the sponsor and a co-sponsor through DH key-exchange. This value is broadcast after being encrypted under the public-keys of nodes that were on the co-path of the leaving node.

Invariant 1. Since Invariant 1 is true for the k member group, a passive outside adversary does not have access to old keys of the group and, therefore, cannot get access to r_{dh}. Thus, he cannot compute any of the new keys. Invariant 1 holds for $k-1$ member group and hence is preserved by the Leave protocol.

Invariant 2. Note that all those members that have access to private-keys of nodes on the co-path of the leaving member (allowing them to decrypt messages and access r_{dh}) are only those nodes that share a key-path node with the leaving member and and hence are authorized to get the updated keys. Thus the invariant is preserved if it was true before the leave protocol.

Group-Key Secrecy. Invariant 1 implies Group-Key Secrecy.

Backward Secrecy. Given that both the invariants and security properties hold for the k member group, and the key generated in the protocol, r_{dh}, is independent of old keys we have that backward secrecy is satisfied by the new group.

Forward Secrecy. Since both the invariants and the four security properties are satisfied by the k member group, and the key generated during the protocol, r_{dh}, is fresh and random the only forward secrecy violation we need to worry about is that of the leaving member computing the new group key used by the $k-1$ member group. Since Invariant 2 is true before the leave event, the leaving member does not have access to private-keys needed to decrypt r_{dh} and, therefore, cannot obtain the new keys.

Given the above claims and the fact that executing a join protocol on a one member group produces a two member group for which the invariants and the security properties hold we argue that inter-leaving the protocols will preserve the invariants and satisfies the security properties. That is, given a two member group that satisfies the invariants and security properties we can either run a Join or a Leave and we will still end up with a group that will satisfy the invariants and security properties according to to claims 1 and 2.

Partial Contributory Nature of DLPKH. A criticism of decentralized key distribution schemes is that they rely on a single entity to generate keys leading to the possibility of weak keys due to potential errors (or malicious acts) in random number generation. To address this concern, contributory key agreement schemes require an equal share from every group member towards key generation. However, in practice this possibility of weak keys is significantly minimized just by having more than one entity generate the key. FDLKH [5] does so by having two sponsors generate a new key via a Diffie-Hellman operation for every key that needs to be updated. DLPKH does the same by having the sponsor and co-sponsor generate the random number for a key update via a Diffie-Hellman operation. However, we take this approach of partial contribution even further because we keep adding each random number generated for a key update for a given membership event to all key updates for all previous membership events. This ensures that even if the sponsor and co-sponsor happen to generate poor random numbers in a given membership event the updated key will still be strong. We argue that this approach suffices in practice and as we shall we see in the next section results in significant reduction of computation costs for decentralized key management via DLPKH.

4 Analytical Comparison

4.1 Complexity Model

The costs of a key management protocol are dominated by communication costs and computation costs, which can often be traded for one another. We measure the efficiency of the DLPKH scheme and compare it against DLKH, FDLKH and TGDH using the cost definitions described below.

Communication Complexity. Communication complexity of a protocol measures the communication cost of the protocol in terms of rounds, messages and bytes as described below. Combined together these parameters provide a representation of the communication cost with the idea being that minimizing all three results in minimization of the energy spent by members for communication during key update operations. These costs are provided in Table 1.

Table 1. Communication costs where n, d, and h have the same meaning as described in Section 3.1 and K denotes the size of a key

Protocol	Operation	Rounds	Max. Messages Sent per Member	Total Messages Sent	Total Bytes on the Network
DLPKH	Join	3	2	4	$n + (3d + 11)*K$
	Leave	2	2	3	$(h + 6)*K$
FDLKH-Dedicated	Join	3	2	$2d + 3$	$n + (4d + 6)*K$
	Leave	2	2	$2h + 3$	$(5h + 4)*K$
FDLKH-Distributed	Join	3	3	$3d + 2$	$n + (6d + 4)*K$
	Leave	3	3	$3h$	$(6h)*K$
DLKH	Join *	3	3	4	$n + (d + 8)*K$
	Leave	3	$h + 3$	$3h + 3$	$(7h + 2)*K$
TGDH	Join	2	1	2	$n + (2d + 4)*K$
	Leave	1	1	1	$(d)*K$

* Join protocol in DLKH does not provide Backward Secrecy and hence the constant computation costs.

Round Complexity. The round complexity of a protocol is the number of rounds it takes before termination. Messages that can be sent simultaneously are considered to occur in the same round. A protocol with a larger round complexity is more expensive especially over networks with high latency.

Message Complexity. We define the message complexity of a protocol in terms of 1) maximum number of messages that need to be transmitted by any single user and 2) the total number of messages transmitted during the execution of protocol. Maximum number of messages that need to be transmitted by any single user characterizes the scalability of the protocol. The total number of messages, even if some of them are sent in parallel, increase the burden on underlying group communication system and hence better characterizes the communication cost. In this paper we will adopt the *broadcast* model [6] where the cost of sending a message to a single party is same as broadcasting the same message to multiple parties.

Byte Complexity. We define the byte complexity of the protocol in terms of number of bytes that need to be transmitted during the protocol. For simplicity, we measure this in terms of the total number of keys that need to be transmitted all the while keeping in mind that symmetric keys are smaller than asymmetric keys for RSA and El Gamal but similar in size to asymmetric keys for Elliptic Curve Cryptography (ECC). For simplicity K denotes the size of all keys but we count an asymmetric key-pair as two keys. We include the bytes needed to provide message authentication, namely, the additional bytes for sending digital signatures. Authenticating messages for key updates is essential and it is natural to include these costs. In addition, we include n bytes for sending the tree-structure to the joining member assuming that it takes 0.5 byte to send information on each node of the tree. If there are optimizations to this then they will apply to all protocols equally as all of them have to send the tree structure to the joining member.

Computational Complexity. Computational complexity measures the computation cost incurred by the protocol. This cost is dominated by expensive cryptographic operations involved and is measured in terms of number of computations involved in generating shared secrets, establishing secure channels, message encryption and decryption, and signing and verifications; e.g., exponentiations in RSA or El Gamal and point multiplications in ECC. We ignore the costs of other operations such as symmetric key operations, additions, multiplications, or point additions as they are insignificant when compared to these expensive operations. For the execution of a complete join and leave operations we assess the maximum number of (1) expensive operations not dealing with authentication performed by any members (for simplicity we denote all such costs under "exponentiations"), (2) signatures for authentication generated by any member, and (3) signature verifications for authentication performed by any member. Unlike communication cost, computation that is done in parallel can be collapsed for the purposes of measuring computational latency of the protocol. Hence we measure total serial computation cost. Furthermore, the number of total expensive operations undertaken by all members during a membership event provides insights into the overall computation costs of the protocol. Combined together these parameters provide a representation of the computation cost with the idea being that minimizing them results in minimization of the energy spent by members for computations undertaken during key update operations. These costs are provided in Table 2.

Table 2. Computation Costs where n, d, and h have the same meaning as described Section 3.1

Protocol	Operation	Exponentiations		Signatures		Verifications		Total Serial Operations	Total Operations*
DLPKH	Join	9	Sponsor	2	Sponsor	3	Co-Sponsor	17	$3n+18$
	Leave	$2h+3$	Sponsor	2	Sponsor	2	Co-Sponsor	$2h+8$	$2n+2h+7$
FDLKH-Dedicated	Join	$d+2$	Joining Mem.	2	Captain	$d+1$	Joining Mem.	$2d+7$	$3n+5d+6$
	Leave	$h+1$	Buddy Captain	3	Buddy Captain	h	Buddy Captain	$2h+4$	$2.5n+6h-3$
FDLKH-Distributed	Join	3	Captain	3	Captain	$d+1$	Join Mem.	$d+11$	$3n+8d+5$
	Leave	3	Captain	3	Captain	h	Member	$h+8$	$3n+4h-5$
DLKH	Join**	2	Leader	3	Leader	3	Join Mem.	7	$2n+10$
	Leave	$h+1$	Leader	$h+3$	Leader	h	Leader	$3h+7$	$2n+8h-1$
TGDH	Join	$2d+2$	Sponsor	1	Sponsor	2	Member	$3d+8$	$4n+2d+4$
	Leave	$2d-2$	Sponsor	1	Sponsor	1	Member	$3d-2$	$3n-5$

* Total computation cost is analyzed for a balanced tree.

** Join protocol in DLKH does not provide Backward Secrecy and hence the constant communication costs.

4.2 Complexity Analysis

Analyzing Communication Costs. From Table 1 we see that all protocols have a constant number of rounds. With the exception of DLKH no member needs to send more than a constant number of messages. However, significant differences appear between the protocols when looking at the total number of messages sent and the total number of bytes on the network. Only DLPKH and TGDH involve a constant number of total messages while others require $O(\log(n))$ messages. DLKH join involves a constant number of total messages, however, if the protocol is extended to support backward secrecy then this cost will also increase to $O(\log(n))$. The reason behind this difference between the protocols is that earlier decentralized key distribution protocols, namely, FDLKH and DLKH, required members to establish secure channels in order to distribute new keys. Using pair-wise channels this naturally required $O(\log(n))$ channels leading to $O(\log(n))$ messages sent on the network to both establish the channels and then to send the updated keys. In contrast, DLPKH (like TGDH) uses a public-key tree so that group members have ready access to public keys that allow them to send keying material securely to an arbitrary subset of group members in a single message. The difference between the protocols in terms of the total bytes on the network is not as big. They all require $O(n)$ bytes for sending the tree structure and then $O(\log(n))$ bytes for sending keys. There are constant differences between the protocols with TGDH sending the least number of bytes followed closely by DLPKH that requires the sending of an additional $(d+7)*K$ bytes for join and $6*K$ bytes for leave. Overall, the large number of messages in FDLKH and DLKH make them significantly inefficient in comparison with DLPKH and TGDH with TDGH being the most efficient.

Analyzing Computation Costs. The first observation from Table 2 is that despite the use of only symmetric key trees, FDLKH and DLKH have a large number of expensive operations overall owing to their need for establishing secure channels and authenticating a large number of messages. In terms of exponentiations FDLKH-distributed comes out ahead with a constant factor followed closely by DLPKH with a constant factor for Join and $O(log(n))$ for Leave. (We discount the constant cost for Join in DLKH because they do not support backward secrecy). DLPKH Leave, FDLKH-dedicated, FDLKH-distributed and TGDH all have $O(log(n))$ costs differing by a constant factor with TGDH performing the worst in this category. For computation costs dealing with authentication DLPKH and TGDH perform significantly better than others with constant costs because they do not require the signing and verification of a large number of messages involved in establishing multiple secure channels. The column presenting total serial operations provides a measure of overall latency in execution of membership changes. Here only DLPKH Join has constant costs while DLPKH Leave and all other the schemes have $O(log(n))$ costs. They all differ by a constant factor with TGDH performing the worst. The last column presenting the total number of expensive operations provides a measure of the overall energy expended by all group members in executing membership changes. All protocols have $O(n + log(n))$ costs, which is the only $O(n)$ cost in the two tables dealing with key exchange (the other $O(n)$ cost involves communication of the tree structure). Ignoring the DLKH join operation (for reasons discussed above) DLPKH has the best performance in this category and indicates its real strengths. When compared with FDLKH-dedicated and FDLKH-distributed, DLPKH performs better by at least a large logarithmic factor. When compared to TGDH, DLPKH performs better by $n - 2d - 14$ operations for Join and by $n - 2h - 12$ operations for Leave. This saving is intuitive in nature because DLPKH involves distribution of keys while TGDH involves contributory key generation.

4.3 Experimental Analysis

To gauge the efficiency of these protocols with increasing group size in practice, we ran experiments to evaluate the total and serial computation cost, and total byte costs of the protocols. Starting with a group size of 16 we doubled the group size at very increment to reach 1024. We conducted the evaluation using two different cryptosystems: (1) Diffie-Hellman (DH) and ElGamal for "exponentiations" and RSA for signatures (i.e., DH/EG-RSA) and (2) ECC for both "exponentiations" and signatures (i.e., ECC-ECC). Measurements with the first cryptosystem reflect a comparison of the protocols as presented by the authors while those with the second reflect a comparison with a communication-efficient cryptosystem that is suitable for constrained devices and networks. We used the MIRACL library to benchmark the cryptographic primitives on a 3.0GHz Intel processor running Linux. We used 163 bit keys for ECC, 1024 bit keys with the exponent 65537 when using RSA for signatures and a 1024 modulus with 160 bit exponents when using ElGamal. We use 128 bit symmetric keys when computing

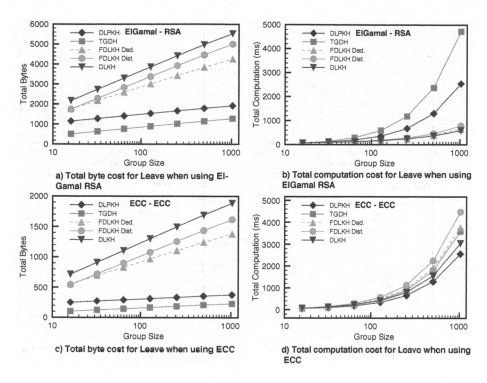

Fig. 5. Total computation and byte costs for Leave using DH/ElGamal-RSA and ECC-ECC

byte costs with symmetric keys. We did not take into account the byte cost for distributing the tree structure as that is common for all protocols.

Figure 5 shows the experimental results for leave protocol. In terms of total byte costs Figures 5a and 5c show that TGDH has the best performance followed closely by DLPKH. DLPKH is a factor of $O(log(n))$ worse, which is consistent with the analysis in Section 4.2. Contrary to the analysis in Section 4.2., Figure 5b shows that DLPKH performs worse, albeit marginally, than FDLKH and DLKH with respect to total computation cost. This is due to the fact that signature verification costs dominate the total computation cost incurred by FDLKH and DLKH and exponentiation costs dominate that of TGDH and DLPKH. RSA signature verification is an order of magnitude cheaper than exponentiation in ElGamal group. For the key sizes used for the experiments, RSA verifications costs $0.2ms$ compared to $2.21ms$ for exponentiation. However, consistent with the analytical results, DLPKH outperforms TGDH in practice, with respect to total computation cost, by a factor of $O(n)$, which is a significant improvement. When we look at results with ECC in Figure 5d, DLPKH outperforms all other protocols, in terms of total computation cost, with results being consistent with analytical ones. These results indicate that in environments where communication savings are important, DLPKH can provide significant savings in both communication and computation. The experimental results for join protocol are similar and are shown in Figure 6.

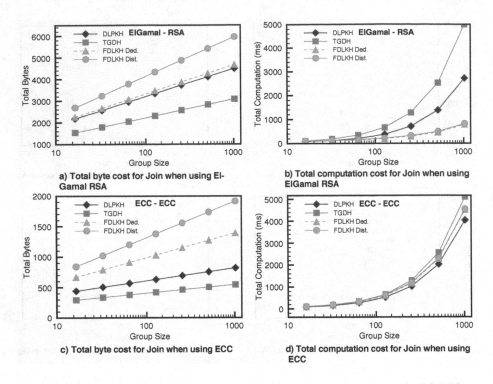

a) Total byte cost for Join when using El-Gamal RSA

b) Total computation cost for Join when using ElGamal RSA

c) Total byte cost for Join when using ECC

d) Total computation cost for Join when using ECC

Fig. 6. Total computation and byte costs for Join using DH/ElGamal-RSA and ECC-ECC

5 Conclusions

In this work we developed a novel decentralized key distribution scheme, DLPKH, that uses public-key trees and obtains partial contributions for key generation. These advances result in a scheme that is efficient, simple and practical. We show that the scheme is secure by analyzing it against a set of desirable properties. The resulting DLPKH scheme is very efficient as demonstrated by an analysis of its computation and communication costs and by experiments. In particular, the scheme provides computation benefits by a factor of $O(n)$ over previous decentralized key distribution schemes as well as over contributory key agreement schemes. These benefits are also clearly demonstrated by experiments.

Acknowledgements. Discussions with Weiting Cao, Neelay Shah and Luke St. Clair inspired and helped the development of ideas in this work. This work was funded by the Office of Naval Research under award numbers N00014-04-1-0562 and N00014-06-1-1108 and by the National Science Foundation under award number CNS-0524695. The views and conclusions contained in this document are those of the authors and should not be interpreted as representing the official policies, either expressed or implied, of the Office of Naval Research, the National Science Foundation or the United States Government.

References

1. Amir, Y., Kim, Y., Nita-Rotaru, C., Tsudik, G.: On the performance of group key agreement protocols. ACM Trans. Inf. Syst. Secur. 7(3), 457–488 (2004)
2. Bresson, E., Catalano, D.: Constant round authenticated group key agreement via distributed computation. In: Public Key Cryptography, pp. 115–129 (2004)
3. Burmester, M., Desmedt, Y.: A secure and efficient conference key distribution system (extended abstract). In: De Santis, A. (ed.) EUROCRYPT 1994. LNCS, vol. 950, pp. 275–286. Springer, Heidelberg (1995)
4. Dutta, R., Barua, R.: Dynamic group key agreement in tree-based setting. In: Boyd, C., González Nieto, J.M. (eds.) ACISP 2005. LNCS, vol. 3574, pp. 101–112. Springer, Heidelberg (2005)
5. Inoue, D., Kuroda, M.: Fdlkh: Fully decentralized key management scheme on logical key hierarchy. In: Jakobsson, M., Yung, M., Zhou, J. (eds.) ACNS 2004. LNCS, vol. 3089, pp. 339–354. Springer, Heidelberg (2004)
6. Katz, J., Yung, M.: Scalable protocols for authenticated group key exchange. In: Boneh, D. (ed.) CRYPTO 2003. LNCS, vol. 2729, pp. 110–125. Springer, Heidelberg (2003)
7. Kim, Y., Perrig, A., Tsudik, G.: Simple and fault-tolerant key agreement for dynamic collaborative groups. In: ACM Conference on Computer and Communications Security, pp. 235–244 (2000)
8. Kim, Y., Perrig, A., Tsudik, G.: Tree-based group key agreement. ACM Trans. Inf. Syst. Secur. 7(1), 60–96 (2004)
9. Rafaeli, S., Hutchison, D.: A survey of key management for secure group communication. ACM Comput. Surv. 35(3), 309–329 (2003)
10. Rodeh, O., Birman, K.P., Dolev, D.: Using avl trees for fault-tolerant group key management. Int. J. Inf. Sec. 1(2), 84–99 (2002)
11. Setia, S., Koussih, S., Jajodia, S., Harder, E.: Kronos: A scalable group re-keying approach for secure multicast. In: SP 2000: Proceedings of the 2000 IEEE Symposium on Security and Privacy, p. 215. IEEE Computer Society, Washington, DC (2000)
12. Sherman, A.T., McGrew, D.A.: Key establishment in large dynamic groups using one-way function trees. IEEE Trans. Software Eng. 29(5), 444–458 (2003)
13. Steer, D.G., Strawczynski, L., Diffie, W., Wiener, M.: A secure audio teleconference system. In: Goldwasser, S. (ed.) CRYPTO 1988. LNCS, vol. 403, pp. 520–528. Springer, Heidelberg (1990)
14. Steiner, M., Tsudik, G., Waidner, M.: Key agreement in dynamic peer groups. IEEE Trans. Parallel Distrib. Syst. 11(8), 769–780 (2000)
15. Wong, C.K., Gouda, M.G., Lam, S.S.: Secure group communications using key graphs. IEEE/ACM Trans. Netw. 8(1), 16–30 (2000)

Inference Control in Logic Databases as a Constraint Satisfaction Problem

Joachim Biskup, Dominique Marc Burgard, Torben Weibert*, and Lena Wiese

Fachbereich Informatik, Universität Dortmund, 44221 Dortmund, Germany
{biskup,burgard,weibert,wiese}@ls6.cs.uni-dortmund.de

Abstract. We investigate inference control in logic databases. The administrator defines a confidentiality policy, i.e., the pieces of information which may not be disclosed to a certain user. We present a static approach which constructs an alternative database instance in which the confidential information is replaced by harmless information. The construction is performed by the means of constraint programming: The task of finding an appropriate database instance is delegated to a hierarchical constraint solver. We compare this static approach to a dynamic inference control mechanism – Controlled Query Evaluation – investigated in earlier work, and we also point out possible extensions which make use of the various opportunities offered by hierarchical constraint solvers.

Keywords: Inference control, confidentiality, logic databases, constraint satisfaction problems, constraint hierarchies.

1 Introduction

A key feature of a secure information system is preservation of *confidentiality*: Each user must only learn the information he is allowed to. Traditional approaches rely on static access rights assigned to the *data*, and suffer from the *inference problem* [1]: The user may combine several pieces of accessible information in order to infer confidential information. For example, the two pieces of data "Alice is a manager" and "a manager's salary is $50,000" can be easily combined to the information that Alice's salary must be $50,000.

This problem can be overcome by a proper *inference control mechanism*: The administrator defines a *confidentiality policy* which specifies which pieces of *information* may not be disclosed. The inference control mechanism will then make sure that this confidential information cannot be inferred from the data returned to the user. Basically, there are *dynamic* and *static* approaches to the inference problem. A dynamic inference control mechanism monitors the queries and answers during runtime, and possibly distorts or filters part of the answers. On the other hand, a static approach modifies the original data such that the confidential information is removed or replaced, and queries can be processed in the ordinary manner without the need for any additional processing at runtime.

---

* This author is funded by the German Research Foundation (DFG) under Grant No. BI-311/12-1.

P. McDaniel and S.K. Gupta (Eds.): ICISS 2007, LNCS 4812, pp. 128–142, 2007.

Controlled Query Evaluation (CQE) [2] has been designed as a dynamic approach to the inference problem in logical databases. After each query, the system checks whether the answer to that query – combined with the previous answers and possible a priori assumptions – would enable the user to infer any secret information. If so, the answer is either refused or modified. Finally, the answer is stored in a log file in order to be accounted for later. CQE has been studied under various parameters [2,3,4], and there is also a static, SAT-solver based approach to CQE [5].

In this paper, we pick up the framework of CQE and present a static approach in which an alternative database instance is constructed from the original instance which does not contain any confidential information anymore. As opposed to [5], finding such a database instance is achieved by modelling the requirements as a *constraint satisfaction problem (CSP)* [6,7]. A *constraint solver* is a piece of software which tries to find an assignment over a set of variables such that a set of user-defined *constraints* is satisfied. In particular, *boolean constraint solvers* operate on the domain {*true, false*} (meaning that each variable is assigned a value of either *true* or *false*), and allows us to specify the constraints as a set of boolean formulas. A problem arises in case the constraints are inconsistent, for example, if one constraint demands that $a = true$, and another constraint demands that $a = false$. In this situation, a *hierarchical constraint solver* can be used to identify an assignment which satisfies only part of the constraints, according to some previously established hierarchy. The concept of constraints can be found in various research fields of security, for example in the context of role-based access control [8,9] or secure workflow models [10].

The paper is outlined as follows: Section 2 presents the logical framework and the declarative requirements for a confidentiality-preserving inference control mechanism. In Section 3, we recall Controlled Query Evaluation as a dynamic enforcement method. The foundations of hierarchical constraint networks are presented in Section 4. In Section 5, we show how to use hierarchical constraint networks in order to construct a suitable alternative database instance. A comparison of this static approach to the existing dynamic mechanisms can be found in Section 6. In Section 7, we propose some extensions which further exploit the abilities of hierarchical constraint solvers. We finally conclude in Section 8.

2 Declarative Framework

We consider complete logic databases, founded on some logic $\mathcal{L}$, for example propositional or first-order logic. Let S model_of Φ denote that the structure S is a model of the sentence Φ wrt. to the semantics of the logic under consideration. Let the logical implication operator $\models$ be defined as usual: A set of sentences Σ implies a single sentence Φ ($\Sigma \models \Phi$) iff each structure which is a model of Σ is also a model of Φ.

Definition 1 (Logic databases and ordinary query evaluation). *A database instance* db *is a structure of the logic under consideration. The* database schema DS *captures the universe of discourse and is formally defined as the set of* *all instances. A* (closed) query *is a sentence* Φ. *It is evaluated within a database instance db by the function*

$$eval(\Phi) : DS \rightarrow \{true, false\} \ with$$

$$eval(\Phi)(db) := \begin{cases} true & \text{if } db \ \texttt{model\_of } \Phi \\ false & \text{otherwise} \end{cases} \tag{1}$$

We also use an alternative evaluation function which returns the query or its negation, respectively:

$$eval^*(\Phi) : DS \rightarrow \{\Phi, \neg\Phi\} \ with$$

$$eval^*(\Phi)(db) := \begin{cases} \Phi & \text{if } db \ \texttt{model\_of } \Phi \\ \neg\Phi & \text{otherwise} \end{cases} \tag{2}$$

Definition 2 (Confidentiality policy). *The* confidentiality policy *is a set*

$$policy := \{\Psi_1, \ldots, \Psi_m\}$$

of potential secrets, *each of which is a sentence of the logic under consideration, with the following semantics: In case* Ψ_i *is true in the actual database instance db, the user may not learn this fact. Otherwise, if* Ψ_i *is false in db, this fact may be disclosed to the user. Accordingly, the user may believe that* Ψ_i *is false even if it is actually true.*

Example 3. Given a database which holds the medical record of some person, the confidentiality policy given by

$$policy := \{aids, cancer\}$$

defines that the user may not learn that the person suffers from aids, and may neither learn that the person suffers from cancer. In case the person does not suffer from one of these diseases, that information may be disclosed to the user.

The aim of an inference control mechanism is to protect the potential secrets in the aforementioned manner. We abstractly formalize an inference control mechanism as a function

$$f(Q, db, prior, policy) := \langle ans_1, \ldots, ans_n \rangle$$

where

- $Q = \langle \Phi_1, \ldots, \Phi_n \rangle$ is a (finite) query sequence,
- *db* is the actual database instance,
- *prior* is the user's *a priori assumptions*, given as a set of sentences in the logic under consideration, and
- *policy* is the confidentiality policy.

The function returns a sequence of answers, where each $ans_i \in \{\Phi_i, \neg\Phi_i\}$.[1] The answers are to be generated iteratively, i.e., the i-th answer must be returned before the $i + 1$-th query is received.

We assume that each enforcement method f goes along with a function

$$precond(db, prior, policy) \in \{true, false\}$$

which defines the admissible arguments for f. For example, an enforcement method could refuse to start a session if any of the potential secrets can already be inferred from the a priori assumptions in the first place. Based on this abstract definition, we can introduce our notion of confidentiality.

Definition 4 (Confidentiality of an enforcement method). *An enforcement method f preserves* confidentiality *if and only if*

for all finite query sequences Q,
for all instances db,
for all confidentiality policies $policy$,
for all potential secrets $\Psi \in policy$,
for all sets of a priori assumptions $prior$
so that $(db, prior, policy)$ satisfies the precondition,
there exists an instance db'
so that $(db', prior, policy)$ satisfies the precondition,
and the following two conditions hold:
(a) [(db, policy) and (db', policy) produce the same answers]
  $f(Q, db, prior, policy) = f(Q, db', prior, policy)$
(b) [Ψ is false in db']
  $eval(\Psi)(db') = false$

Condition (a) guarantees that db and db' are indistinguishable to the user; he cannot tell whether db or db' is the actual database instance. Condition (b) makes sure that Ψ is *false* in db'; as the user considers db' as a possible actual database instance, he cannot rule out that Ψ is actually *false*.

3   A Dynamic Approach – Controlled Query Evaluation

We briefly recall Controlled Query Evaluation, in particular the uniform lying method for known potential secrets in complete databases, as found in [11,2]. This enforcement method keeps a *log file* of the past answers, and uses logical implication in order to detect threats to the confidentiality policy.

The log file log_i is a set of sentences of the logic under consideration, initialized with the a priori assumptions:

$$log_0 := prior$$

---

[1] Previous work [2] additionally uses the special symbol mum to indicate a refused answer; however, the present paper does not consider refusal.

After each query Φ_i, the answer ans_i is added to the log file:

$$log_i := log_{i-1} \cup \{ans_i\}$$

The uniform lying method makes sure that the log file does never imply the information that at least one potential secret must be *true*, by keeping

$$log_i \not\models pot\_sec\_disj \quad \text{with } pot\_sec\_disj = \bigvee_{\Psi \in policy} \Psi$$

as an invariant throughout the query sequence. For the a priori assumptions, the invariant is enforced by the precondition

$$precond(db, prior, policy) := prior \not\models pot\_sec\_disj.$$

Having received the query Φ_i, an appropriate answer is chosen so that the invariant is preserved: If the actual value $eval^*(\Phi_i)(db)$ does not lead to a violation, it is returned to the user. Otherwise, the negation of the actual value is returned as the answer, i.e., a lie is issued.

$$ans_i := \begin{cases} eval^*(\Phi_i)(db) & \text{if } log_{i-1} \cup \{eval^*(\Phi_i)(db)\} \not\models pot\_sec\_disj \\ \neg eval^*(\Phi_i)(db) & \text{otherwise} \end{cases}$$

Theorem 5. *The uniform lying method for known potential secrets preserves confidentiality in the sense of Definition 4.*

The full proof can be found in [2]. We give a short sketch here. Consider that $log_n \not\models pot\_sec\_disj$. This means that there must be a structure db' which is a model of log_n but not a model of pot_sec_disj, and thus also no model of Ψ for each particular $\Psi \in policy$. This satisfies condition (b) of Definition 4. It can also be shown that the same answers are returned under db and db', which satisfies condition (a).

4   Constraint Satisfaction Problems

In this section, we present the fundamentals of constraint satisfaction problems. We first introduce ordinary constraint networks, and then present the concept of hierarchical constraint networks which are able to handle conflicting set of constraints.

4.1   Constraint Networks

Basically, a constraint network consists of a set of variables, each with a specific domain, and a set of constraints over these variables. The task of a constraint solver is to find a variable assignment which satisfies all constraints.

Definition 6 (Constraint network). *A constraint network is a tuple (X, D, C) where*

- $X = \{x_1, \ldots, x_n\}$ *is a set of variables,*
- $D = \{d_1, \ldots, d_n\}$ *specifies the domain of each variable, and*
- $C = \{c_1, \ldots, c_m\}$ *is a set of constraints.*

Definition 7 (Solution of a constraint network). *A* variable assignment θ *for a constraint network* (X, D, C) *is a set*

$$\{(x_1, v_1), \ldots, (x_n, v_n)\},$$

with $\{x_1, \ldots, x_n\}$ *are the variables from* X, *and each* $v_i \in d_i$ *is a value from the respective domain.*

We write $c(\theta) = true$ *to indicate that a variable assignment* θ *satisfies a constraint* $c \in C$, *and* $c(\theta) = false$ *otherwise. A* solution *of a constraint network* (X, D, C) *is a variable assignment which satisfies all constraints from* C, *i. e.,* $c(\theta) = true$ *for all* $c \in C$.

A constraint network may have a unique solution, multiple solutions, or even no solutions, in case the constraints are inconsistent and thus conflicting.

4.2   Constraint Hierarchies

Given a conflicting set of constraints, an ordinary constraint network does not have a solution, because there is no variable assignment which satisfies all constraints at the same time. One could however be interested to find an approximate solution, i. e., a variable assignment which satisfies only some of the constraints. One approach to this problem are *hierarchical constraint networks* [12], which we introduce in this section.

Definition 8 (Hierarchical constraint network). *A* hierarchical constraint network *is a tuple* (X, D, C, H), *where* (X, D, C) *is a constraint network, and* $H = \{H_0, \ldots, H_l\}$ *is a* constraint hierarchy. *The latter defines a partition of the constraint set* C, *assigning a* strength i *with* $0 \leq i \leq l$ *to each constraint* $c \in C$. *In particular, we have*

$$H_i \cap H_j = \emptyset \text{ for all } i \neq j$$

and

$$\bigcup_{H_i \in H} H_i = C.$$

The constraints $c \in H_0$ *are called the* required *constraints.*

The aim is to find a variable assignment which satisfies all of the constraints from H_0, and satisfies the other constraints from $H_1, \ldots, H_l$ "as good as possible". There might be various notions of what a "better" solution is; for the moment, we assume that we have a predicate

$$better(\sigma, \theta, H)$$

saying that σ is a better variable assignment than θ wrt. the constraint hierarchy H. *better* must be irreflexive and transitive. Based on this predicate, we can formally define a solution of a hierarchical constraint network.

Definition 9 (Solution of a hierarchical constraint network). *Let (X, D, C, H) be a hierarchical constraint network. Let*

$$S_0 := \{ \theta \mid c(\theta) = true \text{ for all } c \in H_0 \}$$

be the set of variable assignments which satisfy all required constraints. A solution to the hierarchical constraint network (X, D, C, H) is a variable assignment θ such that

$$\theta \in S_0 \text{ and } \neg better(\sigma, \theta, H) \text{ for all } \sigma \in S_0.$$

A solution satisfies all required constraints from H_0. Regarding the other levels $1, \ldots, l$, we investigate different approaches to define a *better* predicate.

Locally better. A variable assignment σ is *locally better* than a variable assignment θ iff both assignments satisfy exactly the same set of constraints up to some level $k - 1$, and for level k, σ satisfies some constraint $c \in H_k$ which θ does not satisfy, and σ also satisfies any constraint from H_k which θ satisfies. In other words, we only consider the lowest level on which σ and θ differ; any other level $k + 1, \ldots, l$ does not have an influence on the decision. Given an *error function* e with

$$e(c, \theta) := \begin{cases} 0 & \text{if } c(\theta) = true \\ 1 & \text{if } c(\theta) = false, \end{cases}$$

we can formally define the locally-better predicate as follows:

$$\begin{aligned} better_{locally}(\sigma, \theta, H) \ := \ & \exists k > 0 \text{ such that} \\ & \forall i \in \{1, \ldots, k-1\}, \forall c \in H_i : e(c, \sigma) = e(c, \theta) \text{ and} \\ & \exists c \in H_k : e(c, \sigma) < e(c, \theta) \text{ and} \\ & \forall d \in H_k : e(d, \sigma) \leq e(d, \theta) \end{aligned}$$

Globally better. The globally-better predicate is parameterized by a function $g(\theta, H_i)$ which calculates how good a variable assignment θ satisfies the constraints on level i. A variable assignment σ is *globally better* than a variable assignment θ if both have the same quality (according to g) up to level $k - 1$, and σ has a better quality than θ on level k:

$$\begin{aligned} better_{globally}(\sigma, \theta, H) \ := \ & \exists k > 0 \text{ such that} \\ & \forall i \in \{1, \ldots, k-1\} : g(\sigma, H_i) = g(\theta, H_i) \text{ and} \\ & g(\sigma, H_k) < g(\theta, H_k) \end{aligned} \quad (3)$$

A suitable g function could e.g. count the number of constraints satisfied on a given level. (This is different from $better_{locally}$, where the *exact set* of constraints needs to be satisfied in order to have the same quality on some level $i \leq k - 1$.) One could also assign weights to the constraints and calculated the weighted sum of the satisfied constraints. Further options are pointed out in [12].

5   A Static Approach Using a Constraint Network

We present a static inference control method csp using a hierarchical constraint network. First, we show how to construct an alternative database instance db_{alt}, which does not contain any confidential information anymore. Based on this alternative database instance, we can easily construct an enforcement method which satisfies the requirements of Definition 4.

5.1   Construction of db_{alt}

Given a database instance db, a set of a priori assumptions $prior$, and a confidentiality policy $policy$, we construct a hierarchical constraint network $CN(db, prior, policy) = (X, D, C, H)$ as follows:

Variables X**:** The set $X = \{x_1, \ldots, x_n\}$ of variables corresponds to the set of atomic sentences in the corresponding database schema DS. For example, when using propositional logic, X corresponds to the set of propositions.

Domains D**:** Each variable x_i has the domain $d_i = \{true, false\}$.

Constraints C**:** The set C of constraints consists of three subsets C_{ps}, C_{prior} and C_{db}:

1. The potential secrets must not hold in the alternative database instance:

$$C_{ps} := \bigcup_{\Psi \in policy} \{\neg \Psi\} \qquad (4)$$

2. The a priori assumptions must hold in the alternative database instance:

$$C_{prior} := \bigcup_{\alpha \in prior} \{\alpha\}$$

3. All atoms should have the same value as in the original database instance:

$$C_{db} := \bigcup_{x \in X} \{eval^*(x)(db)\}$$

Note that these constraints may be conflicting – in particular, C_{ps} and C_{db} will be inconsistent in case at least one potential secret is $true$ in the original instance.

Hierarchy H**:** We establish the following constraint hierarchy $H = \{H_0, H_1\}$: The constraints from C_{ps} and C_{prior} are the required constraints:

$$H_0 := C_{ps} \cup C_{prior}$$

The constraints from C_{db} are assigned to level 1:

$$H_1 := C_{db}$$

A valid solution to this constraint network is a variable assignment to all atoms of DS, and thus a structure which can be regarded as an alternative database instance db_{alt}. The constraints ensure that none of the potential secrets is *true* in db_{alt}, and that any sentence from *prior* holds in db_{alt}. Finally, db_{alt} should have a minimum distance to the original database instance db, i. e., a minimum number of atoms should have a different truth value in db and db_{alt}. This is achieved by employing the $better_{globally}$ predicate (3) with the underlying function

$$g(\sigma, H_i) := |\{c \in H_i \mid c(\sigma) = false\}|$$

which counts the number of constraints from H_i that are not satisfied (i. e., the number of atoms with a different truth value).

Remark 10. Given a relatively large database schema DS, the number of atoms (and thus the number of variables in X) can become very large. As an optimization, we can restrict X to the *relevant* atoms, i. e., those atoms which appear in at least one sentence of either *policy* or *prior*. The truth value of these relevant atoms will be calculated by the constraint network; all other, non-relevant atoms will have the same truth value in db_{alt} as in the original instance db.

5.2 Enforcement Method Based on db_{alt}

Based on the alternative database instance, we construct an enforcement method *csp*. The algorithm involves a preprocessing step which is initiated prior to the first query. In that step, the alternative database instance is generated with the means of the constraint network described in the previous section. The precondition $precond_{csp}$ is satisfied if a valid alternative database instance was identified. Finally, the evaluation of the query sequence is performed within the alternative database instance db_{alt}, using the $eval^*$ function (ordinary query evaluation).

Definition 11 (Enforcement method csp). *Let Q be a query sequence, db a database instance, prior a set of a priori assumptions, and policy a confidentiality policy. We define an enforcement method csp along with its precondition function $precond_{csp}$ as follows.*

1. **Preprocessing step**
    If $db \models \Psi$ for some $\Psi \in policy$, or $db \not\models \alpha$ for some $\alpha \in prior$, construct an alternative database instance db_{alt} as specified in Section 5.1.
        Otherwise, choose $db_{alt} := db$.
        The precondition $precond_{csp}(db, prior, policy)$ is satisfied iff a valid alternative database instance db_{alt} could be identified. (Note that prior and policy might be inconsistent, so that the constraint network will not have a solution.)
2. **Answer generation**
    All queries are evaluated in the alternative database instance db_{alt} using the ordinary query evaluation function:

$$ans_i := eval^*(\Phi_i)(db_{alt}) \quad for\ 1 \leq i \leq n \tag{5}$$

Theorem 12. *csp preserves confidentiality in the sense of Definition 4.*

Proof. Let Q be a query sequence, db a database instance, $prior$ the a priori assumptions, and $policy$ a confidentiality policy, such that $precond_{csp}(db, prior, policy)$ is satisfied. Let $\Psi \in policy$ be a potential secret.

In the preprocessing step, db_{alt} is either generated by the constraint network (in case at least one potential secret is *true* in the original db, or the a priori assumptions do not hold in db), or is identical to db. Query evaluation is performed within db_{alt} using the ordinary $eval^*$ function.

We show that db_{alt} can be regarded as a database instance db' as demanded by Definition 4, such that $precond_{csp}(db_{alt}, prior, policy)$ is *true*, and both conditions from that definition are satisfied.

Condition (b) [Ψ is *false* in db_{alt}]: If $db_{alt} = db$, then db does not imply any potential secret, in particular $db \not\models \Psi$. Otherwise, if db_{alt} was generated by the constraint network, the constraints in C_{ps} make sure that none of the potential secrets hold in db_{alt}.

Precondition: The preprocessing step for $(db_{alt}, prior, policy)$ will notice that none of the potential secrets holds in db_{alt} (see proof for condition (b) above), and that the a priori assumptions are satisfied in db_{alt} (due to the constraints C_{prior} used for the construction of db_{alt}). It will thus choose db_{alt} as the "alternative" database instance, and will not initiate the generation of a different instance by the constraint solver. Thus, db_{alt} itself will serve as the "alternative" database instance, and the precondition is satisfied for $(db_{alt}, prior, policy)$.

Condition (a) [Same answers]: We have shown above that the "alternative" database instance under $(db_{alt}, prior, policy)$ will then be db_{alt} itself. Consequently, the same answers will be returned as under $(db, prior, policy)$.

6   Comparison

In this section, we compare the static, constraint-based approach from Section 5 to the existing dynamic CQE approach (cf. Section 3).

Generally, the dynamic approach involves a certain overhead at query time:

1. We need to keep a log file of all past answers which consumes space. In particular, when multiple users (with the same confidentiality requirements) query the database at the same time, we need to keep a distinct log file for each user.
2. At each query, an implication problem must be solved, as we need to make sure that the resulting log file does not imply the disjunction of all potential secrets *pot_sec_disj*. However, logical implication can be computationally expensive or even undecidable in certain logics.

On the other hand, the static approach involves the expensive preprocessing phase in which the alternative database instance is generated; there is however no overhead at query time. We can also re-use the alternative database instance for multiple users and/or sessions, given that the users are subject to the same confidentiality policy, and are assumed to have the same a priori assumptions.

Table 1. Answers for the query sequence $Q_1 = \langle a, b \rangle$

Query Φ_i	Dynamic Approach		Static Approach
	Answer ans_i	Log File log_i	Answer ans_i
a	a	$\{a\}$	a
b	$\neg b$	$\{a, \neg b\}$	$\neg b$

Given these considerations, the static approach is more favorable if we expect long query sequences or multiple sessions by users with the same confidentiality requirements.

Although neither approach can anticipate future queries, the dynamic CQE approach can take advantage of that fact that it can dynamically choose when to return a lie, and only issue a distorted answer as a "last resort". This can lead to a gain of availability in certain situations. We demonstrate this by a minimal example in propositional logic.

Example 13. Consider the database schema $DS = \{a, b\}$ and the database instance $db = \{a, b\}$ (both a and b are *true* in db). We assume that the user does not make any a priori assumptions ($prior = \emptyset$), and he is not allowed to know that a and b are both *true*: $policy = \{a \wedge b\}$.

As $eval(a \wedge b)(db) = true$, the preprocessing step of the static approach will need to construct an alternative database instance, using the constraint network (X, D, C, H) with

$$X := \{a, b\},$$
$$D := \{\{true, false\}, \{true, false\}\},$$
$$C := C_{ps} \cup C_{db} \text{ with } C_{ps} = \{\neg(a \wedge b)\} \text{ and } C_{db} = \{a, b\},$$
$$H := \{H_0, H_1\} \text{ with } H_0 = C_{ps} \text{ and } H_1 = C_{db}.$$

This constraint network has two possible solutions:

$$\theta_1 = \{a \to true, \ b \to false\}$$
$$\theta_2 = \{a \to false, \ b \to true\}$$

Both satisfy all constraints from $H_0 = C_{ps}$ and a maximum number of constraints from $H_1 = C_{db}$. We cannot predict which solution will be chosen by the constraint solver. Assume that it will chose θ_1, then we have

$$db_{alt} = \{a, \neg b\}.$$

Consider the query sequence $Q_1 = \langle a, b \rangle$. The respective answers are given in Table 1. The dynamic approach will first return the original answer a, as it does not imply the disjunction of all potential secrets $pot\_sec\_disj = a \wedge b$. However, it returns a lie for the second query b. The static approach with the alternative database instance $db_{alt} = \{a, \neg b\}$ returns exactly the same answers.

Table 2. Answers for the query sequence $Q_2 = \langle b, a \rangle$

Query Φ_i	Dynamic Approach		Static Approach
	Answer ans_i	Log File log_i	Answer ans_i
b	b	$\{b\}$	$\neg b$
a	$\neg a$	$\{b, \neg a\}$	a

When we reverse the query sequence ($Q_2 = \langle b, a \rangle$, cf. Table 2), the static approach returns the same answers: First the lie $\neg b$, then the honest answer a. The dynamic approach however gives the honest answer b first, and then returns the lie $\neg a$. You can see that the dynamic approach uses the lies only as a last-minute action. Nevertheless, both approaches issue the same number of honest and dishonest answers, respectively.

Now imagine the user only issues a single query for b: $Q_3 = \langle b \rangle$. The dynamic approach returns the honest answer b, while the static approach returns the lie $\neg b$. This lie is not necessary to protect the potential secret $a \wedge b$. However, the static approach cannot know that the user will never ask for a, and cannot risk to omit the lie. In this situation, the dynamic approach offers a higher availability.

7 Extensions

The static inference control method presented in Section 5 resembles the dynamic uniform lying method of Controlled Query Evaluation, as summarized in Section 3, as well as the SAT-solver based approach from [5]. Hierarchical constraint networks however offer further possibilities, some of which we point out in this section, as a guideline for future work.

7.1 Explicit Availability Policy

A forthcoming extension of the SAT-solver based approach from [5] offers the ability to specify an explicit availability policy, namely a set $avail$ of sentences for which the system must always return the correct truth value, and which must not be used as a lie in order to protect one of the potential secrets. In the context of our static method, we demand that any sentence from $avail$ must have exactly the same truth value in db_{alt} as in the original instance db:

$$for\ each\ \alpha \in avail : eval(\alpha)(db_{alt}) = eval(\alpha)(db)$$

We can achieve this property by introducing another set of constraints

$$C_{avail} := \bigcup_{\alpha \in avail} \{eval^*(\alpha)(db)\}$$

which is merged into the set of required constraints H_0:

$$H_0 := C_{ps} \cup C_{prior} \cup C_{avail}.$$

The constraint solver will then ensure the desired property. In particular, it will fail to find a solution if the actual truth values of the sentences from *avail* in *db* contradict to the negation of the potential secrets. For example, *avail* = {*aids*} and *policy* = {*aids*} will be inconsistent in case *eval*(*aids*)(*db*) = *true*.

7.2   Multiple Levels of Potential Secrets

The basic approach from Section 5, as well as Definition 4, assumes that each potential secret has the same quality wrt. secrecy: The user may not infer *any* of the potential secrets.

Depending on the application, one could imagine to soften this requirement and establish a *hierarchy* of potential secrets: secrets that the user *must not* learn, secrets that the user *should not* learn, secrets that the user *should rather not* learn, etc. The confidentiality policy is split up into multiple subsets of potential secrets,

$$policy = policy_0 \cup policy_1 \cup policy_2 \cup \ldots \cup policy_l,$$

where $policy_0$ are the *strict potential secrets*, and the potential secrets from $policy_1, \ldots, policy_l$ are called *loose potential secrets*. Similar to (4), we construct a set C_{ps_i} of constraints for each $0 \le i \le l$:

$$C_{ps_i} := \bigcup_{\Psi \in policy_i} \{\neg\Psi\}$$

These constraints, together with C_{prior} and C_{db}, are organized in the constraint hierarchy $H = \{H_0, \ldots, H_{l+1}\}$ as follows: The constraints C_{ps_0} for the strict potential secrets remain in the set of required constraints:

$$H_0 := C_{ps_0} \cup C_{prior}$$

Each set of constraints C_{ps_i} corresponding to a set of loose potential secrets $policy_i$ $(1 \le i \le l)$ is assigned a level of its own:

$$H_i := C_{ps_i}$$

Finally, the constraints C_{db}, demanding a minimum distance to the original database, build the highest level:

$$H_{l+1} := C_{db}$$

It is important to choose a suitable *better* predicate (cf. Section 4) which reflects the desired relationship between the various levels of potential secrets. The $better_{globally}$ predicate (3) may be a good choice; however, it might be favorable to "trade" a non-protected potential secret on some level i against multiple protected potential secrets on a level $k > i$. This would not be possible with $better_{globally}$, and the administrator would have to choose a different predicate.

Alternatively, or in addition to multiple levels of potential secrets, it is also possible to assign a weight to each potential secret. In this case, a suitable g function underlying the $better_{globally}$ predicate (3) must be used which considers these weights. Some possible functions are given in [12].

7.3   Refusal

The present approach constructs an alternative database instance db_{alt} in which the truth values of certain atoms have been *changed* such that none of the potential secrets hold in db_{alt}. This corresponds to the concept of lying in dynamic inference control.

Alternatively, one could *erase* the truth values of particular atoms in order to protect the secret information. This can be easily achieved by allowing an additional value – say, *undef* – for each variable x in the constraint network. The resulting alternative database instance is *incomplete*: The value of certain sentences cannot be determined due to the missing truth values.

Of course, the user expects the answers to originate from a *complete* database. It is therefore not acceptable to disclose that certain information is missing in db_{alt}, and that a query Φ cannot be answered. A possible solution is to pick up the *refusal* approach from Controlled Query Evaluation [11]: In addition to Φ and $\neg\Phi$, we allow the special answer mum indicating a refused answer. Each time the alternative database instance db_{alt} cannot provide the answer to a query Φ, the system returns mum instead.

It is important to avoid harmful *meta inferences*: The user may not conclude from a refused answer that the secret information he might have asked for is actually true. For example, given $policy = \{a\}$ and $db = \{a, b\}$, the alternative database instance could be $db_{alt} = \{b\}$ (with the truth value of a removed). The query $\Phi = a$ will lead to a refusal. The user could then conclude that a must have been true in the original database instance.

To avoid such meta inferences, we must remove the truth value of the potential secret a even if it was *not* true in the original instance, for example in case $db' = \{\neg a, b\}$, which would then lead to the same alternative instance $db_{alt} = \{b\}$. Then, a refused answer does not provide any information about the original query value anymore.

8   Conclusion

We have presented a static approach for inference control in logic databases. The system is supported by a hierarchical constraint solver which generates an alternative database instance in which all confidential information has been replaced by harmless information. In general, this corresponds to the uniform lying approach of the (dynamic) Controlled Query Evaluation framework. In Section 6, we have shown that both approaches have advantages and drawbacks, and that maximum availability (measured by the number of distorted answers) can only be achieved by a dynamic approach, yet with a relatively high runtime complexity. This result justifies the employment of dynamic approaches when maximum availability is an issue.

The use of a constraint solver makes the construction of a suitable alternative database instance rather easy, as we can declaratively define the desired properties for that database instance (which generally correspond to the declarative properties demanded by Definition 4). While the basic static approach from

Section 5 only makes use of the fundamental abilities of hierarchical constraint networks, there are various options to exploit the remaining opportunities, some of which were presented in Section 7. These shall be further investigated in future work.

References

1. Farkas, C., Jajodia, S.: The inference problem: A survey. SIGKDD Explorations 4(2), 6–11 (2002)
2. Biskup, J., Bonatti, P.A.: Controlled query evaluation for enforcing confidentiality in complete information systems. International Journal of Information Security 3, 14–27 (2004)
3. Biskup, J., Bonatti, P.A.: Controlled query evaluation with open queries for a decidable relational submodel. In: Dix, J., Hegner, S.J. (eds.) FoIKS 2006. LNCS, vol. 3861, pp. 43–62. Springer, Heidelberg (2006)
4. Biskup, J., Weibert, T.: Keeping secrets in incomplete databases. Submitted, 2007. In: FCS 2005. Extended abstract presented at the LICS 2005 Affiliated Workshop on Foundations of Computer Security (2005), available from http://www.cs.chalmers.se/~andrei/FCS05/fcs05.pdf
5. Biskup, J., Wiese, L.: On finding an inference-proof complete database for controlled query evaluation. In: Damiani, E., Liu, P. (eds.) Data and Applications Security XX. LNCS, vol. 4127, pp. 30–43. Springer, Heidelberg (2006)
6. Apt, K.: Principles of Constraint Programming. Cambridge University Press, Cambridge (2003)
7. Frühwirth, T., Abdennadher, S.: Essentials of Constraint Programming. Springer, Heidelberg (2003)
8. Ahn, G.J., Sandhu, R.: Role-based authorization constraints specification. ACM Trans. Inf. Syst. Secur. 3(4), 207–226 (2000)
9. Jaeger, T.: On the increasing importance of constraints. In: RBAC 1999. Proceedings of the fourth ACM workshop on Role-based access control, pp. 33–42. ACM Press, New York (1999)
10. Moodahi, I., Gudes, E., Lavee, O., Meisels, A.: A secureworkflow model based on distributed constrained role and task assignment for the internet. In: Lopez, J., Qing, S., Okamoto, E. (eds.) ICICS 2004. LNCS, vol. 3269, pp. 171–186. Springer, Heidelberg (2004)
11. Biskup, J., Bonatti, P.A.: Lying versus refusal for known potential secrets. Data & Knowledge Engineering 38, 199–222 (2001)
12. Borning, A., Freeman-Benson, B.N., Wilson, M.: Constraint hierarchies. Lisp and Symbolic Computation 5(3), 223–270 (1992)

An Improved SCARE Cryptanalysis
Against a Secret A3/A8 GSM Algorithm

Christophe Clavier

Gemalto, Security Labs,
La Vigie, Avenue du Jujubier, ZI Athélia IV,
F-13705 La Ciotat Cedex, France
christophe.clavier@gemalto.com

Abstract. Side-channel analysis has been recognized for several years as a practical and powerful means to reveal secret keys of publicly known cryptographic algorithms. Rarely this kind of cryptanalysis has been applied to reverse engineer a non-trivial part of the specifications of a proprietary algorithm. The target here is no more one's secret key value but the undisclosed specifications of the cryptographic algorithm itself.

In [8], Novak described how to recover the content of one (out of two) substitution table of a secret instance of the A3/A8 algorithm, the authentication and session key generation algorithm for GSM networks. His attack presents however two drawbacks from a practical viewpoint. First, in order to retrieve one substitution table (T_2), the attacker must know the content of an other one (T_1). Second, the attacker must also know the value of the secret key K.

In this paper, we improve on Novak's cryptanalysis and show how to retrieve *both* substitution tables (T_1 and T_2) *without any prior knowledge about the secret key*. Furthermore, our attack also recovers the secret key.

With this contribution, we intend to present a practical SCARE (Side Channel Analysis for Reverse Engineering) attack, anticipate a growing interest for this new area of side-channel signal exploitation, and remind, if needed, that security cannot be achieved by obscurity alone.

Keywords: GSM Authentication, A3/A8, Reverse Engineering, Substitution Table, Side Channel Analysis.

1 Introduction

Secure implementations of cryptographic algorithms on security devices such as smart-cards have been carefully studied, particularly since side-channel attacks were initially proposed by P. Kocher [5]. This kind of attacks derive information about the execution of a sensitive algorithm, either from timing, power consumption or electromagnetic emanation measurements. The signal exploitation may range from simple observations, to more advanced statistical analyses. A simple observation allows distinguishing the rough structure of the algorithm — e.g. the number of round — or detecting the presence/absence of specific instructions or blocks of instructions. Statistical analyses come close to hypothesis testing, either by noise reduction averaging and enhancement of small signal contribution

P. McDaniel and S.K. Gupta (Eds.): ICISS 2007, LNCS 4812, pp. 143–155, 2007.
© Springer-Verlag Berlin Heidelberg 2007

for differential techniques (DPA, DEMA) [6,11], or by more global and robust model fitting for correlation-based analyses (CPA, CEMA) [1]. Though many flavours of these techniques have been proposed for several years, the target was inevitably the recovery of some sensitive user-related data (e.g., a private key).

In [8], Novak exploited side-channel leakage in order to obtain non-trivial details concerning the secret specifications of a block-cipher algorithm. The targeted algorithm is one of the many proprietary instances of the A3/A8 GSM authentication and session key generation algorithm. This opened a breach in a new kind of cryptanalytic attacks: the *Side-Channel Analysis for Reverse Engineering (SCARE) attacks*. Later, Daudigny *et al.* [3] also applied this technique to 'recover' the DES standard algorithm details.

Without disclosing any further details about the targeted algorithm than those found in [8], we present two improvements on Novak's attack. The attack described in Novak's paper recovers the entries of a secret substitution table T_2 from the knowledge of the other secret substitution table T_1 and the secret key K. The SCARE attacks we present in this paper allow to recover the entries of the two secret substitution tables and the secret key altogether from scratch. We therefore widen the applicability of this reverse engineering attack which may thus become more practical. Our attack confirms that security cannot be achieved by obscurity alone. This is even more true because of the SCARE attacks. The security level of proprietary cryptographic algorithms (i.e., with secret specifications) is usually lower than publicly scrutinized algorithms. As SCARE attacks may allow to disclose their secret specifications (substitution tables in our case), those algorithms are more likely at risk to succumb to classical cryptanalytic attacks.

The rest of this paper is organized as follows. In Section 2, we review the principles behind Novak's attack as well as its underlying assumptions. We then propose a graph interpretation of it, and discuss its theoretical feasibility. The next two sections describe our main contributions. Section 3 explains how to recover substitution table T_1 from the sole knowledge of secret key K and Section 4 explains how to do without the secret key knowledge. In Section 5, we discuss the threat of SCARE attacks and suggest practical counter-measures. We finally conclude this paper in Section 6.

2   Retrieving Table T_2 with Known Key K and Known Table T_1

2.1   Description of Novak's Attack

As for any GSM A3/A8 instance, the cryptographic algorithm attacked by Novak in [8] takes a 16-byte challenge $M = (m_0, \ldots, m_{15})$ and a 16-byte secret key $K = (k_0, \ldots, k_{15})$ on input, and produces a 32-bit message authentication code S_{RES} and a 64-bit voice ciphering session key K_C.

Novak's attack relies on three assumptions:

Assumption 1 (Observational). *The attacker is supposed to be able to detect by side-channel analysis whether intermediate values at two given points during the execution of the algorithm are the same.*

While not unrealistic, it may not be so obvious why and when this assumption should be verified in practice. As an illustrative example, this assumption is not verified when the device perfectly leaks according to the linear Hamming Weight model. In that case, two data with equal Hamming weights can not be distinguished from each other by side-channel observation. Nevertheless, we practically checked and confirmed that some experimental settings are compatible with Assumption 1. Indeed, it is possible to detect equality of intermediate results in the Hamming Distance model. This may be achieved by consolidating information of equal Hamming distances with respect to several reference states.

Note that this assumption has previously been used in [9] and [10] to devise collision-based side channel attacks in the classical *key recovery* context.

Assumption 2 (Prior structural knowledge). *The attacker is supposed to know the structure of the very beginning of the proposed target algorithm. Namely, he must know that the application of function f (as depicted in Figure 1) to each one of the pairs* $\{(m_i, k_i)\}_{i=0,\dots,15}$ *forms the very first layer of operations performed onto the input data.*

Note that in his goal to retrieve the value of the substitution table(s), the attacker does not need to know more about the structure of the algorithm. In particular, he does not need to know the number of rounds and (if applicable) the number of sub-rounds per round.[1], nor how is achieved the diffusion process in the algorithm.

Assumption 3 (Prior data knowledge). *In order to retrieve table* T_2, *the attacker is supposed to know the whole content of table* T_1 *and the secret key* K.

This last assumption is by far the main limitation in Novak's attack. In particular, it is hardly plausible that an attacker managed to get the content of T_1, and didn't know T_2. Furthermore, the required knowledge of the secret key constitutes an additional barrier.

In the sequel, *iteration i* refers to an application of f to a pair (m_i, k_i) in the first layer. An observation of two intermediate values for different iterations (resp. for the same iteration) is called a *cross-iteration* (resp. *intra-iteration*) observation.

Definition 1. *Let* $\mathcal{R}^{(2)}_{\alpha,\beta}$ *be the set of input pairs* (m_α, m'_β) *producing two identical values at point* P_2 *(cf. Figure 1) for iterations* α *and* β, *namely*

$$\mathcal{R}^{(2)}_{\alpha,\beta} = \{(m_\alpha, m'_\beta) : T_1(T_2(T_1(m_\alpha \oplus k_\alpha) \oplus m_\alpha)) \oplus (m_\alpha \oplus k_\alpha)$$
$$= T_1(T_2(T_1(m'_\beta \oplus k_\beta) \oplus m'_\beta)) \oplus (m'_\beta \oplus k_\beta)\}.$$

---

[1] A widely used and now public GSM algorithm, COMP128, owns a round structure divided in 5 similar sub-rounds.

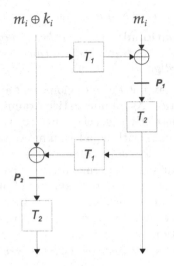

Fig. 1. Synopsis of function f

By Assumption 1, it is possible to collect the set of pairs

$$\mathcal{R}^{(2)} = \bigcup_{\alpha,\beta} \mathcal{R}^{(2)}_{\alpha,\beta}$$

for which an intermediate equality occurs at point P_2 in the first layer.

We note that, by incrementing all message bytes in parallel, only 256 invocations of the algorithm are needed to collect the set of pairs $\mathcal{R}^{(2)}$.

Each one of these pairs links two different entries of T_2 together by the equation:

$$T_1(T_2(x_\alpha)) \oplus T_1(T_2(x'_\beta)) = d \tag{1}$$

with

$$\begin{cases} x_\alpha = T_1(m_\alpha \oplus k_\alpha) \oplus m_\alpha \\ x'_\beta = T_1(m'_\beta \oplus k_\beta) \oplus m'_\beta \\ d = (m_\alpha \oplus k_\alpha) \oplus (m'_\beta \oplus k_\beta) \end{cases} \tag{2}$$

where x_α, x'_β and d are known from Assumption 3.

Each such relation gives the opportunity to link together (if not already done) two different T_2 entries. This decrements by one the degree of freedom (d.o.f.) of the table, that is, the number of remaining independent T_2 entries.

Once the d.o.f. of T_2 is reduced to 1, all T_2 entries may be infered from any of them, e.g. from $T_2(0)$. There so remain 256 possible candidates for the whole content of the table. The attacker may then identify the correct T_2 value by DPA-like [6] or CPA-like (correlation based) [1] techniques.

Alternatively, and only if he knows all other details of the algorithm, the attacker may also identify the correct T_2 value by a classical plaintext/ciphertext comparison. We stress that this knowledge is not mandatory for none of the attacks presented in this paper. Only the knowledge of the structure of the first layer (Assumption 2) is merely required to carry out the attacks.

2.2 Graph Interpretation

In this section, we propose an interpretation of the attack principle in terms of graph, discuss some implementation aspects, and present theoretical arguments for its feasibility.

Observing equal intermediate values at point P_2 links together, by parameter d, two T_2 entries with indices x and x'. This basic relationship suggests a graph interpretation of the current knowledge that the attacker acquired so far about the constraints on T_2.

The graph of constraints on T_2 is a labelled undirected graph $\mathcal{G}^{(2)}$ whose vertices are the indices of the different T_2 entries, and where an edge labelled d between two vertices x and x' (noted $x \overset{d}{\frown} x'$) means that $T_2(x)$ and $T_2(x')$ are linked together by the relation:

$$T_1(T_2(x)) \oplus T_1(T_2(x')) = d \ . \tag{3}$$

At the beginning of the attack, graph $\mathcal{G}^{(2)}$ contains no edge, each vertex from 0 to 255 being apart from each other. This means that each entry is a priori independent of all others (except for the fact that they are all different from each other since T_2 is a permutation). There are 256 different connected components, each containing only one vertex. The d.o.f. of T_2 is then also equal to 256.

Each time a relation like Equation (3) is to be exploited, the attacker connects vertices x and x' (if they were not) by a d-labelled edge. This results in a graph containing one less connected component. Note that the number of independent entries in T_2 (the d.o.f.) still remains equal to the number of connected components in $\mathcal{G}^{(2)}$.

Proposition 1 (Edge transitivity). *For any vertices x, x', x'', and any edge labels d_1 and d_2,*

$$x \overset{d_1}{\frown} x' \text{ and } x' \overset{d_2}{\frown} x'' \implies x \overset{d_1 \oplus d_2}{\frown} x'' \ .$$

Proof. This comes from the fact that

$$\big(T_1(T_2(x)) \oplus T_1(T_2(x'))\big) \oplus \big(T_1(T_2(x')) \oplus T_1(T_2(x''))\big) = T_1(T_2(x)) \oplus T_1(T_2(x''))$$

$$\square$$

This proposition shows that it is possible to ensure that each connected component of $\mathcal{G}^{(2)}$ is fully connected.

2.2.1 Practical Exploitation of Observations

From a practical viewpoint, a possible and memory-efficient way to manage and maintain the information contained in $\mathcal{G}^{(2)}$ is to define two 256-byte arrays, denoted comprep and delta, such that:

– comprep[x] represents an identifier of the connected component $comp(x)$ of x. By convention, it is defined as the least vertex belonging to $comp(x)$. This vertex may be thought of as the representative of $comp(x)$.

– delta[x] represents the d parameter of the relation linking the vertex x and the representative of $comp(x)$ (comprep[x]). In particular,

$$\forall x \in \mathcal{G}^{(2)}, \text{ delta}\big[\text{comprep}[x]\big] = 0.$$

The exploitation process of the relations starts with comprep $= \{0, 1, \ldots, 255\}$ and delta $= \{0, 0, \ldots, 0\}$, meaning that each vertex forms a connected component by itself, of which it is obviously the representative.

Each time a relation is exploited, function AddRelationToGraph(x, x', d) defined in Figure 2 is called and possibly modifies the graph structure by merging together the connected components of x and x', if they were distinct.

Input: $\mathcal{G}$ given by comprep and delta arrays

(x, x', d) an observational $x \overset{d}{\thicksim} x'$ relation

Output: $\mathcal{G}$ with $comp(x)$ and $comp(x')$ merged together

---

if (comprep[x] = comprep[x']) **then return** $\mathcal{G}$
if (comprep[x] > comprep[x']) **then** swap(x, x')
for all $y \in comp(x') \setminus \{x'\}$ **do**
    AddPointToGraph($x, y, d \oplus$ delta[x'] $\oplus$ delta[y])
endfor
AddPointToGraph(x, x', d)
return $\mathcal{G}$

Fig. 2. AddRelationToGraph(x, x', d) function

This operation both preserve the convention that comprep[x] is minimal in $comp(x)$, and the property induced by Proposition 1. It also ensures that all connected components are fully connected.

The process stops, either if there is no more relation to be exploited, or if the graph is fully connected which is detectable by the fact that comprep $= \{0, 0, \ldots, 0\}$. In this later case, delta contains all the information required to infer a possible candidate for T_2 from each possible value t_0 for its first element $T_2(0)$. The attack then succeeds.

Note that in the case of an unfinished attack, the number of possible candidates for T_2 rapidly grows with the number of remaining connected components in comprep (d.o.f.). This may become prohibitive if the number of remaining component is not small enough. This motivates the following study of the connectivity of $\mathcal{G}^{(2)}$ after having exploited all relations.

2.2.2   Resulting Connectivity of $\mathcal{G}^{(2)}$

We first evaluate the number of relations that may be collected for the attack when all possible message bytes are inputed at all possible iterations.

Input: $\mathcal{G}$ given by `comprep` and `delta` arrays
             (x, y, d) a $x \overset{d}{\frown} y$ relation
Output: $\mathcal{G}$ with y added to $comp(x)$

> **if** $(\texttt{comprep}[x] = \texttt{comprep}[y])$ **then return** $\mathcal{G}$
> $\texttt{comprep}[y] \leftarrow \texttt{comprep}[x]$
> $\texttt{delta}[y] \leftarrow \texttt{delta}[x] \oplus d$
>
> **return** $\mathcal{G}$

Fig. 3. $\texttt{AddPointToGraph}(x, y, d)$ function

For any given secret key $K = (k_0, \ldots, k_{15})$, let

$$l_K = \mathrm{Card}(\{k_i\}_{i=0\ldots15})$$

denote the number of distinct bytes of K. Let also $g(m, k)$ denote the value at point P_2 when m and k are the input bytes to the function f.

For each possible intermediate value $z \in \{0 \ldots 255\}$ at point P_2, we also define $\mathcal{S}_K(z)$ as the set of all preimages (m, k) of z at some iteration:

$$\mathcal{S}_K(z) = \{(m, k) : k = k_i \text{ for some } i, \text{ and } g(m, k) = z\}.$$

Finally, let $s_K(z) = \mathrm{Card}(\mathcal{S}_K(z))$.

Each pair $\big((m_\alpha, k_\alpha), (m'_\beta, k_\beta)\big)$ of elements of $\mathcal{S}_K(z)$ induces a local collision at point P_2. According to Equation (2), the corresponding pair (x_α, x'_β) of T_2 inputs forms an edge to be added to the graph of constraints on T_2. The number of such edges for a given z is $\binom{s_K(z)}{2}$ but many of them can be deduced from others due to the transitivity property (Proposition 1). As these edges must not be counted as new relations, the number of independant edges brought by $\mathcal{S}_K(z)$ to the graph $\mathcal{G}^{(2)}$ is only $s_K(z) - 1$.[2] The total number of such edges amounts to

$$n_K = \sum_{z=0}^{255}(s_K(z) - 1) = 256 \cdot l_K - 256 = 256 \cdot (l_K - 1).$$

Assuming that $g(m, k)$ behaves like a random function, sets

$$\{x = T_1(m \oplus k) \oplus m : (m, k) \in \mathcal{S}_K(z)\}_z$$

behave like random samples of vertices, and the evolution of $\mathcal{G}^{(2)}$ can be modeled as a random graph process.

This kind of structure and the evolution of its components have been deeply studied in graph theory. An asymptotic result from P. Erdős and A. Rnyi [4] states that a random graph with n vertices and $m \sim \frac{1}{2} n \log n$ random edges is almost certainly connected when $n \to \infty$.

---

[2] We neglect the very unlikely case when $s(z) = 0$.

For $n = 256$, the graph is connected once it contains $m \approx 710$ edges. Given that ([7])

$$\Pr(l_K = t) = \left\{ {16 \atop t} \right\} \frac{\prod_{k=0}^{15}(256 - k)}{256^{16}}$$

where $\left\{ {16 \atop t} \right\}$ denotes the Stirling number of the second kind, we have

$$\Pr(l_K \geqslant 13) = \Pr(n_K \geqslant 3072) \geqslant 0.999.$$

This states that there are much more relations than needed for $\mathcal{G}^{(2)}$ to be connected. We confirmed this fact by many simulations with random permutations T_1 and T_2 where it appears that the exploitation of only intra-iteration relations is always sufficient to end up with a fully connected graph.

3   Retrieving Table T_1 with Known Key K

The attack presented in [8] assumes the ability to detect equalities of intermediate results at point P_2; the exploitation of such local collisions makes it possible to recover T_2.

In this section, we present a similar method that allows to recover T_1 by observing equalities of intermediate results at point P_1 (see Figure 1).

Compared to Novak's attack, our attack relies on the same observational and structural prior knowledge assumptions (Assumptions 1 and 2). But the prior data knowledge assumption (Assumption 3) is weakened and replaced with the following one:

Assumption 3' ([Weakened] prior data knowledge). *In order to retrieve table T_1, the attacker is supposed to know secret key K. (Knowledge of T_2 is not needed.)*

Definition 2. *Let $\mathcal{R}_{\alpha,\beta}^{(1)}$ be the set of input pairs (m_α, m'_β) producing two identical values at point P_1 (cf. Figure 1) for iterations α and β, namely*

$$\mathcal{R}_{\alpha,\beta}^{(1)} = \left\{ (m_\alpha, m'_\beta) : T_1(m_\alpha \oplus k_\alpha) \oplus m_\alpha = T_1(m'_\beta \oplus k_\beta) \oplus m'_\beta \right\}.$$

Similarly to Section 2.1, each pair $(m_\alpha, m'_\beta) \in \mathcal{R}_{\alpha,\beta}^{(1)}$ links two different entries of T_1 together by the equation:

$$T_1(x_\alpha) \oplus T_1(x'_\beta) = d \tag{4}$$

with

$$\begin{cases} x_\alpha = m_\alpha \oplus k_\alpha \\ x'_\beta = m'_\beta \oplus k_\beta \\ d = m_\alpha \oplus m'_\beta \end{cases} . \tag{5}$$

Here again, parameters x_α, x'_β and d are known by the attacker (Assumption 3').

We make a specific remark concerning this case:

Proposition 2. $\forall \alpha, \beta \in \{0, \ldots, 15\}$, we have[3] $\mathcal{R}_{\beta,\beta}^{(1)} = \mathcal{R}_{\alpha,\alpha}^{(1)} \oplus (k_\alpha \oplus k_\beta)$.

Proof. $\forall m, m' \in \{0, \ldots, 255\}$, we have

$$
\begin{aligned}
(m, m') \in \mathcal{R}_{\alpha,\alpha}^{(1)} \iff & T_1(m \oplus k_\alpha) \oplus m = T_1(m' \oplus k_\alpha) \oplus m' \\
\iff & T_1\big((m \oplus (k_\alpha \oplus k_\beta)) \oplus k_\beta\big) \oplus (m \oplus (k_\alpha \oplus k_\beta)) \\
& = T_1\big((m' \oplus (k_\alpha \oplus k_\beta)) \oplus k_\beta\big) \oplus (m' \oplus (k_\alpha \oplus k_\beta)) \\
\iff & (m \oplus (k_\alpha \oplus k_\beta), m' \oplus (k_\alpha \oplus k_\beta)) \in \mathcal{R}_{\beta,\beta}^{(1)} \\
\iff & (m, m') \oplus (k_\alpha \oplus k_\beta) \in \mathcal{R}_{\beta,\beta}^{(1)} \ . \qquad \square
\end{aligned}
$$

This implies for the attacker that information about T_1 brought by the whole relation set $\mathcal{R}_{\alpha,\alpha}^{(1)}$ is the same as the one brought by each other $\mathcal{R}_{\beta,\beta}^{(1)}$. Thus, it is worth exploiting only one of the 16 intra-iteration relation sets. Hopefully, such a remark does not apply to cross-iteration relation sets. Each one of the cross-iteration relation sets is *a priori* informative. Compared to the case where the attacker retrieves T_2 by observing at point P_2, the number of relation sets to be exploited is reduced from $16 + \binom{16}{2} = 136$ to $1 + \binom{16}{2} = 121$. This does not represent a noticeable penalty to carry out the attack.

The exploitation process of the relations is the same as in Section 2.

The graph $\mathcal{G}^{(1)}$ of constraints on T_1 gathers all edges $x \overset{d}{\sim} x'$ where $T_1(x)$ and $T_1(x')$ are linked together by the relation:

$$
T_1(x) \oplus T_1(x') = d. \tag{6}
$$

The discussion about the connectivity of $\mathcal{G}^{(1)}$ is essentially the same as in Section 2.2.2 — $g(m, k)$ being defined as the value at point P_1, and vertices x being equal to $m \oplus k$ instead of $T_1(m \oplus k) \oplus m$.

$\mathcal{G}^{(1)}$ is still modeled as a random graph, but there are slightly less available random edges due to Proposition 2. Nevertheless, simulations confirmed that this number of observed relations is still large enough to carry out the attack successfully.

4   Retrieving Table T_1 Without Knowing the Key

In the case where he does not know secret key $K = (k_0, \ldots, k_{15})$, the attacker can make guesses about its successive bytes.

By making a guess g_0 about k_0, the attacker is able to exploit relations belonging to $\mathcal{R}_{0,0}^{(1)}$. More generally, by making a guess $g_t = (g_0, \ldots, g_{t-1})$ about the first t bytes $k_t = (k_0, \ldots, k_{t-1})$ of the key, the attacker is able to exploit all relations in

$$
\mathcal{R}_t^{(1)} \triangleq \bigcup_{0 \leqslant \alpha, \beta < t} \mathcal{R}_{\alpha,\beta}^{(1)} \ .
$$

---

[3] By abuse of notations, for a vector x and a scalar δ, $x \oplus \delta$ means that each component of x is $\oplus$-ed with δ, i.e., if $x = (x_0, \ldots, x_t)$ then $x \oplus \delta = (y_0, \ldots, y_t)$ with $y_i = x_i \oplus \delta$.

For any guess g_t, let $\mathcal{G}^{(1)}(g_t)$ denote the graph of constraints on T_1 after having exploited all relations in $\mathcal{R}_t^{(1)}$, and assuming that $k_t = g_t$.

Graph $\mathcal{G}^{(1)}(g_t)$ is said to be *inconsistent* whenever the edge transitivity property (Proposition 1) is not verified; otherwise, it is said to be *consistent*. For any incorrect guess g_t, the odds for graph $\mathcal{G}^{(1)}(g_t)$ to be inconsistent increase with t. This suggests an in-width first searching algorithm to retrieve T_1.

Let $\mathcal{C}_t$ denote the set of all guesses g_t (together with their corresponding graph $\mathcal{G}^{(1)}(g_t)$) for which $\mathcal{G}^{(1)}(g_t)$ is consistent. At depth $t + 1$, when guessing byte k_t with each possible value g_t, each graph $\mathcal{G}^{(1)}(g_t)$ in $\mathcal{C}_t$ is further constrained with all relations in $\mathcal{R}_{t+1}^{(1)} \setminus \mathcal{R}_t^{(1)}$. Provided that it is still consistent, each such updated graph $\mathcal{G}^{(1)}(g_{t+1})$ is then stored (together with g_{t+1}) in $\mathcal{C}_{t+1}$.

Before going further, we give a slight generalization of Definition 2:

Definition 2'. *For any given k, let $\mathcal{R}_{\alpha,\beta}^{(1)}(k)$ be the set of input pairs (m_α, m'_β) producing two identical values at point P_1 for iterations α and β, when the secret key is k.*

Proposition 3. $\forall \alpha, \beta \in \{0, \dots, 15\}, \forall \delta \in \{0, \dots, 255\}$, *we have*

$$\mathcal{R}_{\alpha,\beta}^{(1)}(k \oplus \delta) = \mathcal{R}_{\alpha,\beta}^{(1)}(k) \oplus \delta \ .$$

Proof. $\forall m, m' \in \{0, \dots, 255\}$, we have

$$
\begin{aligned}
(m, m') \in \mathcal{R}_{\alpha,\beta}^{(1)}(k) &\iff T_1(m \oplus k_\alpha) \oplus m = T_1(m' \oplus k_\beta) \oplus m' \\
&\iff T_1\big((m \oplus \delta) \oplus (k_\alpha \oplus \delta)\big) \oplus (m \oplus \delta) \\
&\qquad = T_1\big((m' \oplus \delta) \oplus (k_\beta \oplus \delta)\big) \oplus (m' \oplus \delta) \\
&\iff (m \oplus \delta, m' \oplus \delta) \in \mathcal{R}_{\alpha,\beta}^{(1)}(k \oplus \delta) \\
&\iff (m, m') \oplus \delta \in \mathcal{R}_{\alpha,\beta}^{(1)}(k \oplus \delta) \ . \qquad \square
\end{aligned}
$$

Given that each T_1 entry $x = m \oplus k$ linearly depends on m, Proposition 3 implies the existence of equivalence classes of pairs (table, key). For any δ, the same set of observed relations may suggest a given value for T_1 if the secret key is k, as well as a table deduced from the previous one by XOR-ing its indices with δ if the secret key is $k \oplus \delta$.

The consequence of this is twofold. First, exploiting equalities of intermediate values at point P_1 will, at best, disclose the value of T_1 up to its first element (as in the previously described attacks), but also up to a XOR of its indices with a constant δ. Second, if a secret key k is compatible with observations then each secret key $k \oplus \delta$ is also compatible.

Taking these properties into account, the algorithm described above must be modified in that only one guess about k_0 (say $g_0 = 0$) needs to be considered. The rest of the algorithm remains unchanged.

Note that without any refutation of guesses which reveal their graph as inconsistent, the number of guesses to be considered would increase exponentially with the depth t. Thus, one may wonder whether this in-width search process indeed requires a prohibitive number of guesses g_t to be considered, or if incorrect guesses prove themselves to be inconsistent so rapidly that the attack becomes practicable.

Here again, simulations of this in-width guessing process showed that the recovery of the relative value of T_1 (up to a XOR of entries with $T_1(0)$, and up to a XOR of indices with $\delta = k_0$) is actually effective. At depth $t = 2$, only few (often less than 20) incorrect guesses remain alive, and for $t = 3$ or 4 only the graph of the correct relative guess (up to k_0) usually remains consistent. At that point, the relative value of T_1 is already known, but the attacker may choose to continue this process and exploit relations implying successive iterations in order to retrieve the remaining (relative) bytes of the secret key.

Finally, the relative values of T_1 and K are retrieved, and the attacker only needs to identify by DPA-like or CPA-like techniques (2^{16} candidates about T_1) which $(T_1(0), k_0)$ defines their correct absolute values.

We explained how an attacker may proceed to recover T_1 and K from no particular prior data knowledge. This step may then be followed by the basic Novak's attack in order to retrieve T_2 as well.

5   Counter-Measures

By enhancing Novak's work, the attacks presented in the previous sections make it possible to recover the two substitution tables of a secret algorithm. The exposure of such design details represents a threat at *system level* — as opposed to the *user level* threat in a classical key recovery scenario. As the attacks need to be performed only once, the secrecy of the algorithm specifications directly relates to the protection offered by the *weakest available product* implementing this A3/A8 GSM algorithm.

Fortunately, there are counter-measures preventing our attacks. Side-channel leakage may be reduced via hardware features (including current scrambler or dual-rail logic). Time randomization may be introduced by hardware (e.g., dummy cycles) or software (e.g., random delays) means, making harder the comparison of waveforms at specific points. Finally, masking all intermediate values, which is a classical counter-measure against statistical analysis, should efficiently thwart our attacks, provided that the randomization is refreshed at every iteration. We point the synergy provided by the combination of these protections, each one making it difficult to bypass each other. Provided that such counter-measures are properly implemented, the observational assumption (Assumption 1) do not stand anymore, and the attacker is defeated.

6   Conclusion

A SCARE attack presented in [8] allows an attacker to recover the value of a substitution table T_2 which is part of the secret specifications of a GSM A3/A8 authentication and session key generation algorithm.

We proposed a graph interpretation of this attack and proved, under the random graph model, that the set of relations collectible by side-channel observation is large enough to infer the whole table up to its first element.

Noticing that this first attack needs the knowledge of another substitution table T_1 used in this algorithm as well as the knowledge of the secret key K (Assumption 3), we presented a similar way to retrieve T_1 from the sole knowledge of secret key K. We then improved this later attack to recover T_1 without even knowing secret key K, which is also recovered as a by-product.

Our proposed attacks have been validated by simulation. Providing that the observational assumption (Assumption 1) discussed in [8], and a weak prior structural knowledge assumption (Assumption 2) are satisfied, our last attack allows to recover both substitution tables T_1 and T_2 (as well as secret key K), without additional prior data knowledge.

We stress that, unlike classical attack scenarii in which the target is usually one's cryptographic secret key, SCARE attacks are *one-shot attacks* in that they jeopardize the specifications of the algorithm once for all. Should these specifications be publicized, a further analysis by cryptography researchers may then reveal potential design flaws which will in turn threat all users within the system. The security of a system being that of its weakest link, this type of attacks demonstrates the need for a *generalization* of carefully designed implementations. Also, and despite the progressive replacement of GSM algorithms with open standards such as KASUMI and AES in 3G networks, our work illustrates once again the need to depart from the *security by obscurity alone* paradigm.

We hope that this contribution, together with [3] and [8], will open new perspectives for side-channel analysis applied to reverse engineering.

Acknowledgements

The authors would like to thank the anonymous referees for their useful remarks.

The work described in this document has been financially supported by the European Commission through the IST Program under Contract IST-2002-507932 ECRYPT.

References

1. Brier, E., Clavier, C., Olivier, F.: Correlation Power Analysis with a Leakage Model. In: Joye, M., Quisquater, J.-J. (eds.) CHES 2004. LNCS, vol. 3156, pp. 16–29. Springer, Heidelberg (2004)
2. Chari, S., Jutla, C.S., Rao, J.R., Rohatgi, P.: Towards sound approaches to counteract power-analysis attacks. In: Wiener, M.J. (ed.) CRYPTO 1999. LNCS, vol. 1666, pp. 398–412. Springer, Heidelberg (1999)
3. Daudigny, R., Ledig, H., Muller, F., Valette, F.: SCARE of the DES. In: Ioannidis, J., Keromytis, A.D., Yung, M. (eds.) ACNS 2005. LNCS, vol. 3531, pp. 393–406. Springer, Heidelberg (2005)
4. Erdös, P., Rnyi, A.: On the evolution of random graphs, Magyar Tud. Akad. Mat. Kut. Int. Kzl. 5, 17–61 (1960)

5. Kocher, P.: Timing attacks on implementations of Diffie-Hellman, RSA, DSS, and other systems. In: Koblitz, N. (ed.) CRYPTO 1996. LNCS, vol. 1109, pp. 104–113. Springer, Heidelberg (1996)
6. Kocher, P., Jaffe, J., Jun, B.: Differential power analysis. In: Wiener, M.J. (ed.) CRYPTO 1999. LNCS, vol. 1666, pp. 388–397. Springer, Heidelberg (1999)
7. Menezes, A.J., van Oorschot, P.C., Vanstone, S.A.: Handbook of applied cryptography. CRC Press, Boca Raton (1997)
8. Novak, R.: Side-Channel Attack on Substitution Blocks. In: Zhou, J., Yung, M., Han, Y. (eds.) ACNS 2003. LNCS, vol. 2846, pp. 307–318. Springer, Heidelberg (2003)
9. Schramm, K., Leander, G., Felke, P., Paar, C.: A Collision-Attack on AES Combining Side Channel- and Differential-Attack. In: Joye, M., Quisquater, J.-J. (eds.) CHES 2004. LNCS, vol. 3156, pp. 163–175. Springer, Heidelberg (2004)
10. Schramm, K., Wollinger, T., Paar, C.: A New Class of Collision Attacks and its Application to DES. In: Johansson, T. (ed.) FSE 2003. LNCS, vol. 2887, pp. 206–222. Springer, Heidelberg (2003)
11. Quisquater, J-J., Samyde, D.: A new tool for non-intrusive analysis of smart cards based on electro-magnetic emissions, the SEMA and DEMA methods. In: Preneel, B. (ed.) EUROCRYPT 2000. LNCS, vol. 1807, pp. 14–18. Springer, Heidelberg (2000)

Cryptanalysis and the Improvement of Kim et al.'s Password Authentication Schemes

Debasis Giri and P.D. Srivastava

Department of Mathematics
Indian Institute of Technology, Kharagpur 721 302, India
{dgiri, pds}@maths.iitkgp.ernet.in

Abstract. In 1999, Yang and Shieh proposed two authentication schemes with smart cards, one is timestamp-based password authentication scheme and other is nonce-based password authentication scheme. In 2002, Chan and Cheng pointed out that Yang and Shieh's timestamp-based password authentication scheme is insecure to vulnerable forgery attack. Further, in 2003, Sun and Yeh showed that Yang and Shieh's both schemes are insecure to vulnerable forgery attack. In 2005, Yang et al. proposed the improvement of Yang and Shieh's password authentication schemes to withstand Sun and Yeh's forgery attack. In 2005, Kim et al. pointed out the security weaknesses to forgery attacks on Yang et al.'s schemes and they further proposed the improvement of Yang et al.'s schemes in order to resist their attacks. In this paper, we show that the Kim et al.'s password authentication schemes have security weaknesses to forgery attacks. Further, we propose the improvement of Kim et al.'s schemes in order to eliminate these weaknesses.

Keywords: Authentication, Smart card, Attack, Timestamp, Nonce.

1 Introduction

In a remote user authentication scheme, a remote user can be authenticated by the remote server over a public channel. In 1981, Lamport [1] first proposed a well-known hash-based password authentication scheme to authenticate a remote user by a remote server over an insecure channel. His scheme resists replay attack, but it requires a verification (password) table to verify the legitimacy of a login user. In 2000, Hwang and Li [2] pointed out that Lamport's scheme [1] has weaknesses such as the risk to modify the password table and the cost of managing and protecting the table. After his scheme, several authentication schemes [3,4,5,6] have been proposed. In 1999, Yang and Shieh proposed two password authentication schemes [7] with smart cards which are the timestamp-based and the nonce-based authentication schemes. In 2002, Chan and Cheng [8] pointed out that Yang and Shieh's timestamp-based password authentication scheme [7] is insecure to vulnerable forgery attack. Further, in 2003, Sun and Yeh [9] showed that Yang and Shieh's password schemes [7] are insecure to vulnerable forgery attack. In 2005, Yang et al. [10] proposed the improvement of Yang and Shieh's password based authentication schemes [7] to withstand the forgery

P. McDaniel and S.K. Gupta (Eds.): ICISS 2007, LNCS 4812, pp. 156–166, 2007.

attack of Sun and Yeh [9]. In 2005, Kim et al. [11] found the security weaknesses to forgery attacks on Yang et al.'s schemes [10] and then they proposed the improvement of Yang et al.'s schemes to resist their forgery attacks. In this paper, we demonstrate that the Kim et al.'s password authentication schemes [11] have security weaknesses to forgery attacks. Further, we propose the improvement of Kim et al.'s schemes in order to eliminate these weaknesses.

The remainder of this paper is organized as follows. Section 2 briefly reviews the Kim et al.'s schemes [11]. Section 3 shows the security weaknesses of Kim et al.'s password authentication schemes. In Section 4, we describe our improved schemes. We provide the security analysis for our schemes in Section 5. Finally, Section 6 concludes the paper.

2   Brief Review of Kim et al.'s Schemes

In this section, we briefly review the Kim et al.'s schemes [11], one is timestamp-based password authentication scheme and other is nonce-based password authentication scheme.

2.1   Timestamp-Based Password Authentication Scheme

It consists of three phases, namely, *registration, login* and *verification* phases.

[Registration phase]
If a user U_i wants to register, he first transmits his identity ID_i and password PW_i to the key information center (KIC) by a secure channel. On receiving the registration request, the KIC performs the following operations:

- *Step-1:* Choose two large primes p and q and compute their product as $n = pq$.
- *Step-2:* Choose a prime e as public parameter, where $1 < e < (p-1)(q-1)$ and then compute secret key d as $d = e^{-1} \bmod (p-1)(q-1)$.
- *Step-3:* Choose g as a primitive element on both $GF(p)$ and $GF(q)$, where g is public parameter and $GF(p)$ stands for the Galois field over prime p.
- *Step-4:* Generate a smart card's identifier CID_i, and compute $S_i = ID_i^{CID_i \cdot d} \bmod n$ and $h_i = g^{PW_i \cdot d} \bmod n$.
- *Step-5:* Load the parameters $(n, e, g, ID_i, CID_i, S_i, h_i)$ into the memory of smart card and issue it for U_i.

[Login phase]
If a user U_i wants to login to the KIC, he first inserts his card into a card reader and then submits his identity ID_i and password PW_i. Then, the smart card performs the following steps:

- *Step-1:* Generate a random number r_i.
- *Step-2:* Compute $X_i = g^{PW_i \cdot r_i \cdot e} \bmod n$ and $Y_i = h_i^{r_i} \cdot S_i^T \bmod n$, where T is the current login timestamp.

- *Step-3:* Transmit the login request message $M = \langle ID_i, CID_i, X_i, Y_i, n, e, g, T \rangle$ to the KIC.

[Authentication phase]
On receiving the login message $M = \langle ID_i, CID_i, X_i, Y_i, n, e, g, T \rangle$ at the timestamp T^*, the KIC authenticates the user U_i as follows.

- *Step-1:* Check the validity of ID_i and CID_i. If any one of these two is invalid, the KIC rejects the login request; otherwise go to Step-2.
- *Step-2:* Verify the validity of the time interval between T^* and T. If $T^* - T < \Delta T$, go to Step-3; otherwise the KIC rejects it. ΔT denotes the expected valid time interval for transmission delay.
- *Step-3:* Check whether

$$Y_i^e = X_i^d \cdot ID_i^{CID_i \cdot T} \bmod n. \tag{1}$$

If the above equality holds good, the KIC accepts the login request message; otherwise the KIC rejects it.

2.2   Nonce-Based Password Authentication Scheme

This scheme consists of three phases, namely, *login, registration* and *authentication* phases.

[Registration phase]
This phase is same as registration phase of Kim et al.'s timestamp-based password authentication scheme described in Subsection 2.1.

[Login phase]
If a user U_i wants to login to the KIC, he first inserts his card into a card reader and then submits his identity ID_i and password PW_i. Then, the smart card and the KIC perform the following steps:

- *Step-1:* The smart card transmits the login request message $M_1 = \langle ID_i, CID_i \rangle$ to the KIC.
- *Step-2:* On receiving M_1, the KIC checks the validity of both ID_i and CID_i. If any one of these is invalid, the KIC rejects it. Otherwise, the KIC computes a nonce $N = f(r_j)$ and sends it to the smart card, where r_j is a random number and $f(\cdot)$ is a one-way hash function and go to Step-3.
- *Step-3:* After receiving N, the smart card generates a random number r_i and computes $X_i = g^{PW_i \cdot r_i \cdot e} \bmod n$ and $Y_i = h_i^{r_i} \cdot S_i^N \bmod n$.
- *Step-4:* The smart card then transmits the message $M_2 = \langle X_i, Y_i, n, e, g \rangle$ to the KIC.

[Authentication phase]
On receiving the login request message M_2, the KIC verify the validity of the condition $Y_i^e = X_i^d \cdot ID_i^{CID_i \cdot N} \bmod n$. If the condition is valid, the KIC accepts the login request message; otherwise the KIC rejects it.

3   Cryptanalysis of Kim et al.'s Password Authentication Schemes

In this section, we show two possible attacks on Kim et al.'s timestamp-based password authentication scheme [11]. The details of the attacks are outlined as follows.

Attack-1

In this attack, we show that without stolen a smart card of a user, say, U_i, an adversary can create a forged login request message for any timestamp T^*. Let us consider an adversary $\mathcal{A}$ traps two valid login request messages $M^{[1]} = \langle ID_i,$ $CID_i,\ X_i^{[1]},\ Y_i^{[1]},\ n, e, g, T^{[1]} \rangle$ and $M^{[2]} = \langle ID_i,\ CID_i,\ X_i^{[2]},\ Y_i^{[2]},\ n, e, g, T^{[2]} \rangle$ from the transaction records sent by a user U_i to the KIC over a public channel such that $\gcd(T^{[1]}, T^{[2]}) = 1$. Then, the following steps need to be executed by the adversary $\mathcal{A}$ in order to generate a valid login request message for any timestamp T^*.

- *Step-1:* Choose two integers a and b such that $aT^{[1]} + bT^{[2]} = 1$.
- *Step-2:* Compute $Y_i^* = ((Y_i^{[1]})^a \cdot (Y_i^{[2]})^b)^{T^*} \bmod n$, where $Y_i^{[1]} = h_i^{r_i^{[1]}} \cdot S_i^{T^{[1]}} \bmod n$ and $Y_i^{[2]} = h_i^{r_i^{[2]}} \cdot S_i^{T^{[2]}} \bmod n$.
- *Step-3:* Compute $X_i^* = ((X_i^{[1]})^a \cdot (X_i^{[2]})^b)^{T^*} \bmod n$, where $X_i^{[1]} = g^{PW_i \cdot r_i^{[1]} \cdot e} \bmod n$ and $X_i^{[2]} = g^{PW_i \cdot r_i^{[2]} \cdot e} \bmod n$.
- *Step-4:* Transmit the login request message $M^* = \langle\ ID_i, CID_i, X_i^*,\ Y_i^*,\ n, e, g, T^* \rangle$ to the KIC.

On receiving M^*, according to the Kim et al.'s protocol, the KIC first checks the validity of ID_i, CID_i and $(T' - T^*)$, where T' is the current timestamp of the KIC's machine. Obviously, ID_i and CID_i are valid. In case, to check the validity of $(T' - T^*)$, one should have $(T' - T^*) < \triangle T$. By guessing the value of T', $\mathcal{A}$ can choose T^* in such a fashion that $T' - T^* < \triangle T$ holds. As a result, $T' - T^*$ is valid. Now, we prove that the authentication condition in Eqn. (1) is true, which is shown below. We have,

$$
\begin{aligned}
Y_i^* &= ((Y_i^{[1]})^a \cdot (Y_i^{[2]})^b)^{T^*} \bmod n \\
&= (h_i^{r_i^{[1]}} \cdot S_i^{T^{[1]}})^{a \cdot T^*} \cdot (h_i^{r_i^{[2]}} \cdot S_i^{T^{[2]}})^{b \cdot T^*} \bmod n \\
&= (g^{PW_i \cdot d \cdot r_i^{[1]}} \cdot ID_i^{CID_i \cdot d \cdot T^{[1]}})^{a \cdot T^*} \cdot (g^{PW_i \cdot d \cdot r_i^{[2]}} \cdot ID_i^{CID_i \cdot d \cdot T^{[2]}})^{b \cdot T^*} \bmod n \\
&= g^{PW_i \cdot d \cdot (a \cdot r_i^{[1]} + b \cdot r_i^{[2]}) \cdot T^*} \cdot ID_i^{CID_i \cdot d \cdot (a \cdot T^{[1]} + b \cdot T^{[2]}) \cdot T^*} \bmod n \\
&= g^{PW_i \cdot d \cdot (a \cdot r_i^{[1]} + b \cdot r_i^{[2]}) \cdot T^*} \cdot ID_i^{CID_i \cdot d \cdot T^*} \bmod n, \quad [\text{as}\ \ a \cdot T^{[1]} + b \cdot T^{[2]} = 1\ ]
\end{aligned}
$$
$$(2)$$

and

$$
X_i^* = ((X_i^{[1]})^a \cdot (X_i^{[2]})^b)^{T^*} \bmod n
$$

$$= (X_i^{[1]})^{a \cdot T^*} \cdot (X_i^{[2]})^{b \cdot T^*} \bmod n$$
$$= (g^{PW_i \cdot r_i^{[1]} \cdot e})^{a \cdot T^*} \cdot (g^{PW_i \cdot r_i^{[2]} \cdot e})^{b \cdot T^*} \bmod n$$
$$= g^{PW_i \cdot (a \cdot r_i^{[1]} + b \cdot r_i^{[2]}) \cdot e \cdot T^*} \bmod n. \tag{3}$$

Now, from Eqn. (2) and Eqn. (3), we obtain

$$(Y_i^*)^e = g^{PW_i \cdot (a \cdot r_i^{[1]} + b \cdot r_i^{[2]}) \cdot T^*} \cdot ID_i^{CID_i \cdot T^*} \bmod n$$
$$= (g^{PW_i \cdot (a \cdot r_i^{[1]} + b \cdot r_i^{[2]}) \cdot T^* \cdot e})^d \cdot ID_i^{CID_i \cdot T^*} \bmod n$$
$$= (X_i^*)^d \cdot ID_i^{CID_i \cdot T^*} \bmod n. \tag{4}$$

Therefore, the forged login request message $\mathcal{M}^*$ satisfies the validity of authentication of the KIC. Hence, $\mathcal{A}$ can impersonate as a valid user to login to the KIC. Similarly, this attack can readily be extended to the Kim et al.'s nonce-based password authentication scheme.

Attack-2

Let an adversary $\mathcal{A}$ intercept a login request message $\mathcal{M} = \langle\, ID_i, CID_i, X_i, Y_i, n, e, g, T \,\rangle$ sent by a user U_i to the KIC over a public channel. In order to create a forged login request message, the adversary $\mathcal{A}$ performs the following steps.

- *Step-1:* Choose a number $R, 1 < R < n-1$, and compute $X_i' = X_i \cdot R^{e^2} \bmod n$ and $Y_i' = Y_i \cdot R \bmod n$.
- *Step-2:* Transmit $\mathcal{M}' = \langle\, ID_i, CID_i, X_i', Y_i', n, e, g, T \,\rangle$ to the KIC.

On receiving $\mathcal{M}'$, the KIC verifies the validity of the condition $(Y_i')^e = (X_i')^d \cdot ID_i^{CID_i \cdot T} \bmod n$. Now, we prove that this condition is true, which is shown below:

$$(Y_i')^e = (Y_i \cdot R)^e \bmod n$$
$$= Y_i^e \cdot R^e \bmod n$$
$$= (X_i^d \cdot ID_i^{CID_i \cdot T}) \cdot R^e \bmod n \quad \text{[Using Eqn. (1)]}$$
$$= (X_i^d \cdot R^e) \cdot ID_i^{CID_i \cdot T} \bmod n$$
$$= (X_i \cdot R^{e^2})^d \cdot ID_i^{CID_i \cdot T} \bmod n$$
$$= (X_i')^d \cdot ID_i^{CID_i \cdot T} \bmod n.$$

Hence, the login request message $\mathcal{M}'$ satisfies the validity of authentication of the KIC. Thus, $\mathcal{A}$ can impersonate as a valid user to create forged login request message to the KIC. Similarly, this attack can be mounted on Kim et al.'s nonce-based password authentication scheme.

4   Our Improved Schemes

In this section, we propose the improvement of Kim et al.'s schemes [11] to remedy our forgery attacks described in Section 3.

4.1   Timestamp-Based Password Authentication Scheme

This scheme has three phases, namely, *registration, login* and *verification* phases.

[Registration phase]
This phase remains same as that in Kim et al.'s timestamp-based password authentication scheme [11] described in Subsection 2.1.

[Login phase]
If a user U_i wants to login to the KIC, he first inserts his card into a card reader and then submits his identity ID_i and password PW_i. Then, the smart card performs the following steps:

- *Step-1:* Generate a random number r_i.
- *Step-2:* Compute $X_i = g^{PW_i \cdot r_i} \bmod n$ and $Y_i = S_i^{X_i} \cdot h_i^{r_i \cdot T} \bmod n$, where T is the current login timestamp.
- *Step-3:* Transmit the login request message $\langle ID_i, CID_i, X_i, Y_i, n, e, g, T \rangle$ to the KIC.

[Authentication phase]
On receiving the message $\langle ID_i, CID_i, X_i, Y_i, n, e, g, T \rangle$ at timestamp T', the KIC authenticates the user U_i as follows.

- *Step-1:* Check the validity of ID_i and CID_i. If any one of these two is invalid, the KIC rejects the login request; otherwise go to Step-2.
- *Step-2:* Verify the validity of the time interval between T^* and T. If $T^* - T < \triangle T$, go to Step-3; otherwise the KIC rejects it. Here $\triangle T$ denotes the expected valid time interval for transmission delay.
- *Step-3:* Check whether the condition

$$Y_i^e = ID_i^{CID_i \cdot X_i} \cdot X_i^T \bmod n \qquad (5)$$

is valid or not. If the condition is valid, the KIC accepts the login request; otherwise the KIC rejects it.

We now show the correctness of the condition in Eqn. (5), which is as follows.

$$\begin{aligned}
Y_i^e &= (S_i^{X_i})^e \cdot (h_i^{r_i \cdot T})^e \bmod n \\
&= ID_i^{CID_i \cdot X_i} \cdot g^{PW_i \cdot r_i \cdot T} \bmod n \\
&= ID_i^{CID_i \cdot X_i} \cdot X_i^T \bmod n.
\end{aligned} \qquad (6)$$

4.2   Nonce-Based Password Authentication Scheme

This scheme has three phases, namely, *registration, login* and *verification* phases.

[Registration phase]
This phase is same as that in Kim et al.'s timestamp-based password authentication scheme [11] described in Subsection 2.1.

[Login phase]

If a user U_i wants to login to the KIC, he first inserts his card into a card reader and then submits his identity ID_i and password PW_i. Then, the smart card and the KIC execute the following steps:

- *Step-1 & Step-2:* These steps are same as those in Kim et el.'s nonce-based password authentication scheme [11].
- *Step-3:* On receiving the nonce N, the smart card computes $X_i = g^{PW_i \cdot r_i}$ mod n and $Y_i = S_i^{X_i} \cdot h_i^{r_i \cdot N}$ mod n.
- *Step-4:* The smart cards transmits the message $M_2 = \langle X_i, Y_i, n, e, g \rangle$ to the KIC.

[Authentication phase]

On receiving $M_2 = \langle X_i, Y_i, n, e, g \rangle$, the KIC checks the validity of the condition

$$Y_i^e = ID_i^{CID_i \cdot X_i} \cdot X_i^N \bmod n. \tag{7}$$

If the condition is valid, the KIC accepts the login request; otherwise the KIC rejects it.

The correctness of the condition in Eqn. (7) is shown below:

$$Y_i^e = (S_i^{X_i})^e \cdot (h_i^{r_i \cdot N})^e \bmod n$$
$$= ID_i^{CID_i \cdot X_i} \cdot g^{PW_i \cdot r_i \cdot N} \bmod n$$
$$= ID_i^{CID_i \cdot X_i} \cdot X_i^N \bmod n.$$

5 Security Analysis

In this section, we describe security analysis of our proposed schemes.

In our schemes, since g is a primitive element on both $GF(p)$ and $GF(q)$ and further $n = pq$ is a product of two large prime factors, computation of a discrete logarithm modulo n without knowing the prime factors of n is an infeasible problem, as presented in [12]. That is, the computation of x from given y and n, where $y = g^x$ mod n, is an infeasible problem due to the discrete logarithm problem because of the fact that order of g is large on both $GF(p)$ and $GF(q)$ as well as the factorization of n is computationally hard. As a result, even if $S_i = ID_i^{CID_i \cdot d}$ mod n and $h_i = g^{PW_i \cdot d}$ mod n with ID_i, CID_i and PW_i are known to an adversary, it is computationally infeasible to compute d. In the following, we now describe that the proposed schemes are secure against some possible attacks.

[Forgery attacks]

We describe that our improvement of Kim et al.'s schemes are secure against *Attack-1* and *Attack-2* which have been described in Section 3.

The proposed Attack-1

In the following, we can show that *Attack-1* described in Section 3 is infeasible on our timestamp-based password authentication scheme.

Let us consider an adversary $\mathcal{A}$ traps two valid login request messages $M^{[1]} = \langle ID_i, CID_i, X_i^{[1]}, Y_i^{[1]}, n, e, g, T^{[1]} \rangle$ and $M^{[2]} = \langle ID_i, CID_i, X_i^{[2]}, Y_i^{[2]}, n, e, g, T^{[2]} \rangle$ from the transaction records sent by a user U_i to the KIC such that $\gcd(T^{[1]}, T^{[2]}) = 1$. Then, the adversary $\mathcal{A}$ performs the following steps as attack procedure in our *Attack-1* for any timestamp T^*.

- *Step-1:* Choose two integers a and b such that $aT^{[1]} + bT^{[2]} = 1$.
- *Step-2:* Compute $Y_i^* = ((Y_i^{[1]})^a \cdot (Y_i^{[2]})^b)^{T^*} \bmod n$, where $Y_i^{[1]} = S_i^{X_i^{[1]}} \cdot h_i^{r_i^{[1]} \cdot T^{[1]}} \bmod n$ and $Y_i^{[2]} = S_i^{X_i^{[2]}} \cdot h_i^{r_i^{[2]} \cdot T^{[2]}} \bmod n$.
- *Step-3:* Compute $X_i^* = ((X_i^{[1]})^a \cdot (X_i^{[2]})^b)^{T^*} \bmod n$, where $X_i^{[1]} = g^{PW_i \cdot r_i^{[1]}} \bmod n$ and $X_i^{[2]} = g^{PW_i \cdot r_i^{[2]}} \bmod n$.
- *Step-4:* Transmit the login request message $M^* = \langle ID_i, CID_i, X_i^*, Y_i^*, n, e, g, T^* \rangle$ to the KIC.

We now prove that the authentication condition $(Y_i^*)^e = ID_i^{CID_i \cdot X_i^*} \cdot (X_i^*)^{T^*} \bmod n$ is not valid, which is shown below:

$$
\begin{aligned}
(Y_i^*)^e &= ((Y_i^{[1]})^a \cdot (Y_i^{[2]})^b)^{e \cdot T^*} \bmod n \\
&= ((S_i^{X_i^{[1]}} \cdot h_i^{r_i^{[1]} \cdot T^{[1]}})^a \cdot (S_i^{X_i^{[2]}} \cdot h_i^{r_i^{[2]} \cdot T^{[2]}})^b)^{e \cdot T^*} \bmod n \\
&= (S_i^{X_i^{[1]} \cdot a + X_i^{[2]} \cdot b})^{e \cdot T^*} \cdot (h_i^{r_i^{[1]} \cdot T^{[1]} \cdot a + r_i^{[2]} \cdot T^{[2]} \cdot b})^{e \cdot T^*} \bmod n \\
&= ID_i^{CID_i \cdot (X_i^{[1]} \cdot a + X_i^{[2]} \cdot b) \cdot T^*} \cdot g^{PW_i \cdot (r_i^{[1]} \cdot T^{[1]} \cdot a + r_i^{[2]} \cdot T^{[2]} \cdot b) \cdot T^*} \bmod n,
\end{aligned}
$$
$$(8)$$

$$
\begin{aligned}
(X_i^*)^{T^*} &= ((X_i^{[1]})^a \cdot (X_i^{[2]})^b)^{T^*} \bmod n \\
&= g^{PW_i \cdot (r_i^{[1]} \cdot a + r_i^{[2]} \cdot b) \cdot T^*} \bmod n.
\end{aligned}
$$
$$(9)$$

It is noted that $(Y_i^*)^e \neq ID_i^{CID_i \cdot X^*} \cdot (X_i^*)^{T^*} \bmod n$ from Eqn. (8) and Eqn. (9). Hence, our timestamp-based password authentication scheme is secure against *Attack-1*. In the similar fashion, one can show that this attack can not be mounted on our nonce-based password authentication scheme.

The proposed Attack-2

In the following, we can show that *Attack-2* described in Section 3 is infeasible on our timestamp-based password authentication scheme.

Let an adversary $\mathcal{A}$ intercept a valid login request message $\mathcal{M} = \langle ID_i, CID_i, X_i, Y_i, n, e, g, T \rangle$ sent by a user U_i to KIC over a public channel. In order to create a forge login request message as in our attack procedure in *Attack-2*, the adversary $\mathcal{A}$ executes the following steps.

- *Step-1:* Choose a number $R, 1 < R < n-1$, and compute $X_i' = X_i \cdot R^{e^2} \bmod n$ and $Y_i' = Y_i \cdot R \bmod n$.
- *Step-2:* Transmit $\mathcal{M}' = \langle ID_i, CID_i, X_i', Y_i', n, e, g, T \rangle$ to the KIC.

On receiving $\mathcal{M}'$, the KIC verifies the validity of the condition $(Y_i')^e = ID_i^{CID_i \cdot X_i'}$. $(X_i')^T \bmod n$. We have:

$$(Y_i')^e = (Y_i \cdot R)^e \bmod n$$
$$= Y_i^e \cdot R^e \bmod n$$
$$= ID_i^{CID_i \cdot X_i} \cdot X_i^T \cdot R^e \bmod n \quad [\text{Using Eqn. (5)}]$$
$$= ID_i^{CID_i \cdot X_i} \cdot g^{PW_i \cdot r_i \cdot T} \cdot R^e \bmod n. \tag{10}$$

$$(X_i')^T = (X_i \cdot R^{e^2})^T \bmod n$$
$$= g^{PW_i \cdot r_i \cdot T} \cdot R^{e^2 \cdot T} \bmod n. \tag{11}$$

From Eqn. (10) and Eqn. (11), we conclude that $(Y_i')^e \neq ID_i^{CID_i \cdot X_i'}$. $(X_i')^T$ $\bmod n$. Hence, the forged login request message $\mathcal{M}'$ does not satisfy the validity of authentication of the KIC. Thus, our timestamp-based password authentication scheme is secure against *Attack-2*. Further, this attack can not be mounted on our nonce-based password authentication scheme.

[Password-guessing attack]
In our timestamp-based password authentication scheme, let an adversary $\mathcal{A}$ trap a valid login request message $\mathcal{M} = \langle ID_i, CID_i, X_i, Y_i, n, e, g, T \rangle$ of a user U_i. It is noted that PW_i is embedded in both X_i and Y_i, where $X_i = g^{PW_i \cdot r_i} \bmod n$, $Y_i = S_i^{X_i} \cdot h_i^{r_i \cdot T} \bmod n$, $h_i = g^{PW_i \cdot d} \bmod n$ and $S_i = ID_i^{CID_i \cdot d} \bmod n$. In login phase of our timestamp-based password authentication scheme, since r_i is a random number generated by the smart card, it is infeasible to the adversary $\mathcal{A}$ to guess the password PW_i of the user U_i from $\mathcal{M} = \langle ID_i, CID_i, X_i, Y_i, n, e, g, T \rangle$ without knowing r_i. Similarly, in our nonce-based password authentication scheme, it is also infeasible to guess the password PW_i of the user U_i.

[Smart card loss attack]
It is possible that a user U_i has lost his smart card and an adversary gets it. Another possibility is that an adversary actively steals a smart card of a user U_i. Let an adversary $\mathcal{A}$ get a smart card of the user U_i. Then, $\mathcal{A}$ inserts the card into a card reader and submits identity ID_i. As the *password-guessing attack* is infeasible in our schemes as described in previous attack procedure, the adversary $\mathcal{A}$ needs to choose an arbitrary password, say, PW_A and submits it. Then, the smart card computes $X_i = g^{PW_A \cdot r_i} \bmod n$ and $Y_i = S_i^{X_i} \cdot h_i^{r_i \cdot T} \bmod n$, where $h_i = g^{PW_i \cdot d} \bmod n$ and $S_i = ID_i^{CID_i \cdot d} \bmod n$. We show that these X_i and Y_i do not satisfy the validity condition in Eqn. (5) as follows:

$$Y_i^e = (S_i^{X_i} \cdot h_i^{r_i \cdot T})^e \bmod n$$
$$= ID_i^{CID_i \cdot X_i} \cdot g^{PW_i \cdot r_i \cdot T} \bmod n, \tag{12}$$

$$X_i^T = g^{PW_A \cdot r_i \cdot T} \bmod n. \tag{13}$$

From Eqn. (12), Eqn. (13) and since $PW_A \neq PW_i$, it is clear that $Y_i^e \neq ID_i^{CID_i \cdot X_i} \cdot X_i^T \bmod n$. As a result, $\mathcal{A}$ can not generate a valid login request message to the KIC after getting a smart card of a user and without interacting with that user or the KIC. Similarly, this attack can not be mounted on our nonce-based password authentication scheme.

[Replay attack]
In our timestamp-based password authentication scheme, let an adversary $\mathcal{A}$ attempt to record of the exchanged messages between a user U_i and the KIC. The replay of the old request message $\mathcal{M} = \langle\ ID_i, CID_i, X_i,\ Y_i,\ n, e, g, T \rangle$ sent by the user U_i to the KIC fails because the validity of a message can be checked through the timestamp. As a result, our timestamp-based password authentication scheme is secure against *replay attack*. In our nonce-based password authentication scheme, a nonce N generated by the KIC is used to represent the transaction uniquely between the smart card and the KIC. Let an adversary $\mathcal{A}$ trap $M_1 = \langle ID_i, CID_i \rangle$, N and $M_2 = \langle X_i, Y_i, n, e, g \rangle$ from the previous communications between the smart card of U_i and the KIC over a public channel. Now, $\mathcal{A}$ can try to attack by the following way:

- *Step-1:* $\mathcal{A}$ transmits the login request message $M_1 = \langle ID_i, CID_i \rangle$ to the KIC.
- *Step-2:* On receiving M_1, the KIC checks the validity of ID_i and CID_i. It is obvious that these are valid information. Then, the KIC computes a new nonce $N^* = f(r_j^*)$ after choosing a random number r_j^*.
- *Step-3:* Then, $\mathcal{A}$ transmits old $M_2 = \langle X_i, Y_i, n, e, g \rangle$, which is trapped by $\mathcal{A}$ from previous communications between the smart card of U_i and the KIC.

We show that $Y_i^e \neq ID_i^{CID_i \cdot X_i} \cdot X_i^{N^*} \bmod n$ as follows. We have,

$$Y_i^e = (S_i^{X_i} \cdot h_i^{r_i \cdot N})^e \bmod n$$
$$= ID_i^{CID_i \cdot X_i} \cdot g^{PW_i \cdot r_i \cdot N} \bmod n, \qquad (14)$$

$$X_i^{N^*} = g^{PW_i \cdot r_i \cdot N^*} \bmod n \qquad (15)$$

Since $N^* \neq N$, the replay request message $M_2 = \langle X_i, Y_i, n, e, g \rangle$ does not satisfy the authentication condition shown in Eqn. (5). Hence, our nonce-based password authentication scheme is secure against *replay attack*.

6 Conclusion

In this paper, we have shown that Kim et al.'s password authentication schemes have security weaknesses to forgery attacks. Further, we have proposed the improvement of Kim et al.'s schemes to remedy these weaknesses.

References

1. Lamport, L.: Password authentication with insecure communication. Communications of the ACM 24, 770–772 (1981)
2. Hwang, M.S., Li, L.: A new remote user authentication scheme using smart cards. IEEE Trans. Consumer Electron 46, 28–30 (2000)
3. Chien, H.Y., Jan, J.K., Tseng, Y.M.: An efficient and practical solution to remote authentication: smart card. Computers and Security 21, 372–375 (2002)
4. Shen, J.J., Lin, C.W., Hwang, M.S.: Security enhancement for the timestamp-based password authentication scheme using smart cards. Computers and Security 22, 591–595 (2003)
5. Sun, H.M.: An efficient remote user authentication scheme using smart cards. IEEE Trans. Consumer Electron 46, 958–961 (2000)
6. Yoon, E.J., Ryu, E.K., Yoo, K.Y.: Efficient remote user authentication scheme based on generalized elgamal signature scheme. IEEE Transactions on Consumer Electronics 50, 568–570 (2004)
7. Yang, W., Shieh, S.: Password authentication schemes with smart cards. Computers and Security 18, 727–733 (1999)
8. Chan, C.K., Cheng, L.M.: Cryptanalysis of a timestamp-based password authentication scheme. Computers and Security 21, 74–76 (2002)
9. Sun, H.M., Yeh, H.T.: Further cryptanalysis of a password authentication scheme with smart cards. IEICE Trans. and Comm. E86-B, 1412–1451 (2003)
10. Yang, C.C., Wang, R.C., Chang, T.Y.: An improvement of the yang-shieh password authentication schemes. Applied Mathematics and Computations 162, 1391–1396 (2005)
11. Kim, K.W., Jeon, J.C., Yoo, K.Y.: An improvement on yang et al 's password authentication schemes. Applied Mathematics and Computations 170, 207–215 (2005)
12. Girault, M.: Self-certified public keys. In: Davies, D.W. (ed.) EUROCRYPT 1991. LNCS, vol. 547, pp. 491–497. Springer, Heidelberg (1991)

Information Leakage Via Electromagnetic Emanations and Evaluation of Tempest Countermeasures

Hidema Tanaka

National Institute of Information and Communications Technology, Japan
4-2-1, Nukui-Kitamachi, Koganei, Tokyo 184-8795, Japan

Abstract. It is well known that there is relationship between electro-magnetic emanation and processing information in IT devices such as personal computers and smart cards. By analyzing such electromagnetic emanation, eavesdropper will be able to get some information, so it be-comes a real threat of information security. In this paper, we show how to estimate amount of information that is leaked as electromagnetic em-anation. We assume the area between the IT device and the receiver is a communication channel, and we define the amount of information leakage via electromagnetic emanations by its channel capacity. By some experimental results of Tempest, we show example estimations of amount of information leakage. Using the value of channel capacity, we can cal-culate the amount of information per pixel in the reconstructed image. And we evaluate the effectiveness of Tempest fonts generated by Gaus-sian method and its threshold of security.

Keyword: Electromagnetic emanation, EMC, Tempest, Eavesdropping, Side-channel attack.

1 Introduction

Information leakage via electromagnetic emanations from IT devices is a well known threat. Information concerning man-machine interfaces (such as monitors, keyboards, printers, etc.) cannot be protected by crypto technologies, so they are security risks. In particular, information displayed on a monitor (hereafter called "displayed information") is a very serious one.

An eavesdropper receiving electromagnetic emanations does not leave evi-dence of their activity, and the victim notices nothing. Such a problem is known as a "Tempest", and various countermeasures have been proposed [3] [9] [15] [20]. They can be classified into two categories: hardware based and software based. Almost all hardware-based countermeasures are aimed at preventing electromag-netic emanations. Though the immediate effect is high, these countermeasures are expensive, and the cost effectiveness is low. In addition, they most likely can-not be built into current systems, and further maintenance of the infrastructure would be needed. On the other hand, software-based countermeasures will make it difficult to reconstruct information from received electromagnetic emanations.

P. McDaniel and S.K. Gupta (Eds.): ICISS 2007, LNCS 4812, pp. 167–179, 2007.

Table 1. Tempest countermeasures

	Method	Purpose
Hardware	filter/adapter	prevention of emanation from parts (USB, serial connector etc) of IT devices
	infrastructure	prevention of emanation from the buildings or rooms (e.g. shielded room)
	jamming	interception of the receiving by generating another emanation
Software	image processing	transformation of images which does not generate strong emanation (e.g. TEMPEST fonts [12])

They are cheap and can easily be introduced into existing systems, but the effect they have is limited. Examples are shown in Table 1.

The effectiveness of most countermeasures has been evaluated from the viewpoint of EMC (Electro-Magnetic Compatibility) and experimental results of human subjectivity [5]. There are following major problems.

P1. Electromagnetic emanations from IT devices have a wide frequency band. But they are not limited to the frequency band in which a strong emanation occurs; that displayed information is included.

P2. The effectiveness of countermeasures is judged effective when testees cannot read characters in a reconstructed image. However, the effectiveness does not have any numerical value, and the threshold of successful effectiveness is vague. And there are no method to evaluate for displayed information except characters such as figures, pictures, position of mouse cursor and animation effects of operation such as touch panel.

In addition, the conditions of measurement differ for each proposer of countermeasure, and the verification of an appropriate measurement is not performed. Therefore, a third party cannot do a double check, and different countermeasures cannot be compared. In particular, these problems have not been researched from the viewpoint of information security. Problem P1 is part of the topic focusing on the electromagnetic measurement area. Therefore, details of P1 are not discussed in this paper. Kuhn shows a detailed analysis and constructive proposal to this problem in his paper at CHES 2005 [9]. We contribute to solve problem P2.

In this paper, we describe a method for evaluating the effectiveness of the countermeasures from the viewpoint of information theory. We assume the area between the IT device and the receiver is a communication channel, and we define the amount of information leakage via electromagnetic emanations by its channel capacity. Using the value of channel capacity, we can calculate the amount of information per pixel in the reconstructed image. When the target is a monochrome image, if we can get 1.0[bit] per pixel or more, the image can be successfully reconstructed. If a reconstructed image has 0.0[bit] per pixel, it will be a perfectly random noise image. We show the experimental results of a comparison between the amount of information leakage and the quality of the reconstructed image.

From these results, we conclude that if a countermeasure can archive the reconstructed image with about 0.8[bit] per pixel or less, it will be effective.

2   Information Leakage Via Electromagnetic Emanations

2.1   Channel Capacity of Continuous Channel

When a communication channel is given, the maximum amount of information that a sender can transmit is calculated as the channel capacity. For an additive Gaussian channel with band limited signal, the channel capacity C of continuous channel is calculated as follows [17].

$$C = W \log_2 \left(1 + \frac{S}{N} \right) \quad \text{[bps]}, \tag{2.1}$$

where S denotes the power of the signal, N denotes the power of the noise and W denotes the bandwidth.

We assume the area between the target and the receiver to be an additive Gaussian channel with limited band signal. Thus, we can estimate the amount of information leakage can be received as channel capacity. However, in this case, only the receiver exists, and the target does not generate a signal. We face the following problems.

Q1. What is the signal?
Q2. Which frequency should be received?
Q3. How do we distinguish between signal and noise?

We discuss these problems.

2.2   Q1. What Is the Signal?

Since IT devices leak various kinds of processing information as electromagnetic emanations, eavesdroppers should decide which signal to receive [14] [18]. For a Tempest, the target signal is a video. The eavesdropper receives a video signal from the electromagnetic emanations and gives vertical and horizontal synchronous signals to make the image. As a precondition, the eavesdropper can give the same synchronous signal as the target, but this condition can be easily solved [3] [10] [15] [20]. When the eavesdropper can see the reconstructed information as an image, we can judge that he or she has succeeded in receiving the signal. When the eavesdropper cannot make an image, he or she can be judged to have failed. In this way, especially for information concerning man-machine interfaces, we can easily judge success or failure because successfully reconstructed information can be easily recognized. Therefore we can distinguish signal from noise easily.

2.3   Q2. Which Frequency Should Be Received?

Though the mechanism is not understood, we know based on experiments that some frequency bands include video signal in the case of typical personal computers. Some experimental results have already been published [3] [10] [20].

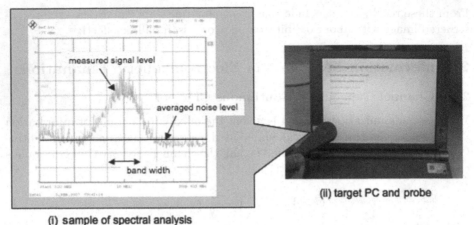

(i) sample of spectral analysis

(ii) target PC and probe

Fig. 1. Spectral analysis of electromagnetic emanation from laptop computer

Therefore, we can determine the frequency and bandwidth for a successful eavesdrop. Also, ITU-T SG5 has started to discuss these problems in regards to protecting against information leakage [5].

2.4   Q3. How Do We Distinguish Between Signal and Noise?

This is the main problem to solve in our paper because from the viewpoint of EMC, all emanation is noise. Fig. 1 shows an experimental result of a spectral analysis of electromagnetic emanations from a laptop computer. In this experiment, we received frequency from 310[MHz] to 410[MHz]. Between about 340[MHz] and 375[MHz], we were able to make a reconstructed image. Therefore, electromagnetic emanation in this frequency range can be judged to be a video signal. In other ranges (310[MHz] ∼ 340[MHz] and 375[MHz] ∼ 410[MHz]), we failed to make the image and therefore judged them to be noise. In our many experiments, we could more easily distinguish the signal from the noise than what we had expected.

2.5   Calculation of Channel Capacity

In the following, we used the measured value for the signal level and defined the noise level to be the average of the signal level judged to be noise in the measured range of frequency. It is difficult problem to determine the accurate value of noise level and standard frequency range to be measured. For some settings of measurement frequency range, noise level is larger than the signal. Such situations have been confirmed by our experiments (e.g. using 500[MHz] of frequency range). Theoretically, it is necessary to decide it by the level at the frequency where the signal and the noise change. In the case of result shown in Fig.1, the noise levels should be determined at 340[MHz] and at 375[MHz]. However we observed some measurement results that the difference between level of low frequency and of high frequency is huge (there were difference of about 8[dB] $\sim$ 14[dB]). So, we experimentally searched for the adequate width of measurement frequency band where the level of noise seems to be constant. After some experiments, we conclude that 100[MHz] of frequency range is appropriate to our purpose. Then we assumed the averaged value to be noise level.

Let $S(f)$ be the measured signal level at frequency $f(f_1 \leq f \leq f_2)$ and N be the averaged noise level (see Fig.1(i)). Then, the channel capacity can be calculated as follows [17].

$$C = \max \int_{f_1}^{f_2} \log_2 \left(1 + \frac{S(f)}{N} \right) df \quad [\text{bit/sec}] \qquad (2.2)$$

There is a relationship between the displayed image and the power of electromagnetic emanations. We confirmed from experiments that the strongest electromagnetic emanations are generated when the image changes from black to white (or from white to black) horizontally [3]. We measured the maximum value of $S(f)$ by choosing the displayed image appropriately (using "maximum hold mode"). Thus, we can calculate channel capacity C using measured $S(f)$.

There are some methods for an accurate calculation of channel capacity from measurement results. In this paper, we used following simple calculation. We describe the accuracy of this method in section 3.2.

1. Since we get the measurement result as gain [dB], the value of the term $\frac{S(f)}{N}$ is calculated as follows.

$$\frac{S(f)}{N} = 10^{\frac{(\text{measured value at } f \text{ [Hz]})-(\text{averaged value } N)}{20}} \qquad (2.3)$$

   Note that gain [dB] $= 20 \log_{10} \frac{y}{x}$, $(x = \text{input}, y = \text{output})$.
2. " df" depends on the sampling rate of the receiver. Our receiver has 500,000 [samples/rate]. Using the receiver for measurement of 100[MHz] frequency range, Δf is calculated as 100[MHz]/500,000=200[Hz].
3. Thus, we can calculate channel capacity as follows.

$$\int_{f_1}^{f_2} \log_2 \left(1 + \frac{S(f)}{N} \right) df$$
$$= \sum_{f_1 \leq f \leq f_2} \log_2(1 + 10^{\frac{(\text{measured value})-(\text{averaged value } N)}{20}}) \times \Delta f \quad (2.4)$$

Let V[bps] be the video signal in the personal computer. When $C \geq V$, the eavesdropper can get information on the video signal and make a sufficiently clear image. When $C < V$, the eavesdropper can get some information and make a vague reconstructed image. When $S(f) = N$, the value of C is the minimum ($C_{\min} = f_2 - f_1$). Then we cannot get any reconstructed image.

3   Experimental Results and Analysis

3.1   Example Experiment

We show an experimental calculation of the channel capacity for a laptop computer (PC), which was the target. The PC displayed the image shown in

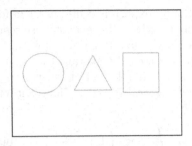

Fig. 2. Displayed image (1024x768[pixel] monochrome). These symbols contain all elements (vertical line, horizontal line, hatched line, and curve) that compose the shape of alphabets.

Fig. 2. We used a near magnetic field probe (Anritsu MP666A) to receive the electromagnetic emanations. We placed the probe directly on PC (see Fig. 1(ii)). The reason why such experiments are appropriate is shown in section 3.3. The amount of information from the video signal, V[bps], is calculated as follows.

$$V = (\text{\# of colors [bit]}) \times (\text{display resolution [pixel]}) \times (\text{frame rate [fps]})$$
$$= 24 \times (1024 \times 768) \times 60 \tag{3.1}$$

However, because Fig. 2 is a monochrome image, we should apply not 24[bit] true-color but 1[bit] monochrome. Therefore, V was calculated as follows.

$$V = 1 \times (1024 \times 768) \times 60$$
$$\simeq 47[\text{Mbps}] \tag{3.2}$$

We obtained the spectral analysis result shown in Fig. 3 (i). The averaged noise level, N, is about 29.4[dBm] from the spectral analysis. The channel capacity, C, was calculated as follows.

$$C = \int_{350}^{370} \log_2 \left(1 + \frac{S(f)}{N}\right) df$$
$$\simeq 100[\text{Mbps}] \tag{3.3}$$

In this experiment, because C is significantly larger than V, we expected a clear reconstructed image. To reconstruct displayed information, we set the bandwidth value of the receiver to 20[MHz] and set the center frequency to 360[MHz] and make the reconstructed image shown in Fig. 3(ii). The horizontal lines, such as baseline of triangle and horizontal lines of square, have disappeared in the reconstructed image. Because electromagnetic emanations are not generated from parts without causing horizontal changes in the image, such parts are not reflected in the reconstructed image. Though such lost data occurred, we were able to get enough semantics from the reconstructed image about the displayed information.

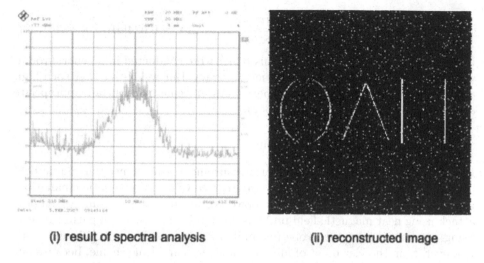

(i) result of spectral analysis   **(ii) reconstructed image**

Fig. 3. Spectral analysis result and reconstructed image for Fig.2

3.2   Analysis of Results

From the value of C, we estimated that Fig. 3(ii) which is a reconstructed image, is constructed using 2.12[bit] per pixel. This value shows the quality of the reconstructed image. We call it Q, which is defined as follows.

$$Q = \frac{C\,[\text{bps}]}{\text{display resolution [pixel]} \times \text{frame rate [fps]}} \quad [\text{bit}] \qquad (3.4)$$

The color information cannot be reproduced in the reconstructed image, and the reconstructed image is expressed only by brightness and contrast. So, the value of Q means the number of steps in the gray scale of the reconstructed image. Therefore, if the value of Q is large, a detailed reconstructed image will be made. We estimate the maximum value of Q will be 8[bit] because each color (red, green, and blue) in the VESA standard was expressed by an 8[bit] value [21]. $Q = 0.0$ is the minimum value and a reconstructed image will be perfectly random noise.

We estimate the value of Q using C which is calculated by the method shown in section 2.5. The error margin of averaged N influences the accuracy of C. Let ΔN be the error margin of N. So , the error margin of Q, ΔQ, is calculated as follows.

$$\Delta Q = \frac{\Delta N \times (f_2 - f_1)}{\text{display resolution [pixel]} \times \text{frame rate [fps]}} \quad [\text{bit}] \qquad (3.5)$$

Under the condition of 1024×768 [pixel], 60 [fps] and bandwidth $f_2 - f_1 = 20$[MHz], when the accuracy of $\Delta Q = 0.01$ is needed, the requirement of the accuracy for ΔN is as follows.

$$0.01 = \frac{\Delta N \times (20 \times 10^6)}{(1024 \times 768) \times 60} \quad \Rightarrow \quad \Delta N \simeq 0.024[\text{dB}] \tag{3.6}$$

Because the experiments shown in this paper were conducted in a general room, we expect that our results have no such accuracy. But we expect that such high accuracy can be achieved if the experiments are conducted in an appropriate environment such as in a shielded room.

3.3 Conditions of Measurement

In this paper, we show the results of measurement using a near magnetic field probe. In the fact, there are various way to receive electromagnetic emanation; using antennas, injection probes for power supply line and so on. A Tempest attack using near magnetic field probe is not realistic threeat comparing attacks using antenna or injection probe (example attacks are shown in [10] and [20]). However, from the viewpoint of measurement, it is an ideal scheme, because our measurement have large signal-noise ratio. We can use the results using near magnetic field probe to estimate the results using other method. We need to refer to [5] to convert the results. Kuhn also refers the appropriate measurement environment and the specification of equipments in [9].

4 Effectiveness of Countermeasures

We hoped that the countermeasure would achieve $Q = 0.0$. However, cost and physical restrictions make it difficult to achieve. Moreover, some cases are secure even when $Q > 0.0$. For example, the eavesdropper succeed in making reconstructed images but he or she could not get any semantics because the shapes of many fonts were broken in reconstructed images. In such a case, Q is larger than 0.0[bit].

"Tempest fonts" are software based countermeasure and they have been developed expecting such effect [8] [12] [20]. We can use them simply by installing them on the system, special equipment is not needed, and they are cheap. We can find some free fonts at "SearchFreeFonts.com". However, the effectiveness is limited as mentioned before. Many methods can be used to make Tempest fonts. In this paper, we evaluate the Gaussian method from the viewpoint of the value of Q [20].

The Gaussian method is a technique for smoothing images by using a Gauss filter. To use the Gauss function for the filter, the value is calculated according to the distance from the center pixel, (x_a, y_b), using the following formula.

$$P(x_a, y_b) = \frac{1}{2\pi\sigma} \sum_i \sum_j e^{-\frac{(x_i - x_a)^2}{2\sigma^2}} e^{-\frac{(y_j - y_b)^2}{2\sigma^2}} P(x_i, y_j), \tag{4.1}$$

where $P(x_i, y_j)$ denotes the value of pixel (x_i, y_j), and σ denotes the standard deviation of the distribution. The distance from (x_a, y_b) is called the radius [pixel].

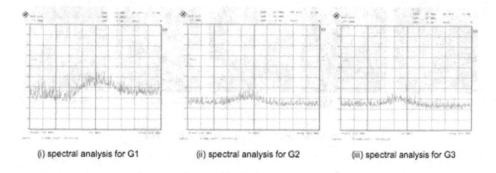

(i) spectral analysis for G1   (ii) spectral analysis for G2   (iii) spectral analysis for G3

Fig. 4. Spectral analysis results for G1, G2 and G3

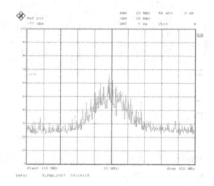

Fig. 5. Spectral analysis result with 10[dB] attenuator

The effectiveness of the Gauss filter is decided based on the radius and deviation. The strongest electromagnetic emanations are generated when the image changes from black to white (or from white to black) directly. But in a black-and-white image through a Gaussian filter, gradation is generated. The power of electromagnetic emanations generated for each step in gradation is smaller than the power generated for direct changes from black to white. Therefore detailed gradation suppresses strong electromagnetic emanations.

We made three images; G1 was made from Fig. 2 through a Gaussian filter with radius=1[pixel], G2 was made through a filter with radius=2[pixel], and G3 was made from G1 through a filter with radius=1[pixel]. The gradation is in the order of G1, G2, and G3. The spectral analysis results are shown in Fig. 4. In addition, the spectral analysis result for Fig. 2 when the gain was reduced with a 10[dB] attenuator is shown in Fig. 5. The reconstructed images are labeled as follows and shown in Fig.6.

R0: reconstructed from Fig. 2
R1: reconstructed from Fig. 2 with 10[dB] attenuator
R2: reconstructed from G1

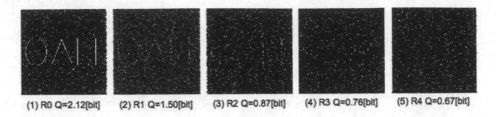

(1) R0 Q=2.12[bit]   (2) R1 Q=1.50[bit]   (3) R2 Q=0.87[bit]   (4) R3 Q=0.76[bit]   (5) R4 Q=0.67[bit]

Fig. 6. Reconstructed images R0 ∼ R4

Table 2. Result of subjective test

Reconstructed image	Channel capacity [bps]	Quality Q [bit]	Result
R0	100.0[Mbps]	2.12[bit]	perfectly readable
R1	69.2[Mbps]	1.50[bit]	almost readable
R2	41.2[Mbps]	0.87[bit]	partially readable
R3	36.2[Mbps]	0.76[bit]	no readable
R4	31.7[Mbps]	0.67[bit]	no readable

R3: reconstructed from G2
R4: reconstructed from G3

Because of the characteristics of reconstructed images, they (especially R2, R3 and R4) may be hard to see on the paper.

We conducted a subjective test. Each testee permuted these images to make the legible order. All testees answered that R0 is the most legible at first. In the same way, they claimed that R1 is also clear image. Though it will be difficult to see in printed images, vertical lines of square in R2 was recognized easily by testees. And they noticed part of circle and hatched lines of triangle after a while. All testees answered that he or she cannot see anything in R3 and R4. Moreover, they could not distinguish R3 and R4 and allocate the order. These results are concluded in Table 2. As the results, we expected that the countermeasure that archives $Q < 0.8$ will be sufficiently effective for Fig.2. After some experiments using other displayed images and using other generating methods of Tempest fonts, we concluded $Q = 0.8$ will be the threshold value that we can determine effective countermeasure. However, we need more discussions about scheme of subjective test and we will need some psychological method such as affordance.

5   Discussion

5.1   Validity of Value Q

From the results of the subjective experiment shown in section 4, we can confirm that the value of Q and the quality of the reconstructed image closely correspond. For instance, there are no opinion that $Q = 0.9$ is more legible than $Q = 1.2$. The effectiveness of the countermeasures (without distinguishing between hardware and software) can be mutually compared when displaying the same image for the same PC by measuring the value of Q.

However, for some cases, the displayed image will change the threshold of Q for an effective countermeasure. For example, the value of Q for effective countermeasures may be different for 10-point and 24-point character fonts. In this case, the value of an effective Q for a 10-point font will be larger than that for a 24-point one. In addition, user-friendliness is an important factor in comparing Tempest fonts. A high effectiveness of countermeasure and legibility may not coexist, so we need to find a balance between the two. Finding solutions to these problems will be part of our future work.

5.2   Increase in the Value Q by Image Processing

A reconstructed image can be made clear by storing the received data and by applying image processing such as averaging to it [20]. As a result, an image where the value of Q increases can be obtained. For example, because Q=2.12 for the results of Fig. 2, we can estimate that the maximum value of Q is reached using data that is stored for about four seconds. Therefore, the resulting image will be a "complete reconstructed image". Even if it is such an image, the color information and horizontal lines disappear. Thus, there is an upper bound in the quality of the reconstructed image. If the upper bound can be estimated, the necessary amount of data that should be stored can be estimated. We will show such an estimation in our future work.

5.3   Evaluation of Physical Security and Side-Channel Attacks

Side-channel attack is a typical physical security topic [1] [4] [6] [16]. Generated physical phenomenon (electric power, electromagnetic emanation, heat, light and so on) when IT devices operate is called side-channel information. The amount of changes of physical phenomenon is related to information that IT devices process. Side-channel attack uses the such changes of side-channel information to derive processing information. From such a viewpoint, Tempest is one of side-channel attacks.

The amount of information leakage as side-channel information can be estimated by channel capacity shown as this paper. For example, in the case of EM side-channel cryptanalysis, we can adapt our method to estimate the amount of information leakage [1] [4] [16] [18]. From the result, we will be able to determine the necessary number of sampling data. The attacker needs one operation of a crypto module for one data sampling, so a huge amount of time is needed. Thus, we want to know the minimum number of samplings for the security evaluation. In addition, we will be able to estimate the effectiveness of countermeasure against EM side-channel cryptanalysis.

For the other side-hannel information, we need to determine the signal and noise appropriately. We will be able to know signal-noise ratio from the difference between operation state and stationary state for power cryptanalysis such as SPA and DPA [6] [7]. In the case of optical side-channel information, it will be able to estimate from the change in the brightness with operation [13] [19]. This theme will also be part of our next work.

References

1. Agrawal, D., Archambeault, B., Chari, S., Rao, J.R.: Advances in Side-Channel Cryptanalysis Electromagnetic Analysis and Template Attacks. RSA Laboratories Cryptobytes 6(1), 20–32 (2003)
2. Chari, S., Rao, J.R., Rohatgi, P.: Template attacks. In: Kaliski Jr., B.S., Koç, Ç.K., Paar, C. (eds.) CHES 2002. LNCS, vol. 2523, pp. 13–28. Springer, Heidelberg (2003)
3. van Eck, W.: Electromagnetic radiation from video display units: An eavesdropping risk? Computers and Security 4 (1985)
4. Gandolfi, K., Mourtel, C., Oliver, F.: Electromagnetic analysis:Concrete results. In: Koç, Ç.K., Naccache, D., Paar, C. (eds.) CHES 2001. LNCS, vol. 2162, pp. 251–261. Springer, Heidelberg (2001)
5. International Telecommunication Union, Telecommunication Standardization Sector (ITU-T) Study Group 5, Protection against electromagnetic environment effects, http://www.itu.int/ITU-T/studygroups/com05/index.asp
6. Kocher, P.: Timing attacks on implementations of Diffie-Hellman, RSA, DSS, and other systems. In: Koblitz, N. (ed.) CRYPTO 1996. LNCS, vol. 1109, pp. 104–113. Springer, Heidelberg (1996)
7. Kocher, P., Jaffe, J., Jub, B.: Differential power analysis. In: Wiener, M.J. (ed.) CRYPTO 1999. LNCS, vol. 1666, pp. 388–397. Springer, Heidelberg (1999)
8. Kuhn, M.: Filtered-tempest fonts, available at http://www.cl.cam.ac.uk/~mgk25/st-fonts.zip
9. Kuhn, M.: Security Limits for Compromising Emanations. In: Rao, J.R., Sunar, B. (eds.) CHES 2005. LNCS, vol. 3659, pp. 265–279. Springer, Heidelberg (2005)
10. Kuhn, M.: Electromagnetic Eavesdropping Risks of Flat-Panel Displays. In: Martin, D., Serjantov, A. (eds.) PET 2004. LNCS, vol. 3424, pp. 88–107. Springer, Heidelberg (2005)
11. Kuhn, M.: Optical Time-Domain Eavesdropping Risks of CRT Displays. In: IEEE Symposium on Security and Privacy, pp. 3–18 (2002)
12. Kuhn, M.G., Anderson, R.J.: Soft Tempest: Hideden Data Transmission Using Electromagnetic Emanations. In: Aucsmith, D. (ed.) IH 1998. LNCS, vol. 1525, pp. 124–142. Springer, Heidelberg (1998)
13. Loughry, J., Umphress, D.A.: Information leakage from optical emanations. ACM Transactions on Information and System Security 5(3), 262–289 (2002)
14. Micali, S., Reyzin, L.: Physically observable cryptography, IACR Cryptology ePrint archive 2003/120
15. National Security Telecommunications and Information Systems Security Instruction NSTISSI No. 7000: TEMPEST Countermeasures for Facilities. National Security Agency, Fort George G. Meade, Maryland, 29, Partially declassified transcript (November 1993), http://cryptome.org/nstissi-7000.htm
16. Quisquater, J.-J., Samyde, D.: Electromagnetic analysis (EMA): measures and countermeasures for smart cards. In: Attali, S., Jensen, T. (eds.) E-smart 2001. LNCS, vol. 2140, pp. 200–210. Springer, Heidelberg (2001)

17. Shannon, C.E.: A Mathematical Theory of Communication. The Bell System Technical Journal 27, 623–656 (1948)
18. Smulders, P.: The threat of information theft by reception of electromagnetic radiation from RS-232 cables. Computer and Security 9 (1990)
19. Skorobogatov, S., Anderson, R.: Optical fault induction attacks. In: Kaliski Jr., B.S., Koç, Ç.K., Paar, C. (eds.) CHES 2002. LNCS, vol. 2523, pp. 2–12. Springer, Heidelberg (2003)
20. Tanaka, H., Takizawa, O., Yamamura, A.: Evaluation and improvement of Tempest fonts. In: Lim, C.H., Yung, M. (eds.) WISA 2004. LNCS, vol. 3325, pp. 457–469. Springer, Heidelberg (2005)
21. Video Electronics Standards Association, http://www.vesa.org/

Data Privacy – Problems and Solutions

Sabrina De Capitani di Vimercati and Pierangela Samarati

Dipartimento di Tecnologie dell'Informazione
Università degli Studi di Milano
Via Bramante 65 - 26013 Crema (CR) - Italy
{decapita,samarati}@dti.unimi.it

Abstract. Nowadays, the global information infrastructure connects remote parties worldwide through the use of large scale networks, relying on application level protocols and services such as the World Wide Web. The vast amounts of personal information thus available has led to growing concerns about the privacy of their users. In this paper, we briefly discuss some privacy issues that have to be considered to address the new needs and desiderata of today's systems and discuss ongoing work.

1 Introduction

The increased power and interconnectivity of computer systems available today provide the ability of storing and processing large amounts of data, resulting in networked information accessible from anywhere at any time [4]. Indeed, thanks to the availability of post-third generation mobile networks, user transactions are no longer bound to the traditional office-centered environment, but can be started virtually anywhere and at any hour [10]. Resources may then be accessed in a variety of contexts, and users requesting access may be required to disclose a rich set of distributed information about themselves, including dynamic properties such as their location or communication device as well as conventional, identity-related user attributes. The vast amounts of personal information thus available has led to growing concerns about the privacy of their users [14,15]. *Personal information privacy* is therefore an issue that most people are concerned about, particularly because the possibilities of information distribution, combination, and reuse have been increased [8,9].

In such a scenario, information privacy is about the collection, processing, use, and protection of personal information and should be addressed also by developing privacy-aware languages and policies that encompass two notions: *i)* guaranteeing the desired level of privacy of information exchanged between different parties and controlling access to services/resources based on this information; and *ii)* managing and storing personal information given to remote parties in a trustworthy way. A privacy-aware solution should combine these two notions and should be simple and expressive enough to support the following functionality.

- *Context (including location)-aware privacy policies*. Context information should be used by the policy infrastructure to allow environment factors

P. McDaniel and S.K. Gupta (Eds.): ICISS 2007, LNCS 4812, pp. 180–192, 2007.

to influence how and when policy is enforced. Generally speaking, context information is a set of metadata identifying and possibly describing entities of interest, such as subjects and objects, as well as any ambient parameters concerning the technological and cultural environment (including *location*), where a transaction takes place. As far as policy enforcement is concerned, context contains information enabling verification of policy conditions and, therefore, it should be made available to any authorized service/application at any time and in a standard format. Still unauthorized information leaks should be prevented, also to avoid loss of privacy, for example, on the user's whereabouts.

– *Data protection*. An important issue that a privacy-aware solution should be taken into consideration is how to protect data while they are being stored, either on the client side or, more important, on the server side. It should be therefore adopted techniques both for limiting the possibility of identifying user [2,7] and for protecting sensitive information about users. These aspects are attracting increasing attention from regulatory bodies and final users, and should be addressed.

In this paper, we illustrate recent proposals and ongoing work addressing privacy issues in emerging applications and new scenarios. The remainder of this paper is structured as follows. Section 2 describes how traditional access control policies can be enriched by using context (location) information. Section 3 presents our proposal for enforcing selective access on the outsourced data. Section 4 presents some challenges to be addressed for protecting data privacy. Finally, Section 5 concludes the paper.

2   Extending Privacy Policies with Context Information

The increasing availability of information about users's context makes it possible to develop context-sensitive services, where access to resources provided/managed by a server is limited depending on a user's context. For instance, a *location-based service* can require a user to be at a particular location to let the user to use or access a resource or learn her friends' location. However, constraining access to a resource based on context information of users could result in privacy violations. For instance, if access is constrained based on the location of a user, granting or rejecting access will provide information about the location of the user and could therefore violate her privacy.

In [3], we address this issue in relation with Location-Based Access Control (LBAC) systems, which support the evaluation of policies also based on conditions, expressed by using *location-based predicates*, on users physical locations.

Location-based predicates. The definition of location-based predicates for access control mechanisms requires to specify the conditions that an authorization language can support and today's location technology can verify. Three main classes of conditions could be identified [3]:

- *position-based* conditions on the location of a user, for evaluating (e.g.,
  whether a user is in a certain building or city or in the proximity of other
  entities);
- *movement-based* conditions on the mobility of a user (e.g., her velocity, ac-
  celeration, or direction where she is headed);
- *interaction-based* conditions relating multiple users or entities (e.g., the number of users within a given area).

With respect to these classes, some specific predicates corresponding to specific conditions can be provided in an authorization language. A language for
location-based predicates should include the following two elements.

- Users is the set of *user identifiers* (UID) that unambiguously identify users
  known to the location services (i.e., the entity that provides the location information). This includes both users of the system (i.e., potential requesters)
  as well as any other known physical and/or moving entity which may need
  to be located (e.g., a vehicle with an on-board GPRS card). A typical UID
  for location-based applications is the SIM number linking the user's identity
  to a mobile terminal.[1]
- Areas is a set of map regions identified either via a geometric model (i.e., a
  range in a n-dimensional coordinate space) or a symbolic model (i.e., with
  reference to entities of the real world such as cells, streets, cities, zip code,
  buildings, and so on) [26].

In the following, we will refer to elements of Users and of Areas as *user* and
area terms, respectively. While we assume such elements to be ground in the
predicates, a language could be readily extended to support variables for them.

All predicates could be expressed as boolean queries, and therefore have the
form *predicate(parameters, value)*. Their evaluation returns a triple [*bool_value*,
$\mathcal{R}$, *timeout*], where the term *bool_value* assumes values *true/false* according to the
corresponding access decision, $\mathcal{R}$ qualifies the accuracy of the predicate evaluation, and *timeout* sets the validity timeframe of the location predicate evaluation.
Our core set of location predicates includes the following predicates.

- A binary *position* predicate inarea(*user, area*) whose first argument *user*
  is a user term and second argument *area* is an area term. The predicate
  evaluates whether a user is located within a specific area (e.g., a city, a
  street, a building).
- A binary *position* predicate disjoint(*user, area*) whose first argument *user*
  is a user term and second argument *area* is an area term. The predicate
  evaluates whether a user is outside a specific area. Intuitively, disjoint is
  equivalent to the negation of inarea.

---

[1] Individual users may carry multiple SIMs and SIMs may be passed over to other
users. We shall not elaborate on these issues, since they are outside the scope of this
paper.

- A 4-ary *position* predicate distance(*user*, *entity*, *min_dist*, *max_dist*) whose first argument *user* is a user term, second argument *entity* is either a user or area term (identifying an entity in the system), while the third argument *min_dist* and fourth argument *max_dist* are two numbers specifying the minimum and maximum distance, respectively. The semantics of this predicate is to request whether the user lies within a given distance from the specified entity. The entity involved in the evaluation can be either stable or moving, physical or symbolic, and can be the resource to which the user is requesting access.
- A ternary *movement* predicate velocity(*user*, *min_vel*, *max_vel*) whose first argument *user* is a user term, and second argument *min_vel* and third argument *max_vel* are two numbers specifying a minimum and maximum velocity, respectively. The semantics of the predicate is to request whether the user speed lies within a given range of velocity.
- A ternary *interaction* predicate density(*area*, *min_num*, *max_num*) whose first argument *area* is an area term, while second argument *min_num* and third argument *max_num* are numbers specifying a minimum and maximum number of users. The semantics of the predicate is to request whether the number of users currently in an *area* lies within the interval specified.
- A 4-ary *interaction* predicate local_density(*user*, *area*, *min_num*, *max_num*) whose first argument *user* is a user term, the second argument *area* is a "relative" area with respect to the user, and third argument *min_num* and fourth argument *max_num*) specify a minimum and maximum number of users, respectively. The semantics of the predicate is to evaluate the density within an area surrounding the user.

Example 1. Let Alice be an element of Users, and Milan and Meeting_Office be two elements of Areas (specifying two symbolic characterizations corresponding to two known ranges of spatial coordinates).

- inarea(Alice,Milan) = [True,0.9,2007-10-05_11:10am]
  means that the location service assesses as true the fact that Alice is located in Milan with a confidence of 0.9, and that such an assessment is to be considered valid until 11:10am of October 5, 2007.
- velocity(Alice,70,90) = [True,0.7,2007-10-04_03:00pm]
  means that the Location Service assesses as true the fact that Alice is traveling at a speed included in the range [70,90] with a confidence of 0.7, and that such an assessment is to be considered valid until 3:00pm of October 4, 2007.
- density(Meeting_Office,0,1) = [False,0.95,2007-10-03_06:00pm]
  means that the Location Service assesses as false the statement that there is at most one person in the Meeting_Office and believes that two or more persons are in the office with an accuracy of 0.95. Such an assessment is to be considered valid until 06:00pm of October 3, 2007.

Location-based access control policies. Several existing authorization languages could be enriched with location-based predicates (e.g., [5,23,30]). We propose a model where location-based authorization rules can be defined as follows.

Definition 1 (Location-based authorization rule). *A location-based authorization rule is a triple of the form* ⟨subject_expression, object_expression, actions⟩, *where:*

- subject_expression *is a boolean formula of terms that allows referring to a set of subjects depending on whether they satisfy or not certain conditions that could evaluate traditional user's credentials and location predicates;*
- object_expression *is a boolean formula of terms that allows referring to a set of objects depending on whether they satisfy or not certain conditions that could evaluate traditional user's credentials and location predicates;*
- actions *is the action (or set of actions) to which the policy refers.*

Each user is assigned an identifier or pseudonym. Besides their identifiers (or pseudonym), users usually have other properties (e.g., name, address, and date of birth) that can be transmitted through digital certificates and are grouped into a *user profile*. Objects are data/services which users may ask to access to. Properties of an object are grouped into an *object profile*. Each property into user or object profiles are referenced with the traditional dot notation. Also, to make it possible to refer to the user and object of the request being evaluated without introducing variables in the language, we rely on the **user** and **object** keywords. For instance, **user.Affiliation** indicates the property **Affiliation** within the profile of the user whose request is currently processed.

Example 2. Consider a medical research laboratory that conducts research on the neuropathology of schizophrenia. The following are examples of location-based authorizations rules that can be expressed in our model.

- The access to the objects of type 'Tests' must be granted to doctors and must be performed when they are in the **TestRoom** only.
  ⟨**user.Role**='Doctor'∧inarea(**user.sim**, TestRoom), **object.type** = 'Tests', read⟩
- The access to the patient-related information must be granted to doctors only when they are in the building of the medical research laboratory (area MRL) and if there is nobody near them.
  ⟨**user.Role**='Doctor'∧inarea(**user.sim**, MRL)∧local_density(**user.sim**, CloseTo,1,1), **object.type** = 'PatientsInfo', read⟩

In [3], we also describe how to solve a basic problem: location-based predicates appear in rules as parts of a boolean formula, while the responses to boolean location queries are in the form of a triple [*bool_value, $\mathcal{R}$, timeout*]. To process a response from the location service, the LBAC system will need to assign a truth value to it. Intuitively, the transformation of a location predicate's value into a boolean value requires the LBAC system to determine whether or not the value returned by the location service can be considered valid for the purpose of controlling access.

3   Data Protection

The evolution of computer technology promises to offer inexpensive storage, with capacities considerably greater than the bandwidth of the network connecting the users accessing the resources. This permits the creation and distribution of huge collections of information, which need to be protected by third parties different from the owner of the data. Organizations have to add data storage (and skilled administrative personnel) at a high rate to store the increasing amount of information that is part of their information systems. A solution to the problem, which is becoming increasingly popular, as it saves costs and provides service benefits, is represented by *data outsourcing*, where data are stored together with application front-ends at the sites of external servers who take full responsibility of their management. However, in such a scenario the external server, which is relied upon for ensuring high availability of the outsourced data, cannot always be trusted with the confidentiality of data content (i.e., the server may be *honest but curious*). Besides well-known risks of confidentiality and privacy breaks, threats to outsourced data include improper use of information: the server could extract, resell, or commercially use substantial parts of a collection of data gathered and organized by the data owner, potentially harming the data owner's market for any product or service that incorporates that collection of information. Since traditional access control techniques cannot prevent the server itself from making unauthorized access to the outsourced data, data are encrypted and techniques are needed for enabling external service providers to execute queries on encrypted data [13,18,19,20]. The main drawback of all these existing proposals is that data are encrypted using a single key; knowledge of the key grants complete access to the data. Clearly, such an assumption does not fit real world applications, which demand for selective access by different users, groups of users, or applications. We now describe our approach for solving such a problem.

3.1 Selective Encryption

Given a system composed of a set $\mathcal{U}$ of users and a set $\mathcal{R}$ of resources, the data owner may want to define and enforce a policy, stating which user $u_i \in \mathcal{U}$ is allowed to access which resource $r_j \in \mathcal{R}$. Note that since the solution that we will describe do not depend on the granularity level to which the access control policy is defined, in the remainder of this section, we will continue to use the generic term resource to generically indicate any element on which authorizations can be specified.

The set of authorizations defined by the data owner are represented through a traditional *access matrix* $\mathcal{A}$, with a row for each user in $\mathcal{U}$, a column for each resource in $\mathcal{R}$, and such that $\mathcal{A}[u_i, r_j] = 1$, if u_i is allowed to access r_j; $\mathcal{A}[u_i, r_j] = 0$, otherwise. In the following, given an access matrix $\mathcal{A}$ over sets $\mathcal{U}$ and $\mathcal{R}$, $acl(r_j)$ denotes the *access control list* of resource r_j, that is, the set of users that can access r_j. For instance, Figure 1 represents an access matrix for a system with four users, namely Alice (A), Bob (B), Carol (C), and David (D), and four resources (r_1, r_2, r_3, and r_4). Here, for example, $acl(r_1)$={B,C}.

The naive solution for enforcing access control through selective encryption consists in using a different key for each resource in the system, and in communicating to each user the set of keys associated with the resources she can

	r_1	r_2	r_3	r_4
Alice	0	1	1	1
Bob	1	0	1	0
Carol	1	1	0	1
David	0	1	1	1

Fig. 1. An example of access matrix

access. This solution correctly enforces the policy, but it is very expensive since each user needs to keep a number of keys that depends on her privileges. That is, users having many privileges and, probably, often accessing the system, will have a greater number of keys than users having a few privileges and, probably, accessing only rarely the system. To reduce the number of keys a user has to manage, we propose to use a *key derivation method*. A key derivation method is basically a function that, given a key and a piece of publicly available information, allows the computation of another key. The basic idea is that each user is given a small number of keys, from which she can derive all the keys needed to access the resources she is authorized to access.

To the aim of using a key derivation method, it is necessary to define which keys can be derived from another key and how. Key derivation methods proposed in the literature are based on the definition of a *key derivation hierarchy*. Given a set of keys $\mathcal{K}$ in the system and a partial order relation $\preceq$ defined on it, the corresponding key derivation hierarchy is usually represented as a pair $(\mathcal{K}, \preceq)$, where $\forall k_i, k_j \in \mathcal{K}$, $k_j \preceq k_i$ iff k_j is derivable from k_i. Any key derivation hierarchy can be graphically represented through a directed graph, having a vertex for each key in $\mathcal{K}$, and a path from k_i to k_j only if k_j can be derived from k_i. Depending on the partial order relation defined on $\mathcal{K}$, the key derivation hierarchy can be: a *chain* [27] (i.e., $\preceq$ defines a total order relation); a *tree* [17,27,28]; or a *directed acyclic graph* [1,6,11,16,21,22,24,25,29] (DAG).

When choosing a key derivation method for the outsourcing scenario, it is necessary to take into consideration two different aspects: *1)* the client overhead and *2)* the cost of managing access control policy updates. The client overhead is mainly the communication and computation time for getting from the server the public information that is needed in the derivation process. Since the key derivation hierarchy is used to correctly enforce the access control policy specified by the data owner, the cost of enforcing access control policy updates is the cost of updating the key derivation hierarchy. Intuitively, if the access control policy is likely to change over time, the hierarchy needs to re-arrange accordingly (i.e., insert or delete vertices, and modify keys). An important requirement is then to minimize the amount of re-encrypting and re-keying need in the hierarchy re-arrangement. Indeed, any time the key of a vertex is changed, at least the resources encrypted with that key need to be re-encrypted by the data owner, and the new key should be given to all users knowing the old one. By analyzing the most important key derivation methods, we can observe that the key derivation methods operating on trees or DAGs allow insertion and deletion of leaf vertices, without need of changing other keys. If, instead, an internal vertex v is inserted

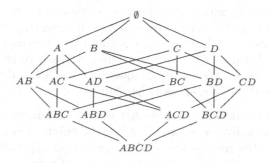

Fig. 2. An example of user hierarchy

or deleted, all the keys of the vertices in the subtree rooted at v must be updated accordingly, and all resources previously encrypted by using the old keys must be re-encrypted. However, there are methods operating on DAGs and associating public information with edges in the graph (e.g., Atallah's et al. [6]) that allow insertion and deletion of vertices without need of re-keying operations. These methods are therefore appropriate for the purpose of minimizing the cost of enforcing policy updates. In particular, we adopt the method proposed in [6] that maintains a piece of public information, called *token*, associated with each edge in the hierarchy. Given two keys, k_i and k_j arbitrarily assigned to two vertices, and a public label l_j associated with k_j, a token from k_i to k_j is defined as $T_{i,j}=k_j \oplus h(k_i,l_j)$, where $\oplus$ is the n-ary xor operator and h is a secure hash function. Given $T_{i,j}$, any user knowing k_i and with access to public label l_j, can compute (derive) k_j. All tokens $T_{i,j}$ in the system are stored in a *public catalog*.

Key derivation hierarchy. An access control policy $\mathcal{A}$ is enforced by defining a *user-based hierarchy*[2], denoted UH, that is a pair $(P(\mathcal{U}), \preceq)$, where $P(\mathcal{U})$ is the set containing all possible sets of users in the system, and $\preceq$ is the partial order relation induced by the set containment relation ($\subseteq$). More precisely, $\forall a, b \in P(\mathcal{U})$, $a \preceq b$ if and only if $b \subseteq a$. The user-based hierarchy contains therefore the set of all subsets of $\mathcal{U}$ and the corresponding DAG has $2^{|\mathcal{U}|}$ vertices. For instance, Figure 2 represents a user-based hierarchy built over a system with four users A, B, C, and D. To correctly enforce the access control policy, each vertex in the hierarchy is associated with a key, each resource in the system is encrypted by using the key of the vertex representing its *acl*, and each user is given the key of the vertex representing herself in the hierarchy. From the key of vertex u_i, user u_i can then derive the keys of the vertices representing groups of users containing u_i and therefore she can decrypt all the resources she can access (i.e., belonging to her capability list). Note that the empty set vertex represents a key known only to the data owner, and it is used to encrypt resources that nobody can access. As an example, consider the policy in Figure 1 and the hierarchy in Figure 2. Resource r_1 is encrypted with key k_{BC} of vertex BC, r_2 with k_{ACD},

---

[2] Note that a dual approach can be applied by defining a *resource-based hierarchy*, where the access control policy $\mathcal{A}$ is modeled as a set of capabilities.

r_3 with k_{ABD}, and r_4 with k_{ACD}. Each user knows the key associated with the vertex representing herself and there is a path connecting each user's vertex with all the vertices representing a group containing the user. For instance, if we consider user A, from vertex A it is possible to reach vertices AB, AC, AD, ABC, ABD, ACD, and $ABCD$. Consequently, user A can decrypt r_2, r_3, and r_4, which are exactly the resources in her capability list.

Hierarchy reduction. It is easy to see that the solution described above defines more keys than actually needed and requires the publication of a great amount of information on the remote server, thus causing an expensive key derivation process at the client-side. The higher is the number of users, the deeper is the key derivation hierarchy (the hierarchy height is equal to the number of users in the system). As an example, consider the user-based hierarchy in Figure 2 and, in particular, consider user A. To access resource r_3, A has to first derive k_{AD} that in turn can be used for deriving k_{ABD}, which is the key needed for decrypting r_3. However, in this case, vertex AD makes only the derivation process longer than needed and therefore it can be removed without compromising the correctness of the derivation process.

Since an important goal is to reduce the client's overhead, it is possible to simplify the key derivation hierarchy, removing non necessary vertices, while ensuring a correct key derivability. Therefore, instead of representing all the possible groups of users in the DAG, it is sufficient to represent those sets of users whose key is relevant for access control enforcement. Intuitively, these groups are those corresponding either to the *acl* values or singleton sets of users. The vertices corresponding to *acl*s and to users are necessary because their keys are used for resource encryption and allow users to correctly derive all the other keys used for encrypting resources in their capabilities, respectively. This set of vertices needs then to be correctly connected in the hierarchy. In particular, from the key of any user u_i it must be possible to derive the keys of all those vertices representing a group that contains u_i[3]. Another important observation is that when building the key derivation hierarchy, other vertices can be inserted, which are useful for reducing the size of the public catalog, even if their keys are not used for derivation. As an example, consider a system with five users and three *acl* values: ACD, ABD, and ADE. If vertices A, B, C, D, and E are connected directly with ACD, ABD, and ADE, the system needs nine tokens. If instead a new vertex AD is inserted and connected with the three *acl* values, A and D do not need an edge connecting them directly to each *acl* value, but they only need an edge connecting them with AD. In this case, the system needs eight tokens. Therefore, any time three or more vertices share a common parent, it is useful to insert such a vertex for saving tokens in the public catalog. Figure 3 illustrates the hierarchy corresponding to the access control policy in Figure 1 and containing only the vertices needed for a correct enforcement of the policy. The problem of correctly enforcing a policy through a key derivation graph while

---

[3] Note that it is not advisable to connect each user's key directly with each group containing the user itself because any time a client needs to derive a key, it queries the remote server to gain the tokens necessary for derivation.

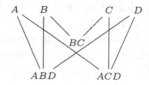

Fig. 3. An example of simplified hierarchy enforcing the access control policy in Figure 1

minimizing the number of edges in the DAG is however *NP-hard*. In [12] we have solved this problem through an approximation algorithm.

4 Research Challenges

We now outline some of the key aspects and challenges to be addressed in the context of privacy-aware location-based services and data outsourcing scenarios.

- *Secure infrastructure for contextual information.* A globally accessible, secure infrastructure for distributing context information, involving a variety of devices from portable computers to mobile phones and seamlessly dealing with their different standard formats, should be available. Also, information generated from different applications should not remain restricted to the local context; integrating context information with user profiles paves the way to advanced applications where user context can be exploited for service discovery and composition. To achieve these goals, context representation must be semantically unambiguous, interoperable, human readable and processable by machines.
- *Definition of privacy preferences.* An important aspect for the success of privacy-aware location-based services is the definition of a mechanism for the specification of user privacy preferences that should be easy to use to nonspecialists in the field. This issue has received little attention in existing proposals on location privacy.
- *Balancing location privacy and accuracy.* Location privacy solutions should be able to balance the need of privacy protection required by users and the need of accuracy required by service providers. Location privacy techniques, which are mostly focused on users needs, could make service provisioning impossible in practice due to an excessive degradation of the accuracy of location measurement.
- *Write authorizations.* The proposals for enforcing selective access on outsourced data treat only read authorizations. This is justified by practical considerations, as currently applications are mostly read-only. Moreover, read authorizations permit also a simpler description of the approach. However, there are situations where it is needed to support write authorizations. In this case, an important security concern in data outsourcing is also integrity.

- *Policy changes.* A limitation of current proposals for enforcing access control on outsourced data is that they require the owner, in case of updates of the authorization policy, to re-encrypt the resources and resend them to the server. Therefore, a crucial problem to be addressed in this context concerns the enforcement of selective authorization policies and the support of policy updates in dynamic scenarios.
- *Partial encryption.* From a data access point of view, dealing with encrypted information represents a burden since encryption makes it not always possible to efficiently execute queries and evaluate conditions over the data. The assumption underlying approaches in the data outsourcing scenario is that all the data are equally sensitive and therefore encryption is a price to be paid to protect them. This assumption is typically an overkill in many scenarios. As a matter of fact, in many situations data are not sensitive per se; what is sensitive is their association with other data (e.g., in a hospital the list of illnesses cured or the list of patients could be made publicly available, while the association of specific illnesses to individual patients must be protected). An interesting evolution would be therefore the development of new solutions where encryption should be applied only when explicitly demanded by the privacy requirements.

5   Conclusions

The protection of privacy in today's global infrastructure requires the combined application solution from technology (technical measures), legislation (law and public policy), and organizational and individual policies and practices. The privacy problem therefore covers different and various fields and issues on which much is to be said. In this paper, we have highlighted the critical necessity for privacy protection and identified some research challenges to be looked at.

Acknowledgments

This work was supported in part by the European Union under contract IST-2002-507591, and by the Italian Ministry of Research, within program PRIN 2006, under project "Basi di dati crittografate" (2006099978).

References

1. Akl, S., Taylor, P.: Cryptographic solution to a problem of access control in a hierarchy. ACM Transactions on Computer System 1, 239 (1983)
2. Ardagna, C.A., Damiani, E., Cremonini, M., De Capitani di Vimercati, S., Samarati, P.: CAS++: an open source single sign-on solution for secure e-services. In: Proc. of the 21st IFIP TC-11 International Information Security Conference, Karlstad, Sweden (May 2006)

3. Ardagna, C.A., Damiani, E., Cremonini, M., De Capitani di Vimercati, S., Samarati, P.: Supporting location-based conditions in access control policies. In: ASIACCS 2006. Proc. of the ACM Symposium on InformAtion, Computer and Communications Security, Taipei, Taiwan (March 2006)
4. Ardagna, C.A., Damiani, E., De Capitani di Vimercati, S., Foresti, S., Samarati, P.: Trust management. In: Petkovic, M., Jonker, W. (eds.) Security, Privacy and Trust in Modern Data Management, Springer, Heidelberg (2007)
5. Ardagna, C.A., Damiani, E., De Capitani di Vimercati, S., Samarati, P.: Towards Privacy-Enhanced Authorization Policies and Languages. In: Proc. of the 19th IFIP WG11.3 Working Conference on Data and Application Security, Storrs, Connecticut USA (August 2005)
6. Atallah, M.J., Frikken, K.B., Blanton, M.: Dynamic and efficient key management for access hierarchies. In: CCS 2005. Proc. of the 12th ACM conference on Computer and Communications Security, Alexandria, VA, USA (November 2005)
7. Cimato, S., Gamassi, M., Piuri, V., Sassi, R., Scotti, F.: Privacy issues in biometric identification. Information Security (October 2006)
8. Ciriani, V., De Capitani di Vimercati, S., Foresti, S., Samarati, P.: K-anonymity. In: Jajodia, S., Yu, T. (eds.) Security in Decentralized Data Management, Springer, Heidelberg (2007)
9. Ciriani, V., De Capitani di Vimercati, S., Foresti, S., Samarati, P.: Microdata protection. In: Jajodia, S., Yu, T. (eds.) Security in Decentralized Data Management, Springer, Heidelberg (2007)
10. Corallo, A., Cremonini, M., Damiani, E., De Capitani di Vimercati, S., Elia, G., Samarati, P.: Security, privacy, and trust in mobile systems. In: Mobile and Wireless Systems beyond 3G: managing new business opportunities, Idea Group Inc., USA (2004)
11. Crampton, J., Martin, K., Wild, P.: On key assignment for hierarchical access control. In: CSFW 2006. Proc. of the 19th IEEE Computer Security Foundations Workshop, Venice, Italy (July 2006)
12. Damiani, E., De Capitani di Vimercati, S., Foresti, S., Jajodia, S., Paraboschi, S., Samarati, P.: Selective data encryption in outsourced dynamic environments. In: VODCA 2006. Proc. of the Second International Workshop on Views On Designing Complex Architectures, Bertinoro, Italy (September 2006)
13. Damiani, E., De Capitani di Vimercati, S., Jajodia, S., Paraboschi, S., Samarati, P.: Balancing confidentiality and efficiency in untrusted relational DBMSs. In: CCS 2003. Proc. of the 10th ACM Conference on Computer and Communications Security, Washington, DC, USA (October 2003)
14. De Capitani di Vimercati, S., Samarati, P.: Privacy in the electronic society. In: Bagchi, A., Atluri, V. (eds.) ICISS 2006. LNCS, vol. 4332, Springer, Heidelberg (2006) (invited talk)
15. De Capitani di Vimercati, S., Samarati, P.: Protecting privacy in the global infrastructure. In: Proc. of the International Conference on Information Security and Computer Forensics, Chennai, India (December 2006) (invited talk)
16. De Santis, A., Ferrara, A.L., Masucci, B.: Cryptographic key assignment schemes for any access control policy. Inf. Process. Lett. 92(4), 199–205 (2004)
17. Gudes, E.: The design of a cryptography based secure file system. IEEE Transactions on Software Engineering 6, 411 (1980)
18. Hacigümüs, H., Iyer, B., Li, C., Mehrotra, S.: Executing SQL over encrypted data in the database-service-provider model. In: Proc. of the ACM SIGMOD 2002, Madison, Wisconsin, USA (June 2002)

19. Hacigümüs, H., Iyer, B., Mehrotra, S.: Providing database as a service. In: Proc. of 18th International Conference on Data Engineering, San Jose, California, USA (March 2002)
20. Hacigümüs, H., Iyer, B., Mehrotra, S.: Ensuring integrity of encrypted databases in database as a service model. In: Proc. of the IFIP Conference on Data and Applications Security, Estes Park, Colorado, USA (August 2003)
21. Harn, L., Lin, H.: A cryptographic key generation scheme for multilevel data security. Computers and Security 9, 539 (1990)
22. Hwang, M., Yang, W.: Controlling access in large partially ordered hierarchies using cryptographic keys. The Journal of Systems and Software 67, 99 (2003)
23. Jajodia, S., Samarati, P., Sapino, M.L., Subrahmanian, V.S.: Flexible support for multiple access control policies. ACM Transactions on Database Systems 26(2), 214–260 (2001)
24. Liaw, H.T., Wang, S.J., Lei, C.L.: On the design of a single-key-lock mechanism based on newton's interpolating polynomial. IEEE Transaction on Software Engineering 15, 1135 (1989)
25. MacKinnon, S., Taylor, P.D., Meijer, H., Akl, S.G.: An optimal algorithm for assigning cryptographic keys to control access in a hierarchy. IEEE Transactions on Computers 34(9), 797–802 (1985)
26. Marsit, N., Hameurlain, A., Mammeri, Z., Morvan, F.: Query processing in mobile environments: a survey and open problems. In: DFMA 2005. Proc. of the First Inernational Conference on Distributed Framework for Multimedia Applications, Besancon, France (February 2005)
27. Sandhu, R.S.: On some cryptographic solutions for access control in a tree hierarchy. In: Proc. of the 1987 Fall Joint Computer Conference on Exploring Technology: Today and Tomorrow, Dallas, Texas, USA (1987)
28. Sandhu, R.S.: Cryptographic implementation of a tree hierarchy for access control. Information Processing Letters 27, 95 (1988)
29. Shen, V.R.L., Chen, T.S.: A novel key management scheme based on discrete logarithms and polynomial interpolations. Computer and Security 21, 164 (2002)
30. van der Horst, T.W., Sundelin, T., Seamons, K.E., Knutson, C.D.: Mobile trust negotiation: Authentication and authorization in dynamic mobile networks. In: Proc. of the Eighth IFIP Conference on Communications and Multimedia Security, Lake Windermere, England (September 2004)

Secure Chaotic Synchronization Using Negative Feedback of Super-Positioned Signals

G.K. Patra, V. Anil Kumar, and R.P. Thangavelu

CSIR Centre for Mathematical Modelling and Computer Simulation,
Bangalore, India
{gkpatra, anil, thangam}@cmmacs.ernet.in
http://www.cmmacs.ernet.in

Abstract. Chaotic synchronization is a potential candidate for a stream cipher cryptosystem. However, many of the proposed schemes do not posses the required security level to be used in real implementations. One of the major threats to such cryptosystems based on chaotic synchronization is the parameter estimation method both in on-line and off-line forms. In this paper we propose a new method of feedback synchronization, in which instead of a single variable feedback, we propose to use a superposition of multiple variable values. As super-positioning is an irreversible computation, it dilutes the information content of the various parameters of the chaotic system. We show in this paper that an identical chaotic system (parameters are same) can still synchronize, while a non-identical system (parameters are different) will fail. We have demonstrated the robustness of the proposed system from well-known on-line and off-line attacks.

Keywords: Chaotic Synchronization, Chaotic cryptosystems, Super-positioned signal, Stream ciphers.

1 Introduction

In the last few years many chaos-based cryptosystems have been proposed for both analog and digital communication [1,2,3,4]. Most analog chaos-based cryptosystems are meant for secure communication for noisy channels, while digital chaos-based cryptosystems are meant for digital computers. Almost all the chaos based cryptosystems, whether analog or digital are based on chaotic synchronization. Synchronization of two identical chaotic systems by transmitting only a subset of the state space variable is well-known [5,6,7]. This phenomenon has been tried in building an end-to-end secure communication channel. A good review can be found in reference [4].

Synchronization using a single time dependent variable continuously in a one-way interaction has been the most widely used method. Based on this continuous synchronization process many chaos-synchronization-based cryptosystems such as chaotic masking [1], chaotic switching [8], chaotic modulation [2], chaos-based pseudo-random number generators [9], block ciphers etc have been proposed. Continuous synchronization can be achieved using various techniques.

P. McDaniel and S.K. Gupta (Eds.): ICISS 2007, LNCS 4812, pp. 193–207, 2007.

Researchers have proposed various synchronization schemes and have studied their advantages and disadvantages. The most used synchronization scheme is the feedback scheme [10], where one of the state space values is continuously sent from the transmitter to the receiver and the receiver uses the difference with respect to its own value as a feedback to the system. It has been observed that by continuously feeding the signal back, the two chaotic systems are synchronized. This means that all the state space variables converge and start following the same trajectory [3].

For achieving secure communication the synchronization process has to be secure. In a one-way coupled system the master (transmitter), is static, so most of the attacks are aimed at parameter estimation of the masters system by using the time series obtained from the public state space variable. There are two types of attackers normally studied, one is off-line, where the attacker does a time series analysis [11] and tries to get the parameter of the master system, while in case of on-line attacks [12,13], the attacker tries to synchronize the variables as well as the parameters with the master's using some minimization methods. Though the expected advantages from the chaos-based cryptosystems are quite encouraging, lack of proper security has prevented these methods from hardware implementation so far [11,14,15,16].

In this paper, we propose a negative feedback scheme, in which instead of transmitting only a single state space variable, a superposition of two or more state space variables are transmitted. We show that synchronization can be achieved using this proposed scheme. We have discussed various properties and advantages of the proposed synchronization scheme. To end the paper we have carried out a security analysis and have discussed its robustness against some of the well known off-line and on-line attacks.

2   A Typical Synchronization Scheme and Its Vulnerabilities

Before presenting the new scheme let us look at the current synchronization schemes and the possible threats. There are two types of synchronization schemes. One is the complete replacement [3] and the other is feedback [10]. In a complete replacement scheme the public state space variable of the transmitter replaces the receivers same state space variable. This reduces the problem to a five equation system. In feedback synchronization scheme the difference of the public state space variable value of receiver and transmitter is fedback continuously at the receiver end to achieve synchronization. Fig. 1 shows the synchronization of all state space variable values using a three variable Lorenz system as given in Eq. 1 (a) complete replacement scheme (b) feedback scheme. In both the scheme of synchronization the value of only a single state space variable of the transmitter is made public.

$$\dot{x}_1 = \sigma(x_2 - x_1) \ \ \dot{y}_1 = \sigma(y_2 - y_1) \ .$$
$$\dot{x}_2 = \rho x_1 - x_2 - x_1 x_3 \ \ \dot{y}_2 = \rho y_1 - y_2 - y_1 y_3 \ .$$
$$\dot{x}_3 = x_1 x_2 - \beta x_3 \ \ \dot{y}_3 = y_1 y_2 - \beta y_3 \ .$$

$$(1)$$

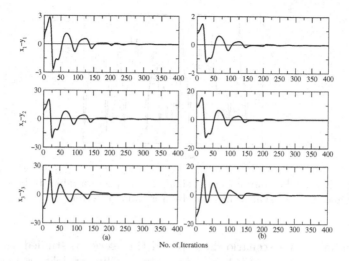

Fig. 1. Differences in all the three state space variable values between the receiver and the transmitter with number of iterations (a) complete replacement scheme (b) feedback scheme. All the differences converge to zero indicating synchronization.

A typical time series available publicly is shown in fig. 2. This is the only information an attacker can use to estimate the unknown information about the chaotic system which has generated the signal. It is well-known that a great deal of information about the chaotic system is contained in the time series of its variables. Parameter estimation [11,13,17,18] using time series is one of the most important research topics in chaos. This has many applications in fields other than cryptosystems. However, in case of chaotic cryptosystems the parameter estimation techniques are treated as possible threats.

The public time series is important information to an off-line attacker. Using various time series analysis techniques the attacker tries to exploit its vulnerabilities. In the literature there are many analyses proposed on chaotic synchronization [11,18] schemes, of which many are not practical either because they consume a lot of time or need a long portion of data. In 2003 Vaidya [11] proposed a faster parameter estimation method on a three parameter Lorenz system with access only to a short portion of the data. The attack proposed consists of four steps. The first is to find the first three derivatives from the received samples of public signal. The second is to from a set of tri-linear equations by transforming the Lorenz equations. The third step is to recast these as linear equations with four unknowns. In the fourth step the unknown parameters are determined using a generalized inverse of a matrix. By using a short portion of data from the public signal shown in fig. 2, they could successfully estimated the parameters with sufficient accuracy. The assumption in this attacking strategy is that the attacker has knowledge of the functional form of the chaotic system.

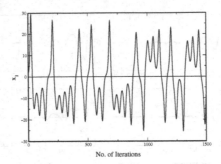

Fig. 2. Publicly available information (a single state space variable) to be exploited by an attacker and used for synchronization by a genuine receiver

In an on-line attack scenario the exposed time series is studied as and when the synchronization process is happening. Most on-line attacks are synchronization based [13,17], where the attacker uses a similar chaotic system (with random initial condition and random unknown static parameters) to minimize the error in the public state space variable value (time series). Many on-line methods proposed are unsuitable to estimate all the parameters of a chaotic system. In 2005 Konnur [13] proposed a least square approach to drive a system of differential equations which govern the temporal evolution of the parameters. He showed that asymptotic convergence to the true parameter values can be achieved by solving those equations. Fig. 3 shows the convergence of the parameters as well as the state space variables using the above technique. To overcome these vulnerabilities many suggestions were made such as sporadic driving [19], exchange of information at longer intervals [20], alternatively switched bi-directional coupling [21,22], techniques for rapid synchronization [20] etc. We propose a simple modification to the feedback mechanism to protect the synchronization from these vulnerabilities.

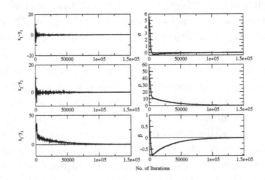

Fig. 3. Difference in the parameters as well as the state space variable values of an on-line attacker and genuine transmitter in a typical feedback synchronization scenario. The convergence to zero in all the variables are an indication of successful attack.

3   The Concept of Super-Positioned Feedback

Chaotic synchronization is achieved by driving the receiver system with the value of one or more state space variables. However, in applications such as secure communication, one has to give as little information as possible to an eavesdropper. So normally only one variable is transmitted to achieve synchronization between the receiver and the transmitter. The time series which is made public provides enough information about the chaotic system. In an alternative feedback mechanism, we modify the public signal in such a way that the information content becomes too low to be exploited by an attacker without compromising on the efficiency of the synchronization process. We looked at using a signal, which is an additive linear superposition of two or more state space variables as given in eq. 2.

$$S = \frac{1}{\sum_i a_i} \sum_i a_i x_i. \tag{2}$$

where S is the super-positioned signal which will be made public and a_i is the strength of contribution of the signal x_i in the super-positioned signal. In case of a Lorenz system the value of i is equal to 3. Eq. 2 suggests that the normal synchronization process of using one state space variable is a special case of S, where except one all other coefficients are equal to zero.

Now let us discuss the properties and advantages of using a super-positioned signal as feedback instead of a single variable feedback. As the superposition considered here is linear it only provides a time series which is a combination of two signals with different strengths. As it is an additive combination, which is an irreversible process, the new signal cannot be uniquely decomposed to its individual components. This is an advantage as the information about the system parameters are diluted, especially in the areas where the signal have opposite sign. By keeping the values of the coefficient a_i secret (which can be treated as one of the secret parameter) the attacker can be kept completely in the dark about the constituents of the signal. The other advantage which is worth discussing is the verification of synchronization. From the definition of synchronization, we say two identical chaotic systems are synchronized, if all the time dependent variables follow the same trajectory. That means for a three variable Lorenz system as shown in Eq. 1 synchronization means $x_i - y_i \to 0$ for i=1 to 3. In the case of a super-positioned signal the verification of synchronization indicates testing convergence of multiple variables at the same time. The feedback signal to the receiver system is seen as

$$\frac{\alpha}{\sum_i a_i} \sum_i a_i (x_i - y_i). \tag{3}$$

In the case of super-positioned feedback, Eq. 3 should damp out and converge to zero. The only situation, where it can give false illusion about the synchronization is, when the Eq. 3 is 0, inspite of few of $(x_i - y_i)$'s non zero. However, as that point will not be a stable point, it can be clearly identified. The only precaution one needs to take in deciding the values of a_i, is that a particular signal does not dominate the resultant super-positioned signal, which will reduce the scheme to a normal synchronization with already known vulnerability.

4   Synchronization Methodology and Its Advantages

The most important question that needs to be addressed is whether super-positioned feedback can lead to synchronization or not. We will discuss it analytically and also numerically. Let us look at the system of equations of transmitter(x) and the receiver(y) as shown below

$$\dot{x}_1 = \sigma(x_2 - x_1) \quad \dot{y}_1 = \sigma(y_2 - y_1) - R \, .$$
$$\dot{x}_2 = \rho x_1 - x_2 - x_1 x_3 \quad \dot{y}_2 = \rho y_1 - y_2 - y_1 y_3 \, . \tag{4}$$
$$\dot{x}_3 = x_1 x_2 - \beta x_3 \quad \dot{y}_3 = y_1 y_2 - \beta y_3 \, .$$

$$R = \left[\frac{\alpha}{\sum_i a_i} \sum_i a_i y_i \right] - \left[\frac{\alpha}{\sum_i a_i} \sum_i a_i x_i \right] \, .$$

Let us consider the simplest case of super-positioned signal i.e super position of only two variables with $a_1 = 1$, $a_2 = 1$ and $a_3 = 0$, so that we get $R = 0.5\alpha (y_1 + y_2 - x_1 - x_2)$. To show that the damping term damps down to zero, we need to show that the Jacobean matrix associated with the three element error vector e_1, e_2, e_3 (which are equal to $x_1 - y_1$, $x_2 - y_2$ and $x_3 - y_3$ respectively) has eigen values, whose real parts are negative. The Jacobean matrix for the above system is given by [23]

$$\begin{pmatrix} -\sigma - \frac{\alpha}{2} & \sigma - \frac{\alpha}{2} & 0 \\ \rho - <x_3> & -1 & -<x_1> \\ <x_2> & <x_1> & -\beta \end{pmatrix}$$

Here $< x >$ denotes the time average on the invariant measure along the driving trajectory for the x variable. This needs to be numerically estimated for a sufficiently long period. The eigen values λ for the above mentioned Jacobean matrix are given by [23]

$$\lambda_1 = -\beta \, .$$
$$\lambda_2 = \frac{-(\sigma + 1 + 0.5\alpha)}{2} + \frac{1}{2}\sqrt{(\sigma + 0.5\alpha - 1)^2 + 4(\sigma - 0.5\alpha)(\rho - <x_3>)} \, . \tag{5}$$
$$\lambda_3 = \frac{-(\sigma + 1 + 0.5\alpha)}{2} - \frac{1}{2}\sqrt{(\sigma + 0.5\alpha - 1)^2 + 4(\sigma - 0.5\alpha)(\rho - <x_3>)} \, .$$

In order to make sure that the feedback perturbation will damp out, the largest transverse exponent should be negative. We looked at the natural measures on the chaotic attractor [23]. The value of α for which all the eigen values will have negative real part, for guaranteed synchronization can be derived form Eq. 5. The critical value of α for which synchronization will occur is give by

$$\alpha \geq -2\sigma \frac{\rho - <x_3> -1}{1 + \rho - <x_3>} \, . \tag{6}$$

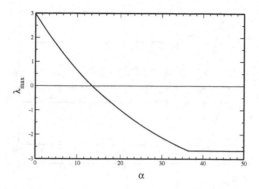

Fig. 4. The effect of coupling strength on the largest Lyapunov exponent. Negative largest Lyapunov exponent indicates guaranteed synchronization.

The dynamics of the Lorenz system has a chaotic attractor for $\sigma = 10, \beta = 8/3$ and $\rho = 60$. The numerically calculated [23] values of $< x_1 >, < x_2 > and < x_3 >$ are 0, 0, 54.81 respectively. So for synchronization to happen for the above case the value of α should be greater than 13.6. A similar derivation can be made for feedback to the y_2 and y_3 equations at the receiver end. For same feedback given at y_2 equation α should be greater than or equal to $\rho - < x_3 > -1(\approx 4.2)$. However, feedback to y_3 equation shows that synchronization cannot be achieved. To show the effect of the coupling strength on the real part of largest eigen value we plotted (fig. 4) λ_{max} for different α with y_2 fedback.

As a numerical example we considered a typical case with initial conditions $(1.874, 2.056, 19.142)$ and $(2.125, -6.138, 34.672)$ for the transmitter and receiver

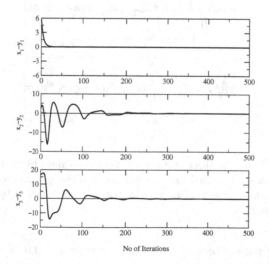

No of Iterations

Fig. 5. Differences in all the three state space variable values between transmitter and receiver, when a super-positioned signal is fed-back to the y_1 equation of the receiver's Lorenz equations. The convergence to zero indicates synchronization.

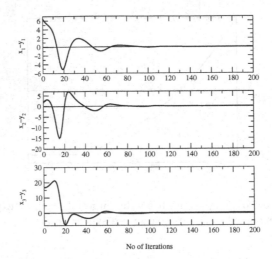

Fig. 6. Differences in all the three state space variable values between transmitter and receiver, when a super-positioned signal is fed-back to the y_2 equation of the receiver's Lorenz equations. The convergence to zero indicates synchronization.

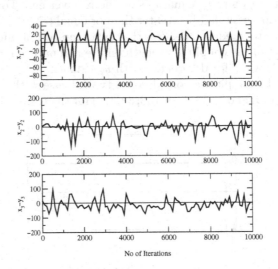

Fig. 7. Differences in all the three state space variable values between transmitter and receiver, when a super-positioned signal is fed-back to the y_3 equation of the receiver's Lorenz equations. This shows synchronization cannot be achieved by feed backing the signal to the y_3 equation.

respectively. The parameters of the system are ($\sigma = 10.0, \beta = 2.667$ and $\rho = 60.0$) which are exchanged using an alternate method of key exchange. The transmitter and receiver calculate their trajectory by solving the Lorenz equation (Eq.4) using the 4th order Runge-Kutta procedure. Fig. 5 and fig. 6 shows the

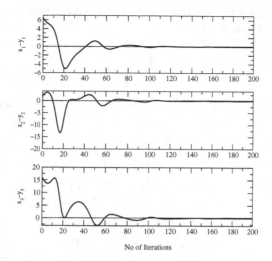

Fig. 8. Differences in all the three state space variable values between transmitter and receiver, when a super-positioned signal is fed-back to both the y_2 and y_3 equations of receiver's Lorenz equations. The convergence to zero suggests that the feedback at y_3 does not disturb the synchronization.

e_1, e_2, e_3 converging to zero for the super-positioned feedback in y_1 equation and y_2 equations respectively. Fig.7 shows the same for super-positioned feedback in y_3 equation, which shows that synchronization cannot be achieved. However, as shown in fig. 8, if the feedback is given to multiple equations in addition to the y_3 equation then synchronization can still be achieved.

5   Security Analysis

Our main aim is to achieve a secure synchronization mechanism. In this section we will look at the robustness of the synchronization scheme from both off-line and on-line attacks. As already discussed earlier the most successful off-line attack is proposed by Vaidya [11], which needs access to only a small portion of data. According to the attack, the variables of Lorenz equation should be transformed to a new set of variables, which will be related to each other through a tri-linear equation such that they can be used to form a matrix to be solved to find out the unknown parameters [11]. Let us consider the transformation of the state space variables x_1, x_2, x_3 in to A,B,C as follows

$$A = x_1 + x_2 .$$
$$B = (\rho x_1 - x_2 - x_1 x_3) + \sigma(x_2 - x_1) . \tag{7}$$
$$C = \rho\sigma(x_2 - x_1) - \rho x_1 + x_2 + x_1 x_3 - x_1(x_1 x_2 - \beta x_3) - \sigma x_3(x_2 - x_1) + \sigma\big[(\rho x_1 - x_2 - x_1 x_3) - \sigma(x_2 - x_1)\big] .$$

This transformation has an inverse if $A \neq 0$. With this transformation, the Lorenz equation takes the form

$$\frac{d}{dt}A = B .$$
$$\frac{d}{dt}B = C .$$
$$\frac{d}{dt}C = D = Px_1{}^3 + Qx_1{}^2 + Rx_1 + S + Tx_1{}^{-1} + Ux_1{}^{-2} .$$

where

$$P = -6\sigma .$$
$$Q = 7\sigma A - B .$$
$$R = 2\beta\rho\sigma + 2\beta\sigma - 4\sigma^2 - 2\sigma A^2 .$$
$$S = 2\sigma^2 A - \beta\sigma A - \beta\rho\sigma A - B - \sigma B - \sigma C .$$
$$T = \sigma B^2 + CA - 2\sigma AB - 2\sigma^2 AB .$$
$$U = \sigma^2 A^2 - \sigma A^2 - \sigma AB .$$

and x_1 is the solution of the quartic

$$x_1{}^4 + Lx_1{}^3 + Mx_1{}^2 + Nx_1 + O = 0 . \tag{8}$$

where

$$L = -A .$$
$$M = 2\sigma - \beta - \beta\rho .$$
$$N = 2\sigma^2 - \sigma B - A\sigma - C - A .$$
$$O = \sigma AB + \sigma A^2 - \sigma^2 A^2 .$$

The above equation leads to a complex relation between the unknown parameters, which cannot be embedded into a multidimensional unique equation. So a generalized matrix problem, which gives an estimate of the parameters, can not be formed with sufficient accuracy and uniqueness. Further, conflicting checks for computation conditions makes it impossible to satisfy all the criteria for a successful estimation. Though the above analysis of a particular attack does not necessarily show the robustness against all off-line attacks, it gives an indication of the complexity involved in time series analysis attacks. This attack which is very successful against a one variable feedback scheme by just using a small portion of the large time series available publicly, is unsuccessful against a super-positioned feedback as the feedback signal by virtue of its superposition property loses some information. Further if the coefficient a_i can be kept secret an attacker cannot perform time series analysis.

Now let us analyze the synchronization based on-line parameter estimation strategy on feedback synchronization using super-positioned signals. Let the chaotic systems at the transmitter, the receiver and the attacker be represented by the following system of ordinary differential equations

$$\dot{x} = f(x, p) \, .$$
$$\dot{y} = f(y, p) \, . \tag{9}$$
$$\dot{z} = f(z, q) \, .$$

It is already clear that $y - x \to 0$ as $t \to \infty$. An attacker to synchronize in a similar way will have to minimize $(z - x)^2$ for the variable which is made public for the purpose of synchronization. The feedback signal is a superposition of x_1 and x_2 values. The objective of the analysis is to see whether the information content is the public signal is sufficient to estimate the parameters even without knowing the time independent parameters. We formulated a system of differential equations governing the evolution of the model system parameters based on the Konnur[13] approach. Our objective is to design a strategy that drives the measured synchronization error. For this we have consider the following minimization problem, for the specific feedback discussed above.

$$G = min\left[(z_1 + z_2 - x_1 - x_2)\right]^2 . \tag{10}$$

The minimization problem in Eq. 10 can be rewritten as the following system of differential equations

$$\dot{q}_j = \frac{\partial G}{\partial q_j} = -2\epsilon_j(z_2 + z_1 - x_2 - x_1)\left[\frac{\partial z_2}{\partial q_j} + \frac{\partial z_1}{\partial q_j}\right] . \tag{11}$$

The positive term ϵ_j is introduced to control stability. The knowledge of the variational derivative $\frac{\partial z_i}{\partial q_j}$ is required for solving this system of equations. Since the functional form of the model is known, these derivatives are given by

$$\frac{d}{dt}\left(\frac{\partial z_i}{\partial q_j}\right) = \sum_{k=1}^{n} \frac{\partial f(z, q)}{\partial z_k}\frac{\partial z_k}{\partial q_j} + \frac{\partial f(z, q)}{\partial q_j} - F\left[\frac{\partial z_1}{\partial q_j} + \frac{\partial z_2}{\partial q_j}\right] . \tag{12}$$

Here F is the feedback vector which decides the equation to which the value is to be fed-back. For numerically showing that the attacker cannot synchronize to the genuine values, let us consider the worst case of attack, where the attacker already has two of the three unknown parameters. The above mentioned minimization problem is reduced to estimate only the value of one of the unknown parameters say σ. From eq. (10-12) we get the following differential equation [17] to estimate σ.

$$\dot{\sigma} = -\frac{\epsilon}{2}(z_1 + z_2 - x_1 - x_2)(z_2 - z_1) . \tag{13}$$

Here ϵ is the stiffness constant. Fig. 9 shows the difference in σ and the other variables (between attacker and transmitter) for a normal synchronization scheme (a) and the newly proposed method (b). It is seen that the attacker is not able to estimate the unknown parameter by using the synchronization based parameter estimation method in the case of a super-positioned feedback. This can also be attributed to diluted information because of superposition. In this worst case of attack, we have shown that even after having knowledge of the majority of the parameters, an attacker is unsuccessful in estimating remaining parameters. In the case of a Lorenz system the analysis can be extended to cases, where the attacker has to estimate two or all parameters [17]. However, by considering the worst case for our analysis, we have ruled out the possibility of success in estimating multiple parameters.

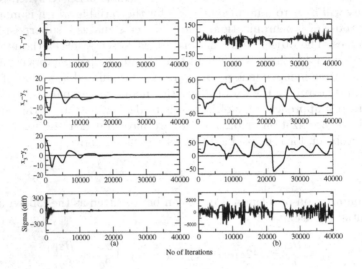

Fig. 9. Differences in all the three state space variables as well as the σ parameter values of the attacker and the transmitter (a) for a normal one variable feedback synchronization (b) for the proposed super-positioned feedback synchronization. Non-convergence of these values in case of the super-positioned feedback indicates un-successful attack.

It can also be argued that, while the analysis suggests that the information is diluted, the receiver is still able to synchronize by using the same information. This suggests that the super-positioned time series does still have sufficient information about the unknown parameters of the chaotic system. However, this can be explained by emphasizing the advantage a genuine communicator has over an attacker. The successful synchronization of the genuine communicators suggests that the diluted information is sufficient to drive an identical system (where the parameters are same), while an non-identical system (at least one parameter is different, even with same mathematical formulation) cannot successfully synchronize.

Further in our analysis and discussion, we have considered the simplest form of super-positioned feedback, while the feedback system can be made more complicate by designing a feedback signal with different coefficients. By keeping the coefficient secret these attacks can be completely eliminated.

Further, in addition to having better security than the normal synchronization schemes, there are many other advantages from the cryptographic implementation point of view. The most important advantage is the speed of synchronization.

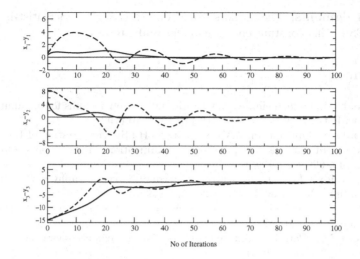

Fig. 10. Number of steps required for synchronization in case of normal one variable feedback (dotted lines) and super-positioned feedback (Solid lines). Super-positioned feedback shows faster synchronization.

It is noticed that the synchronization time in case of a super-positioned feedback is less than the normal synchronization time. This makes it more practical to implement. A typical scenario is shown in fig. 10, where, a super-positioned feedback to the y_2 evolution equation is compared with a normal feedback synchronization.

6   Conclusion

We have proposed a new feedback scheme for chaotic synchronization, which has potential to be used in secure communication. In this scheme instead of using a single variable feedback, a superposition of multiple variables is fed-back in order to dilute the information content in the public signal. Through analysis it has been shown that the diluted information is sufficient to drive an identical chaotic system (having the same parameter values) to synchronize but not otherwise. Parameter estimation through time-series analysis or through an on-line synchronization method are un-successful because of the diluted information, diluted by the law of superposition/averaging. These systems may still be vulnerable, if proper superposition strengths are not selected. Hence, utmost care should be taken in choosing the controlling parameters, that govern the process of synchronization. In addition to enhancing the security of the synchronization process it also has the advantage of providing fast synchronization. This makes it suitable to practical implementations. This can be used as random key stream generator, which can be used for designing stream ciphers. This method can be seen as a potential replacement to the binary shift registers.

Acknowledgments. The authors would like to thank the Scientist-in-Charge, C-MMACS for his constant encouragement and support.

References

1. Cuomo, K.M., Oppenheim, A.V.: Chaotic signals and systems for communications. In: Proc. IEEE ICASSP III, vol. III, pp. 137–140 (1993)
2. Cuomo, K.M., Oppenheim, A.V., Strogatz, S.H.: Synchronization of Lorenz-based chaotic circuits with applications to communications. IEEE Trans. On Circuits Systems 40, 626–633 (1993)
3. He, R., Vaidya, P.G.: Implementation of chaotic cryptography with chaotic synchronization. Phys. Rev. E. 57, 1532–1535 (1998)
4. Yang, T.: A survey of chaotic secure communication systems. Int. J. Comput. Cognition 2, 81–130 (2004)
5. Pecora, L.M., Carroll, T.L.: Synchronization in chaotic systems. Phys. Rev. Lett. 64(8), 821–824 (1990)
6. Pecora, L.M., Carroll, T.L.: Driving systems with chaotic signals. Phys. Rev. A. 44(4), 2374–2383 (1991)
7. Carroll, T.L., Pecora, L.M.: Synchronizing chaotic circuits. IEEE Trans. Circ. Syst. 38(4), 453–456 (1991)
8. Kocarev, L., Halle, K.S., Eckert, K., Chua, L.O., Parlitz, U.: Experimetal demonstration of secure communications via chaotic synchronization. Int. J. Bifurc. Chaos. 2, 709–713 (1992)
9. Zhou, H., Ling, X.: Generating chaotic secure sequences with desired statistical properties and high security. Int. J. Bifurc. Chaos. 7, 205–213 (1997)
10. Pecora, L.M., Carroll, T.L., Johnson, G.A., Mar, D.J.: Fundaments of synchronization in chaotic systems, concepts, and applications. Chaos 7(4), 520–542 (1997)
11. Vaidya, P.G., Angadi, S.: Decoding chaotic cryptography without access to the super key. Chaos, Solitons and Fractals. 17(2-3), 379–386 (2003)
12. Parlitz, U.: Estimating Model Parameters from Time Series by Auto synchronization. Phys. Rev. Lett. 76(8), 1232–1235 (1996)
13. Konnur, R.: Estimation of all parameters of model from discrete scalar time series mesurement. Phys. Lett. A. 346, 275–280 (2005)
14. Alvarez, G., Montoya, F., Romera, M., Pastor, G.: Cryptanalysis of a chaotic secure communication system. Phys. Lett. A. 306(4), 200–205 (2003)
15. He, R., Vaidya, P.G.: Analysis and synthesis of synchronous periodic and chaotic systems. Phys. Rev. A. 46, 7387–7392 (1992)
16. Alvarez, G., Montoya, F., Romera, M., Pastor, G.: Cryptanalysis of a chaotic secure communication system. Phys. Lett. A. 306(4), 200–205 (2003)
17. Maybhate, A., Amritkar, R.E.: Use of synchronization and adaptive control in parameter estimation from a time series. Phys. Rev. E. 59, 284 (1999)
18. Alvarez, G., Montoya, F., Romera, M., Pastor, G.: Breaking parameter modulated chaotic secure communication system. Chaos, Solitons and Fractals. 21, 783–787 (2004)
19. Toni, S., Kocarev, L., Parlitz, U., Harris, R.: Sporadic driving of dynamical systems. Phy. Rev. E. 55(4), 4035–4045 (1996)

20. Vaidya, P.G.: Monitoring and speeding up chaotic synchronization. Chaos, Solitons and Fractals 17(2), 433–439 (2003)
21. Patra, G.K., Ramamohan, T.R., Anil Kumar, V., Thangavelu, R.P.: Improvement in Security Level of First Generation Chaotic Communication System by Mutual Synchronization. In: Proceedings ADCOM 2006, pp. 195–198. IEEE Press, Los Alamitos (2006)
22. Patra, G.K., Anil Kumar, V., Thangavelu, R.P.: Analysis of Synchronization-based Parameter Estimation Attack on Switched Bidirectional Chaotic Key Stream Generator. In: Proc. of ICIP-2007, pp. 298–307. I. K. International Publisher (2007)
23. Brown, R., Rulkov, N.F.: Synchronization of chaotic systems: Transverse stability of trajectories in invariant manifolds. Chaos 7(3), 395–413 (1997)

A Secure and Efficient Multi-authority Proactive Election Scheme

Ashish Kumar Singh[1] and Priya Chandran[2]

[1] National Institute of Technology, Calicut, 673601, Kerala, India
[2] National Institute of Technology, Calicut, 673601, Kerala, India
priya@nitc.ac.in
http://www.nitc.ac.in

Abstract. In this paper we present a new secret-ballot multi-authority election scheme that is proactive and guarantees privacy, universal verifiability and robustness. In our scheme, a voter posts a single encrypted message as the ballot, accompanied by a non-interactive proof that it contains a valid vote. Our scheme is an efficient modification of the result by [CGS97]. The process of key recovery for decryption of votes in our scheme requires only $O(r)$ steps, where r is the number of authorities required to decrypt the key, and the number of messages required for initial setup of the scheme is $O(n)$, where n is the total number of authorities. The time complexity of key recovery in [CGS97] is $O(r\log^2 r)$ and the complexity of number of messages is $O(n^2)$. Thus the proposed scheme is more efficient in terms of time complexity and number of messages required to be sent. We also outline a simple and elegant technique to make our scheme proactive. Our implementation results demonstrate the improved time complexity of the proposed scheme.

1 Introduction

Electronic voting protocols are known to be the epitome of secure multi-party computations. An electronic voting protocol, also informally termed as an 'election scheme', can be used to conduct an online voting on some topic, or more importantly, to computerize the general elections of a country where issues such as privacy of the voter and the verifiability of the final tally are of utmost importance.

The idea of an (n,r) threshold cryptosystem — where a single key could be shared among n authorities such that r out of them were required to recover the key — was put forward in [SHA79]. That system was used in [PED91] to explain how the key could be distributed without any trusted party among the authorities, using Lagrange's interpolation. Later the idea of [PED91] was used in [CGS97] for an election scheme that provided privacy, universal verifiability, robustness and prevented vote duplication. Another (n,r) threshold cryptosystem was put forward in [AB83]. The notion of proactive security in a secret sharing scheme was explained in [HJKY95].

P. McDaniel and S.K. Gupta (Eds.): ICISS 2007, LNCS 4812, pp. 208–218, 2007.
© Springer-Verlag Berlin Heidelberg 2007

Our voting protocol provides privacy, universal verifiability and robustness, as these are the primary properties to be considered when conducting general elections.

Section 1 of the paper defines the properties that our election scheme provides and introduces our contribution. Section 2 describes the election scheme of [CGS97]. Section 3 explains our election scheme. Section 4 illustrates how proactive security could be incorporated into our system. Section 5 demonstrates that our election scheme satisfies the three properties that we have considered. Section 6 provides the results of the analysis of a prototype of our scheme which demonstrates the improved time complexity of our system.

1.1 Properties of Elections

Below we define the properties of an election scheme that we have considered for our scheme:

- **Privacy-** The privacy of an individual vote should be assured against any reasonably sized coalition of parties (not including the voter himself). i.e., unless the number of colluding parties exceeds a certain threshold, different ballots should be indistinguishable irrespective of the number of votes cast.
- **Universal Verifiability-** It ensures that any party, including a passive observer, can check that the election is fair, i.e. whether the published final tally is consistent with the correctly cast ballots. This property also includes the fact that any party can check whether ballots are correctly cast, and that only invalid ballots are discarded.
- **Robustness-** Robustness with respect to voters means that no coalition of (malicious) voters of any size can disrupt the election. Robustness with respect to the authorities means that faulty behavior of a threshold number of authorities can be tolerated.

1.2 Our Contributions

The main result of our paper is a fair and efficient election scheme in which the process of key recovery for decryption of votes requires only $O(r)$ steps as compared to $O(r\log^2 r)$ for [CGS97], where r is the number of authorities required to decrypt the key in an (n,r) threshold scheme ([SHA79]). Also, the number of messages required to be sent between the authorities for initial setup of the election scheme is $O(n)$, as compared to $O(n^2)$ in [CGS97]. We also came up with a simple and efficient technique to make our scheme proactive(proactive techniques are described in [HJKY95]).

2 Election Scheme by R. Cramer et al.

The following describes the election scheme put forward in [CGS97], the scheme on which our election scheme is based.

2.1   The Building Blocks

El-Gamal Cryptosystem. The El-Gamal cryptosystem works for any family of groups for which the discrete logarithm is considered intractable. The construction works in subgroups G_q of order q of Z_p, where p and q are large prime numbers such that $q|p-1$. The primes p and q and a generator g of G_q are the system parameters. The key pair of the receiver consists of a randomly chosen element s as the private key and $h = g^s$ as the public key which is announced to the participants. Given a message $m \in G_q$ the encryption proceeds as follows. The sender chooses a random $\alpha \in G_q$ and sends pair $(x, y) = (g^\alpha, mh^\alpha)$ as the cipher text. To decrypt the cipher text (x, y), the receiver recovers m as:

$$m = y/x^s.$$

Bulletin Board. All the communication in our election scheme takes place through a public broadcast channel with memory, which is called a bulletin board. Any communication through the bulletin board is public and can be read by any party (including passive observers). No party can erase any information from the bulletin board, but each active participant can append messages to its own designated section.

Robust Threshold El-Gamal Cryptosystem. In an (n,r) threshold cryptosystem, if $2r - 1 = n$, then we have a system where more than half the number of authorities must work together to recover the key. i.e., the system can tolerate $\lfloor n/2 \rfloor$ number of dishonest authorities.

The main protocols of a threshold cryptosystem are:

- A key generation protocol to generate the private key jointly by the receivers and
- A decryption protocol to jointly decrypt the cipher text without explicitly rebuilding the private key. The solution to both of the above are described in [PED91].

Both of the above protocols are described below:

Key Generation. As part of the set-up procedure of the election scheme, the authorities execute a key generation protocol described in [PED91]. The result of the key generation protocol is that each authority A_j possesses a share $s_j \in Z_q$ of a secret s. The authorities are committed to these shares as the values $h_j = g^{s_j}$ are made public. Furthermore, the shares s_j are such that the secret s can be reconstructed from any set of t shares using appropriate Lagrange coefficients.

Decryption. To decrypt a cipher text $(x, y) = (g^\alpha, h^\alpha m)$ without reconstructing the secret s, the authorities execute the following protocol:

- Each authority A_j broadcasts $w_j = x^{s_j}$ and proves in zero-knowledge that

$$log_g h_j = log_x w_j \tag{1}$$

– Let Λ denote any subset of t authorities who passed the zero knowledge proof. By raising x to both sides of above equation, it follows that the plain text can be recovered as:

$$m = y/ \prod_{j \in \lambda} w_j^{\lambda_{j,\Lambda}} \qquad (2)$$

where,

$$\lambda_{j,\Lambda} = \prod_{l \in \frac{\lambda}{j}} \frac{l}{l-j} \text{ is the Lagrange Coefficient used.} \qquad (3)$$

Equation (1) can be proved in zero knowledge as:

Prover		Verifier
$[(x,y) = (g^\alpha, h^\alpha)]$		
$w \in Z_q$		
$(a,b) \leftarrow (g^w, h^w)$	$\xrightarrow{\quad a,b \quad}$	
	$\xleftarrow{\quad c \quad}$	$c \in Z_q$
$r \leftarrow w + \alpha c$	$\xrightarrow{\quad r \quad}$	$g^r == ax^c \ \&\& \ h^r == by^c$

Homomorphic Encryption. Our election scheme uses yet another property of encryption called Homomorphic Encryption, due to [CGS97]. Let E denote a probabilistic encryption scheme. Let M be the message space and C the cipher text space such that M is a group under operation $\oplus$ and C is a group under operation $\otimes$. We say that E is a $(\oplus, \otimes)$- homomorphic encryption scheme if for any instance E of the encryption scheme, given $c_1 = E_{r_1}(m_1)$ and $c_2 = E_{r_2}(m_2)$, there exists an r such that $c_1 \otimes c_2 = E_r(m_1 \oplus m_2)$. Now given an ElGamal encryption (x_1, y_1) of m_1 and an ElGamal encryption (x_2, y_2) of m_2, we see that $(x_1 x_2, y_1 y_2)$ is an ElGamal encryption of $m_1 m_2$.

In order to make the ElGamal cryptosystem homomorphic, we change our message space from G_q, to Z_q with addition modulo q as group operation. Given a fixed generator $G \in G_q$, the encryption of a message $m \in Z_q$ becomes the ElGamal encryption of G^m. So given two such encryptions of m_1 and m_2, respectively, the product will be an encryption of $(m_1 + m_2) \bmod q$.

Proof of Validity of the Vote. Assuming the voter has a choice between two options, each voter will post an El-Gamal encryption of either m_0 or m_1, where m_0 and m_1 are distinct elements of G_q. The values of m_0 and m_1 can be as follows:

$m_0 = G$ and
$m_1 = 1/G$ where G is a fixed generator of the group G_q

Thus a ballot can be prepared as an El-Gamal encryption of the form

$$(x,y) = (g^\alpha, h^\alpha G^b) \quad \text{for random } b \in \{1, -1\} \qquad (4)$$

Now the encryption should be accompanied by a proof of validity that proves that the encryption indeed contains one of these values, without revealing the value itself.

Consider an ElGamal encryption of the following form:

$$(x, y) = (g^\alpha, mh^\alpha), \quad \text{with } m \in \{m_0, m_1\} \tag{5}$$

where the prover knows the value of m. To show that the pair (x, y) is indeed of this form without revealing the value of m boils down to a proof of knowledge of the following relation:

$$log_g\ x = log_h\ (y/m_0) \lor log_g\ x = log_h\ (y/m_1) \tag{6}$$

The prover either knows a proof for the left part or a proof for the right part (but not both at the same time), depending on the choice for m. By the technique in [CGS97], we can obtain an efficient witness indistinguishable proof of knowledge for the above relation, as shown below:

Voter			Verifier
$v = 1$	$v = -1$		
$\alpha, w, r_1, d_1 \in Z_q$	$\alpha, w, r_2, d_2 \in Z_q$		
$x \leftarrow g^\alpha$	$x \leftarrow g^\alpha$		
$y \leftarrow g^\alpha G$	$y \leftarrow g^\alpha/G$		
$a_1 \leftarrow g^{r_1} x^{d_1}$	$a_1 \leftarrow g^w$		
$b_1 \leftarrow h^{r_1}(yG)^{d_1}$	$b_1 \leftarrow h^w$		
$a_2 \leftarrow g^w$	$a_2 \leftarrow g^{r_2} x^{d_2}$		
$b_2 \leftarrow h^w$	$b_2 \leftarrow h^{r_2}(y/G)^{d_2}$	$\xrightarrow{x, y, a_1, b_1, a_2, b_2}$	
		$\xleftarrow{c}$	$c \in Z_q$
$d_2 \leftarrow c - d_1$	$d_1 \leftarrow c - d_2$		$c == d_1 + d_2$
$r_2 \leftarrow w - \alpha d_2$	$r_1 \leftarrow w - \alpha d_1$	$\xrightarrow{d_1, d_2, r_1, r_2}$	$a_1 == g^{r_1} x^{d_1}$
			$b_1 == h^{r_1}(yG)^{d_1}$
			$a_2 == g^{r_2} x^{d_2}$
			$b_2 == h^{r_2}(y/G)^{d_2}$

In order to make the above proof of validity non-interactive, we can assume the presence of a trusted beacon that broadcasts random values of c at regular intervals. Each challenge c should be made voter-specific, i.e., the challenge c should be computed for voter V_i as $H(ID_i, x, y, a_1, b_1, a_2, b_2)$, where ID_i is a unique public string identifying V_i. The transcripts of the proof of validity should appear on the bulletin board. This shows to any observer that the final tally is consistent with the number of valid votes cast.

The main steps of the voting protocol now are:

- Voter V_i posts a ballot (x_i, y_i) to the bulletin board accompanied by a non-interactive proof of validity.

- When the deadline is reached, the proofs of validity are checked by the authorities and the product

$$(X, Y) = (\prod_{i=1}^{l} x_i, \prod_{i=1}^{l} y_i) \quad \text{is formed.} \tag{7}$$

- Finally, the authorities jointly execute the decryption protocol for (X, Y) to obtain the value of

$$W = \frac{Y}{X^s} \tag{8}$$

A non-interactive proof of knowledge is used in Step 1 of the decryption protocol.

We thus get $W = G^T$ as the final decrypted message. Since the generator G is known to the authorities, the number T (which denotes the final tally of the election) can be easily determined.

3   The New Election Scheme

We came up with a new election scheme, which is based on the scheme described above. The difference between the two lies in the threshold scheme used. The scheme of [CGS97] uses a key distribution and decryption protocol that is based on interpolating polynomials, and lagrange's interpolation formula. The key recovery through interpolation requires at least $O(r\log^2 r)$ steps, where r is the threshold number of authorities required to recover the key.

Instead, we use the (t,n) threshold scheme described in [AB83], which requires $O(r)$ steps to recover the key. We describe the scheme below.

3.1 (t, n) Threshold Scheme

The basic method is as follows:

A set of integers $p, m_1 < m_2 < m_3 < ....m_n$ is chosen subject to the following three conditions:

$$(m_i, m_j) = 1 \; \forall \; i \neq j \tag{9}$$

$$(p, m_i) = 1 \; \forall \; i \tag{10}$$

$$\prod_{i=1}^{r} m_i > p \prod_{i=1}^{r-1} m_{n-i+1} \tag{11}$$

Let

$$M = \prod_{i=1}^{r} m_i \tag{12}$$

Key Distribution. Let x be the key such that $0 \leq x < p$. Let $y = x + Ap$ where A is an arbitrary integer such that $0 \leq y < M$. Then $y_i \equiv y \bmod m_i$ are the shadows (or shares) given to each authority i.

Key Recovery. To recover x, it suffices to recover y. If $y_{i_1}, y_{i_2}, . y_{i_r}$ are known, then by the Chinese Remainder Theorem, y is known modulo $N_1 = \prod_{j=1}^{r} m_{i_j}$. As $N_1 \geq M$, this uniquely determines y and hence x (as $x \equiv y (mod\ p)$). If $r - 1$ shadows are available, no information can be recovered. If $y_{i_1}, y_{i_2}, . y_{i_{r-1}}$ are known then all we have is $y(mod\ N_2)$ where $N_2 = \prod_{j=1}^{r-1} m_{i_j}$. Since $M/N_2 > p$ and $(N_2, p) = 1$, the collection of numbers n_i with $n_i = y(mod\ N_2)$ and $n_i \leq M$ cover all congruence classes $mod\ p$, hence no useful information is available without r shadows.

Extension to Multi-Way Elections. Instead of a choice between two options, it is often required that a choice between several options can be made. Here we present a simpler method of achieving that, as compared to the method of [CGS97]. To get an election for a 1-out-of-K choice, we simply take K (independently generated) generators G_i, $1 \leq i \leq K$. Now if each of these generators are prime, then at the end of election we get the final decrypted message M as:

$$M = G_1^{T_1} G_2^{T_2} ..... G_K^{T_K} \tag{13}$$

Then since the generators G_i, $1 \leq i \leq K$ are known to the authorities, the authorities can easily determine the final tally $(T_1, T_2, ...T_K)$.

The proof of validity of a ballot (x, y) becomes a proof of knowledge of

$$log_g\ x = log_h\ (y/G_1).... \lor ....log_g\ x = log_h\ (y/G_K) \tag{14}$$

Since the voter can only generate this proof for at most one generator G_i, it is automatically guaranteed that the voter cannot vote for more than one option at a time.

4   Proactive Security

If the voting system has to be in place for a long time, then the techniques of proactive security can be used for enhanced security. Such a scenario is typical in online elections, or in general elections of a country where utmost precautions are being taken and the shadows with authorities are being refreshed in every 1 hour, for example. In proactive security, the shares of the private key available with the authorities are refreshed after a specific amount of time without affecting the actual private key, so that an adversary does not have the privilege of sufficient time to attack the threshold number of authorities and recover the key. We came up with a simple and efficient way of achieving the above, as follows:

The key distribution protocol of (n,r) threshold system used in our election scheme(Section 3.1) involves calculation of a variable $y = x + Ap$, where x is the chosen private key, A is a random number, and p is the chosen prime number. The only condition to y is $0 \leq y < M$. If the random number A is changed periodically so that the new value of y still conforms to the condition $0 \leq y < M$, then the new value of y would result in new shadows for the authority, without affecting the public and private key of the system in any sort (as $x \equiv y(mod\ p)$). Once the old shadows of the private key are replaced with the new values (made from the new value of A), the old shadows become useless, and the attacker needs to start collecting shadows from scratch.

So, implementing proactive security boils down to changing the random number A periodically.

5   Discussion

What follows, describes how our system conforms to the three properties we had considered.

- Universal verifiability is achieved because any observer can check the proofs of validity for the ballots which are posted at the bulletin board. It is also clear to any observer if the final tally is correct with respect to all valid ballots.
- Privacy of individual votes is guaranteed partly by the security of the El-Gamal cryptosystem used to encrypt the votes. This is true because we assume that no more than $r - 1$ authorities conspire, since r authorities can reconstruct the secret key used in the scheme. Other than the encrypted votes, a voter casts a proof of validity. But this is useless in order to break the privacy since such proof is witness indistinguishable.
- Robustness with respect to malicious voters is achieved by means of the soundness of the proof of validity, which ensures that voters cannot submit bogus ballots. Robustness with respect to at most $n - r$ malicious authorities is inherited from the robustness of the key generation and decryption protocols.

6   Implementation

In order to quantitatively compare our scheme and the election scheme presented in [CGS97], we implemented both the schemes in Java. The authorities and voters were simulated as threads. All the communication between the authorities were implemented using shared memory. The *main* thread acted as the central authority in the implementation of our scheme. We also implemented the verification of authorities and voters. We did not implement the proactive techniques.

There were five threads acting as authorities, out of which three were required to recover the key. A separate class was acting as the bulletin board. A common secret key of value 20 was assumed. Three votes(one for each of the available voting choices) were cast by the program. Any random number required at any stage was assumed to be a constant. Figure 1 shows the thread structure of our implementation.

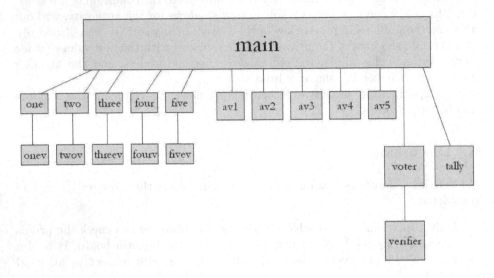

Fig. 1. Thread structure

The *main* thread spawns five authorities named *one, two....five*. The authority side of authority verification is implemented using threads *onev, twov....fivev*. The verifier side of authority verification is implemented using the threads *av1, av2...av5*. Voter is implemented by the thread *voter*, and the verifier side of voter verification is simulated using the thread *verifier*. *Tally* denotes the thread that calculates the final tally.

The two election schemes were analyzed using netbeans 5.5 profiler, on a 2.4 GHz, 256 MB RAM machine. The result was that our scheme took lesser time than the scheme by [CGS97], as shown in Table 1.

As evident from the table, the scheme of [CGS97] took a total time of 4 minutes and 1.625 seconds, whereas our scheme took a total time of 1 minute and 18.625 seconds.

The purpose of our implementation is solely to demonstrate the improvement provided by our scheme over [CGS97] even with a modest computational infrastructure. The results provide a practical manifestation of the improved efficiency of our technique, which is theoretically analyzed and proved. The scalability of our technique is shown by the improved time and message complexities, and can be practically demonstrated by an implementation on a more advanced computing environment.

Table 1. Time taken by each thread in the two schemes

Thread Name	Basic Scheme min:sec	New Scheme min:sec
one	1.093	00.547
two	1.640	00.547
three	1.640	00.547
four	1.640	00.437
five	1.109	00.437
av1	18.109	1:13:047
av2	29.063	1:12.718
av3	1:16.469	1:12.500
av4	1:26.531	1:18.625
av5	4:01.625	1:12.500
onev	10.172	1:09.578
twov	10.516	1:09.578
threev	11.063	1:09.578
fourv	11.813	1:09.688
fivev	12.797	1:09.688
main	12.156	1:12.782
verifier	00.688	01.453
verifier	00.765	00.688
verifier	00.625	00.672

7 Conclusion

In this paper, we have presented an efficient election scheme for safely and fairly conducting general elections. Our scheme has a key recovery protocol of time complexity $O(r)$ as compared to $O(r\log^2 r)$ provided by [CGS97] and message complexity of $O(n)$ as compared to $O(n^2)$ provided by [CGS97]. The quantitative analysis conducted further reinforces the fact that our scheme is better. We also have a very efficient and easy way of making our election scheme proactive. The reason for the improved performance of our election scheme over the election scheme presented in [CGS97] is the replacement of the (n,r) threshold cryptosystem used in [PED91] with a different technique (explained in [AB83]).

The scheme of [AB83] requires a trusted party for initial key distribution among the authorities, as opposed to the former election protocol, which doesn't require a trusted party for that stage. But since both of the (n,r) schemes require a trusted party for the recovery of the key, it is not a serious drawback. [AB83] uses Chinese Remainder Theorem for recovering the distributed key giving the key recovery protocol a time complexity of $O(r)$ as compared to the time complexity of $O(r\log^2 r)$ provided by the earlier scheme. This also causes the message complexity of the initial key distribution protocol to reduce from $O(n^2)$ to $O(n)$.

In addition, by simply changing a random number, we can periodically refresh the shares given to each authority with a new share, without affecting the actual key and hence improving the security of the system.

References

[SHA79]   Shamir, A.: How to share a secret. Communications of the ACM 22(11), 612–613 (1979)

[PED91]   Pedersen, T.: A threshold cryptosystem without a trusted party. In: Davies, D.W. (ed.) EUROCRYPT 1991. LNCS, vol. 547, pp. 522–526. Springer, Heidelberg (1991)

[CGS97]   Cramer, R., Gennaro, R., Schoenmakers, B.: A Secure and Optimally Efficient Multi-Authority Election Scheme. European Transactions on Telecommunications 8(5), 481–490 (1997)

[HJKY95]   Herzberg, A., Jarecki, S., Krawczyk, H., Yung, M.: Proactive Secret Sharing Or: how to cope with perpetual leakage. In: Coppersmith, D. (ed.) CRYPTO 1995. LNCS, vol. 963, pp. 339–352. Springer, Heidelberg (1995)

[AB83]   Asmuth, C., Bloom, J.: A modular approach to key safeguarding. IEEE Transactions on Information Theory IT-29(2), 208–211 (1983)

Secure Transaction Management Protocols for MLS/DDBMS

Navdeep Kaur, Rajwinder Singh, Manoj Misra, and A.K. Sarje

Department of Electronics and Computer Engineering,
Indian Institute of Technology Roorkee, Roorkee, India
{nrwsingh,rwsingh}@yahoo.com

Abstract. Majority of the research in multilevel secure database management systems (MLS/DBMS) focuses primarily on centralized database
systems. However, with the demand for higher performance and higher
availability, database systems have moved from centralized to distributed
architectures, and the research in multilevel secure distributed database
management systems (MLS/DDBMS) is gaining more and more promi-
nence. Traditional transaction management protocols (i.e., concurrency
control and commit protocols) are important components of database systems. The most important issues for these protocols in MLS database system are the covert channel problem [2] and starvation of high security level
transactions [10]. To address these problems, first we propose new correctness criteria for multilevel secure multiversion concurrency control protocol, called read-down conflict serializability. It is the extended definition
of one-copy serial (or1-serial) that allows a transaction to read older versions, if necessary. If a concurrency control protocol allows transaction to
read older versions, we can obtain better throughput and response time
than the traditional multiversion concurrency control protocols. We show
that multiversion schedule based upon proposed criteria is also one-copy
serializable. Secondly, this paper proposes a secure multiversion concurrency control protocol for MLS/DDBMSs that is only free from covert
channels but also do so without starving high security level transactions,
in addition to ensure the proposed serializability. Further, in distributed
database systems, an atomic commitment protocol is needed to terminate
distributed transactions consistently. To meet MLS requirements and to
avoid database inconsistencies 2PC commit protocol is also modified.

Keywords: Multilevel security, concurrency control, commit protocol,
covert channel, distributed database system.

1 Introduction

In many applications such as military, government agencies, hospitals, security
is an important requirement since the database system maintains sensitive data.
Many of these applications are inherently distributed in nature. One common
technique for supporting the security can be a multilevel security (MLS). The
basic model of MLS was introduced by Bell and LaPadula. The Bell -LaPadula

P. McDaniel and S.K. Gupta (Eds.): ICISS 2007, LNCS 4812, pp. 219–233, 2007.

model [1] is stated in terms of objects and subjects. In a multilevel secure distributed database model a security level is assigned to each transaction (subject) and data item (object). A security level for a transaction represents its clearance level and the security level for a data represents its classification level. Classifications and clearances are collectively known as security levels and are partially ordered [1]. An MLS distributed database management system (MLS/DDBMS) can be shared by users at different clearance levels and contains distributed database consisting of data at different classification levels. The sensitive data in MLS/DDBMS is protected by controlling the access to data based on the security level of users submitting the transactions and the security level of data. The Bell-LaPadula model prevents direct flow of information from a security level (high) to another non-dominated security level (low). However, it is not sufficient to guard against illegal information flows through covert channels [2].

Applications interact with the database system through transactions. A transaction consists of a sequence of read and writes operations performed on data items. In a typical database system, several transactions execute concurrently in order to achieve high throughput and fast response time. When transactions execute concurrently and share data items, conflicts among them are often unavoidable. Concurrency control protocol is used to manage the concurrent execution of operations by rejecting or delaying the conflicting operations such that consistency is maintained [7], [8], and an atomic commitment protocol [16] is needed to terminate distributed transactions consistently. Transaction management techniques are fairly well understood for traditional distributed database systems, this is not the case for multilevel secure distributed database systems. Traditional transaction management protocols (i.e., concurrency control and commit protocols) such as Two Phase Locking (2PL) and Early Prepare (EP) [?]protocols cannot be used directly for multilevel secure DDBMSs (MLS/DBMSs) as they cause covert channels.

Transaction management protocols for MLS/DBMSs must ensure data consistency as well as security. Several secure transaction management protocols for MLS/DBMS have been proposed in the literature [2],[3],[4],[9],[11],[12],[17]. Majority of the research in MLS/DBMSs focuses primarily on centralized database systems. Secure concurrency control protocols can be classified into two categories based on the number of data item version they allow. Some of them use only a single version whereas other uses multiple data versions. Most of single version protocols [10] achieve correctness and security at the cost of declined performance of high security level transactions i.e., the high security level transactions suffers from starvation. To eliminate the problem of covert channel and starvation of high security level transaction, some secure multiversion concurrency control protocols have been proposed [2],[4],[12]. The use of multiple versions prevents high security level transactions from interfering with low security level transactions, in that high security level transactions are given older versions of low security level data. Therefore, a low security level transaction is never delayed or aborted because of the concurrent execution of a high security level transaction thus both covert channels and starvation are eliminated.

Maintaining multiple versions may not add much to the cost of concurrency control, because the versions may be needed by the recovery algorithm [4]. However, a major concern of these protocols is how to select a correct version in order to ensure correct execution of transactions and security. A correct version of a data item is the version, which a transaction would have used if it would run serially. The requirement of security especially impacts serializability, which is the usual notion of concurrent executions of transactions. No prior work has been reported that extends the secure multiversion concurrency control for MLS/DDBMS.

To address above issues, we propose a multilevel secure multiversion concurrency control protocol for MLS/DDBMSs. It prevents covert channels and starvation of high security level transactions that may often occur in existing multilevel secure concurrency control protocols in addition to ensure the proposed serializability. Moreover, our protocol can provide higher degree of concurrency than traditional multiversion concurrency control protocols. In distributed database systems, an atomic commitment protocol is needed to terminate distributed transactions consistently. The two-phase commit protocol (2PC) is the most popular atomic commit protocol. Since proposed protocol uses V-Locks in addition to conventional locks, therefore 2PC cannot be integrated with proposed protocol in its present form. We modify 2PC to avoid database inconsistencies.

The remainder of the paper is organized as follows. In Section 2, we discuss the correctness criteria for multiversion concurrency control and then propose Read-down Conflict-preserving serializability. Section 3 presents MLS Distributed Database Model. Section 4 presents multilevel secure multiversion concurrency control and commit protocol for MLS/DDBMS. Simulation model of MLS/ DDBS and Performance results of proposed protocol are presented in section 5. Section 6 concludes the paper.

2   Read-Down Conflict-Preserving Serializability

One-copy serializability [15] is strictly established correctness criterion for traditional multiversion concurrency control protocols where correctness alone was the prime concern. In order to prove that multiversion concurrency control protocol is correct, we must show that each of MV histories produced by protocol is equivalent to a serial single version (SV) history [15]. An MV history and a SV history are equivalent, if they have the same reads-from relationships. An MV history is serial if for every two transactions T_i and T_j that appear in H, either all of T_i's operations precede all of T_j's or vice versa. A serial MV history is one-copy serial (or 1-serial) if for all i, j and some data item x, if Ti reads x from Tj, then i = j, or T_j is the last transaction preceding Ti, that writes into any version of x. This means that each transaction is permitted permit to read the most recent versions of data items. An MV history is one-copy serializable (or 1SR) if its committed projection is equivalent to a l-serial MV history. However, there are many one-copy serializable MV histories which are not one-copy serial. Let us consider the following histories H_1 and H_2 over transaction T_1, T_2 and

T_3. $r_i[x_j]$ represents Ti reads x written by T_j, $w_i[x_i]$ represents T_i writes x and c_i represents commitment of T_i .

$H_1 = w_1[x_1]w_1[y_1]c_1r_2[x_1]r_2[y_1]w_2[x_2]w_2[y_2]c_2r_3[x_2]r_3[y_2]c_3$
$H2 = w_1[x_1]w_1[y_1]c_1r_2[x_1]r_2[y_1]w_2[x_2]w_2[y_2]c_2r_3[x_1]r_3[y_1]c_3$

In above histories, H_1 is one-copy serial while H_2 is not one-copy serial because T_3 does not read the most recent version. However, the MV history H_2 is equivalent to a serial SV history $T_1T_3T_2$ and thus, H_1 and H_2 are 1SR histories. Multiversion concurrency control protocol in MLS/DBSs, in addition to ensure the correct execution of concurrent transactions, must also preserve security. Unfortunately, one-copy serializability dose not provide acceptable performance in MLS multiversion database systems because one-copy serializability was originally introduced for traditional multiversion database systems (Single security level systems). In this section, we propose a new serializability, called read-down conflict-preserving serializability (RD-CSR) for multiversion concurrency control protocol in MLS/DBSs. RD-CSR eliminates the limitation of traditional multiversion concurrency control protocol that transactions must read the most recent committed versions of data items. By relaxing this restriction, we can obtain higher degree of concurrency since transactions are unnecessarily blocked or aborted in traditional concurrency control protocols. RD-CSR allows a transaction to read older version of data item when the transactions cannot read the most recent version. "1-copy serial" can be redefined in terms of "RD-serial" as follows: A multiversion history over a transaction set T is 1-copy serial, if for each transaction in T and some data item x, the first read operation of a transaction selects the most recent version of data item of x or the version written by itself and each of the following read operations of transaction selects most recent versions created before the next new version of x.

2.1   Distributed MLS Database Systems

Transactions executing in distributed database systems may require to access (either read or write) data items from more than one site. Each distributed transaction, consist of a process called coordinator that execute at the site where the transaction is submitted, and a set of other process, called cohorts that execute at various sites (participant sites) where the required data items reside. Cohorts may be executed in sequential or parallel manner. To extend the protocol given in [2] for MLS/DDBSs additional communications between the coordinator and the participants is required to determining the timestamp of a transaction since every transaction must be assigned a timestamp such that it is smaller than the timestamps of all active transactions executing at all lower security levels. Otherwise, it is possible that a lower security level transaction with a smaller timestamp at some other site may issue write operations that can invalidate the read operations of high security level transaction. In addition to that it has the drawback that transactions at a higher security level are forced to read far outdated values due to timestamp assignment. Protocol describe in [5] can be easily extended to handle distributed transactions, but it has the drawback that the high security level transaction T_i is re-executed if a low level transaction T_j writes a value, read by T_i such that $ts(T_j) < ts(T_i)$ and requires T_i to wait for its commit until all transactions at all sites with smaller timestamps than that of T_i commit.

Protocol proposed in [12] cannot be easily extended to handle distributed transactions. Suppose that every site in the MLS/DDB uses Kim et al. protocol for concurrency control. There are two sites A and B in a DDBS. Let T_i and T_j be the distributed transactions that originate at site A and site B respectively such that $L(T_j) < L(T_i)$. Each distributed transaction consists of two cohorts: c_i^a, c_i^b, and c_j^a, c_j^b, with c_i^a, and c_j^a, executing at Site A, and c_i^b, and c_j^b, executing at Site B, respectively. Among the data items accessed by T_i and T_j are x, y and z with $L(x) = L(y) = L(z) = L(T_j)$. Data item x and y are at Site A while z is at Site B. cr_i is the certifying operation of C_i and indicates that the cohort has completed execution and sent a WORKDONE message to the coordinator. $L(T)$ and $L(x)$ be the security level of transaction and data item respectively. The order of execution of each cohort is shown in Fig. 1.

Site A

C_i^a: $r_i(x_0)$ $r_i(y_0)$ cr_i

C_j^a : $w_j(x_j)$ $w_j(y_j)$ cr_j

Site B

C_i^b : $r_i(z_j)$ cr_i

C_j^b : $w_j(z_j)$ cr_j

Fig. 1. An example history illustrating the problem of retrieval anomaly

Note that when c_j^a is submitted to scheduler at site A, it blocks c_i^a to execute c_j^a in order to avoid a covert channel. The values written by c_j^a are not visible to c_i^a when it resumes its execution in order to avoid retrieval anomaly as it added into **C-set**c_i^a (conflict transaction set). On the other hand at site B, c_i^b read values written by c_j^b.

3   MLS Distributed Database Model

We use the MLS distributed database model given in [9]. It consists of a set N of sites, where each site $N\epsilon$ N is an MLS database. Each site has an independent processor connected via secure (trusted) communication links to other sites. Thus no communication between two sites is subject to eavesdropping, masquerading, reply or integrity violations. The MLS distributed database is modeled as a quadruple $<D, \tau, S, L >$, where D is the set of data items, τ is the set of distributed transactions, S is the partially ordered set of security levels with an ordering relation $\leq$, and L is a mapping from $D \bigcup T$ to S. Security level S_i is said to dominate security level Sj if $S_j = S_i$. Every data object x, as well as every distributed transaction τ, has a security level associated with it, i.e., for every x ε D, $L(x)\varepsilon$ S, and for every τ ε τ, $L(\tau)$ ε S. Each MLS database N is also mapped to an ordered pair of security classes $L_{min}(N)$ and $L_{max}(N)$. Where $L_{min}(N)$,

$L_{max}(N) \, \varepsilon \, S$, and $L_{min}(N) = L_{max}(N)$. In otherwords, every MLS database in the distributed database has a range of security levels associated with it. For every data item x stored in an MLS database N, $L_{min}(N) = L(x) = L_{max}(N)$ Similarly, for every transaction T executed at N, $L_{min}(N) = L(T) = L_{max}(N)$. A site N_i is allowed to communicate with another site N_j only if $L_{max}(N)i = L_{max}(N)j$. The security policy used is based on the Bell-LaPadula model.

3.1   Distributed Transaction Model

Each distributed transaction has single process, called the master (coordinator), that executes at the originating site of the transaction and multiple other processes, called cohort that execute at the various sites where the required data items reside. The transaction manager at a site is responsible for creation of master process and cohort processes for each transaction submitted to that site. Master forward cohorts to the appropriate concurrency control manager by sending the STARTWORK message when some data item at the site is to be accessed. Generally, there is only one cohort on behalf of the transaction at each site. When a cohort completes its data access and processing requirements, it sends a WORKDONE message to the master and waits for the master process to initiate commit protocol. The master process provides the coordination of cohort processes; the master process commits a transaction only if all cohorts of the transaction are ready to commit, otherwise it aborts. Therefore, a commit protocol is needed to ensure that all cohorts and the master reach a uniform decision. There are two types of distributed transaction execution model i.e. sequential and parallel. In sequential execution model, only one cohort is active at a time and master send the subsequent STARTWORK message only after the previous cohort has completed the work assigned to it. On the other hand in parallel execution model the master send the STARTWORK messages to all cohorts together. After successful execution of the master's request at cohort, sends a WORKDONE message to the master.

Each distributed transaction T submitted to its coordinator and coordinator assign a unique timestamp to it. The coordinator divides the distributed transaction into cohorts and forwards them to appropriate site. The distributed transaction's timestamp and security level is also assigned to all its cohorts. Each cohort is executed under local concurrency control. We use notation T_i (C_i) to represent a transaction (its cohort) with timestamp i (or TS). The commit timestamp of a transaction depends on its commit time i.e. if i <j for two transactions T_i and T_j then $c(T_i)< c(T_j)$ where c(T) represents the commit time of transaction T.

4   Secure Multiversion Locking Concurrency Control Protocol

In this section, we present a secure multiversion concurrency control protocol based on read-down conflict-preserving serializability for MLS/DDBSs. The proposed concurrency control protocol is based on the Bell-LaPadula security model (Restricted Write Model) to prevent direct flow of information from a high security level transaction to low security level transaction. The security model allows a transaction to issue read-equal, read-down and write-equal operations. Consequently, following conflicts may occur:

1. Read-down conflict among different security levels
2. Read-write conflict at same security level
3. Write-write conflict at same security level.

To close all covert channels, read-down conflict is the only case that needs to be treated differently from the conventional conflict in MLS database systems.

Proposed concurrency control protocol is primarily based on multiversion locking protocol [15]. In case of same security level data conflicts, (Read-write conflict and Write-write conflict at same security level) conflicts are resolved using traditional multiversion two phase locking (MV2PL) protocol, since there is no security problem within same security level. MV2PL protocol, relaxes the rule of two phase locking (2PL) so that the conflicts between read and write or write and write are eliminated. Hence, each data item may have many versions that are created by active cohorts, called uncertified versions. However, cohorts are allowed to read only the most recent version of each data item in order to ensure the correct execution of cohorts. Three types of locks are used: read, write and certify. Read and write locks are set as usual for two-phase locking protocol, but when commit operation is sent to the concurrency control manager, all write-locks are converted into certify locks. And a certify lock is used to delay the commitment of a transaction until there is no active reader of data items that are about to overwrite. Certify locks only conflict with read locks and other certify locks. However, in order to prevent covert channels, certify locks are granted to low security level cohorts in proposed protocol, upon the conflicts between read and certify locks at different security levels.

Assumptions

1. The DBS uses Lamport clock to generate consistent timestamps across different sites.
2. Cohorts are executed sequentially.

Basic Idea

The proposed protocol uses a secure version of MV2PL for concurrency control that uses version locks, similar to Kim's t-lock to reduce the number of high security level (HL) transactions that are aborted due to read-down conflicts with low security level (LL) transactions. Existing secure concurrency control protocols for distributed MLS /DBS grant write lock to LL transactions Tj on a data item x (say on sit A) even when x has a read lock by some HL transaction T_i. This is done to avoid covert channel. Further to avoid database inconsistencies T_i is aborted and re-executed.

The proposed protocol instead of aborting Ti and re-executing it, sets V-locks on values written by T_j and all transactions dependent on T_j (on site

A) so that these values are not visible to Ti. However Ti may still read a data item y written by T_j or a transaction dependent on T_j on some other site, say B (retrieval anomaly [5]). To handle this Ti records the version numbers of all low data items, it reads directly or indirectly on different sites. During commit the coordinator of T_i uses this information to detect the retrieval anomaly, if any, and commit / aborts T_i accordingly.

This allows all those HL transactions T_i's to commit (without re-executing) that do not read values written or write values read / written by LL transaction T_j or transactions dependent on it on more than one site.

Requirement: If transaction Ti depends on another transaction T_j , $c(T_i)$ ¡ $c(T_j)$. Where c(T) represents the commit time of transaction T.

Algorithm Data Structures: Let C_i^a represent the cohort of T_i executing at site A. Each HL transaction T_i (and not each cohort) maintains two data structures CS[i] and Low-RS[i] defined as follows:

1. CS[i] = j if C_j^* (we use * to represent any site) is the LL cohort with lowest TS on the current site or on some previous site that gets a certify lock on some LL data item x read locked by T_i. It is 0 otherwise.
2. Set Low-RS$_a$[i] contains j (!=0) if T_i reads version j of a low level data item directly or indirectly (T_i reads a HL data item x having Low-TS$[x]$ = (j, write)). Following additional information is stored along with each data item x:

1. Write-TS$[x]$: When a transaction T is certified each data item x written by T is assigned a timestamp (version)$Write - TS[x] = commit_time(T)$. Following additional information is stored along with each HL data item x:
2. Low-TS[x]: When a high level transaction Ti reads / writes x it also stores (at the time of commit) Low-TS$[x]$ = (largest entry in Low-RS$_a$[i], read/write). // HL transaction writes HL data items only.

In addition to above, coordinator of $T_i$has maintain every site in MLS/DDBS has to maintain V-LockTable.

1. V-LockTable contains (data version, list of transactions not allowed to read this version).

Since cohorts of a transaction are executed sequentially data structures CS[i] and Low-RS[i] can be passed on from first cohort to second, then to third and so on through coordinator. If CS[i] is non-zero cohorts read LL data items with version $\leq$ CS[i] only, otherwise they read most recent certified version. This reduces the abortion rate of high security level transactions due to read-down conflicts with low security level transactions. However if the ith cohort in sequence reads a LL data item x and then a LL cohort C_a^j gets a write lock on x, Low-RS[i] is checked for an entry $\geq$ j. If it is there, transaction is aborted otherwise the execution may continue.

Concurrency Control: The proposed concurrency control algorithm uses following rules to get a lock on data item x:

Rule 1 (Cohort C_i^a requests for a read lock on data item x)
   HL Cohort (HL or LL data):
   CS[i] $== 0$: get lock as per MV2PL // (get the read lock on latest certified value if there is no certify lock)
   HL Cohort (CS[i] $== j$) / HL or LL data:
     if (LL data) get the lock on the latest certified value $< j$;
     if (HL data) get the lock on latest certified value with Low-TS[x] $< (j$, write)
   Modify Low-RS$_a$[i];
   LL Cohort / LL data:
     get lock as per MV2PL;
Rule 2 (Cohort C_i^a requests for a write lock on data item x)
  C_i^a creates a new version of x; // there is no conflict between write and other operations.
Rule 3 (Cohort C_i^a requests for a certify lock on data item x)
   LL Cohort (HH Cohort C_a^j already has a read lock on LL data)
     get certify lock without any delay;
   HL(LL) Cohort (HL (LL)Cohort already has a read lock or certify lock on HL(LL) data)
     get lock as per MV2PL;
Modified 2PC Coordinator (Ti)
Send the STARTWORK message along with CS[i] and Low-RS[i] to next participant
Wait for WORKDONE message
if (last participant)
   send request for VOTE to all participant
   wait for VOTE from all cohorts
     if (all voted YES)
       send COMMIT
  else
       send ABORT.
Participant (C_i^a)
 wait for STARTWORK message from coordinator;
Complete processing;
if (HL Cohort)
 if (CS[i]$\neq 0$) and (Low-RS$_a$[i] contains an entry $\geq$ CS[i])
   send ABORT message;
 else send WORKDONE message;
else send WORKDONE message;
wait for request for VOTE;
if (request for VOTE) and can commit: send YES;
else send ABORT
wait for COMMIT
if (COMMIT)
 Modify values and the Write-TS;

if (HL Transaction) Modify Low-TS[x] for each x written;
if ((LL data item)and (read lock by a HL transaction C_j^a))
        Add i into CS[j]; // add LL Cohort id into Conflict Set of HH Cohort;
        Set V-lock on all certified versions written by LL Cohort;
else Abort.

5   Performance Evaluation

In this section, we evaluate the performance of proposed concurrency control protocol. We extend the protocol given in [5] for distributed databases, called SMVTO. We compare the performance of proposed secure concurrency control protocol with SMVTO by means of simulation.

5.1   Simulation Model

Our simulation model is similar in many aspects to the distributed database model presented in [13], which has also been used in several other studies of distributed database system behavior. It consists of MLS database that is distributed, in a non-replicated manner, over N homogenous sites connected by a secure network. Thus no communication between two sites is subject to eavesdropping, masquerading, reply or integrity violations. Each site in the model has six modules. In addition to these per site components, the model also has a network manager which models behavior of the communications network. All the modules in the database systems are assumed to be trusted. In this, we are concerned only with providing security at concurrency level. Fig. 2 presents simulation model of a site. Other sites of the network are identical.

Transaction Generator: The transaction generator is responsible for generating the workload for each data site. Transactions are generated as a Poisson stream with mean equal to ArriRate. All sites receive the same workload, i.e. have an identical transaction arrival rate. Each transaction in the system is distinguished by a globally unique transaction id. The id of a transaction is made up of two parts: a transaction number, which is unique at the originating site of the transaction and the id of the originating site, which is unique in the system.

Database Model: The database is modeled as a collection of DBSize pages. These pages have been assigned ClassLevels and are uniformly distributed in a non-replicated fashion across all the NumSites sites, so that each data item is managed by only one site. Accesses to data pages are distributed uniformly over the entire database, i.e. each data page is accessed with equal probability. The database is equally partitioned into ClassLevels security classification levels (e.g. if database has 1000 pages and number of classification is 2, pages 1 through 500 belongs to level 1, pages 501 through to 1000 belongs to level 2). Table 1 summarizes the parameters of simulation model.

Transaction Manager: Each distributed transaction in the workload has single process, called the master or coordinator, that executes at the originating site of

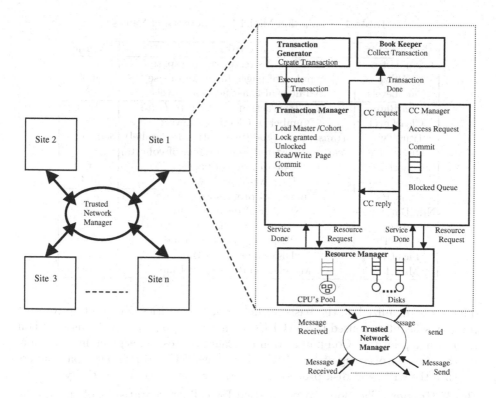

Fig. 2. Simulation Model of the DDBMS

the transaction and multiple other processes, called cohort that execute at the various sites where the required data pages reside. The transaction manager at a site is responsible for creation of master process and cohort processes for each transaction submitted to that site. The cohorts are created dynamically as need. There can be at most one cohort of a transaction at each site. If there exists any local data page in the access list of the transaction, one cohort will be executed locally. When a cohort completes its data access and processing requirements, it waits for the master process to initiate commit protocol. The master process provides the coordination of cohort processes; the master process commits a transaction only if all cohorts of the transaction are ready to commit, otherwise it aborts and restarts the transaction after a delay and makes the same data accesses as before.

Concurrency Control Manager. Concurrency Control Manager is responsible for handling concurrency control requests made by the transaction manager, including read and write access requests, requests to get permission to commit or abort a cohort, and several types of master and cohort management requests to initialize and terminate master and cohort processes.

Resource Manager. The resource manager manages the physical resources of each site. The physical resources at each site consist of NumCPUs processors, NumDataDisks data disks and NumLogDisks log disks. Both CPU and IO

Table 1. Simulation Model Parameters and Values

Parameter	Meaning	Value
NumSites	Number of sites in the database	8
DBSize	Number of pages in the database	4000
ClassLevels	Number of Classification Levels	2
ArriRate	Mean transaction arrival rate / site	1-10
ClearLevel	Number of Clearance Levels	2
TransType	Transaction Type (Sequential or Parallel)	Sequential
DistDegree	Degree of Distribution (number of cohorts)	3
CohortSize	Cohort size (in pages)	6
WriteProb	Page write probability	0.4
NumCPUs	Number of processors per site	2
NumDataDisks	Number of disks per site	4
NumLogDisks	Number of log disks per site	1
PageCPU	CPU page processing time	5ms
PageDisk	Disk page access time	20ms
MsgCPU	Message send / receive time	5ms

queues are organized on the basis of the cohort's priorities. Preemptive-Resume priority scheduling is used by the CPUs at each site; preemptions being based on transaction priorities. Communication messages processing is given higher priority than data processing at the CPUs. The PageCPU and PageDisk parameters capture the CPU and disk processing times per data page, respectively.

Book Keeper. The Book keeper is used for collecting statistics of the site. It counts the number of transactions completed and aborted at each security level and the average execution time.

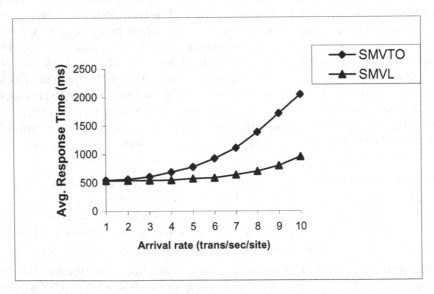

Fig. 3. Average Response Times

Network Manager. We assumed a reliable and secure system, in which no site failures or communication network failures occur. The communication network is simply modeled as a switch that routes messages without any delay [14] since we assume a local area network that has high bandwidth. However, the CPU overheads of message transfer, message transfer are taken into account at both the sending and the receiving sites. This means that there are two classes of CPU requests - local data processing requests and message processing requests. The CPU overheads for message transfers are captured by the MsgCPU parameter.

5.2 Simulation Results

For each experiment, we ran the simulation with the same parameters for four different random number seeds. Each simulation run was continuing up to 2,000 transactions of each security level were committed. The results depicted are the average over the four runs. All the data reported in this section have 95 perctange confidence intervals.

Fig. 3 depicts the average response times of SMVL and compared with SMVTO as a function of overall transaction arrival rate per site. In figure, we observe that at low arrival rates, the response times are more or less the same for both protocols. This is because contention levels are low, and majority of the time is spent in disk access and CPU access rather than in resource queues, locks queues, or transactions abort. The impact of these factors increases as the arrival rate increases that result in different response times for all protocols. We observed from figure that SMVL has better response time than SMVTO. This is because in SMVTO, high security level transaction T_i wait for its commit until all transactions at all sites with smaller timestamps than that of T_i commit and if a data item read by

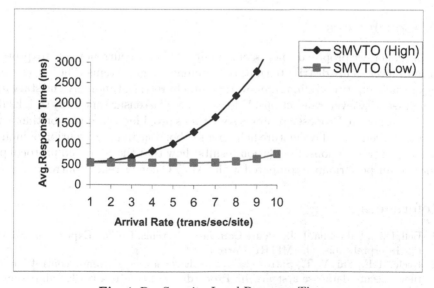

Fig. 4. Per Security Level Response Time

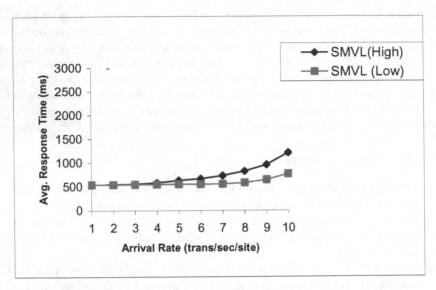

Fig. 5. Per Security Level Response Time

a T_i is updated and invalidated by a low security level transaction, then T_i is re-executed. In Fig. 4 and Fig. 5 we present the average transactions response times per-security level of SMVTO and SMVL protocols as a function of overall transaction arrival rate per site.

We observe that in SMVTO concurrency control protocol the response time of high security level transactions is significantly higher than that of low security level transactions throughout the arrival rates.

6   Conclusions

In this paper, we proposed a new secure multiversion concurrency control protocol for multilevel secure distributed database management systems. They ensure one-copy serializability and eliminate covert channels, retrieval anomaly and starvation of high security level transactions. V-locks are used to ensure one-copy serializability of transaction. Proposed protocol sometimes provides a data version that is not the most recent one. This feature helps avoid abortion and re-execution of high security level transactions. Simulation results show that the proposed protocol provides better performance compared with SMVTO concurrency control protocol.

References

1. Bell, D.E., LaPadula, L.J.: Secure Computer Systems: Unified Exposition and Multics Interpretation. The MITRE Corp. (1976)
2. Keefe, T.F., Sai, W.T., Sarivastva, J.: Multiversion concurrency control for multilevel secure database systems. In: Proceedings of the 10th IEEE Symposium on Security and Privacy, Oakland, California, pp. 369–383 (1990)

3. Atluri, V., Jajodia, S., Keefe, T.F., McCollum, C., Mukkamala, R.: Multilevel secure transaction processing: Status and Prospects. In: Proceedings of the tenth annual IFIP TC11/WG11.3 International Conference on Database Security X: Status and Prospects, Como, Italy, pp. 79–98 (1996)
4. Maimone, W.T., Greeberg, I.B.: Single level multiversion schedulers for Multilevel Secure Database Systems. In: Proceedings of 6th Annual Computer Security Application Conference, Tucson, pp. 137–174 (1990)
5. Atluri, V., Jajodia, S., Bertino, E.: Alternative correctness criteria for concurrent execution of transactions in MLS databases. IEEE Transactions on Knowledge and Data Engineering 8(5), 839–854 (1996)
6. Keefe, T.F., Tsai, W.T., Srivastava, J.: Database concurrency control in multilevel secure database management systems. IEEE Transactions on Knowledge and Data Engineering 5(6), 1039–1055 (1993)
7. Bernstein, A., Hadzilacos, V., Goodman, N.: Concurrency Control and Recovery in Database Systems. Addison-Wesley, Massachusetts (1987)
8. Ceri, S., Pelagatti, G.: Distributed Databases Principles and Systems. McGraw-Hill Book Company, New York (1984)
9. Ray, I., Mancini, L.V., Jajodia, S., Bertino, E.: ASEP: A secure and flexible commit protocol for MLS distributed database systems. IEEE Transactions on Knowledge and Data Engineering 12(6), 880–899 (2000)
10. Kaur, N., Sarje, A.K., Misra, M.: Performance evaluation of secure concurrency control algorithm for multilevel secure distributed database systems. In: Proceeding of IEEE the International Conference on Information Technology: Coding and Computing, pp. 249–254. Las Vegas, Nevada (2005)
11. Atluri, V., Jajodia, S., Bertino, E.: Transaction processing in multilevel secure databases using kernelized architecture: challenges and solutions. IEEE Transactions on Knowledge and Data Engineering 9(5), 697–708 (1997)
12. Kim, H.T., Kim, M.H.: Starvation-free secure multiversion concurrency control. Information Processing Letters, vol. 65, pp. 247–253. Elsevier, Amsterdam (1998)
13. Carey, M.J., Livny, M.: Conflict detection tradeoffs for replicated data. ACM Transactions on Database Systems 16(4), 703–746 (1991)
14. Carey, M.J., Franklin, M., Zaharioudakis, M.: Fine Grained Sharing in a Page-Server OODBMS. In: Proceedings of ACM-SIGMOD International Conference on Management of Data, Minneapolis, Minnesota, pp. 359–370 (1994)
15. Bernstein, P.A., Hadzilacos, V., Goodman, N.: Concurrency Control and Recovery in Database Systems. Addison-Wesley, Reading (1987)
16. Samaras, G., Britton, K., Citron, A., Mohan, C.: Two-Phase commit optimizations in a commercial distributed environment. International Journal on Distributed and Parallel Databases 3(4), 325–361 (1995)
17. McDermott, J., Jajodia, S.: Orange locking: channel-free database concurrency control via locking. In: Proceeding of 6th Working Conference of IFIP Working Group 11.3 on Database Security on Database Security, VI: Status and Prospects, Vancouver, Canada, pp. 267–284 (1995)

The Curse of Ease of Access to the Internet

Kotagiri Ramamohanarao, Kapil Kumar Gupta, Tao Peng,
and Christopher Leckie

Department of Computer Science and Software Engineering
NICTA Victoria Research Laboratory
The University of Melbourne
{rao,kgupta,tpeng,caleckie}@csse.unimelb.edu.au

Abstract. Since the day the Internet was made public, it has evolved as one of the most convenient, easily available and low cost media that help us to get connected to a vast variety of data and information. Its vast size and the ease of access of resources have made the Internet one of the most popular and widely used media for information exchange. However, this does not mean that it is free from any problems. Ensuring continuity of services and security of data is one of the most critical issues that must be resolved before the real power of the Internet can be harnessed. With more and more attacks emerging on a daily basis, it becomes necessary to analyze their root causes rather than to try and eliminate the attacks individually. Hence, in this paper we identify various factors responsible for the current state of insecurity and discuss the main categories of threats which span over the possible attacks that persist over the Internet. We also discuss the major limitations and challenges that need to be resolved to provide a better and a safe Internet.

1   Introduction

The Internet has emerged as one of the most convenient and widely used media for exchanging information. The amount of information that it contains is unprecedented, compared to any other media source and this information increases rapidly every day. The Internet is the newest and the fastest growing media for information flows and its size was estimated to be about 532,897 Terabytes in the year 2002 [2]. On top of this scalability, the main factor that led to its success is the ease with which anyone can access this information. Today, it is hard even to imagine a business running without making use of the Internet. However, the Internet of today is faced with many challenges, largely due to the vast size, ease of access, anonymity enjoyed by an individual and the open architecture of the Internet. One of these most daunting challenges is to ensure security, i.e., to ensure continuity of services, and the confidentiality and integrity of the available data [8], [1] while maintaining ease of access. New and unseen attacks emerge even when existing security systems are unable to detect the present attacks reliably [13]. Security becomes an important issue the moment we think of resource sharing. This is because every single piece of information has an owner attached to it and it is up to the owner to decide whether that information is

P. McDaniel and S.K. Gupta (Eds.): ICISS 2007, LNCS 4812, pp. 234–249, 2007.

shareable or not and if so, then to whom and under what conditions. Even for a stand alone computer which is shared by multiple users, restricting access to important information from others is important and hence security becomes an important factor that must be addressed. Ensuring this is relatively easy on a single computer, but when we connect it to the Internet, we cannot be sure of the associated risks.

The Internet, then known as ARPANET, was brought online in 1969 by the Advanced Research Projects Agency (ARPA) which initially connected four major computers at universities in the southwestern United States of America [24], [15]. The idea of developing the Internet was to provide a communications network that could work even if some of the sites were destroyed. The main feature for such a network was that the live nodes could communicate regardless of the state of the overall network [23]. This requirement affected the design of the Internet in two ways. First, to achieve this high level of interconnection, a packet switched architecture was selected as opposed to the circuit switched network used in traditional telephony [21]. This ensured that the packets could reach from one node to any other node even if multiple nodes between the two were down. This is because there was no direct connection between any two nodes at any point in time and multiple paths existed for the packets to travel from the source to reach the destination. Hence, packets can take different paths when traveling between two fixed nodes. This is known as the multi-path routing [25]. Second, to avoid any single point of failure for the entire Internet, each node in the network was considered as important as any other node in the network. Hence, the network could work even if a few nodes were not active. This resulted in a decentralized architecture for the Internet.

During the initial stages of the development of the Internet, it was not meant to be a public network and hence security was not considered as a major factor in its design [16]. The idea was to provide a simple, fast and reliable media for data transfer. However, Internet soon became a major public communication network and by then it was too late to redesign the entire Internet to add the required security functions. Hence, all the security features are left to be implemented at the user end rather than in the backbone of the Internet. This is because it is difficult to implement the security solutions at the core, as it has high bandwidth and huge amount of data, as compared to the edges of the Internet where the data flow is limited. The Internet Protocol does not implicitly provide any mechanism for security though it is one of the most desired features for any individual or organization accessing the Internet. This necessitates deploying expensive security mechanisms at the target so as to protect malicious attackers from gaining illegal access to private data and to ensure the continuity of services provided to the clients. Even then, no security administrator can ensure complete network and data security. In this paper, our focus is to identify various causes of security threats over the Internet in order to categorize the attacks and to highlight the challenges for resolving the root causes of these attacks.

The rest of the paper is organized as follows. We discuss various causes for attacks over the Internet in Section 2 where we highlight how the features and the architecture of the Internet enables the attacks to succeed. In Section 3 we categorize the main types of attacks and analyze the associated challenges along with possible solutions. We then discuss the core issues that needs to be addressed to improve security over the Internet in Section 4. We discuss the possible future directions for minimizing various security issues thereby increasing security over the Internet in Section 5. We then conclude in Section 6.

2   Causes for the Attacks over the Internet

Given that the Internet Protocol by itself does not provide any security mechanism to ensure data security and continuity of services, it is prone to a number of attacks such as Denial of Service and data theft. Theoretically, the problem of security can be eliminated if the software were "perfect" without any bugs and there were no implementation errors when configuring various systems and granting access rights. However, the notion of a perfect software is an ill-defined problem, as it is a semantic notion and it is very hard if not impossible to verify the semantics of a non-trivial software system. Even if the systems were "perfect", they would require defence against Denial of Service attacks (in the form of bandwidth attacks) and errors arising due to poor management of the systems.

The Internet, in its present state, not only provides a wide variety of tools that make the task of an attacker fast and easier, it offers a favourable environment for an attacker to launch such attacks and get away without even being identified. There are a number of drawbacks in the current Internet architecture which mainly arise in order to satisfy other requirements such as the ease of access, redundancy, openness, scalability and being a low cost medium for data transfer. In order to find out the possible solutions for this state of insecurity, it is very important to first figure out the root causes for this state and then search for mechanisms that can at least mitigate the risks if not completely eliminate them. We now discuss how different features of the current Internet actually provide an easy medium to launch attacks that compromise confidential data and disrupt services over the Internet. This discussion is motivated by the survey in [20]. Interested readers are encouraged to refer to the CERT website to find out the latest security threats and their impact [6].

2.1   Lack of Traceability of Packets

As any other network, the Internet is designed to have very high capacity core networks and low capacity edge networks. The data moves between any two distant edge networks via the core networks. Hence, the core links must be of very high capacity which need to accommodate heavy traffic from many sources and then deliver the same to one or more destinations. In contrast, an edge network only needs to support its end users, which requires less bandwidth. As we mentioned before, the Internet is based upon packet switching and multi-path routing of packets. This ensures that only the source and destination are important in any communication regardless of the path taken by the message to reach the destination. Thus, the data can be transmitted via different routes between the same source and destination. Multi-path routing also provides load balancing capability as the packets can be routed via different links in order to avoid congestion on a single link between the source and the destination. Both packet switching and multi-path routing make the Internet very robust when compared to the existing telephone networks.

While this flexibility of forwarding the IP packets based on their destination address rather than forwarding them on a predefined path helps make the Internet robust, it comes with the cost of loss of traceability of packets making it extremely hard to identify the complete route traversed by a packet. The problem of traceback primarily exists due to the possibility of *IP packet spoofing*. IP spoofing refers to creating an IP packet containing fake information. IP source address spoofing occurs when an IP packet is generated using a different source IP address than the actual address assigned to the source computer. Without an integrity check for each IP packet, attackers can spoof any field of an IP packet and inject it into the Internet.

A simple approach to recover the complete path traversed by any packet would be to ensure that every router that forwards the packet also tags it with a unique router specific code. This, however, involves the core routers making it an unattractive solution. This is because the amount of packets to be marked at the core would significantly degrade the performance over the Internet. Thus the routers only look at the destination address for a packet and route them to the next hop without any authentication. Further, since the volume of traffic they handle is so large, keeping a history of every packet or even the state of connections over the router is generally not practical. Methods need to be developed that are capable to trace the path of the packet reliably without significantly affecting the performance. As we discuss later, methods such as the probabilistic traceback of IP packets proposed in [18] show how to efficiently traceback the path traversed by a packet. The current methods, however, try to trace the complete path in order to reach the actual malicious source. On the other hand, if we can reliably identify the malicious source directly without the knowledge of the complete path traversed by the packet it will not only save the core routers from extra processing, in the form of authentication of the source, but will also provide immediate response when the malicious packet is discovered. Ingress filtering is the most effective method that can be used for this, though it has its own drawbacks. Ingress filtering, even if employed globally, can only be implemented at the level of the sub-net. It can not identify the unique node generating the attack traffic. Nonetheless, in practical situations it is sufficient to reach to the sub-net that is closest to the attacking source.

The ideal solution for packet source identification and traceback is a combination of ingress filtering (to drop the packets close to their source if possible) and an efficient packet marking scheme which does not involve the core routers (so as to recover the complete attack path without affecting the efficiency at the Internet backbone). This requires a clear definition (or boundary) of the edges over the Internet and then developing efficient switches which mandatorily mark every packet with a unique identification based upon the hardware. Further, since the packets are marked at the switches near to the source of the attack, the switches themselves must not be compromised by the attacker so that they can be trusted and relied upon. This approach will also minimize the role of global legislations which, anyways, is very hard to arrive at. This solution is bound to be effective because the packet marking is done very close to the source of the packet and it involves only the edge routers and switches where the traffic is limited as compared to any other present packet marking schemes for IP traceback.

2.2 Decentralized Management

The Internet is an aggregation of an extremely large number of networks which are interconnected to provide global access to the end users [17]. With no central authority or management hierarchy in the Internet each interconnected network is managed locally. This resulted in the rapid growth of the Internet since there were no restrictions and the network administrators were free to set up a network as per their requirements. In order to connect to the Internet and communicate with other networks, a network just needs to understand the Internet Protocol [3]. There is no rule that enforces a network to have a fixed network structure with a predefined set of features.

Decentralized management, however, has also provided the attackers with easy-to-access resources as there is no restriction on the content that is available over the Internet. Lack of standards and compliance often leads to configuration errors which are exploited resulting in security breaches. To counter many threats such as a Distributed Denial of Service attacks, it becomes necessary to make a cooperative effort for global deployment of defense solutions. But with the lack of interest and no administrative control over other's networks, cooperative defence mechanisms becomes extremely difficult to implement, making global deployment of the solution an unattractive alternative. Moreover, due to privacy and other commercial concerns, network service providers are generally reluctant to provide detailed information about the traffic patterns within their networks and do not cooperate in tracing attack sources. A global effort is often necessary because the distributed nature of many attacks renders a single-point solution ineffective. Further, a single point solution can only be implemented at the destination and not close to the source of the attack. It is important to implement the solution close to the source so as to reduce the impact of the attack. Also, since an Internet attack can be launched from a node anywhere in the world, it becomes very hard to first of all track the actual attacker and then to pursue legal actions against the attacker as this would involve international legal systems and cooperation among different governments which may not always be easy without international regulations.

2.3 Resource Sharing

The Internet helps to share resources among users. This, however, results in a situation where the actions of a single user affect the entire network. A simple example is that of a network printer where a single print job given by an individual user can affect the availability of the printer to all the other users in the network. Similarly, a single malicious user can occupy the shared resources as in a typical Denial of Service attack, thereby, disrupting the service to the legitimate users. As there is no quality-of-service guarantee provided to the users, there is no mechanism for enforcing traffic admission controls. This inter-user dependency is a fundamental factor that enables bandwidth attacks [11].

2.4 Vulnerability in Software and Poor Maintenance of Machines

The Internet provides a huge pool of computers and networks that can be exploited and controlled to launch powerful attacks. The software, including both the applications and the operating systems, often have a number of vulnerabilities which can be exploited. Since it is not practical to build "perfect" software, a number of vulnerabilities exist in many widely deployed software platforms. Further, computer networks and personal computers also suffer from configuration errors and poor maintenance resulting in more vulnerabilities.

Such vulnerable computers fall victim to the attacker resulting in an attacker taking control of the machine and turning it into a "zombie" under their control [7]. The attacker can then either create a large army of such zombies by exploiting the same vulnerability in other nodes to launch highly distributed and powerful bandwidth attacks which can be difficult to detect and hence difficult to prevent. Moreover, attackers can simply enter into a private network to obtain valuable information by hiding their identity with the help of the zombie thereby minimizing their chances of being identified [13]. Although, this is not a weakness of the design of the Internet, the vast size of the Internet provides an attacker with a pool of potential victims which can significantly ease the task of the attacker by providing easy targets.

It is important to note that, in case, when a single packet may result in shutting down the entire system or lead to loss of information, it becomes necessary to prevent such an attack by building real time and effective intrusion detection systems [12]. Tracing the source may only help in pursing legal actions as the damage caused by the attack can not be mitigated by identifying the attacker after the attack is successful. Damage can only be prevented if the attack itself is prevented.

2.5 Ease of Phishing

Phishing is an attempt to acquire sensitive personal information by tricking an individual to enter their credentials by masquerading as a true entity or to trick an individual to visit a dummy web location which can install malicious software that can be used to acquire sensitive information. The information acquired may then be used to cause the actual damage at some later stage [4]. The vast size of the Internet and the ease of obtaining a domain name over the Internet provides an easy means to set up such a phishing website that can result in compromising confidential information often resulting in monetary losses.

The vast size of the Internet and the curiosity of users are major factors that make phishing possible. This is because once an individual receives a phishing message, it is either too similar to the legitimate message that one cannot distinguish between the original and the fake message or it appears too exciting that one falls into the trap of such phishing attempts. Phishing, like other attacks, is more of a social engineering problem rather than a drawback in the Internet. However, the enormous size of the Internet and the ease of acquiring a domain name and setting up a phishing website often makes the task of an attacker much easier.

Given the above causes for the attacks over the Internet and that the security mechanisms are implemented at the target, the situation is contrary to the ideal one, i.e., the security methods should be enforced at the edge close to the source in order to prevent the spread of malicious attacks. This not only overwhelms small individual networks with the additional task of providing security, no mechanism is supported to trace back the attacker and pursue legal action. The only option left is to deploy expensive security mechanisms which do not even guarantee to identify the attacks reliably. Another possible solution is to redesign the Internet as the authors propose in [9]. However, in this paper we restrict our efforts to provide security mechanisms for the current Internet.

3   Major Threats over the Internet

Given the current Internet is plagued with a number of attacks and security risks, it is very important to eliminate these risks so as to ensure a safe computing environment. From the users' perspective, they are interested in two things; first, they must be able to access the information or avail of any service that they are authorized to access at any point in time and second, they must be ensured that their details are not compromised, i.e., their details should be accessible to only those individuals who are authorized to do so. Similarly, from an organization's perspective, it must be able to ensure continuity of the services that it is providing to its customers such that its resources are not exploited and no external or unauthorized entity can access the confidential information of its subscribers or illegally access its own confidential documents. This means that the threats fall in two major categories. The first being the Denial of Service attacks and the second being the attacks on Information Systems (or the data thefts which are illegal access to confidential or secure data). Though both of these are equally important, in this paper, we shall mainly focus on the Denial of Service attacks and describe them in detail. We shall only briefly mention about the Information attacks.

3.1   Denial of Service Attacks

A Denial of Service attack aims to flood the target with useless requests leading to depletion of its resources such that the target cannot serve the legitimate requests resulting in loss of services [11]. Such attacks are also known as the Bandwidth attacks. The Denial of Service attacks may also aim to bring down a service itself by exploiting a vulnerability such that the service is unavailable to the intended users.

With the emergence of the Internet as one of the very convenient media to provide customized services to individuals, be it in the form of publishing news, sending and receiving emails, online shopping, personal banking or searching information, a large number of businesses now depend upon the services offered over the Internet. Even a small disruption of these services may result in huge losses and throw an organization out of business. Hence, preventing such attacks is one of the most important challenges faced by a security administrator.

A Denial of Service attack can be launched in two ways [14]. First, it can be launched by sending a carefully crafted packet that exploits a software vulnerability that crashes the target. Second, it can be launched by sending massive volumes of traffic to the target, thus consuming the valuable resources, ultimately resulting in loss of services. The resources that may be depleted as a result of a bandwidth attack may include CPU capacity of a server, stack space in network protocol software or the Internet access link. To generate the enormous amount of traffic, the attack is often launched in two steps; control a large number of zombies by exploiting some vulnerabilities and then instruct the zombies to launch the attack on the target. This is known as the Distributed Denial of Service attack and is much more powerful than a Denial of Service attack.

Problem: The problem is to identify the bad requests from a stream of good and bad requests such that the bad requests may be blocked and good requests are allowed.

Challenges: The main challenge is to minimize the false alarms, or the false positives, i.e., to minimize the labeling of non legitimate requests as legitimate, because this will result in loss of service to a genuine user and partially fulfil the objective of an attacker. Another challenge is to identify the bad behaviour or bad requests close to the source and far away from the target of the attack. This is important because a Denial of Service attack is visible easily as the system performance degrades which is detectable. However, by this time it is too late since the resources have already been depleted and the system finally stops responding. Detecting the attacks close to the source can eliminate this situation. Other challenges that also need to be addressed include the capability of the system to cope up with the ever increasing traffic to analyze, to do this in real time, to minimize the cost involved, to identify how often one needs to retrain the system or update the signatures depending upon whether the system is anomaly based or signature based, to sketch out an efficient intrusion response mechanism and to ensure that the system is light weight and scalable for future expansions. Though all of these challenges need to be addressed, the most important and critical challenge is to differentiate between good and bad requests close to the attacker rather than detecting at the target.

Approaches for Defending against Denial of Service Attacks: The methods to defend against the Denial of Service attacks fall into one of four categories:

1. *Attack Prevention:* It aims at stoping the attack before it reaches the target. The most effective technique is to filter out the traffic with spoofed packets close to the attacker. Present methods such as ingress filtering or router based filtering require universal deployment, which is difficult to ensure in practice. The only option for implementing attack prevention schemes is the introduction of legislation that necessitates their global deployment [20].

2. *Attack Detection:* This aims to detect when a Denial of Service attack occurs. It is very important to detect an attack as soon as possible as it is only after the detection of an attack that the counter measures and responses can be activated. All the current methods such as the MULTOPS, SYN detection, Batch detection, Spectral analysis, Kolmogorov test and time series analysis are based on one or more assumptions which are not always reliable. Hence, the capabilities of current methods are questionable [20].

3. *Attack Source Identification:* Identification of the attack source aims to locate the actual source of the packet, regardless of the source information in the packet. This is because very often the source address as obtained from the packet is spoofed. It is very important to identify the actual source of the attack to activate global responses, if possible, and prevent further traffic from the target and hence minimize future damage from the same source. In Section 2.1 we introduced this problem and discussed the present methods and possible approaches for the attack source identification. Current methods that aim to identify the attack source includes IP trace back by active interaction, probabilistic packet marking schemes and hash-based traceback schemes [20] cannot guarantee the traceback granularity to a single host and are not effective at detecting attacks launched from compromised hosts.

   Nonetheless, methods such as the adjusted probabilistic packet marking for IP traceback [18], show how to efficiently traceback the path traversed by a packet. In the paper the authors show that with their marking scheme the number of packets needed by the victim to reconstruct the attack path is significantly reduced. This method therefore helps to minimize the overhead involved in marking the packets by the router.

4. *Attack Suppression:* This aims to remove the effects of the attack, i.e., recover from the damage caused and update (patch) the system so as to protect it from same or similar attacks in the future. Attack reaction methods include bottleneck resource management, intermediate network reaction and source end reaction [20]. All of these are themselves based upon one or more of the previous mentioned unsolved issues such as differentiating between attack and legitimate traffic and detecting the actual source of the attack. Hence, to completely rely upon the attack reaction methods is not recommended.

3.2   Information Attacks

An information attack is the retrieval and(or) modification of data by unauthorized personnel.

Networks of today are a storehouse of an unprecedented amount of data and information and such data can either be freely accessible to every individual or a person may require special privileges to access it. This depends on two factors, the owner of the data and the nature of the data. It is for the owners of the data to decide whether their data should be accessible to others or not. Similarly, critical data can be exploited if available freely and hence the nature of the data also defines its access privileges. Information sources are often targeted either to manipulate the freely available information or to access and(or) modify secure information [22]. Hence, data security generally involves ensuring integrity and confidentiality of data. Information systems may also be a victim of Denial of Service attacks where the objective is to simply hinder the services provided by the information system to its authorized users.

Problem: The problem is two fold; first, to identify the individual and ensure only the authorized individual is able to access and(or) modify the available information and second, to identify malicious requests from legitimate requests as in typical Denial of Service attack detection.

Challenges: The challenge is to accurately identify the user who is trying to access or modify the information and ensure that the user is authorized to do so. Other challenges are similar to those for fighting against a Denial of Service attack with an additional requirement that the users must also be identified along with their actions which should conform to the installed security policy.

Approaches for Defending against Information Attacks: Methods for defending against Information attacks include *Access Control* (which is based on authentication and authorization [24], [10] including biometric and multi factor authentication [5] along with user profiling schemes), *Providing a Secure Communication Medium* (which includes various Cryptographic methods [24]) and *Secure Management of Information System.*

4   Core Issues - Why Do the Attacks Succeed?

In the light of the two major threats over the Internet and how various features of the current Internet allow an attacker to launch a successful attack, the main question that needs to be addressed is, can we really build a system that can protect our networks from malicious attacks? Further, what are the factors that need to be considered for building any such system? However, before we even attempt to build such a system, we must carefully analyze the challenges and identify various requirements that need to be met by any defense mechanism. We now give a detailed analysis of these issues and identify their domain which is necessary for effectively resolving them.

4.1   How to Trace Back the Actual Source?

To traceback the actual source that is sending malicious packets is critical in order to ensure that the source may be blocked and appropriate legal action may be taken. However, this becomes very hard as the present Internet architecture provides no reliable means to trace the source. This is one of the important areas that certainly needs special attention as this can be achieved. However, current solutions available to handle this problem require global measures which become difficult to implement because the solutions span over different countries with conflicting interests. In the absence of a central governing authority this solution does not seem very promising. We need to somehow trace the source without international cooperation and without taxing the available resources. We discussed one such method in Section 2.1.

4.2   What Is Good and What Is Bad?

The most important challenge is to quantify what is good and what is bad, i.e., when do we call a packet or a request as legitimate and when do we call it as malicious. Further, is it possible to describe them in a sensible way? If yes, what attributes must be monitored to do so? Is there any justification for the same? Very often, a single event may be considered as a normal event with regards to a set of underlying criteria, but the same may be considered anomalous when the criteria are changed. How do we define such criteria?

4.3   Can We Really Authenticate?

Authentication means that every user of any secure system must possess some unique characteristics that must be verified every time the user tries to access the system. Hence, a human is authenticated based on some characteristic features supplied to the system. This does not ensure that only an authorized person can be authenticated. Present systems lack the association of the supplied credentials to a human user, making identity theft a possibility. Though authentication methods have improved significantly, they can still be violated. Does this mean that identity theft cannot be completely prevented? Further, user profiling techniques try to analyze a user by constantly monitoring the user's activities and comparing the current profile to the historic profile. Can we formally prove that the current behaviour is a reflection of past behaviour? How much can the current behaviour deviate from the past behaviour to be considered as normal?

4.4   Can We Eliminate Phishing?

The idea behind phishing is to trick people to enter confidential identification credentials which can be later utilized to launch actual attacks. Phishing attacks are generally focused on acquiring bank account details leading to banking fraud. However, phishing can also be used to trick an individual to acquire sensitive information, disclosure of which can result in other major security issues. Defending against phishing often requires a global effort and such efforts have now started to emerge. The current methods are generally based on creating a huge database of known phishing web sites which are blacklisted and blocked by the browser itself. However, the issue still remains unsolved as the size of the Internet is enormous and it is difficult to build a database of such malicious websites. Further, to provide a real time response by analyzing the requested web URL would become a major challenge as the size of this database would increase. The ease with which an individual can acquire a new domain name and set up a malicious website further exacerbates the situation. Assuming that we can somehow setup such a database and provide a real time analysis for the requested web URL, can we really trust the same, given the database may be biased or is itself a target of an attack? For effective resolution all of such inherent limitations in the solutions must be properly addressed. The possible solutions may be based upon building trust among the entire Internet rather than trusting a single third party.

Phishing problem can be considered as the authentication problem. The only difference is that, instead of authenticating an individual, the system needs to authenticate the requested resource. The system must ensure two things; first, the user is requesting an authentic resource, i.e., the requested resource is not a phishing source and second, the system fetches the same resource that the user requested. Thus, to eliminate Phishing reliable authentication methods must be developed.

4.5   How Can We Protect the Systems from Spyware?

Spyware is software that is installed on a computer without its user's consent, leading to loss of confidential information. Unlike phishing, where a user visits an external phishing website, spyware gets installed on the local machine, though they both serve the same purpose. Spyware is often bundled with other software and is installed automatically along with the installation of the infected software. Many tools are available that claim to remove or block spyware, but all of these are based on building some underlying database of known spyware. Again, is it possible to create a complete list of spyware? Further, how can one be sure that such a list is unbiased and not motivated by financial gains? Providing real time response to the user would becomes a major issue as the size of this list would increase.

4.6   Removing Spam?

Electronic spam refers to sending unsolicited messages over the communication medium. Spam affects the Internet in three ways. First, since spam is something that is useless, it leads to wasting of the critical resources as it increases the amount of traffic that must be routed to the destination. Second, the user has to spend time and filter out the spam from the useful messages. This reduces the performance and efficiency of an individual. Finally, the amount of spam can overwhelm the number of legitimate messages and this may result in loss of important messages mainly due to errors in filtering out the spam. Automatic tools can be employed to filter out the spam but their success depends upon proper definition of spam, which is not clear. Generally, a spam filter is based upon matching of certain keywords. However, the presence of certain words does not necessitate that the message is a spam. Further, this involves more of human behaviour analysis as a particular message may be a spam for one individual but the same may be something useful for another.

The question is: based upon individual user preferences can we identify spam close to its source rather than identifying it at the destination? This is important because the delivery of spam consumes a lot of valuable resources over the Internet. Effective removal of the spam at its source based upon individual user preferences will not only save these resources, for other critical tasks, but will also reduce human involvement in their removal.

5   Future Directions

With the number of attacks over the Internet on the rise, Intrusion Detection Systems now play a significant role in defining the security policy for any organization. Intrusion Detection aims to detect Denial of Service and(or) Information attacks, ideally in real time while the attack is still in progress so that appropriate intrusion response mechanisms can be activated to minimize the impact of the attack. A number of methods have been proposed for building robust and efficient Intrusion Detection Systems, which include various methods from the machine learning domain to data mining and pattern matching.

One of the recently introduced methods for detecting intrusions in an efficient and effective manner is based on conditional random fields [12]. The system is based on the observation that the attacks are often the result of a number of sequential events that are correlated. Thus, a system must be able to analyze such a sequence of events for better attack detection accuracy. Any such method is focused on building a better detector (also known as the analysis engine) of the Intrusion Detection System.

Complementary to such approaches, methods such as distributed intrusion detection [19] and collaborative intrusion detection using peer-to-peer networks [26] are based on correlating the alerts generated by individual Intrusion Detection Systems to reach a global consensus about the possible attack detected by one or more individual systems. Such systems help to analyze the individual alerts generated by different systems in order to invoke a global response mechanism against the attacks.

Given the causes for attacks over the Internet and various open issues for research, we now give some future directions for better resolving these issues. However, to build a security system that can ensure complete security is very hard to achieve. Nonetheless, to start with, an effective approach would be to address the core issues by analyzing them in detail, rather than working to protect the Internet from already known individual attacks. Analyzing and eliminating the root causes would not only prevent the Internet from the known attacks but will also reduce the possibility of future attacks and thus strengthen the Internet.

We broadly classify the problem areas for improving security over the Internet into three categories, each of which may span over multiple disciplines. They are as follows:

1. To reduce the vulnerabilities that can be attacked, better software engineering methods are required to build reliable software. Further, proper system

configuration and maintenance would also prevent the increase in vulnerabilities. Effective solutions for this problem completely lie within the computational science domain. Reducing vulnerabilities would help to prevent Denial of Service attacks and unauthorized access and(or) modification to the data.

2. To provide an environment for global countermeasures against attacks as opposed to local defence mechanisms. The issues are covered both under the legislative domain, as well as through developments in the computational sciences. Examples for this include reliable source identification and the collaborative intrusion detection and response system. Solutions in this area would help to fight the bandwidth attacks to ensure availability of resources. Efforts are, however, required to provide effective solutions from the computational science domain itself in order to reduce the dependence on global regulations.

3. To provide stronger authentication by introducing methods that are difficult to forge. A typical example may be multi-factor authentication. Methods need to be developed that are secure as well as simple and cost effective to implement. The possible solutions span over both the computational and the biological sciences domain. Solutions would help to defend against Phishing, Spyware and Spam as well as help to provide confidentiality and integrity to data.

To help address these problem areas, we are building on our research into more accurate detectors [12], together with our own methods for distributed detection and alert correlation [19], [26], in order to develop robust and scalable detection platforms by using evidence from networks on a global scale. Solution, thus, lies in proper tuning and analysis of the current methods such as discussed in [12], [19] and [26] to effectively resolve the core problems discussed above.

6   Conclusions

In this paper we have discussed various causes for attacks over the Internet with special regards to the weaknesses in the architecture of the Internet that enable an attacker to launch successful attacks and get away without being identified. We also classified the attacks as belonging to two major categories, Denial of Service attacks and Information attacks, and discussed the associated problems and challenges. Finally, we gave possible directions to minimize these security issues for building a better and safer computing environment.

References

[1] CIA Triad; Confidentiality, Integrity, Availability (Last assessed: August 23, 2007), http://en.wikipedia.org/wiki/CIA_Triad
[2] How Much Information? (Last assessed: August 23, 2007) (2003), http://www2.sims.berkeley.edu/research/projects/how-much-info-2003/printable_report.pdf

[3] Internet Protocol. RFC 791 (Last assessed: August 24, 2007) (September 1981), http://www.ietf.org/rfc/rfc791.txt

[4] Phishing: How Not to Get Hooked by a Phishing Scam (Last assessed: August 24, 2007), http://www.onguardonline.gov/docs/onguardonline_phishing.pdf

[5] Two-Factor Authentication (Last assessed: August 24, 2007), http://en.wikipedia.org/wiki/Strong_authentication

[6] Welcome to CERT (Last assessed: August 24, 2007), http://www.cert.org/

[7] Zombie Computer (Last assessed: August 24, 2007), http://en.wikipedia.org/wiki/Zombie_computer

[8] FIPS PUB 199. Standards for Security Categorization of Federal Information and Information Systems. Technical report, National Institute of Standards and Technology. Federal Information Processing Standards Publication (Last Accessed: August 23, 2007) (2004), http://csrc.nist.gov/publications/fips/fips199/FIPS-PUB-199-final.pdf

[9] Clark, D., Sollins, K., Wroclawski, J., Faber, T.: Addressing Reality: An Architectural Response to Real-World Demands on the Evolving Internet. In: ACM SIGCOMM, FDNA Workshop (2003) (Last Accessed: August 29, 2007), http://www.isi.edu/newarch/DOCUMENTS/Principles.FDNA03.pdf

[10] Ferraiolo, D.F., Kuhn, D.R.: Role Based Access Control. In: Proceedings of 15th National Computer Security Conference (1992), http://csrc.nist.gov/rbac/ferraiolo-kuhn-92.pdf

[11] Gligor, V.D.: A Note on Denial-Of-Service in Operating Systems. IEEE Transactions on Software Engineering 10(3), 320–324 (1984)

[12] Gupta, K.K., Nath, B., Ramamohanarao, K.: Conditional Random Fields for Intrusion Detection. In: AINAW 2007. Proceedings of 21st International Conference on Advanced Information Networking and Applications Workshops, pp. 203–208. IEEE Press, Los Alamitos (2007)

[13] Gupta, K.K., Nath, B., Ramamohanarao, K., Kazi, A.: Attacking Confidentiality: An Agent Based Approach. In: Mehrotra, S., Zeng, D.D., Chen, H., Thuraisingham, B., Wang, F.-Y. (eds.) ISI 2006. LNCS, vol. 3975, pp. 285–296. Springer, Heidelberg (2006)

[14] Hussain, A., Heidemann, J., Papadopoulos, C.: A Framework for Classifying Denial of Service Attacks. In: Proceedings of the ACM SIGCOMM Conference, pp. 99–110. ACM, New York (2003)

[15] Leiner, B.M., Cerf, V.G., Clark, D.D., Kahn, R.E., Kleinrock, L., Lynch, D.C., Postel, J., Roberts, L.G., Wolff, S.: A Brief History of the Internet (Last assessed: August 23, 2007), http://www.isoc.org/internet/history/brief.shtml

[16] Longstaff, T.A., Ellis, J.T., Hernan, S.V., Lipson, H.F., Mcmillan, R.D., Pesante, L.H., Simmel, D.: Security of the Internet. Technical Report The Froehlich/Kent Encyclopedia of Telecommunications. CERT Coordination Center vol. 15 (Last Accessed: August 18, 2007) (1997), http://www.cert.org/encyc_article/tocencyc.html

[17] Mirkovic, J., Reiher, P.: A taxonomy of DDoS attack and DDoS defense mechanisms. ACM SIGCOMM Computer Communication Review 34(2), 39–53 (2004)

[18] Peng, T., Leckie, C., Ramamohanarao, K.: Adjusted Probabilistic Packet Marking for IP Traceback. In: Proceedings of the Second IFIP Networking Conference (Networking 2002), pp. 697–708 (2002)

[19] Peng, T., Leckie, C., Ramamohanarao, K.: Information Sharing for Distributed Intrusion Detection Systems. Journal of Network and Computer Applications (2005)

[20] Peng, T., Leckie, C., Ramamohanarao, K.: Survey of network-based defense mechanisms countering the DoS and DDoS problems. ACM Computing Surveys 39(1),
3 (2007)

[21] Roberts, L.G.: The Evolution of Packet Switching. Proceedings of the
IEEE 66(11), 1307–1313 (1978)

[22] Siponen, M.T., Oinas-Kukkonen, H.: A Review of Information Security Issues and
Respective Research Contributions. SIGMIS Database 38(1), 60–80 (2007)

[23] Sterling, B.: Short History of the Internet (Last assessed: August 23, 2007),
http://w3.aces.uiuc.edu/AIM/scale/nethistory.html

[24] Tanenbaum, A.: Computer Networks. Prentice Hall PTR, Englewood Cliffs (2002)

[25] Thaler, D., Hopps, C.: Multipath Issues in Unicast and Multicast Next-Hop Selection. RFC 2991, Publiched online November 2000 (Last assessed: August 24,
2007), http://www.faqs.org/rfcs/rfc2991.html

[26] Zhou, C.V., Karunasekera, S., Leckie, C.: Evaluation of a Decentralized Architec-
ture for Large Scale Collaborative Intrusion Detection. In: The Tenth IFIP/IEEE
International Symposium on Integrated Network Management, pp. 80–89. IEEE
Press, Los Alamitos (2007)

A Structured Approach to Detect Scanner-Printer Used in Generating Fake Document

G. Gupta[1], R. Sultania[1], S. Mondal[1], S.K. Saha[1], and B. Chanda[2]

[1] CSE Department, Jadavpur University, Kolkata, India
sks_ju@yahoo.co.in
[2] ECS Unit, Indian Statistical Institute, Kolkata, India

Abstract. With the advent of modern scanning and printing technology, it is quite easy to make fraudulent copies of sensitive documents. It is very difficult to identify them in the conventional approach. In this work, we present a novel and structured scheme to detect the fake document and the printer-scanner used in generating the same.

Keywords: digital forensic, fake document, printer detection, scanner detection.

1 Introduction

The hardcopy of a document can be captured through scanner, tampered using a software and printed. Such malpractices are referred as *digitized document fraud*. Such documents are so realistic that detection becomes extremely difficult and as a result, a new paradigm called *Digital Image Forensic* has evolved. Authenticity of a transmitted digitized document is verified using a key-based hash scheme [1]. But, it may fail due to transmission error. watermarking is also [2] tried. But, it may introduce distortion. Classifier based schemes are also reported [3]. To detect the camera used for capturing a document, camera modeling parameters like colour filter array pattern [4], camera sensor noise [5] etc. are used.

In this work, we deal with fake documents generated using the scanner and printer. The scope and the proposed methodologies are detailed in section 2. Section 3 presents the experimental results and the concluding remarks.

2 Proposed Methodology

In the fraudulent documents under consideration, the only distortion present is due to *device introduced imperfection*. Thus, the conventional notion of tampered document is changed. Here, we try to *detect whether the document in question is genuine or fake* and to *identify the scanner and printer used to generate the fake document*. The current work considers only inkjet colour printers.

Detection of Fake Document: In order to make the impact of the devices visible, the document is to be magnified even upto 100 times. It is done by high

P. McDaniel and S.K. Gupta (Eds.): ICISS 2007, LNCS 4812, pp. 250–253, 2007.

resolution LEICA microscopes. A small patch of the document is chosen and magnified. This is referred as the document/data under analysis. In connection with the detection of fake document, couple of observations have been made [6]. The observation like *increased number of colour present in the fake document* is a general characteristic that can serve the purpose for wide range of documents. We also adhere to the same feature. $\frac{|C_o - C_q|}{C_o}$ is taken as the measure to detect the fake document. C_o and C_q denote the count of distinct R, G, B combination for original and questioned document respectively.

Detection of Printer: The fake document will have the impact of both the devices embedded in it and those are not readily separable. As the impurities caused by the printer is imposed on top of the scanned output, it is more likely that its impact will be readily visible in the final document. This observation has motivated us to detect the printer first.

Overall Similarity (G_s) is measured based on the observation that the colour inkjet printers put additional coloured dots in the document [6] as its signature. To quantify the observation, hue histogram based feature is considered. Let, H_o and H_q denote the histogram for the original and questioned version of a document respectively. Then, $G_s = \sum_i | (H_{o_i} - H_{q_i}) |$ is considered as the measure of overall similarity.

Similarity in Coarse Area (C_s) is more focused on the noise/impurities introduced by the printer in the document. The coloured dots bearing the signature of the inkjet printers are more pronounced in the relatively smooth region and introduces additional coarseness/noise in the image. In order to provide a measure specific to such noise, first of all the coarse region is extracted as follows.

Extraction of Coarse Region is done using gray-scale morphological closing and opening operation. $F \bullet S$ and $F \circ S$ denote closing and opening operation on the gray-scale image F by a structuring element (SE) S. The RGB document image, F is converted into gray-scale image, F_g. The smooth image, F_m is $((F_g \bullet S) \circ S)$ where, S is the SE of size $k \times k$. The difference image, F_d is such that, $F_d(i,j) = | F_g(i,j) - F_m(i,j) |$. The coarse image F_c is obtained by considering the pixels in F_d satisfying $F_d(i,j) > t$. t is the threshlod of very low value and taken as 1 in our experiment.

Although F_c is mostly due to the impurities induced by the the inkjet printer, but other noise in the form of small dots may appear. To minimize such effect, if any, we further refine F_c and obtain $F_{temp} = ((F_c \circ S_1) \bullet S_1)$ where, S_1 be the SE of size $k_1 \times k_1$ such that $k_1 < k$. The final coarse image, F_c^p is obtained by retaining the R, G, B values from F for the pixels satisfying $F_{temp}(i,j) > 0$.

In our experiment, the values for k and k_1 are chosen as 7 and 3 respectively. $C_s = \sum_i | (H_{o_i}^c - H_{q_i}^c) |$ forms the measure of similarity in coarse area where, $H_{o_i}^c$ and $H_{q_i}^c$ denote the histogram value of i-th bin of the coarse region in the original and questioned document respectively.

Detection of Scanner: Once the printer is identified, with that prior knowledge we proceed to determine the scanner used in the process. The scanner is detected based on the introduced impurities affecting colour saturation and

Table 1. Percentage Change of Colour Present in Fake Documents

Document	% Change in Colour Present for Different Setup			
	P1S1	P1S2	P2S1	P2S2
a	28.79	09.85	38.29	33.52
e	72.01	85.79	63.03	64.41
8	126.76	115.40	93.82	107.10
19	196.10	204.25	128.67	98.08

intensity variance. In order to compute the features, we obtain the residual image, F_s by excluding the coarse region from the document. By applying a filter on F_{s_g} (the gray-scale version of F_s), the denoised image, F_{dn} is formed. Finallly, the noise image, F_n is obtained such that $F_n(i,j) =| F_{s_g}(i,j) - F_{dn}(i,j) |$. The R, G, B values from F are retained in F_n for the pixels satisfying $F_n(i,j) > 0$. In our work, we have used mean, median and Gaussian filter. The median filter helps to model the impulsive noise and others model high frequency noise.

Let, I_{o_i} and I_{q_i} denote the standard deviation of i-th channel intensity for the original and questioned document respectively. Accordingly, S_{o_i} and S_{q_i} are the average saturation for them. Thus, for scanner detection, $I_v = \sum_i | (I_{o_i} - I_{q_i}) |$ and $S_v = \sum_i | (S_{o_i} - S_{q_i}) |$ represent the features.

Table 2. G_s and C_s [see text] for Printer Identification

Document	Printer-Scanner combination							
	P1S1		P2S1		P1S2		P2S2	
	G_s	C_s	G_s	C_s	G_s	C_s	G_s	C_s
a	.21	.21	.07	.04	.36	.42	.16	.21
e	.22	.51	.13	.36	.16	.48	.12	.40
8	.44	.41	.17	.25	.45	.45	.38	.36
19	.42	.47	.30	.33	.49	.58	.33	.34

3   Experimental Results and Conclusion

In our experiment, fake documents are generated using two different HP scanners (referred as **S1** and **S2**) and two different HP printers (referred as **P1** and **P2**). Table 1 shows the Change in colour present for the fake documents with respect to the original document which is quite high and helps in detection. Table 2 shows the values of G_s and C_s for different documents. A careful look into the data reveals that irrespective of the scanner used, the printer **P2**, in comparison to **P1**, maintains the hue distribution closer to the original one. Table 3 shows that given a particular printer, the scanner **S1**, in comparison to **S2**, maintains the closeness to original document in terms of intensity deviation and average saturation.

Table 3. I_v and S_v [see text] for Scanner Identification

Document	Printer	Scanner	Mean Filter		Median Filter		Gaussian Filter	
			I_v	S_v	I_v	S_v	I_v	S_v
a	P1	S1	11.90	.05	12.01	.04	10.10	.03
		S2	17.25	.07	17.21	.06	16.16	.05
	P2	S1	04.46	.07	04.41	.06	04.76	.07
		S2	12.83	.11	12.94	.10	11.48	.09
e	P1	S1	27.63	.07	28.85	.04	13.21	.04
		S2	56.61	.13	57.48	.11	36.09	.10
	P2	S1	12.84	.03	13.16	.02	04.20	.03
		S2	27.23	.06	27.37	.05	05.78	.05
8	P1	S1	20.21	.15	20.04	.14	04.34	.11
		S2	22.97	.19	23.36	.18	04.24	.15
	P2	S1	12.67	.14	12.53	.13	12.71	.11
		S2	25.74	.18	25.53	.17	19.58	.16
19	P1	S1	17.85	.21	16.93	.20	13.77	.16
		S2	22.08	.21	21.18	.20	18.21	.19
	P2	S1	10.19	.16	09.19	.15	03.40	.13
		S2	28.97	.18	28.02	.17	20.49	.15

Thus, it is concluded that the methodology presented in this work can detect the fraud documents and also can identify the printer and scanner used in the generation process. A simple measure based on colour count detects the fake document and then a morphology based scheme has been proposed to extract the coarse region where the signature of the printer dominates. Once printer is detected, scanner characteristics is looked in to the residual image. The experimental result also shows the effectiveness of the scheme.

References

1. Swaminathan, A., Mao, Y., Wu, M.: Robust and secure image hashing. IEEE Trans. on Information Forensics and Security (June 2006)
2. Fridrich, J.: Image watermarking for tamper detection. In: Proc. IEE Intl. Conf. on Image Processing, vol. 2, pp. 404–408 (1998)
3. Farid, H., Lyu, S.: Steganalysis using higher-order image statistics. IEEE Trans. on Information Forensics and Security 1(1), 111–119 (2006)
4. Bayram, S., Sencar, H.T., Memon, N., Avcibas, I.: Source camera identification based on cfa interpolation. In: Proc. IEE Intl. Conf. on Image Processing (2005)
5. Lukas, J., Fridrich, J., Goljan, M.: Digital camera identification from sensor noise. IEEE Trans. on Information Security and Forensics 1(2), 205–214 (2006)
6. Gupta, G., Mazumdar, C., Rao, M.S., Bhosale, R.B.: Paradigm shift in document related frauds: Characteristics identification for development of a non-destructive automated system for printed documents. Digital Investigation 3, 43–55 (2006)

A Zero Knowledge Password Proof Mutual Authentication Technique Against Real-Time Phishing Attacks

Mohsen Sharifi, Alireza Saberi, Mojtaba Vahidi, and Mohammad Zorufi

Computer Engineering Department, Iran University of Science and Technology
msharifi@iust.ac.ir,
{a_saberi, mojtabavahidi, zorufi}@comp.iust.ac.ir

Abstract. Phishing attack is a kind of identity theft trying to steal confidential data. Existing approaches against phishing attacks cannot prevent real-time phishing attacks. This paper proposes an Anti-Phishing Authentication (APA) technique to detect and prevent real-time phishing attacks. It uses 2-way authentication and zero-knowledge password proof. Users are recommended to customize their user interfaces and thus defend themselves against spoofing. The proposed technique assumes the preexistence of a shared secret key between any two communicating partners, and ignores the existence of any malware at client sides.

1 Introduction

Phishing is a branch of internet crimes. In these attacks, users' sensitive information such as passwords and credit card details are captured. Attackers use social engineering in their attacks to masquerade themselves as legitimate servers [1].

In a phishing attack, the attacker spoofs a trusted website and then sends e-mail(s) to users. An encouraged user clicks on a link embedded in the email. By following the link, the unaware user is redirected to a fake website. Due to the similarity between this site and the trusted one, user may enter the phisher's desired information. In this stage, phisher has gained sufficient information and may forge user's identity or withdraw from victim's internet banking account [2, 3].

In traditional phishing attacks, phisher is only connected to the user and saves captured user sensitive information. After that, in a suitable time, phisher sends this information to forge user's identity and abuse the victim's resources. Almost all existing solutions are designed to fight against traditional phishing attacks.

In real-time phishing, phisher stands in the middle of communication between a user and a trusted web site. After getting user's information, phisher sends them to the trusted web site and replays the reply to the user. Detection of real-time phishing attacks is harder than detection of traditional ones. Nearly none of the existing methods are able to detect real-time phishing attacks. This paper proposes an Anti-Phishing Authentication (APA) technique for fighting against real-time phishing.

P. McDaniel and S.K. Gupta (Eds.): ICISS 2007, LNCS 4812, pp. 254–258, 2007.

The paper is structured as follows. Our proposed technique and the way it deals with phishing are discussed in Sections 2. The implementation is presented in Section 3. Sections 4 and 5 are devoted to the evaluation of the proposed technique and conclusions.

2 The Proposed Method

In this section, our Anti-Phishing Authentication (APA) mechanism is proposed. A short secret key (e.g. password) is assumed between a user and a trusted website.

APA is based on SPEKE [8] which is a cryptographic method for password authentication key agreement. SPEKE uses passwords to resist against man in the middle attacks. It performs a 2-way authentication and resists on-line and off-line dictionary attacks [8]. SPEKE is used in APA with some modifications.

SPEKE has two phases. The two sides of communication are user and (web) server. First, user and server start to create a session key (k) using password. Then, each side authenticates itself to the opposite party using the session key.

APA only enhances the second phase of SPEKE. Table 1 describes the symbols used in subsequent tables. Table 2 explains the second phase of authentication process in APA. Using SPEKE, APA allows communicating parties to authenticate each other without revealing passwords, i.e. by zero knowledge password proof.

Table 1. Symbols used in authentication scenario [8]

Symbol	Description
R_U, C_U	Random numbers generated by user
R_{AS}, C_{AS}	Random number generated by server
$E_k(m)$	Symmetric encryption of message m using key k
$D_k(m)$	Symmetric decryption of message m using key k
$U => AS: m$	User sends message m to server
$AS => U: m$	Server sends message m to user
K	Session key
AS_{IP}	IP address of server
PH	Phisher

Table 2. The second phase of authentication in APA

#	Action	Description
1	$U=>AS: E_K(C_U, AS_{IP})$	User generates random number C_U then encrypts C_U and IP address of opposite side. User encrypts message m using key k and sends it to opposite side.
2	$AS: D_K(E_K(C_U, AS_{IP}))$	Server decrypts user's message. If the IP inside the message does not match with its IP address, authentication fails.
3	$AS=>U: E_K(C_U, C_{AS})$	Server generates the random number C_{AS} and encrypts C_U and C_{AS}. Server encrypts message m using key k and sends message to user.
4	$U: D_K(E_K(C_U, C_{AS}))$	User decrypts server's message to validate legitimacy of C_U.
5	$U => AS: E_K(C_{AS})$	User encrypts C_{AS} and sends it to server. From user point of view authentication finished successfully.
6	$AS: D_K(E_K(C_{AS}))$	Server decrypts user's message. Authentication is successful if the received C_{AS} matches the sent C_{AS}.

2.1 Prevention from Traditional Phishing Attacks

Users under traditional attacks conceive phishers as trusted servers and reveal their passwords. But by using APA, attackers are unaware of password and cannot generate session key and therefore are defeated in the first phase of authentication.

APA takes advantage of SPEKE by forcing phishers to generate a session key without knowing the password at the end of the first phase of SPEKE. This task entails lots of computational time (say in orders of months using a single computer) and the session key is valid only for the short period of this session; i.e. even if the session key can be generated, it is useless since the validity of the key must have been expired a long time ago. The time complexity of these attacks against SPEKE is noted in [8, 9].

2.2 Prevention from Real-Time Phishing Attacks

In real-time phishing attacks, phisher is located in the middle of communication between user and server, and replays the received information from one side to another. On-line (real-time) phishing attacks can be run only in two ways.

In the first way, phisher is located in the middle of user and server, and introduces himself/herself as a user to server and vice versa and starts authentication with both sides *simultaneously* and *separately*. As in traditional phishing, due to unawareness of password, attacker cannot generate a suitable session key. Therefore, user and server will detect the existence of attacker in the middle of communication and can stop the authentication.

In the second scenario, phisher is located in the middle of user and server and replays the messages between user and server without any modification. At the end of the first phase of APA authentication process, user and server generate a session key (k) without being aware of phisher's existence in the middle of their communication.

In this scenario, phisher just replays packets between user and server without modification and as a result he/she would be unaware of password. It is impossible for attacker to generate a session key without information about password. As in the previous scenario, this is equal to finding a session key during the first phase of SPEKE without awareness of password. We know that session key generation in a limited period of session key validation is impossible. Although at the end of the first

Table 3. Prevention of real-time phishing in the second phase by APA

	Action	Description
1	$U \Rightarrow PH: E_K(C_U, PH_{IP})$	User generates the random number C_U, encrypts C_U and IP of the opposite side. User encrypts message m using key k and sends it to the opposite side.
2	$PH \Rightarrow AS: E_K(C_U, PH_{IP})$	Phisher does not know the key session so he cannot manipulate message. Phisher can only replay message to server.
3	$AS: D_K(E_K(C_U, PH_{IP}))$	Server decrypts user's message. The IP inside the message (PH_{IP}) does not match with servers IP (AS_{IP}). From server point of view authentication fails.
4	wait	User does not receive any message so after a while, "Connection Time Out" occurs and from user point of view authentication fails.

phase, the attacker is hidden from user and server, but because of unawareness of session key, attacker cannot read the messages of the second phase or modify them.

Table 3 shows the steps that lead to detection of the second real-time phishing scenario by APA.

3 APA Implementation

APA toolbar implementation has two components: one to be located in server to do authentication, and one to be installed on user's web browser for authentication.

Users should enter the user name and password in the APA toolbar. To prevent forging the toolbar by attackers, a personalization facility is added to the toolbar in which user can put an image to make it harder to forge the toolbar. Authentication in server side is implemented as library functions. Programmer needs only to call the functions in the login page. So, APA can be employed in all current web based applications; by only changing the login form of web applications, one can use APA.

4 Evaluation

Since APA is based on password, it is required that a shared password exists between server and user. Furthermore, APA cannot defend against malware. But if phishers want to masquerade themselves as real servers to users, they have to overcome APA authentication mechanism that is equivalent to attacking SPEKE. Since no serious flaws have been reported against SPEKE yet [8], APA is secure too.

There exists a method [5] against real-time phishing attacks, which needs costly hardware token. APA implementation does not require any hardware. Despite proposed methods in [6, 7], APA does not need initial setting for each site. In addition, users are not required to specify their sensitive information initially such as in [4]. Despite location based approaches [4, 6, 7], users may employ any computer without limitation. APA does not require Certificate Authority or authentication centers. Since there is no need to send password, APA is also immune against eavesdropping. Attacker may not get password by sniffing network. APA also resists against DNS poisoning attacks known as Pharming. In this type of attack, user trusted internet address is redirected to phisher computer. Without dependency on SSL or Certificate Authority, APA can prevent from such attacks.

5 Conclusion

The increased number of phishing attacks and identity theft has increased demands for effective mechanisms to fight against them. Although various approaches have been introduced to counter phishing, most of them are not immune against real-time phishing or are expensive to use. In this paper, a method called APA was proposed. In addition to real-time and traditional phishing prevention, APA has simple implementation. It is possible to employ APA in all current sites and is inexpensive.

References

1. Chou, N., Ledesma, R., Teraguchi, Y., Mitchell, J.C.: Client-Side Defense against Web-Based Identity Theft. In: 11th Annual Network and Distributed System Security Symposium, San Diego, USA (February 2004)
2. Dhamija, R., Tygar, J.D., Hearst, M.: Why Phishing Works. In: CHI Conference on Human Factors in Computing Systems, Montreal, Canada (2006)
3. Kirda, E., Kruegel, C.: Protecting Users against Phishing Attacks with AntiPhish. In: 29th IEEE Annual International Computer Software and Applications Conference, UK (2005)
4. Anti-Phishing Working Group: Phishing Activity Trends Report (2005),
   http://antiphishing.org/reports/APWG_Phishing_Activity_Report_May_2005.pdf
5. Anti-Phishing Working Group: Phishing Activity Trends Report (2006),
   http://antiphishing.org/reports/apwg_report_May2006.pdf
6. Herzberg, A., Gbara, A.: TrustBar: Protecting Web Users from Spoofing and Phishing Attacks. Cryptology ePrint Archive, Report 2004/155 (2004),
   http://www.cs.biu.ac.il/ herzbea/TrustBar/
7. Yee, K., Sitaker, K.: Passpet: Convenient Password Management and Phishing Protection. In: Second symposium on Usable privacy and security, Pittsburgh, Pennsylvania, USA (2006)
8. Jablon, D.: Strong Password-Only Authenticated Key Exchange Computer Communication Rev. ACM SIGCOMM 26, 5–26 (1996)
9. Zhang, M.: Analysis of the SPEKE Password-Authenticated Key Exchange Protocol. Communications Letters 8(1), 63–65 (2004)

Simulation of Dynamic Honeypot Based Redirection to Counter Service Level DDoS Attacks

Anjali Sardana and Ramesh Chandra Joshi

Department of Electronics and Computer Engineering,
Indian Institute of Technology, Roorkee
Roorkee-247 667, Uttarakhand, India
anjlsdec@iitr.ernet.in, rcjosfec@iitr.ernet.in

Abstract. DDOS attacks generate flooding traffic from multiple sources towards selected nodes which may be targets of opportunity or targets of choice. The latter reflects service level attacks aimed to disrupt services. Array of schemes have been proposed for defense against DDOS attacks in real time. Low rate DDOS attacks lead to graceful degradation while high rate attacks leave network functionally unstable. Our scheme uses three lines of defense. The first line of defense detects the presence of attacks. The second line of defense identifies and tags attack flows in real time. As the last line of defense, a model for dynamic honeypot routing and redirection has been proposed in response to identified attacks that triggers the automatic generation of adequate nodes to service client requests and required number of honeypots that interact with attackers in contained manner. The judicious mixture of servers and honeypots at different time intervals provide stable network functionality at ISP level. We validate the effectiveness of the approach with analytical modeling on Internet type topology and simulation in ns-2 on a Linux platform.

1 Introduction

Denial-of-Service (DoS) is an intentional attempt by attacker to compromise availability of a service to legitimate users [1]. Distributed Denial-of-Service attacks (DDoS) degrade or completely disrupt services to legitimate users by eating up communication, computational, and or memory resources of the target through sheer volume of packets. DDoS attacks are amplified form of DOS attacks where attackers direct hundreds or even thousands of compromised "zombie" hosts against a single target [2].

Our scheme works at ISP level and serves on three lines of defense to protect a public domain server. Firstly, entropy variations at a POP identify the presence of attack [3]. Secondly the flows are tagged as attacks in subsequent time windows [3]. As the last line of defense, we propose dynamic honeypot [4] based routing and redirection where honeypot changes in number in accordance with network load providing deterrence from public domain server. It ensures

P. McDaniel and S.K. Gupta (Eds.): ICISS 2007, LNCS 4812, pp. 259–262, 2007.

reasonable performance for network under attack. Connection retention with attack flow is to obtain information about the attackers by logging their actions. Hence, the model adopts a proactive behavior to circumvent any anticipated attacks.

The remainder of this paper is organized as follows. Section 2 discusses related work. Section 3 describes the environment used as testbed. Section 4 explains the methodology. Section 5 discusses the results. Finally section 6 concludes the paper.

2   Related Work

A commonly used detection approach is either signature-based or anomaly-based. Signature-based approach inspects the passing traffic and searches for matches against already-known malicious patterns. In practice, several signature-based detection systems [5] have been developed and deployed at firewalls or proxy servers. By contrast, an anomaly based detection system observes the normal network behavior and watches for any divergence from the normal profile. Most of DoS detection systems are anomaly based [6]. However, their normal traffic models are mainly based on flow rates.

Static honeypots [7] [8] have been used to defend against a variety of attacks. However because of their deployment at fixed and detectable locations, they may be compromised by sophisticated attacks. Khattab et. al. [9], proposed the proactive server roaming mechanism. In [10], hybrid architecture has been suggested for defense against DoS attacks, where a passive honeypot has been used for protection against relatively static attacks.

The work presents a comprehensive solution to prevent, detect and react to DDoS attacks ensuring reasonable performance in an ISP domain.

3   The Environment: ISP Network

For simulation purpose, we have simplified ISP level network with four cooperative ISP domains (1, 2, 3, and 4) where each domain has 10 POPs as shown in Fig 1. We assume a pool of N homogenous, geographically dispersed servers.

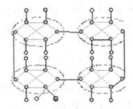

Fig. 1. ISP Network Topology

4 Autonomic Dynamic Honeypot Based Redirection

After detection and characterization [3] we propose dynamic honeypot generation in response to flows identified as attacks in FL (Flow List). Table 1 is used
for mapping CL (Client Load) and AL (Attack Load) to right combination of
servers and honeypots, NS and NH respectively.

Table 1. Mapping load to honeypots and servers

AL	CL	Honeypots	Servers
Low	Low	Low	2 moderate - low
Low	Moderate	Low	2 moderate - low
Low	High	Low	2 moderate - low
Moderate	Low	Moderate	Moderate - low
Moderate	Moderate	Moderate	Moderate
Moderate	High	(Moderate - low;Moderate)	(Mod; Moderate + low)
High	low	2 moderate - low	Low
High	Moderate	(moderate;mod + low)	(moderate - low; Mod)
High	High	Moderate	Moderate

5 Results and Discussion

Figure 2 shows results for variation in goodput with client and attack load. Six
cases have been simulated. (a) Ideal goodput values, (b) No distributed denial of
service attacks, (c) Best defense, which categorizes traffic with entropies between
8.40 to 8.41 as normal i.e. f = .2, (d) Normal defense, which categorizes traffic
with entropies between 8.39 to 8.42 as normal i.e. f = 1.5, (e) Nave defense which
categorizes traffic with entropies between 8.37 to 8.44 as normal i.e. f = .1 (f)
No Defense.

In case of low client load, best, normal and nave defense schemes give maximum goodput which is equal to ideal goodput and goodput with no DDoS.

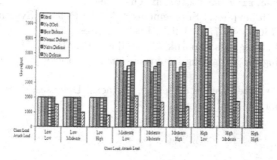

Fig. 2. Variation of goodput with varying client load and attack load

In case of moderate client load, goodput of node for network under no DDoS is equal to ideal goodput. For moderate client and particular value of attack, best defense gives lower goodput than nave defense. In case of high client load, goodput in absence of attack is slightly lesser than ideal goodput. For high client load and a particular value of attack load, best defense gives higher goodput than nave defense. We note that average response time and goodput are independent of attack load.

6   Conclusions

Our scheme gives stable network functionality in case of a smooth change in client load. In case of abrupt changes, it has a tendency to adapt itself according to network. High client load produces a tradeoff between response time and goodput.

References

1. CERT Coordination Center. Denial of Service Attacks,
   http://www.cert.org/techtips/denialofservice.html
2. Mirkovic, J., Reiher, P.: A Taxonomy of DDoS Attack and DDoS defense Mechanisms. ACM SIGCOMM Computer Communications Review 34 (April 2004)
3. Sardana, A., Joshi, R.C., Kumar, K.: Detection and Honeypot Based Redirection to Counter DDoS Attacks in ISP Domain. In: IAS 2007. International Symposium on Information Assurance and Security, IEEE CSI Press, Los Alamitos (to appear, 2007)
4. Kuwatly, I., Sraj, M., Masri, Z.A., Artail, H.: A Dynamic Honeypot Design for Intrusion Detection. In: ICDCS 2004. Proceedings 24th International Conference on Distributed Computing Systems (2004)
5. Paxson, V.: Bro: A System for Detecting Network Intruders in Real-Time. Computer Networks 31(23-24), 23–24 (1999)
6. Gil, T.M., Poletto, M.: Multops: a data-structure for bandwidth attack detection. In: Proceedings of 10th USENIX Security Symposium (2001)
7. Spitzner, L.: Honeypots: Simple, Cost-Effective Detection,
   http://www.securityfocus.com/infocus/1690
8. Zhiguang, L.: Honeypot: A Supplemented Active Defense System for network Security, vol. 0-7803-7840-7/03. IEEE, Los Alamitos (2003)
9. Khattab, S.M., Sangpachatanaruk, C., Melhem, R., Mosse', D., Znati, T.: Proactive Server Roaming for Mitigating Denial-of-Service Attacks. In: Proceedings of ITRE 2003 (2003)
10. Jones, J.: Distributed Denial of Service Attacks: Defenses, A Special Publication. Technical report, Global Integrity (2000)

A New Concept of Key Agreement Using Chaos-Synchronization Based Parameter Estimation

G.K. Patra, V. Anil Kumar, and R.P. Thangavelu

CSIR Centre for Mathematical Modelling and Computer Simulation,
Bangalore, India
{gkpatra,anil,thangam}@cmmacs.ernet.in
http://www.cmmacs.ernet.in

Abstract. Search for a key agreement algorithm not based on traditional number theoretic problem is a challenging area of research in information security. In this paper we present a new concept of key agreement, using synchronization based parameter estimation of two chaotic systems. In this short paper, we only introduce the concept, which shows promise of a new mechanism.

Keywords: Key Agreement Algorithms, Chaotic Synchronization, Parameter Estimation.

1 Introduction

Designing a secure key exchange mechanism is an important and challenging research problem in information security. The security of almost all currently used methods are based on the computationally unbreakable mathematical functions of number theory. Recently proposals like Neural Cryptography [1] have introduced new concept of key exchange, the security of which does not depend on number theory. In this paper, we propose another such mechanism of non-number theoretic key exchange by public discussion.

2 Chaotic Synchronization and Key Agreement

Synchronization of two identical chaotic systems by exchanging only a subset of time dependent information is not new [2]. This can be explained by using a three parameter Lorenz attractor[3] at the transmitter (x) and the receiver (y).

$$\dot{x}_1 = \sigma_t(x_2 - x_1) \quad \dot{y}_1 = \sigma_r(y_2 - y_1) - k(y_1 - x_1) \,.$$
$$\dot{x}_2 = \rho_t x_1 - x_2 - x_1 x_3 \quad \dot{y}_2 = \rho_r y_1 - y_2 - y_1 y_3 \,. \tag{1}$$
$$\dot{x}_3 = x_1 x_2 - \beta_t x_3 \quad \dot{y}_3 = y_1 y_2 - \beta_r y_3 \,.$$

This system behaves chaotically, for some values of σ, ρ and β. Two identical chaotic systems ($\sigma_t = \sigma_r$, $\rho_t = \rho_r$ and $\beta_t = \beta_r$) starting from two different initial conditions can be synchronized by transmission of one of the time

P. McDaniel and S.K. Gupta (Eds.): ICISS 2007, LNCS 4812, pp. 263–266, 2007.

dependent variable (like x_1) from the transmitter to the receiver in a master-slave mode. Recently new mechanisms like mutual interaction and alternately switched bi-directional coupling [4,5] has been proposed to achieve better security in applications like secure communications. Parameter estimation methods, which can estimate all the parameters of a chaotic system are potential threats to these communication systems based on chaotic synchronization. In contradiction we will uses these parameter estimation methods as a new mechanism for key exchange.

In a typical synchronization scenario identical systems are ensured by exchanging σ, ρ and β (the keys) values using some alternate method of key exchange. Here, we will consider two chaotic systems, which have the same functional structure, possessing different parameter values. We will define a mechanism by which the two chaotic systems in addition to synchronizing their time dependent values will also converge in their parameter values. Let us consider the system $\dot{x} = f(x, p)$ at the transmitter and $\dot{y} = f(y, q)$ at the receiver end. Here x and y are the time dependent variables, while p and q are the private parameters of the transmitter and receiver respectively. We have to achieve $(x - y) \to 0$ and $(p - q) \to 0$ as $t \to \infty$. For achieving this we have used the synchronization based parameter estimation [6,7] combined with the concept of alternately switched bi-directional coupling[4,5] to the three variable Lorenz systems given in Eq. 1. To simplify our explanation we consider a feedback synchronization scheme, and assumed that only one of the parameter is unknown ($\sigma_t \neq \sigma_r$, $\rho_t = \rho_r$ and $\beta_t = \beta_r$). We have then extended it to multiple parameter estimation. To achieve synchronization we need to minimize the synchronization error [7], $e(\sigma, n) = (y_1 - x_1)^2$ considering feedback in x_1/y_1 equations alternately. The modified x_1 and y_1 equation is as follows

$$\dot{x}_1 = \sigma_t(x_2 - x_1) - 0.5N_1\alpha(x_1 - y_1) \text{ and } \dot{y}_1 = \sigma_r(y_2 - y_1) - 0.5N_2\alpha(y_1 - x_1). \quad (2)$$

Where $N_1 = (-1)^n + 1$ and $N_2 = (-1)^{n+1} + 1$. Here, α is the feedback constant and n is the iteration number used to account for the alternately switched bi-directional coupling [4]. Now by minimizing the synchronization error, we get the following evolution equation for σ_t and σ_r.

$$\dot{\sigma}_t = 0.5N_1\delta(x_1 - y_1) \text{ and } \dot{\sigma}_r = 0.5N_2\delta(y_1 - x_1). \quad (3)$$

Here, δ is the stiffness constant used for stability in the updation process. We implemented these equations along with the Lorenz feedback system, with parameter values $\rho = 60$ and $\beta = 8/3$. The private values of σ_t and σ_r are 19.142 and 10.142 respectively. The transmitter and receiver are selected to start their evolution process from random initial conditions (9.874, 2.056, 29.142) and (2.874, 1.056, 12.142). The feedback constant considered is 20 and the stiffness constant considered is 0.5. The 4th Order Runge-Kutta procedure was used to solve the system of differential equations. Fig. 1 shows the synchronization of all the three variables along with the convergence of the unequal parameter σ, and hence key agreement. Mathematically we can derive the condition for key-exchange by considering the Conditional Lyapunov Exponents (CLE) for

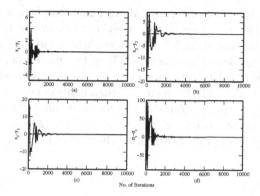

Fig. 1. The synchronization of the three variables and convergence of the unequal parameter

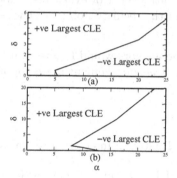

Fig. 2. Conditional Lyapunov Exponent (CLE) in (α, δ) plane for (a)x_1/y_1 (b)x_2/y_2 driving

the error system, which have to be negative for assured synchronization. The Jacobean matrix J for the error system $(x_1 - y_1, x_2 - y_2, x_3 - y_3, \sigma_t - \sigma_r)$ is given by [7].

$$
\begin{pmatrix}
-\sigma - \alpha & \sigma & 0 & < x_1 - y_1 > \\
\rho - < x_3 > & -1 & - < x_1 > & 0 \\
< x_2 > & < x_1 > & -\beta & 0 \\
-\delta < x_1 - y_1 > & 0 & 0 & 0
\end{pmatrix}
$$

The values $< x >$ are the time average on the invariant measure along the driving trajectory, which needs to be numerically estimated for a sufficiently long period. A similar key exchange can be achieved by synchronizing two chaotic system with only ρ unknown by using the following updation formula.

$$\dot{\rho}_t = 0.5 N_1 \delta \sigma x_1 \text{ and } \dot{\rho}_r = 0.5 N_2 \delta \sigma y_1 . \tag{4}$$

Fig. 2 (a) and (b) shows the curve along which the largest conditional Lyapunov exponents become 0 for σ and ρ estimation, in the (α, δ) plane [7]. So by suitably selecting the α and δ from the right hand side of the graph one can agree on common secret parameters. These two parameter estimation mechanisms can be combined to estimate both σ and ρ by choosing proper values of α and δ, which will satisfy both the synchronization criteria. However, it has been observed that all three parameter cannot be estimated using x_1/y_1 driving, while using x_2/y_2 driving it can be achieved after a long time. Further, it is also observed that synchronization cannot be achieved using x_3/y_3 driving.

3 Conclusions

We proposed a new concept of key agreement algorithm using parameter estimation by chaotic synchronization, of which the security does not depend on any assumption about the attacker. However, this proposal is still a concept and needs to be analyzed from the security point of view.

Acknowledgments. The authors would like to thank the Scientist-in-Charge, C-MMACS for his constant encouragement and support.

References

1. Metzler, R., Kinzel, W., Kanter, I.: Interacting Neural Networks. Phys. Rev. E. 62, 2555 (2000)
2. Pecora, L.M., Carroll, T.L.: Driving systems with chaotic signals. Phys. Rev. A 44(4), 2374–2383 (1991)
3. Cuomo, K.M., Oppenheim, A.V., Strogatz, S.H.: Synchronization of Lorenz-based chaotic circuits with applications to communications. IEEE Trans. On Circuits Systems 40, 626–633 (1993)
4. Patra, G.K., Ramamohan, T.R., Anil Kumar, V., Thangavelu, R.P.: Improvement in Security Level of First Generation Chaotic Communication System by Mutual Synchronization. In: Proceedings ADCOM 2006, pp. 195–198. IEEE Press, Los Alamitos (2006)
5. Patra, G.K., Anil Kumar, V., Thangavelu, R.P.: Analysis of Synchronization-based Parameter Estimation Attack on Switched Bidirectional Chaotic Key Stream Generator. In: Proc. of ICIP-2007, pp. 298–307. I. K. International Publisher (2007)
6. Konnur, R.: Estimation of all parameters of model from discrete scalar time series measurement. Physics Letters A 346, 275–280 (2005)
7. Maybhate, A., Amritkar, R.E.: Use of synchronization and adaptive control in parameter estimation from a time series. Phys. Rev. E 59, 284 (1999)

On Knowledge-Based Classification of Abnormal BGP Events

Jun Li, Dejing Dou, Shiwoong Kim, Han Qin, and Yibo Wang*

University of Oregon
{lijun, dou, shkim, qinhan, wangyibo}@cs.uoregon.edu

1 Introduction

One key factor that ensures smooth data delivery over the Internet and keeps the Internet healthy is the well-being of the Internet's inter-domain routing. In today's Internet, the *de facto* standard inter-domain routing protocol is the Border Gateway Protocol, or BGP, that keeps every BGP router updated about which BGP router is the next hop in reaching a particular network and which autonomous systems (AS), in order, it has to cross. Unfortunately, various abnormal events—such as fast-spreading worms or large-scale power outages—can affect the normal operation of BGP. Not only can these events cause routers or BGP sessions between routers to go down—a denial-of-service attack, but they can also create havoc as the scale of damage rises.

It is therefore critical to investigate how such events may impact BGP and whether or not different events can be classified into different types so that proper actions can be taken. Some may argue that the occurrence of such events is uncommon, and once they occur, people will easily know them anyway because of their large-scale damage. However, even if BGP anomalies may be uncommon today, they can have disastrous results once they occur tomorrow. It is also likely that the increased Internet complexity and the continuing challenges to make BGP secure and robust will cause future BGP anomalies both more common and more damaging.

We have designed an *Internet Routing Forensics* framework to provide a new, systematic approach to detecting the occurrence of abnormal events that impact BGP [1]. Basically, we are able to apply data mining techniques to BGP data corresponding to already-known abnormal events, discover rules about how BGP data may differ from the norm during those events, and then further use those rules to detect the occurrence of abnormal events from the past or in the future.

What remains unclear, then, is whether different abnormal events can be further differentiated from each other, and if so, how. In addition to obtaining rules to effectively capture the existence of anomalies in BGP data (BGP updates in particular), it is important to learn whether we can also obtain rules to indicate the disparity—as well as commonality—between, say, a large-scale power outage and a fast-spreading worm, or between different worms.

---

* This material is based upon work supported by the National Science Foundation under Grant No. 0520326.

P. McDaniel and S.K. Gupta (Eds.): ICISS 2007, LNCS 4812, pp. 267–271, 2007.
© Springer-Verlag Berlin Heidelberg 2007

2 Approach

In [2], we have studied a *data-driven* approach to identifying the specific type of an abnormal event without knowledge of BGP. In this paper, we devise an approach that relies on BGP knowledge to classify different abnormal events that impact BGP, i.e., a *knowledge-driven* approach. As events at the global level tend to affect the largest number of networks over the Internet, in this paper we focus on these events, and study how to develop accurate classification rules to describe each individual class of them. In order to support real-time applicability, our basis for classification is the observable impact on BGP from abnormal events that can be measured in real time.

Knowledge-based classification requires knowledge of abnormal BGP events before we try to obtain rules of different classes of these events. The knowledge can be simply the class name of a particular type of events. In this case, we can treat all classes of abnormal events at the same level and conduct i.e., **flat classification**. Or, our knowledge about abnormal BGP events can be enriched by knowing the hierarchical relationship of different classes of abnormal BGP events, allowing us to obtain and test rules for a hierarchy of abnormal event classes, i.e., **hierarchical classification**.

Our BGP data are BGP updates from the periods of the events as well as normal periods, archived by RouteViews [3] or RIPE [4]. We calculate the per-minute values of the most relevant attributes (selected through information gain measure) about these BGP updates, and arrange these values in a chronological sequence of 1-minute bins. If a 1-minute bin is known to correspond to a specific class of abnormal event, we label it with the name of that class.

We then conduct a training process to obtain rules for different classes of abnormal events, using the *C4.5* classification algorithm [5].

In applying these rules against testing bins from a certain event period, we use a probabilistic approach. As a rule is not typically 100% accurate, and a testing bin may match to more than one rule for different classes, or match no rule at all, we design an alert algorithm as follows: If more than Γ percentage of testing bins have a probability matching class C higher than ϵ, we raise an alert than an event of class C occurs. We use 40% for Γ and 0.5 for ϵ in this paper.

3 Case Studies

We conduct case studies on six abnormal events: Code Red worm, Nimda worm, Slammer worm, East Coast blackout, Florida blackout, and Katrina blackout.

With flat classification, we obtain rules for seven classes at the same level: CODERED, NIMDA, SLAMMER, EAST-COAST, FLORIDA, KATRINA, and NORMAL. Table 1 shows the percentage of "hits" in a test set for each of the seven classes, i.e., the γ values (Section 2). Here, the flat classification is effective in distinguishing the three worm-related classes—CODERED, NIMDA, SLAMMER—as well as the NORMAL class. However, it is not effective in telling the three blackout-related classes apart (we explain this toward the end of this section).

Table 1. γ values (percentages) for test sets in the case study using flat classification

Test set	CODERED	NIMDA	SLAMMER	EAST-COAST	FLORIDA	KATRINA	NORMAL
Code Red worm	**82.3**	5.4	0.0	0.8	0.0	0.8	13.1
Nimda worm	0.8	**84.6**	10.8	0.0	0.0	0.0	3.8
Slammer worm	0.0	13.8	**86.2**	0.8	0.0	0.8	0.8
East Coast blackout	0.0	0.0	0.0	**61.5**	0.0	47.7	34.6
Florida blackout	0.0	0.0	0.8	0.8	**36.9**	0.8	49.2
Katrina blackout	0.0	0.0	0.8	0.0	7.7	**0.0**	40.8
Normal	0.0	0.0	0.8	4.5	7.6	4.5	**51.5**
Alert Threshold $\Gamma = 25\%$							

Table 2. γ values (percentages) for test sets in the case study using hierarchical classification at a *high* level

Test set	WORM	BLACKOUT	NORMAL
Code Red worm	**85.4**	1.5	14.6
Nimda worm	**96.2**	0.8	4.6
Slammer worm	**99.2**	1.5	0.0
East Coast blackout	0	**75.4**	27.7
Florida blackout	0.77	**68.5**	25.4
Katrina blackout	2.31	**66.9**	26.9
Normal	0.0	22.0	**45.5**
Alert Threshold $\Gamma = 25\%$			

With hierarchical classification, we have two high-level classes—**WORM** and **BLACKOUT**, three sub-classes of the WORM class—**WORM.CODERED**, **WORM.NIMDA** and **WORM.SLAMMER**, and three sub-classes of the BLACKOUT class—**BLACKOUT.EAST-COAST**, **BLACKOUT.FLORIDA**, and **BLACKOUT.KATRINA**. Table 2 shows that the hierarchical classification case study can distinguish between WORM and BLACKOUT (and also as opposed to the NORMAL class). Moreover, the three WORM subclasses can be distinguished (Table 3), and so can the three BLACKOUT subclasses (Table 4).

As our results above show, the hierarchical classification is more accurate than the flat classification. It does not need to train many classes altogether, an advantage when the difference between different classes are small. In our case studies, as opposed to seven classes in flat classification, the hierarchical classification only needs to train two or three each time. The hierarchical structure of classes also helps incorporate a new class more efficiently: We only need to re-generate rules for classes at the level of the new class on a hierarchy, as opposed to all classes in the flat classification.

The hierarchical classification is also more efficient as it checks less number of classes. A simplified comparison is as follows: Assume that the cost of verifying rules associated with every class is the same. In hierarchical classification, every non-leaf class has m sub-classes, level i has m^i classes, and there are a total of

Table 3. γ values (percentages) for each test set in the case study using hierarchical classification at a *specialized* level for worm-related classes

Test set	WORM.CODERED	WORM.NIMDA	WORM.SLAMMER	NORMAL
Code Red worm	**66**	1.2	0.6	31.5
Nimda worm	0.6	**69.1**	14.2	6.8
Slammer worm	0	2.3	**95.4**	0.8
Normal	0	2.1	0	**95.1**
Alert Threshold $\Gamma = 25\%$				

Table 4. γ values (percentages) for each test set in the case study using hierarchical classification at a *specialized* level for blackout-related classes

Test set	BLACKOUT.EAST-COAST	BLACKOUT.FLORIDA	BLACKOUT.KATRINA	NORMAL
East Coast blackout	**54.6**	0.8	0.0	39.2
Florida blackout	0.0	**30.8**	0.0	58.5
Katrina blackout	0.0	4.6	**40.0**	52.3
Normal	13.1	4.6	6.2	**64.6**
Alert Threshold $\Gamma = 25\%$				

L levels. In flat classification, there are, in total, m^L classes (equivalent to the number of leaf classes in hierarchical classification). During hierarchical classification, we need to check rules of all m classes from level 1, find the matching class, check rules of all its m sub-classes, and repeat until we find out which leaf class matches the testing data. We thus need to check $m \times L$ classes. On the other hand, during flat classification, we need to check against the rules of all m^L classes. Clearly, in most cases, $m \times L \ll m^L$.

4 Summary

In this paper, we proposed a knowledge-based classification approach to distinguishing abnormal events that affect BGP. We demonstrated that we can obtain classification rules about every different abnormal event class, and use the rules to report the occurrence of an abnormal event of a certain class. Our approach further encompasses two classification methodologies: flat classification and hierarchical classification, and our case studies show that the hierarchical classification, in general, is more accurate, efficient, and scalable.

A direct implication of this work is the real-time application in detecting BGP anomalies caused by certain events, an important but missing component in today's Internet. In the future, we will investigate how our studies can complement other work on BGP anomalies and BGP dynamics root cause analysis, and further explore how to quantify the impact on BGP by abnormal events.

References

1. Li, J., Dou, D., Wu, Z., Kim, S., Agarwal, V.: An Internet routing forensics framework for discovering rules of abnormal BGP events. ACM SIGCOMM Computer Communication Review 35(5), 55–66 (2005)
2. Dou, D., Li, J., Qin, H., Kim, S., Zhong, S.: Understanding and utilizing the hierarchy of abnormal BGP events. In: SIAM International Conference on Data Mining, Minneapolis, Minnesota, pp. 457–462 (April 2007) (short paper)
3. University of Oregon Route Views Project,
   http://antc.uoregon.edu/route-views/
4. RIPE NCC, RIPE routing information service raw data,
   http://data.ris.ripe.net/
5. Quinlan, J.: C4.5: Programs for Machine Learning. Morgan Kaufmann Publishers, San Francisco (1993)

Towards Automated Privilege Separation

Dhananjay Bapat, Kevin Butler, and Patrick McDaniel

Department of Computer Science and Engineering
The Pennsylvania State University
University Park, PA 16802 USA
{dbapat,butler,mcdaniel}@cse.psu.edu

1 Introduction

Applications are subject to threat from a number of attack vectors, and limiting their attack surface is vital. By using privilege separation to constrain application access to protected resources, we can mitigate the threats against the application. Previous examinations of privilege separation either entailed significant manual effort or required access to the source code. We consider a method of performing privilege separation through black-box analysis. We consider similar applications to the target and infer *states* of execution, and determine unique *trigger* system calls that cause transitions. We use these for the basis of state-based policy enforcement by leveraging the *Systrace* policy enforcement mechanism. Our results show that we can infer state transitions with a high degree of accuracy, while our modifications to Systrace result in more granular protection by limiting system calls depending on the application's state. The modified Systrace increases the size of the Apache web server's policy file by less than 17.5%.

2 Related Work

Running an untrusted application on a machine opens it to data and system compromise. As a result, application confinement is an area of sustained research.

System calls are the only way for an application to get access to the privileged kernel operations, hence they are important in identifying malicious behavior. Forrest et al. [3] used system call monitoring to identify intrusion detection attempts in a system, creating a system call database of normal behavior and comparing the active system call trace to the database. Any deviation from the database indicated ongoing intrusion.

Privileged and daemon programs in UNIX are the source of most security flaws, and the large codebase of application programs makes it difficult to identify those flaws. Fink et al. [2] use specifications against which a program is *sliced* to significantly reduce the size of code that needs to be checked for flaws [2]. Similarly, privilege separation creates a smaller trust base that is more easily secured. Provos et al. [5] demonstrated that SSH could be privilege-separated through

P. McDaniel and S.K. Gupta (Eds.): ICISS 2007, LNCS 4812, pp. 272–276, 2007.

extensive manual techniques. Brumley et al. considered automated privilege separation [1] and developed a prototype, which works on annotated source code for an application and creates a master and a slave application. Their tool, *Privtrans*, performs inter-procedural static analysis and C-C translation to achieve the goal. A disadvantage of this approach is that the authors of the application must conform and identify higher privileged variables and code for the tool to work. All of the privilege separation mechanisms discussed require access to the program's source code. We have built a privilege separation tool that performs a black-box analysis on an application, with policy enforcement provided by *Systrace* [4].

3   Privilege State Identification and Analysis

3.1   Introduction

Traditionally, privileges within an application were identified as either root or non-root privileges. We extend this concept by considering the state of an application to be its privilege level, such that every application can be described in terms of its state machine. While privilege separation in previous approaches was achieved by physically separating parts of application, we can achieve similar results by identifying states in an application and by enforcing a specific application policy for each of the states.

States in an application can be identified by looking at the source code and by identifying major steps an application takes. However, we wanted our approach to be usable for legacy applications where source code may not be available, such that a black-box analysis would be necessary. Hence, to identify states in an application, we looked at the externally observable behavior of an application, i.e., system call traces.

3.2   Environment

To collect system call traces, we used a Linux machine running the Debian/GNU 2.4.27 distribution. System call traces were generated with the *strace* utility found in Linux.

We generated traces of server executions under a variety of configurations. We found that system call traces were largely independent of changes in server configuration by changing numerous variables such as timeout period, maximum number of child processes, listening port, and password-protecting some files. Our results showed that 93% of system calls remained the same for Apache Web server while 92% remained the same for the Caudium Web server. While system call traces will vary with the kind of workload[1] run on the Web server, our representative workloads capture all system calls made by the server.

---

[1] A web server's workload refers to factors such as the number of requests and amount of data served, and how frequently these requests occur.

Table 1. Web server: Number of unique system calls per state

Application	Start	Listen	Accept
Apache	64	11	12
Caudium	134	33	16
dhttpd	8	29	7
lighttpd	21	5	7
luahttpd	50	0	11
nullhttpd	16	4	16
thttpd	49	18	8
xshttpd	25	1	29

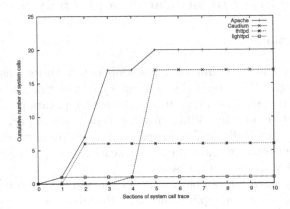

Fig. 1. Cumulative number of **bind** system calls for variety of Web servers

3.3   Observations

To identify states, we first looked to find system calls that can be used to indicate that state transitions have occurred; we term these system calls *triggers*. We attempted to find individual system calls rather than a sequence of system calls to act as trigger. We also do not consider arguments to the system call for simplicity. Certain system calls occur rarely during the Web server's execution. For example, in the Apache Web server, the `listen` system call occurs only once. Since it is a significant event and can be related to the operation of Web server, it can be considered a trigger. We identified system calls that were rarely called during application execution, and used this set of calls to form an initial set for determining triggers.

An important factor in determining whether a system call is a trigger is the point in the application's execution where the call occurs, and whether it repeats (i.e., the *locality* of the call relative to application execution). To further investigate this, we collected system call traces of multiple web servers given the workload of a single user browsing a variety of web pages. We divided the execution trace into ten equal stages to simplify discussion about where state

Table 2. Difference (in number of system calls) between our inferred state transition and where the transition actually occurs in code

Web server	tclhttpd	Abyss	Boa	Cherokee
Listen	0	4	0	11
Accept	24	0	21	126

transitions occur. Figure 1 shows when during execution the `bind` system call occurs. `Bind` system calls start early in the execution trace for most web servers.

3.4   State Analysis and Verification

States of an application should possess features that distinguish them from neighboring states. States may differ in ways that include the types of resources accessed, type of user interface presented, amount of resources accessed, amount of network activity, or the type and number of system calls called. These unique characteristics support the idea that each state in the application is a privilege level.

We identified three states for Web servers: `start`, `listen`, and `accept`. Table 1 shows number of unique system calls per state for the applications we tested. We consider a system call to be unique if using the *Systrace* utility, a new policy is created for the call in automatic policy generation mode.

We verified the inferred state engine on a different set of web servers, as shown in Table 2. The `listen` transition occurs when the application has loaded all of its libraries and is opening a socket to listen for incoming connections. An `accept` state transition coincides with the server entering an unbounded loop where it handles incoming HTTP requests. We inserted dummy system calls in the code for the two new web servers where server initialization is performed and where the server begins its loop of accepting connections, to determine how close our state identification came to the transition in the code itself. Table 2 describes the offset (in the number of system calls) between where we inferred a state identification and where the code transition occurred. The transition into the `listen` state is detected at the same time it occurs in code. Detection of the accept state is more variable, but the offset is still less than 0.5% of the total system calls observed in the trace. Thus, there is a high correlation between our inferred state transitions and their actual occurrence in code, making black-box analysis possible. In the next section, we use these state transitions to demonstrate how policy enforcement can be implemented.

4   Implementation

Having described how to identify states in an application, we are interested in using these as part of a policy enforcement infrastructure. We leverage the *Systrace* policy enforcement framework, which we use because of its clean policy semantics. Systrace policies describe the desired behavior of user applications on the system call level, which are enforced to prevent operations that are not explicitly permitted. Our prototype only modifies the policy semantics of Systrace while keeping the enforcement infrastructure intact.

To create privilege separation in an application, we use the states identified in a program's execution as the basis for different policy enforcement parameters, such that at different points through the execution, we can constrain access to resources. The goal of our implementation is to integrate Systrace with our privilege state engine to simplify privilege separation in the application. This entails modifying Systrace to understand the concept of states and vary enforcement mechanisms depending on the state of the application.

5   Evaluation

We created a prototype of the modified Systrace. In this section, we evaluate different characteristics of the modified Systrace. The number of policy statements is an important performance criterion, as the larger the policy file, the more time is required for the policy engine to search for a policy statement for a given system call. We created policies for couple of Web servers with our modified Systrace. Policies increase in size with the addition of privilege state to the system call policies, and increased by an average of 15 statements.

6   Conclusion

Securing applications is a two-step process involving creating an effective policy enforcement mechanism as well as creating good policies. We also simplified privilege separation processes through inferring state transitions with high accuracy, enabling black-box analysis of the application. In addition, we found that by modifying the Systrace utility, we could provide policy enforcement over the defined states with a less than 17% increase in the size of the Systrace policy file for the Apache web server.

References

1. Brumley, D., Song, D.: Privtrans: Automatically Partitioning Programs for Privilege Separation. In: Proceedings of the 13th USENIX Security Symposium, pp. 57–72 (2004)
2. Fink, G., Levitt, K.: Property Based Testing of Privileged Programs. In: Proceedings of the 10th Annual Computer Security Applications Conference, pp. 154–163 (1994)
3. Hofmeyr, S., Forrest, S., Somayaji, A.: Intrusion Detection using Sequences of System Calls. Journal of Computer Security 6, 151–180 (1998)
4. Provos, N.: Improving Host Security with System Call Policies. In: Proceedings of the 12th USENIX Security Symposium, pp. 257–272 (August 2003)
5. Provos, N., Friedl, M., Honeyman, P.: Preventing Privilege Escalation. In: Proceedings of the 12th USENIX Security Symposium, pp. 231–242 (August 2003)

Constructing a "Common Cross Site Scripting Vulnerabilities Enumeration (CXE)" Using CWE and CVE

K. Sivakumar and K. Garg

Dept. of Electronics & Computer Engg., Indian Institute of Technology, Roorkee
ksivadec@iitr.ernet.in, kgargfec@iitr.ernet.in

Abstract. It has been found that almost 70% of the recent attacks in Web Applications have been carried out even when the systems have been protected with well laid Firewalls and Intrusion Detection Systems. Advisories sites report that more than 20% of the attacks have originated from Cross Site Scripting (XSS) vulnerabilities. Our analysis has shown that more than 40% of the vulnerabilities that are confirmed in Common Vulnerability Exposures (CVE), were based on PHP Script in the year 2006. Out of these PHP based vulnerabilities, 45% are classified under XSS. By organizing these errors into a simple taxonomy and mapping CVE with the Common Weakness Enumeration (CWE) of Mitre Corp, we have constructed a Common XSS vulnerability Enumeration (CXE). With the help of CXE, security practitioners can recognize the common types of developer patterns leading to coding errors in PHP, that result in XSS vulnerability, while developers can identify and rectify existing errors as they build software.

Keywords: Web Security, Secure code, XSS, PHP Vulnerabilities, CVE, CWE.

1 Introduction

Building secure applications is very difficult [1]. The increasing complexity of secure software applications has given rise to potential security flaws within the source code. The necessity for software developers to consistently produce secure code continues to increase as software becomes progressively more immersed in every day public life. Vulnerability is defined as a weakness in some aspect or feature of a system that makes a threat possible. A vulnerability might exist at the network, host, or application levels. An introduction to Web Applications security and Cross site scripting follows next.

1.1 Web Applications Security and Vulnerabilities

Many applications, especially Web based ones, are prevalent with vulnerabilities ranging from Input validation [3] to insecure configuration management.

P. McDaniel and S.K. Gupta (Eds.): ICISS 2007, LNCS 4812, pp. 277–291, 2007.

Although Web applications help expedite business processes, they, at the same time, expose organizations to a considerable amount of security risk. In many cases, the organizations that automate business processes using Web Applications, do not establish the strong security controls and auditing functions needed to mitigate the risks, which can result in serious reputation and financial damage. From an application perspective [1,2], vulnerability identification is absolutely critical and often overlooked as a source of risk. Unverified parameters, broken access controls, buffer overflows and Cross Site Scripting, are few types of potential security vulnerabilities found in complex business applications developed internally. Unfortunately, commercially developed applications are often equally insecure, thereby requiring an in-depth knowledge of dangerous vulnerabilities and their management process. If software developers were warned of potential security vulnerabilities [1,2,3,6,?] and provided with the explanation based on a standard enumeration and taxonomy, we believe that even novice software developers could produce applications free from commonly exploited, known security vulnerabilities.

1.2   Cross Site Scripting (XSS) Vulnerability

A According to Klein [14], Cross Site Scripting, abbreviated as XSS, is one of the most common application level attacks that hackers use to sneak into web applications today. The attack can take place only at the victim's browser that is used to access the site. XSS vulnerabilities are caused by a failure in the web application to properly validate user input. Additionally, the most popular scheme for stealing an Internet user's cookies, involves exploiting Cross-Site Scripting vulnerabilities. Attackers often perform XSS exploitation by crafting malicious URLs and tricking users into clicking on them. These links cause client side scripting languages (VBScript, JavaScript, PHP script etc.) of the attacker's choice to execute on the victim's browser. There are numerous ways to inject PHP Script (any script) code into URLs, for the purpose of a XSS attack. By causing the user's browser to execute rogue script snippets under the same permissions of the web application domain, an attacker can bypass the traditional security restrictions. This can result not only in cookie theft but account hijacking, changing of web application account settings, spreading of a web mail worm, etc. [13,15,16]. The following are some examples of XSS attack from [18].

Example link in e-mail

```
<A HREF="http://../comment.cgi?par=<SCRIPT SRC='http://../badfile'>
</SCRIPT>">Click here</A>
```

Here the source of the malicious code is from another site, hence the name XSS.

XSS attacking cookies

```
setcookie("admin",$password);
```

Trusted website uses the cookie in a later session:

```
if (isset($_COOKIE["admin"]))
$password=$_COOKIE["admin"];
```

Attacker tries to steal the cookie, by having the victim click on the following link:

```
http://www.win.tue.nl/.../index.php?
 id=<script>document.location.replace
 ('http://.../log.php?c='%2Bdocument.cookie)
 </script>">DO THE BAD GUY</a>
```

The attacker script log.php writes the cookie to an attacker accessible:

```
<?php
    $ip = getenv("REMOTE_ADDR");...
    fwrite($f, "cookie:($_GET['c']} IP: $ip");
    ?>
```

By organizing these errors into a simple taxonomy and mapping CVE with CWE, we have constructed a Common XSS vulnerability Enumeration (CXE). With the help of CXE, security practitioners can recognize the common types of developer patterns leading to coding errors in PHP, that result in XSS vulnerability, while developers can identify existing errors as they build software.

The rest of this paper is structured as follows. Section 2 discusses the related work that helps in creating the CXE. Section 3 shows the process of constructing the CXE using CVE and CWE. It provides in detail, the analysis that we have carried out with XSS and other useful parameters. The performance evaluation of our approach is also described in this section. Section 4 compiles the limitations and future direction of our approach. A comprehensive conclusion is made in section 5.

2   Related Work

Organizations want assurance that the software products they acquire and develop are free of known types of security weaknesses [21]. High quality tools and services for finding security weaknesses in code are new. The question as to which tool/service is appropriate for a particular job is hard to answer, given the lack of structure and definition in the software product assessment industry. There are several ongoing efforts to begin to resolve some of these shortcomings, including the US Department of Homeland Security (DHS) [13], National Cyber Security Division (NCSD)-sponsored Software Assurance Metrics and Tool Evaluation (SAMATE) project [7] led by the National Institute of Standards and Technology (NIST). Past attempts at developing this kind of effort have been limited by a very narrow technical domain focus or have largely focused on high-level theories, taxonomies, or schemes that do not reach the level of detail or variety of security issues that are found in today's products. The following subsection discusses CVE and CWE that are major initiatives focused on improving the utility and effectiveness of code based security assessment technology.

2.1   Common Vulnerability Exposure (CVE)

As an alternate approach, under sponsorship of DHS NCSD, and as part of MITRE's [11] participation in the DHS-sponsored NIST SAMATE effort, MITRE investigated the possibility of leveraging the Common Vulnerabilities and Exposures (CVE) initiative's experience in analyzing more than 20,000 real-world vulnerabilities reported and discussed by industry and academia. As part of the creation of the CVE list [11], that is used as the source of vulnerabilities for the National Vulnerability Database [25], MITRE's CVE initiative, during the last six years, has developed a preliminary classification and categorization of vulnerabilities, attacks, faults, and other concepts that can be used to help define this arena. The preliminary classification and categorization work used in the development of CVE was revised to address the types of issues discussed in Preliminary List of Vulnerability Examples for Researchers (PLOVER) [10] PLOVER was a document that listed more than 1,500 diverse, real-world examples of vulnerabilities identified by their CVE name. The work from PLOVER also became the major source of content for Draft 1 of the CWE dictionary.

2.2   Common Weaknesses Enumeration (CWE)

As part of the DHS SwA [8] working groups and the NIST SAMATE project, MITRE fostered the creation of a community of partners from industry, academia and government, to develop, review, use, and support a common weaknesses dictionary that can be used by those looking for weaknesses in code, design, or architecture, as well as those teaching and training software developers about the code [4], design, or architecture weaknesses that they should avoid due to the security problems they can have on applications, systems and networks. This effort is called the Common Weakness Enumeration (CWE) initiative. All the publicly available source content is being hosted on the site for anyone to review or use for their own research and analysis. The vulnerabilities are organized within a detailed conceptual framework that enumerates individual types of weaknesses that cause the vulnerabilities. The weaknesses were simply grouped within the higher-level categories with a large number of real-world vulnerability examples for each type of weakness. Draft 6 of CWE is now available on the Internet [9]. The CWE list brought together as much public content as possible, using the three primary sources given below.

- The Preliminary List of Vulnerability Examples for Researchers (PLOVER) collection which identified over 300 weakness types created by determining the root issues behind 1,400 of the vulnerabilities in Common Vulnerabilities and Exposures (CVE) List [10].

- The Comprehensive, Lightweight Application Security Process (CLASP) from Secure Software, which yielded over 90 weakness concepts [16].
- The issues contained in "Fortify's Seven Pernicious Kingdoms" papers, which contributed over 110 weakness concepts [3].

3   Constructing a CXE Using CVE and CWE

It is true that software developers play a crucial role in building secure computer systems. Because roughly half of all security defects are introduced at the source code level [5], coding errors (bugs) are a critical problem in software security. In defining this taxonomy of coding errors, our primary goal is to organize sets of security rules that can be used to help software developers understand the kinds of errors that have an impact on security. By better understanding how systems fail, developers will better analyze the systems they create, more readily identify and address security problems when they see them, and generally avoid repeating the same mistakes in the future. Publication of such a taxonomy should provide tangible benefits to the software security community. Defining a better classification scheme can also lead to better tools: a better understanding of the problems will help researchers and practitioners create better methods for ferreting them out [3]. Our approach in constructing the Common Cross Site Scripting Vulnerability Enumeration (CXE) is briefly described below.

3.1   Our Approach

Our objective is to build a CXE for XSS vulnerabilities originated from PHP script codes, based on the developers' coding pattern. The method we have chosen is simple but sufficient to accommodate any language or script. The steps in our approach are:

1. Make an elaborate study on Vulnerabilities and their taxonomy (as much as possible).
2. Identify the sources to get hands-on updated information about vulnerabilities.
3. Choose a reliable and standard resource (open source with required information is preferred).
4. Download XML feeds from the resource (We chose NVD-CVE).
5. Use a parser (we have developed a parser in PHP) and parse each file.
6. Create a database with required fields (we used MySql for db).
7. Populate the database with data parsed from XML feeds through a Server (we have used Apache server to link PHP and MySql).
8. Analyze the records for the type of vulnerability to which CXE is to be created (we chose XSS vulnerability: analysis details in section 3.2).
9. Frame the constraints to filter the heavy dataset available to reduce it (for convenience, but sufficient to derive objective).
10. Analyze the vulnerability with respect to the various parameters (eg: PHP script).

11. Make a study of similar, existing enumerations from a reliable source (CWE in our case).
12. Make a mapping between the vulnerability database and the enumeration. (in our case it is CVE and CWE)
13. Compare and contrast, argue and analyze, explore and create/update a new enumeration (CXE in our case).
14. Analyze the new enumeration, extract the developers pattern for the language chosen (PHP in our case).
15. Allow findings to be sent for an experts' view and referral.
16. Use the feedback for future development and for fine tuning the model.

3.2   Analyzing XSS Vulnerabilities in CVE from a Different Angle

Approximately 20 service providers and organizations are effectively involved in producing alerts and advisories on vulnerabilities. We have chosen the CVE database available on site [11]. In the first instance, we want to satisfy ourselves that our choice to create a CXE for XSS vulnerabilities in PHP script is right.

MITRE Corporation, in its document, version 1, on Vulnerability type distributions in CVE [19], has analyzed different types of vulnerabilities. But in our analysis, the Common Vulnerability Scoring System (CVSS) score occupies a predominant place. The reason for giving importance to CVSS can be seen from the following paragraphs.

The National Vulnerability Database (NVD) supports the CVSS standard for all CVE vulnerabilities. NVD provides CVSS 'base scores' which represent the innate characteristics of each vulnerability. NVD provides a CVSS score calculator to allow adding temporal data and even to calculate environmental scores (scores customized to reflect the impact of the vulnerability on your organization). General information on CVSS is available in [26]. A description of CVSS impact vector is given below.

CVSS Base Vectors

CVSS vectors containing only base metrics take the following form:

(AV:[R,L]/AC:[H,L]/Au:[R,NR]/C:[N,P,C]/I:[N,P,C]/A:[N,P,C]/B:[N,C,I,A])

The letters within brackets represent possible values of a CVSS metric. Exactly one option must be chosen for each set of brackets. Letters not within brackets are mandatory and must be included in order to create a valid CVSS vector. Each letter or pair of letters is an abbreviation for a metric or metric value within CVSS. These abbreviations are defined below.

```
Example 1: (AV:L/AC:H/Au:NR/C:N/I:P/A:C/B:C)
Example 2: (AV:R/AC:L/Au:R/C:C/I:N/A:P/B:N)"

Metric: AV = AccessVector (Related exploit range)
Possible Values: R = Remote, L = Local
```

```
Metric: AC = AccessComplexity Required attack complexity)
Possible Values: H = High, L = Low
Metric: Au = Authentication (Level of authentication needed to
exploit)
Possible Values: R = Required, NR = Not Required
Metric: C= ConfImpact (Confidentiality impact)
Metric: I = IntegImpact (Integrity impact)
Metric: A = AvailImpact (Availability impact)
Possible Values: N = None, P = Partial, C = Complete
Metric: B =ImpactBias (Impact value weighting)
Possible Values:
N=Normal,C=Confidentiality,I=Integrity,A=Availability
```

NVD provides severity rankings of "Low", "Medium", and "High" in addition to the numeric CVSS scores, but these qualitative rankings are simply mapped from the numeric CVSS scores:

- "Low" severity if they have a CVSS base score of 0.0-3.9.
- "Medium" severity if they have a base CVSS score of 4.0-6.9.
- "High" severity if they have a CVSS base score of 7.0-10.0.

The files downloaded from [11] to carry out different analysis on XSS and PHP vulnerabilities are *nvdcve-2002.xml, nvdcve-2003.xml, nvdcve-2004.xml, nvdcve-2005.xml, nvdcve-2006.xml, nvdcve-2007.xml.*

In our approach, when steps 5 through 9 are completed, the required data for analysis is made available. Different analysis and tables used for this are discussed next.

Vulnerability types are given as the row heading in Table 1. Vulnerabilities with confirmed CVE number and CVSS score are alone considered for our analysis. The number of vulnerabilities for all CVSS scores and for CVSS scores ≥ 7 are given for the respective years in the column. It is evident from the Table 1 that XSS has made an entry from year 2000 and gathered momentum from 2002. It has made its presence felt strongly in year 2006 by occupying the first position in list of vulnerabilities (upholding ours choice of selecting XSS vulnerabilities).

Our analysis enters into the next phase as we compare the vulnerability counts among the existence of XSS in PHP, JavaScript and Ajax. (Though XSS in ASP is high, it is not within our scope). We have chosen to compare with JavaScript and Ajax because many current websites are dependent on JavaScript & PHP and futuristic Web 2.0 sites are expected to be developed using Ajax. Tables 2 and 3 are similar, except that the former gives the number of vulnerabilities counted for all values of CVSS score and the latter is only for CVSS values ≥ 7. Table 4 is the condensed form of Table 3 where vulnerabilities are given in percentages.

Figures 1 and 2 are the graphs drawn for the corresponding values from Tables 2 and 3 respectively. Figure 3 is the graph drawn for Table 4. The values in the Y-axis represent the percentage of vulnerabilities. It can be observed from

Table 1. Number of Vulnerabilities until year 2002 reported in NVD on May 12, 2007 (for all CVSS values and CVSS values ≥ 7)

YEAR	≤ 2000		2001		2002		≤ 2002	
VULN. TYP	All	≥7	All	≥7	All	≥7	All	≥7
PHP only	19	8	70	39	179	86	268	133
JavaScript only	12	2	24	13	46	20	82	35
Ajax only	0	0	0	0	0	0	0	0
XSS only	1	0	8	1	98	23	107	24
XSS and PHP	0	0	6	0	27	4	33	4
XSS and JS	0	0	1	1	14	1	15	2
XSS and Ajax	0	0	0	0	0	0	0	0
XSS & PHP & JS	0	0	0	0	5	0	5	0
Others	..	..	..	..	..	..	..	..
Overall	2801	1213	1531	729	2156	1013	6488	2955

Table 2. Number of Vulnerabilities in different years reported in NVD on May 12, 2007 (for all CVSS values from 0 to 10)

YEAR Languages	≤2002	2003	2004	2005	2006	2007
PHP only	268	94	391	1150	2811	927
XSS only	107	89	274	714	1274	259
XSS and PHP	33	25	117	291	689	127
JavaScript only	82	9	22	49	93	32
XSS AND JS	15	2	6	22	62	5
XSS & PHP & JS	5	0	0	2	24	1
Ajax only	0	0	0	3	8	7
XSS and Ajax	0	0	0	1	7	3
Others	..	..	..	..	..	..
Overall	6488	1219	2578	4631	6974	2399

these graphs that growth of XSS is phenomenal in 2006 and early 2007. More specifically, the growth of XSS in PHP script is remarkable.

3.3   XSS in CWE's Classification

Step 11 of our approach given in section 3.1 is about imbibing necessary knowledge about Common Weakness Enumeration. We insist on having a specific study about XSS in CWE. Given below is the short representation of XSS in draft 6 of CWE [8]. The numbers given within the brackets are the CWE ID given for each enumeration.

- Cross-site scripting (XSS) - (79)
- Basic XSS - (80)
- XSS in error pages - (81)

Table 3. Number of Vulnerabilities in different years reported in NVD on May 12, 2007 (for CVSS ≥7 only)

YEAR Languages	≤ 2002	2003	2004	2005	2006	2007
PHP only	133	54	170	565	1475	599
XSS only	23	43	60	52	302	88
XSS and PHP	4	12	22	21	175	49
JavaScript only	35	5	7	7	31	6
XSS AND JS	2	0	2	1	17	0
XSS & PHP & JS	0	0	0	0	7	0
Ajax only	0	0	0	0	6	5
XSS and Ajax	0	0	0	0	5	1
Others	..	..	..	..	..	..
Overall	2955	615	1059	1756	2908	1208

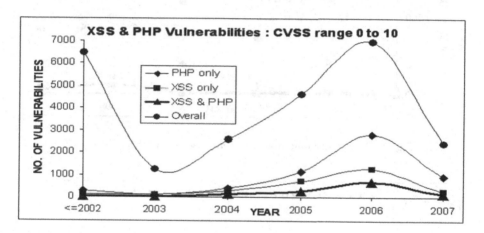

Fig. 1. Growth of vulnerabilities in year wise for all CVSS values

- Script in IMG tags - (82)
- XSS using Script in Attributes - (83)
- XSS using Script Via Encoded URI Schemes- (84)
- Doubled character XSS manipulations, e.g. 'ii script' - (85)
- Invalid Characters in Identifiers - (86)
- Alternate XSS syntax - (87)

3.4   Mapping CVE with CWE for XSS Vulnerabilities

The core part of our work is the mapping among CVE, CVE and XSS vulnerabilities in PHP script. The results of the steps 12 through 14 mentioned in our approach are given in Tables 5 & 6. Table 6 provides the CWE ID with respective number of vulnerabilities classified to it from the ones identified for XSS

Table 4. Percentage of Vulnerabilities in different years reported in NVD on May 12, 2007 (for CVSS values ≥7 only)

YEAR Languages	≤ 2002	2003	2004	2005	2006	2007
PHP only	4.5	8.8	16.1	32.2	50.7	49.6
XSS only	0.8	7.0	5.7	3.0	10.4	7.3
XSS and PHP	0.1	2.0	2.1	0.7	6.0	4.1

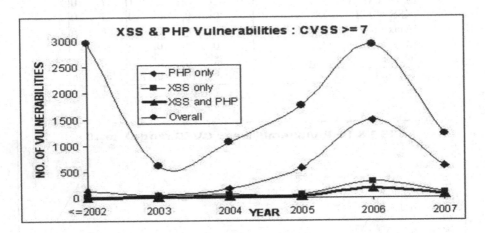

Fig. 2. Growth of vulnerabilities year wise (for CVSS values ≥ 7)

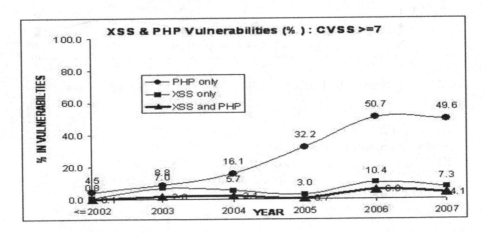

Fig. 3. Growth of vulnerabilities (in %) year wise (for CVSS values ≥7)

and PHP in Table 3 (i.e. adding values in 3rd row = 283 vulnerabilities for all the years). The description provided for the CWE ID is also given in Table 3.

Table 5. CVE-CWE mapping for the XSS Vulnerabilities (CVSS $\geq$7) listed in Table 3

CWE ID	VULN. COUNTS	CWE Dictionary Description
79	25	Cross-site scripting weakness occurs when dynamically generated web pages display input, such as login inform., that is not properly validated, allowing an attacker to embed malicious scripts into the generated page and then execute the script on the machine of any user that views the site. If successful, XSS vulnerabilities can be exploited to manipulate or steal cookies, create requests that can be mistaken for those of a valid user, compromise confidential inform., or execute malicious code on the end user systems for a variety of nefarious purposes. **CVE-2007-2431**
80	163	'Basic' XSS involves a complete lack of cleansing of any special characters, including the most fundamental XSS elements such as "<", ">", and "&".This is an explicit weakness resulting from behavior of the developer. **CVE-2007-2098**
81	7	This Weakness occurs when a web developer displays input on an error page (e.g. a customized 403 Forbidden page). If an attacker can influence a victim to view/request a web page that causes an error, then the attack may be successful. **CVE-2007-0364**
82	3	A Web application that trusts input in the form of HTML IMG tags is potentially vulnerable to XSS attacks. Attackers can embed XSS exploits into the values for IMG attributes (e.g. SRC) that is streamed and then executed in a victim's browser. Note that when the page is loaded into a user's browsers, the exploit will automatically execute. **CVE-2006-3767**
83	59	The software does not filter "javascript:" or other URI's from dangerous attributes within tags, such as onmouseover, onload, on error, or style. **CVE-2007-1305**
84	9	The web application fails to filter input for executable script disguised with URI encodings **CVE-2007-0483**
85	1	The web appln. fails to filter i/p for executable script disguised using doubling of the involved characters. **CVE-2007-2206**
86	13	The software does not strip out invalid characters in the middle of tag names, schemes, and other identifiers, which are still rendered by some web browsers that ignore the characters **CVE-2007-2265**
87	3	The software fails to filter alternate script syntax provided by the attacker. **CVE-2005-4748**
Total	283	

It can be observed from Table 5 that the number of vulnerabilities that are mapped to CWE ID 80 is 163. An example is provided for each ID with CVE reference. From the description provided in CWE dictionary, ID 80 is allotted for the basic XSS type. It is primarily concerned with unsanitized input given through the basic elements, such as parameters and attribute values. We have made an elaborate analysis and found that some common pattern exists in the

Table 6. Developer's coding pattern in assigning Parameter names identified in the XSS vulnerabilities (CVSS≥7) listed in Table 5

PARAMETER NAMES	VULN.COUNTS	CVE EXAMPLE
Admin	12	CVE-2007-0567
Calendar	4	CVE-2007-1234
File	5	CVE-2007-2600
Guest	3	CVE-2007-0542
Id	18	CVE-2007-2102
Image	6	CVE-2006-5532
Index	38	CVE-2007-2562
Input	1	CVE-2007-2245
Log	3	CVE-2007-0186
Module	6	CVE-2006-6734
Msg	3	CVE-2006-6520
Name	4	CVE-2006-6348
News	4	CVE-2006-2721
Page	5	CVE-2007-2099
Search	16	CVE-2007-1240
String	2	CVE-2007-0331
Title	6	CVE-2007-0807
General	27	CVE-2007-2098
Total	163	

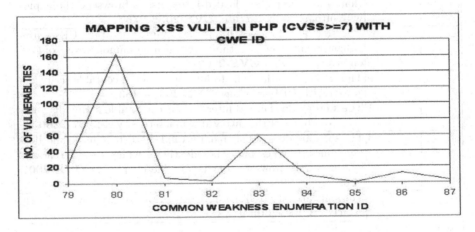

Fig. 4. Mapping XSS vulnerabilities in PHP (CVSS ≥7) with CWE IDs. For XSS.

way developers assign their parameter names and attribute values. Our findings are tabulated in Table 6. It can be seen from Table 6 that most of the vulnerability is reported from the "Index", "Id", "Search", "Admin" parameters. Thus, the CXE for XSS vulnerabilities originated from PHP scripts are created by

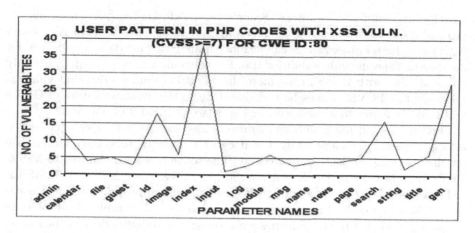

Fig. 5. Developers code pattern in assigning parameter names in PHP scripts leading to XSS vulnerabilities. (for CVSS ≥7 and CWE ID: 80)

appending these new parameter patterns within the CWE for ID 80. The graphical representations of Tables 5 & 6 are given in Figures 4 & 5.

3.5   Performance Evaluation

We have tested our approach with two different applications written by two PHP programmers. It can be noticed from the Table 7, that the number of XSS vulnerabilities found while scanning those application is reduced to almost 50% when the programmers are educated with our findings and are asked to alter their programs accordingly. The performance of our approach would be increased further when we include vulnerabilities with all CVSS values in our analysis given at section 3.3.

Table 7. Number of vulnerabilities found before and after implementing our findings

PHP Programmers	No. of Vuln. before the awareness	No. of Vulnerabilities after correcting their programs using our findings
A	16	9
B	11	6
Total	27	15

4   Limitations and Future Direction

Our approach is limited in that, at present, we have populated the database through the xml feeds available freely from only NVD. More precise findings can be made if the database is populated from other sources like Secunia [22],

CERTs [24] of different countries, Securityfocus [23], OVDB [27], and some additional resources from closed vendors and paid service providers of Alerts and Advisories. Better observations can be made if analysis were done for OS, Vendor and product specific vulnerabilities also. For convenience, we have analyzed only vulnerabilities with CVSS rating more than 7. It is recommended that vulnerabilities with all CVSS values be included. Due to the dynamic nature of CVE's xml feed, we admit to a variance ranging between 1 and 2 in our counts.

Further, we had made our enumeration based on the developer's pattern in assigning parameter names only, but it can be extended to various factors like naming methods, Object parameters etc. The scope is not only limited to XSS & PHP, it can be extended to XSS & JavaScript, XSS & Ajax, XSS & ASP, XSS & JSP and, etc. Further, by working with industry, an appropriate method could be developed for collecting, abstracting and sharing code samples from the code of the products that the CVE names are assigned to, so that they could be shared as part of the reference dataset and aligned with the vulnerability taxonomy [3]. These samples would then be available as tailoring and enhancement aides to the developers of software assessment security tools.

5   Conclusion

By using CVE-CWE-CXE-based relationships, a high quality collection of sample vulnerabilities dataset can be created. We have devised a mechanism that is used to exploit the various CWEs of Cross Site Scripting Vulnerabilities, for the purpose of helping to clarify the CWE groupings specifically for PHP script codes. This work should able to help, shape and mature the code security assessment industry. These domains and profiles could provide a valuable tool to security testing strategy and for improving the accuracy of the software product security assessment tools in testing their own product's code by the developer's community.

References

1. Lucca, G.A., Fasolino, A.R., et al.: Identifying Cross Site Scripting Vulnerabilities in Web Applications. In: Proceedings of the Sixth IEEE International Workshop on Web Site Evolution, pp. 71–80
2. Huang, Y., Tsai, C., Lin, T., Huang, S., Kuo', D.T.: A testing framework for Web application, security assessment. Computer Networks 48, 739–761 (2005)
3. McGraw, G., Chess, B., Tsipenyuk, K.: Seven Pernicious Kingdoms: A Taxonomy of Software Security Errors. In: NIST Workshop on Software Security Assurance Tools, Techniques and Metrics, Long Beach, CA, (November 2005)
4. Martin, R.A., Christey, S., Jarzombek, J.: The Case for Common Flaw Enumeration. In: NIST Workshop on Software Security Assurance Tools, Techniques, and Metrics, Long Beach, CA (November 2005)
5. Weber, S., Karger, P.A., Paradkar, A.: A Software Flaw Taxonomy: Aiming Tools at Security. In: SESS 2005. ACM Software Engineering for Secure Systems - Building Trustworthy Applications, St. Louis, Missouri, USA (June 2004)

6. Dehlinger, J., Feng, Q., Hu, L.: SSVChecker: Unifying Static Security Vulnerability Detection Tools in an Eclipse Plug-In. In: ETX 2006. Eclipse Technology Exchange Workshop at OOPSLA 2006, Portland (October 22-23, 2006)
7. The Software Assurance Metrics and Tool Evaluation (SAMATE) project, National Institute of Science and Technology (NIST), http://samate.nist.gov
8. The OMG Software Assurance (SwA) Special Interest Group, http://swa.omg.org
9. The Common Weaknesses Enumeration (CWE) Initiative, MITRE Corporation, http://cve.mitre.org/cwe
10. The Preliminary List Of Vulnerability Examples for Researchers (PLOVER), MITRE Corporation, http://cve.mitre.org/docs/plover
11. The Common Vulnerabilities and Exposures (CVE) Initiative, MITRE Corporation, http://cve.mitre.org
12. OWASP Top Ten Most Critical Web Application Security Vulnerabilities, http://www.owasp.org/documentation/topten.html
13. Department of Homeland Security National Cyber Security Division's Build Security In (BSI) web site, http://buildsecurityin.us-cert.gov
14. Klein, A.: Cross Site Scripting Explained, Sanctum Security Group, http://www.crypto.stanford.edu/cs155/CSS.pdf
15. Endler, D.: The Evolution of Cross-Site Scripting Attacks iDEFENSE Labs, http://www.cgisecurity.com/lib/XSS.pdf
16. Spett, K.: Are your web applications vulnerable, http://www.spidynamics.com/whitepapers/SPIcross-sitescripting.pdf
17. Viega, J.: The CLASP Application Security Process, Secure Software, Inc., http://www.securesoftware.com
18. Mauw, S.: PHP vulnerabilities 2IF30. In: ECSS group, Eindhoven University of Technology, The Netherlands, http://www.win.tue.nl/_ecss
19. Christey, S.M.: Vulnerability Type Distributions in CVE Document version: 1.0 (October 4, 2006), http://cve.mitre.org/docs/docs-06/vuln-trends.html
20. Barnum, M.: Being Explicit About Security Weaknesses Robert
21. Managing Application Security in Business Processes, http://www.verisign.com/managed-security-services/information-security/vulnerabilty-assessment/index.html
22. Secunia vulnerability advisories Bugtraq, http://www.secunia.com
23. Vulnerability advisories, http://www.securityfocus.com
24. Certcoordination centre, http://www.cert.org
25. National Vulnerability Database, http://nvd.nist.gov
26. Common Vulnerability Scoring System, http://www.first.org/cvss
27. Open Source Vulnerability Database, http://osvdb.org

Performance Analysis for Multi Sensor Fingerprint Recognition System

Shimon Modi, Stephen Elliott[1], and Hakil Kim[2]

[1] Purdue University, West Lafayette IN 47907, USA
[2] INHA University, Incheon, South Korea

Abstract. The increasing use of distributed authentication architecture has made interoperability of systems an important issue. Interoperability of systems reflects the maturity of the technology and also improves confidence of users in the technology. Biometric systems are not immune to the concerns of interoperability. Interoperability of fingerprint sensors and its effect on the overall performance of the recognition system is an area of interest with a considerable amount of work directed towards it. This research analyzed effects of interoperability on error rates for fingerprint datasets captured from two optical sensors and a capacitive sensor when using a single commercially available fingerprint matching algorithm. The main aim of this research was to emulate a centralized storage and matching architecture with multiple acquisition stations. Fingerprints were collected from 44 individuals on all three sensors and interoperable False Reject Rates of less than .31% were achieved using two different enrolment strategies.

1 Introduction

The landscape of authentication technologies has changed in the last decade. Increased use of information technology in an increasingly networked world has reduced the usefulness of monolithic and centralized authentication architectures. Todays networked world requires distributed authentication architecture which is scalable and takes advantage of various technological advancements. But attempting to mix disparate authentication systems raises the issue of interoperability. The effect of interoperability on the authentication results is an issue which needs to be considered when deploying such authentication systems. There are three main methods of authentication: 1) using something known only to the authorized individual e.g. password 2) using something in possession of only the authorized individual e.g. smartcard 3) using physical or behavioral characteristics of the authorized individual i.e. biometrics. Knowledge based and token based authentication systems do not face the same types of interoperability challenges as biometric systems. This issue is of particular relevance to biometric systems because it is dependent heavily on human interaction and human characteristics. A typical biometric system consists of an acquisition subsystem, a feature extraction subsystem, a storage subsystem, a matching subsystem, and a decision subsystem. A fingerprint recognition system can use fingerprint sensors based on a variety of different technologies such as optical, capacitive, thermal,

P. McDaniel and S.K. Gupta (Eds.): ICISS 2007, LNCS 4812, pp. 292–305, 2007.

or others. The physics behind these technologies introduces distortions and variations in the captured images which are characteristic of the technology, and since the acquisition subsystem is the first point of contact between the user and the systems, it is responsible for introducing part or all of the distortion. Fingerprint recognition systems are the most widely deployed and commercially available biometric systems, which makes interoperability germane for a number of constituencies [4]. Taking a financial institution as an example of the need for interoperability, some institutions are starting to deploy Automated Teller Machines (ATM) which use fingerprint recognition for authenticating customers. Such a system can be designed to take advantage of distributed acquisition architecture and use a centralized storage and matching architecture. Without proper understanding of how fingerprints captured from different sensors affect the overall recognition rates, the financial institution would be forced to deploy the same fingerprint sensor at all the ATMs. The effect of using different fingerprint sensors for enrolment and recognition purposes on recognition rates is understood but not well enough for it to be estimable. This requires an extraordinary level of confidence and trust in the fingerprint sensor manufacturer in order to choose just a single manufacturer. This could also be a hurdle to mass absorption of this technology. If the sensor manufacturer was to stop supporting the particular fingerprint sensors, the financial institution would be forced to replace all the sensors and re-enrol all its clients. This could be a massive capital and labor cost and could be a deterrent to using this technology. There is need to understand the effect of different fingerprints on recognition rates not just from an algorithm advancement perspective, but also from a technology usage perspective. The focus of this study was to gain further understanding into effect of sensor specific distortions on recognition error rates and understand how to lower recognition error rates for fingerprint datasets acquired from different fingerprint sensors. This study did not attempt to study or examine sensor specific variations and distortions on the fingerprint images itself. This study used two optical sensors and a capacitive sensor and the results illustrated that fingerprint sensor effects have a significant impact on error rates for different fingerprint datasets.

2   Review of Related Research

The majority of precision and consistency of feature extraction and matching in fingerprint recognition depends on the ability of the fingerprint sensor to acquire the fingerprint images. Fingerprint image acquisition is heavily affected by interaction and contact issues [8]. Inconsistent contact, non-uniform contact and irreproducible contact are specific issues which can affect fingerprint image acquisition [3]. The mapping of a 3-D fingerprint shape onto a 2-D image introduces distortions which are not uniform across different sensor technologies. The inconsistencies introduced during the capture process affect how fingerprints captured on different sensors are assessed. Jain and Ross evaluated the error rates for fingerprint matching for fingerprints captured on an optical and capacitive sensor [6]. Their results showed that Equal Error Rate (EER) for matching images collected from the optical sensor was 6.14% and EER for matching images collected from the capacitive sensor was 10.39%. The EER for the matching images collected from optical sensor to capacitive sensor was 23.13%. Nagdir and Ross have proposed a non-linear calibration scheme based on thin plate splines to facilitate sensor interoperability for fingerprints [10]. Their calibration model was designed to be applied to the minutiae dataset and to the fingerprint image itself. They applied the minutiae and image calibration schemes to fingerprints collected from an optical sensor and capacitive sensor and matched the calibrated images from the two sensors against each other. Their results showed an increase in Genuine Accept Rate from approximately 30% to 70% for VeriFinger matcher after applying the minutiae calibration model. Ko and Krishnan illustrate the need to understand the impact on error rates of fingerprints captured by a new fingerprint sensor which is integrated into an existing fingerprint recognition system infrastructure [7]. Their examination of the U.S. Department of Homeland Securitys Biometric Identification System recommended measures to facilitate maintenance and matcher accuracy of large scale applications. The quality of fingerprint images heavily influences performance of fingerprint recognition systems. Modi and Elliott observed that image quality and performance of fingerprint dataset collected from an 18-25 year population is better than fingerprint dataset collected from 62 years and above population [9]. The authors of [2] presents a methodology to compensate for image resolution and distortion differences for fingerprints from different fingerprint sensors. By calculating the resolution and distortion information of fingerprint sensors, the statistical analysis of compensated images from different sensors showed a reduction in differences of features between the images from different sensors. NIST conducted the MINEX Test in 2004 which assessed the error rates for fingerprint templates created from different template generators and matched on different matchers [1]. Their observations showed a significant difference in error rates for fingerprint datasets which used different template generators and matchers. These previous studies show a higher error rate for matching fingerprints collected from different types of scanners. With distributed authentication architectures becoming more pervasive, interoperability will become a paramount concern. The results from these previous studies indicated a need to analyze and understand the difference in error rates for fingerprint images captured from different sensors.

3   Sensor Technologies

The study was conducted using two types of fingerprint sensor technologies: optical and capacitance. Most optical sensors are based on the phenomenon of frustrated total internal reflection (FTIR) [11]. This technology utilizes a glass platen, a light source and a CCD, or a CMOS camera for constructing fingerprint images [11]. Optical sensors introduce distortions which are characteristic of its technology. The edges of fingerprint images captured using optical sensors have a tendency of getting blurred due to the setup of the lenses. Optical physics could potentially lead to out of focus images which can be attributed to the curvature of the lens. Sometimes residual incident light is reflected from the ridges which can lead to a low contrast image [12]. A phenomenon called Trapezoidal Distortion is also noticed in fingerprint images due to the unequal optical paths between each point of the fingerprint and the image focusing lens [5]. Capacitance sensors are constructed using a two-dimensional array of conductive plates [13]. When a finger is placed on a surface above the array the electrical capacitance of these plates is affected. The sensor plates under the ridge will have a larger capacitance than the sensor plates beneath the valley. Air has lower permittivity than skin, which leads to an increased capacitance in plates under the skin. Capacitance sensors do not produce geometric distortions, but they are prone to introduce distortions due to the electrical nature of the capture technology. Electrostatic discharge can affect the resulting image since the conductive plates are sensitive to it. Capacitance sensors can also be affected from the 60Hz power line and electrical noise from within the sensor [10]. Both these sensor technologies are affected by leftover residue on the surface and skin conditions like sweat and oiliness. These technologies introduce distortions on the resulting image and reduce its fidelity to the original source and also increase inconsistencies in resulting images.

4 Instrumentation, Data Collection and Dataset Summary

The analysis for this study was conducted using fingerprints collected from three different fingerprint sensors. The three fingerprint sensors used were DigitalPersona U.are.U4000a, Identix DFR 2080, and Authentec AF-S2. The DigitalPersona U.are.U4000a and Identix DFR 2080 sensors are optical sensors, and Authentec AF-S2 is a capacitive sensor. Table 1 shows the specifications for the three fingerprint sensors. 44 subjects provided 6 fingerprint samples of their right index finger on these three sensors which resulted in total of 264 fingerprints from each sensor.

Table 1. Fingerprint Sensor Information

SensorName	*SensorType*	*Resolution*	*CaptureArea(mm)*
DigitalPersona U.are.U4000	Optical Sensor	512 dpi	14.6X18.1
Authentec AF-S2	Capacitive Sensor	250 dpi	13X13
Identix DFR 2080	Optical Sensor	500 dpi	15X15

VeriFinger 5.0 SDK was used to perform the feature extraction and matching. This setup simulates one of the main objectives of the experiment: capture fingerprints from different fingerprint sensors and use the same feature extraction and matching algorithm, thus simulating a centralized storage and matching

architecture. The fingerprint images were not translated, rotated or altered during the fingerprint extraction and matching operations; all operations were performed on the raw fingerprint images. The three sensors will be referred to as follows for the rest of the paper: DigitalPersona U.are.U4000a as D, Identix DFR 2080 as I, and Authentec AF-S2 as A.

5   Image Quality and Minutiae Count Analysis

The first step of the research was to analyze the basic features of the fingerprint: image quality and minutiae count. Image quality scores for the three fingerprint datasets were generated using commercially available software. The scores were analyzed to test for statistical difference in image quality score. The Kruskal Wallis statistical test of image quality scores demonstrated a statistically significant difference in image quality at a 95% confidence level between the three fingerprint datasets. The distribution of image quality scores for the three fingerprint datasets can be seen in Fig. 1. Analysis of minutiae count was also

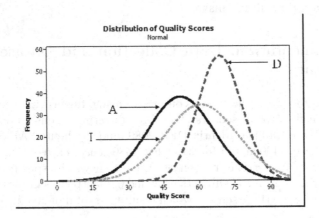

Fig. 1. Distribution of Image Quality Scores

performed to observe the differences in minutiae count for the three fingerprint datasets. The Kruskal- Wallis test showed a statistically significant difference in minutiae count at 95% confidence level across all the datasets. The distribution of minutiae count for the three fingerprint datasets can be seen in Fig. 2. The distribution of the image quality scores and minutiae counts illustrated a clear difference in all the three fingerprint datasets. Combined with the results which showed a difference in image quality and minutiae between the three datasets, and results from previous studies which have shown an increase in error rates of matching datasets collected from different fingerprint sensors, the researchers designed a template generation methodology of combining multiple fingerprints in order to achieve better interoperability rates. This methodology is explained in the next section.

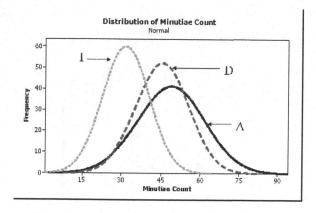

Fig. 2. Distribution of Minutiae Count

6   Methodology and Results

A fingerprint template for an individual can be created from multiple finger-prints. This mode of template generation allows it to account for more finger-print features. Using multiple images can also remove any spurious minutiae which cannot be detected from a single image, but are easier to identify using multiple images. The template generator used for this study has the ability to create a generalized template using a collection of features from multiple fin-gerprints. The first strategy involved using three images from the same sensor to create a generalized template for each individual and the second strategy involved using one image each from the three different sensors to create a gener-alized hybrid template for each individual. False Match Rates (FMR) and False Non Match Rates (FNMR) were calculated using these two different strategies. A detailed discussion of methodology and results is presented in the following sub-sections.

6.1   Generalized Template Methodology

The fingerprint datasets consisted of 44 subjects who provided 6 fingerprint images on each of the three different sensors. The first three images for each subject were separated for use as enrolment images, and the final three im-ages for each subject were kept for testing purposes. The enrolment template from each dataset was compared to the testing images from all three datasets, thus providing FMR and FNMR for native datasets and interoperable datasets. Native datasets are the ones for which the enrolment and testing images are collected using the same sensor. Interoperable datasets are the ones for which the enrolment and testing images are collected using different datasets. Fig. 3 illustrates the analysis methodology for this strategy.

Table 2 summarizes the failure to enrol (FTE) for each dataset, the num-ber of total subjects used for the analysis, and number of testing images from

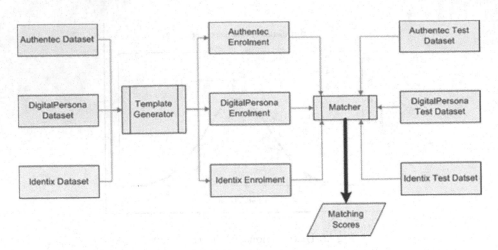

Fig. 3. Generalized Template Test/Analysis Methodology

Table 2. FTE Summary

Dataset	FTE	Total Enroled Subjects	Number of testing images
A	5	39	117
I	1	43	129
D	1	43	129

each dataset. The enrolment strategy used multiple images which required each fingerprint image used in enrolment to be consistent for the software to extract features in order to create a generalized template. This is an internal quality control component which is required. For the testing images if the software could not extract features a failure to match was recorded. A one way analysis of variance (ANOVA) test was performed to test differences in genuine and imposter match scores between the native and interoperable datasets, Fingerprint sensor interoperability can be described as consistency of performance of the matcher for native and interoperable fingerprint datasets. In statistical terms, this can be examined by testing for a significant difference of the mean genuine match scores and mean imposter match scores between native and interoperable fingerprint datasets.

The diagnostic tests for normality, independence, and constancy of variance of error terms did not show any violations which implied that the parametric one way test could be performed. Three different ANOVA tests were performed on genuine match scores: one test for A enrolment dataset, one test for D for enrolment dataset and one test for I enrolment dataset. The tests were performed at $\alpha = .05$ and results are shown in Table 3. μnative is the average genuine match score for matching enrolment images and testing images captured from the same sensor. μinteroperable1 and μinteroperable2 are the average genuine matching scores for matching enrolment images and testing images captured from different sensors. The native subscript refers to the sensor in the Enrolment dataset column in Table 3.

Table 3. ANOVA Results

EnrolmentDataset	NullHypothesis	P − value
A	μnative$\neq$ μinteroperable1$\neq$ μinteroperable2	0.75
I	μnative$\neq$ μinteroperable1$\neq$ μinteroperable2	0.0
D	μnative$\neq$ μinteroperable1$\neq$ μinteroperable2	0.0

The results show there was no statistically significant differences in genuine match scores for A enrolment dataset. There was a statistically significant difference in genuine match scores for enrolment performed with D and I, but it was not strong enough to draw any conclusions based on this sample size. The distributions of genuine scores below illustrate this difference. It can be observed in the distribution of genuine scores for A enrolment dataset that there is a greater overlap of the match scores for the three distributions. The distribution of genuine match scores for I enrolment dataset shows a distinct difference in the three distributions. Three different ANOVA tests were performed on imposter match scores: one test for A enrolment dataset, one test for D for enrolment dataset and one test for I enrolment dataset. The tests were performed at $\alpha = .05$ and results are shown in Table 4. μnative is the average imposter match score for matching enrolment images and testing images captured from the same sensor. μinteroperable1 and μinteroperable2 are the average imposter matching scores for matching enrolment images and testing images captured from different sensors. The native subscript refers to the sensor in the Enrolment dataset column in Table 4.

The three ANOVA tests showed that mean imposter scores were statistically significant for each test. The statistical tests provide insight into difference between mean scores of genuine match scores and imposter match scores. The statistical tests are important as they indicate a change in threshold will result in unpredictable changes in error rates for the three different datasets. Due to the differences in distributions of genuine and imposter match scores, a change in the decision threshold for the matcher will not change the error rates for each dataset at a predictable rate. The next step was to analyze the differences relative to the threshold and determine the different error rates. In order to analyze the change in error rates, FNMR matrices were generated from the match scores. The rows of the error rate matrices represent the enrolment dataset and the columns represent the testing dataset. The diagonal of the error rate matrix represent FNMR for the native datasets and all the cells off the diagonal represent FNMR for interoperable datasets. Three FNMR matrices were created

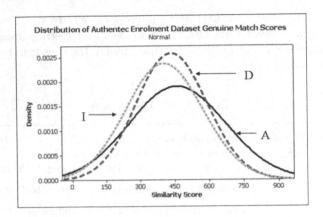

Fig. 4. Distribution of Genuine Match Scores: A Enrolment Dataset

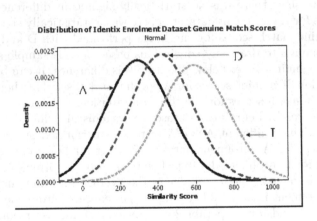

Fig. 5. Distribution of Genuine Match Scores: I Enrolment Dataset

Table 4. ANOVA Results

$Enrolment Dataset$	$Null Hypothesis$	$P - value$
A	μnative$\neq$ μinteroperable1$\neq$ μinteroperable2	0.25
I	μnative$\neq$ μinteroperable1$\neq$ μinteroperable2	0.0
D	μnative$\neq$ μinteroperable1$\neq$ μinteroperable2	0.0

at three different FMR operational points: .00%, .01% and 1% to provide an evaluation of genuine and imposter match scores for the datasets.

The results showed that highest FNMR was .031% for FMR of .001%. The interoperable A testing set for FMR of .001% showed FNMR of .031% and .023%

Table 5. FNMR Matrix at .001% FMR

	I	D	A	
I	0	.015%	.023%	
D	0	.015%	.031%	Enrolment Dataset
A	.0096%	0	.0096%	
	Testing Dataset			

Table 6. FNMR Matrix at .01% FMR

	I	D	A	
I	0	.015%	.023%	
D	0	.015%	0%	Enrolment Dataset
A	.0096%	0	0%	
	Testing Dataset			

Table 7. FNMR Matrix at 1% FMR

	I	D	A	
I	0	0%	0%	
D	0	0%	0%	Enrolment Dataset
A	0%	0	0%	
	Testing Dataset			

with the interoperable optical datasets. These error rates are significantly lower compared to previous studies related to interoperability of fingerprint [6]. The FNMR matrix for FMR of 1% showed a FNMR of 0% for native and interoperable datasets. The A enrolment dataset showed a relatively low FNMR with the interoperable optical datasets in Table 5 which was an interesting result. Contrarily, the A testing dataset showed the highest FNMR in Table 5. The optical sensor datasets showed a relatively low FNMR for interoperability tests compared to the FNMR for interoperability tests between optical and capacitive sensor datasets. The trend of these results is similar to previous studies, although this approach achieved considerably lower FNMR compared to previous studies. The distributions of minutiae count and quality scores for the capacitive sensor dataset were the most variable, and the capacitive dataset showed the highest FNMR with the optical interoperable datasets. This relationship is interesting as it indicates a possibility for improving performance of interoperability datasets by controlling for minutiae count and quality of input samples relative to the native dataset.

6.2   Generalized Hybrid Template

The analysis of results from the generalized simple template methodology led the researchers to test a hybrid template strategy. This strategy involved generating a hybrid template from three fingerprints images, where each fingerprint image was collected from a different sensor. To achieve this, one image from each dataset was used to create the enrolment template, and the remaining 5 images for each subject from each dataset were used as test images. Out of 44 subjects, 2 subjects could not be enroled because of image quality issues. Fingerprint images from the remaining 42 subjects were used to generate the matching scores.

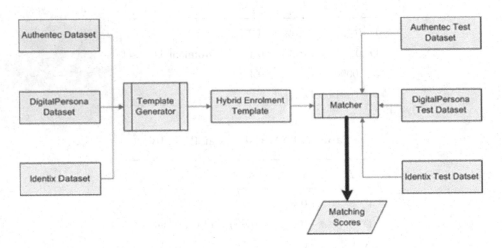

Fig. 6. Generalized Hybrid Template Test/Analysis Methodology

It was observed from the statistical analysis that genuine match scores and imposter match scores for the three test datasets were statistically significant in their differences. The distribution of genuine scores in Fig. 7 indicated that distributions of genuine match scores for D and I test dataset overlapped while the distribution of genuine match scores for A differed. The statistical tests indicated a difference in mean genuine match scores, but we needed to ascertain the error rates due to the differences relative to the threshold. FNMR were calculated for three operational FMR points of .001%, .01%, and 1% similar to the previous section. Due to use of a hybrid template there were no native enrolment datasets which resulted in three FNMR for each operational point.

D test dataset showed an improvement and the A dataset showed a worsening in FNMR using this strategy. I test dataset did not show any difference in error rates between the two strategies. Although there was a positive and negative change in error rates they were not relatively large. At 1% FMR all three datasets

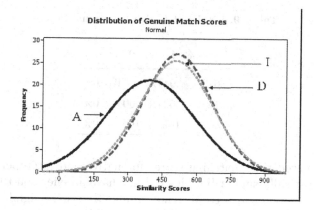

Fig. 7. Distribution of Genuine Match Scores

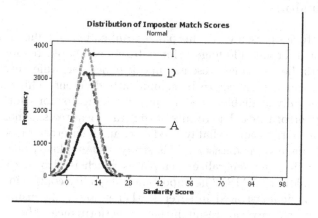

Fig. 8. Distribution of Imposter Match Scores

Table 8. ANOVA Results Summary

Genuine Match Scores	P-value = 0.25
Imposter Match Scores	P-value = 0.0

showed a 0% FNMR. This result was consistent with observations from the previous section. It was observed earlier that the distribution of A genuine match scores did not overlap as much as the distributions for I and D. This can be directly related to the low FNMR for D and I test datasets and the slightly higher FNMR for A dataset. The lower resolution and smaller image size of fingerprint images from sensor A compared to fingerprint images from other sensors made this result predictable. Results from both the template generation

Table 9. FNMR at FMR Operational Points

FMR%	A	D	I
.001%	.044%	.004%	0%
.01%	.024%	.004%	0%
1%	0%	0%	0%

techniques showed that matching scores for native and interoperable datasets were not statistically similar but this did not have an effect on the error rates. Although the matching scores were not similar they were significantly greater than the threshold to have a 0% FNMR at 1% FMR.

7   Conclusions

Both the strategies presented in this paper resulted in a significant improvement in FNMR for interoperable fingerprint datasets compared to previous studies. Although both the strategies presented in this paper were different, the difference in error rates did not appear to be significantly different. This novel approach using commercially available tools is a positive indicator for efforts to lower interoperability error rates. The results of the statistical tests demonstrate a need to further understand and reliably predict changes in error rates for matching interoperable fingerprint datasets. This study also employed quality control as part of generating the generalized templates which is also one the factors responsible for a lower FNMR. The importance of quality control in lowering error rates has been demonstrated in several other studies, and using it as part of the enrolment strategy can result in better performance. The use of multiple fingerprints to capture more features of the fingerprint resulted in better performance compared to the use of a single fingerprint. Analyzing the minutiae count distribution and the error rate matrices indicates that overlap of minutiae distribution can potentially reduce error rates for interoperable databases. Such a strategy would require minutiae count distribution of interoperable datasets be compared to some reference database. The ANSI INCITS 378-2004 fingerprint minutiae data interchange format explicitly states the usage of only basic minutiae information like x coordinate, y coordinate, angle, type and minutiae quality to be used in the matching process. Using a template generalization technique while controlling for minutiae distribution for generation of INCITS 378-2004 fingerprint templates in an interoperability scenario would be an interesting experiment. The importance of interoperability is becoming evermore evident, and so is the importance of finding a solution to alleviate its problems. There are several ongoing efforts which are attempting to reduce the error rates for interoperability datasets. Normalization of fingerprint images collected from sensors of different technologies which result in images of different resolution and sizes is also an ongoing effort [2]. An extension of this work would be to apply the image normalization technique and then follow the template generalization methodology to assess any differences in error rates. This paper presents a practical approach for improving performance of interoperable fingerprint datasets and also brings to light several issues which need to be investigated to reduce the effects of interoperability on performance.

References

1. Grother, P., Wilson, C., Tabassi, E., Indovina, M., Flanagan, P., Salamon, W., Newton, E., McCabe, M., Watson, C.: Minex performance and interoperability of the incits 378 fingerprint template. Technical report, NIST, Gaithersburg Maryland (2006)
2. Han, Y., et al.: Resolution and distortion compensation based on sensor evaluation for interoperable fingerprint recognition. In: International Joint Conference on Neural Networks, Vancouver Canada (2006)
3. Hass, N., Pankanti, S., Yao, M.: Automatic Fingerprint Recognition Systems. In: Fingerprint Quality Assessment, p. 55. Springer, NY (2004)
4. IBG. Biometrics market and industry report, p. 224 (2007)
5. Igaki, S., et al.: Real time fingerprint sensor using a hologram. Applied Optics 31, 1974 (1992)
6. Jain, A., Ross, A.: Biometric sensor interoperability. In: BioAW 2004, vol. 3067, p. 134. Springer, Berlin (2004)
7. Ko, T., Krishnan, R.: Monitoring and reporting of fingerprint image quality and match accuracy for a large user application. In: Applied Imagery Pattern Recognition Workshop, Washington, DC (2004)
8. Kukula, E.: Impact of fingerprint force on image quality and detection of minutiae. Purdue University, INHA University, p. 7 (2007)
9. Modi, S., Elliott, S.: Impact of imagery quality on performance: Comparison of young and elderly fingerprints. In: 6th International Conference on Recent Advances in Soft Computing, Canterbury, UK (2006)
10. Nagdir, R., Ross, A.: A calibration model for fingerprint sensor interoperability. In: SPIE Conference on Biometric Technology for Human Identification III, Orlando, USA (2006)
11. O'Gorman, L., Xia, X.: Innovations in fingerprint capture devices. Pattern Recognition 36, 361 (2001)
12. Secugen. Seir optical technology. Technical report, Secugen (2007)
13. Setlak, D.: Automatic Fingerprint Recognition Systems. In: Advances in Fingerprint Sensors Using RF Imaging Techniques, p. 27. Springer, NY (2004)

Use of Dimensionality Reduction for Intrusion Detection

Subrat Kumar Dash[1], Sanjay Rawat[2], and Arun K. Pujari[1,*]

[1] Artificial Intelligence Lab, Dept. of CIS,
University of Hyderabad, India
`subrat.dash@gmail.com`, `akpcs@uohyd.ernet.in`
[2] Dipartimento di Ingegneria e Scienza dell'Informazione
Università di Trento, Italy
`tosanjayr@gmail.com`

Abstract. Dimensionality reduction is crucial when data mining techniques are applied for intrusion detection. Usually, the Host based intrusion detection problem is formulated as a classification problem and different classification algorithms are applied to high dimensional vectors that represent the system call sequences. Any such classification algorithm demands repeated computation of similarity between pairs of vectors and the computational overhead increases with the increase in the dimensionality of the vectors. Here, we believe that dimensionality reduction of these vectors will help in classification. However, the choice of dimensionality reduction method critically depends on preservation of similarity for efficient classification. We show that Locally Linear Embedding (LLE) preserves the similarity in this context. In this paper, we examine its applicability in two different approaches for system call data with benchmark dataset.

Keywords: Data Mining, Dimensionality Reduction, Locally Linear Embedding, System Calls, Host Based IDS.

1 Introduction

In the past few years data mining approach for intrusion detection has been the main focus of research in the area of information security. Several results are published proposing novel data mining techniques for Masquerade detection[3], Host based intrusion detection (HIDS)[15], Network based intrusion detection (NIDS)[12] etc. In most of these cases the objective is to classify an entity (a user or a process) to be either legitimate or intrusive. Different data mining techniques such as supervised classifications including SVM, neural networks; unsupervised methods such as clustering and sequence mining have been developed for several types of data that capture the behaviour of a process or a user. These data include system call sequences, user command sequences, click streams, network

---

* Current Address is LNMIIT, Jaipur - 303 012, INDIA.

P. McDaniel and S.K. Gupta (Eds.): ICISS 2007, LNCS 4812, pp. 306–320, 2007.

packet information etc. For HIDS, system call sequences have been acknowledged as the most effective set of data that can capture the behaviour of a process.

System calls are functions, which a process calls to invoke different operating system routines/services. When a process executes, depending upon its use of operating system services, it generates a *trace* - an ordered list of system calls. There are many tools such as *strace* and *truss* which can record the sequence of system calls made by a running process.

It is observed that any normal execution of a process follows a pattern and hence the normal behaviour of a process can be profiled by a set of predictable sequences of system calls. Any deviation in this sequence of system calls is termed as intrusion in the framework of anomaly-based IDS. [17] Thus the problem of identifying intrusive process, which are measurably different from the normal behavior, becomes detecting anomalous sequence of system calls. Normally the length of the sequence varies from session to session. Some researchers have proposed to convert the sequence into a set of fixed length subsequences or as vector of fixed size. The aim is to represent the sequences in a form suitable for data mining algorithms.

Dimensionality reduction is aimed at mapping high dimensional data points to a lower dimension preserving certain geometrical properties. It is important in many areas such as machine learning, text processing, data mining, clustering, pattern recognition, bioinformatics, content based retrieval and intrusion detection. Data analysis or pattern recognition algorithms require repeated computation of similarities or distances in the original data source. It is desirable, in such cases, that the similarity is preserved (at least in a neighborhood) while reducing the dimension so that several machine learning tasks like clustering or classification can still be carried out at lower dimension.

Manifold learning is a machine learning based dimensionality reduction that learns the low dimensional manifold structure from the data. It is a non-linear dimensionality reduction technique where every neighborhood of a point in high dimension can be embedded into a linear manifold in a lower dimension. This technique maintains the local neighborhood geometry while embedding. The local geometry is traditionally based on Euclidean geometry in the sense that the distances in higher and lower dimensions are taken as Euclidean distance. Several research papers demonstrating important and effective use of manifold learning for dimensionality reduction, visualization, classification etc. in various domains are published recently [14][16][24].

System call data has been used for different data mining techniques by representing it as vectors, invariably high dimensional vectors. We explore the effectiveness of applying dimensionality reduction for these high dimensional vectors before applying any classification technique. We address the following problem in this study. Is it worthwhile to reduce the dimension by some dimensionality reduction technique for successful intrusion detection?

We observe that in the context of intrusion detection, the need for dimensionality reduction can not be less emphasized. There have been some attempts based on SVD in this direction earlier [18]. However, realizing that manifold learning, LLE in specific, provides a better and robust dimensionality reduction technique, we, in this paper investigate LLE for HIDS using system call data. System call data can be represented in vector form in several ways. We, in this present study, examine two different approaches. We propose two new algorithms for HIDS based on dimensionality reduction. Interestingly, for the known benchmark data, our method gives best possible accuracy and false positive rate.

Rest of the paper is organized as follows: Section 2 gives an overview of research work in this area. A description of LLE including Incremental LLE is given in section 3. In section 4, we describe about two different representations of sequences of data. We describe our proposed approaches in sections 5 and 6. The experimental setup and results are provided in section 7, which is followed by section 8, which concludes the paper.

2   Related Work

Here we give a brief review of work done on system calls and data mining. Forrest *et al.* [5][6], initiated the *time-delay embedding (tide)* approach, where short sequences of system calls are used to profile a normal process using look-ahead pairs. A fixed length sliding window is used to record the correlations between the system call of the process under consideration and the normal sequences of system calls. Anomalies are accumulated over the entire sequence and an alarm is raised if the anomaly count exceeded the threshold. It is extended by Hofmeyr *et al.* [8] by using a technique called *sequence time-delay embedding (stide)*. In this approach, a database of unique sequences of fixed length is formed during training. An anomaly count is defined as the number of mismatches in a temporally local region and if it exceeds a predefined threshold, the sequence is flagged as anomalous. *stide with frequency threshold (t-stide)* [22] works on the premise that rare sequences are suspicious.

All these methods concentrate on fixed length subsequences during training. But, some better results are found if the length of the subsequence is not fixed [23]. *Anomaly Dictionaries* as *self* for anomalous sequences is proposed [1], which contain short sequences of system calls spawn by processes under attack. Lee *et al.* [11], propose RIPPER, a rule learner, to form the rules for classification. It transform the normal processes into sequences of fixed length and each sequence is turned into a RIPPER sample by treating all system calls as attributes, except the last in the sequence which is denoted as the target class.

All of the above approaches concentrate only on the sequences of system calls. Tandon and Chan [20][21] propose to consider system calls arguments and other parameters, along with the sequences of system calls. They make use of the variant of a rule learner LERAD *(Learning Rules for Anomaly Detection)*. Three variants of LERAD are proposed to generate rules under different inputs - S-LERAD for sequences of system calls only, A-LERAD for system call arguments and other key attributes and M-LERAD for argument information and sequences of system calls. A total of six system calls are used in training - first five as conditions and sixth one as decision. In A-LERAD, system calls are taken as pivotal attributes. Any value for other arguments (path, return value, error status), given a system call, which was never encountered in the value for a long time, would trigger an alarm. M-LERAD merges both S-LERAD and A-LERAD. Each input comprises of system call, arguments, path, return value, error status and the previous five system calls.

Artificial neural networks have also been used for anomaly detection [7] due to their ability to learn behavior and generalize from this learning. In this approach, Ghosh and Schwartzbardhey, use the Leaky Bucket Algorithm to capture temporal locality. A new scheme based on the kNN Classifier is proposed by Liao and Vemuri [13], in which each process is treated as a document and each system call as a word in that document. The process is converted into a vector and cosine similarity measurement is used to calculate the similarity among processes. Bag of System calls representation is investigated by Kang *et al.* for classification[9].

In a recent paper [17], an efficient scheme is proposed by Rawat *et al.* using Rough set theory. They propose that reasonably small sequences of system calls better identify abnormality in a process. They make use of Rough set theory for identifying rules from pool of sequences for intrusion detection. Use of Singular value decomposition (SVD), a dimensionality reduction technique for fast detection of intrusion is proposed in [18]. It uses SVD as a preprocessing step to reduce the dimensionality of system generated data, which makes the data noise free in addition to reducing the dimensionality, thus minimizing the computational time.

3   Locally Linear Embedding (LLE)

Recently, Roweis and Saul [19] proposed locally linear embedding algorithm, an unsupervised learning algorithm that can compute low dimensional, neighborhood-preserving embeddings of high dimensional data. The basic idea of LLE is global minimization of the reconstruction error of the set of all local neighbors in the dataset. The steps of LLE are given below.

Input X: $N \times D$ matrix consisting of N data items in R^D
Output Y: $N \times d$ matrix consisting of $d \ll D$ dimensional embedding coordinates for the input points.
Step 1: The K nearest neighbors of each data point x_i are computed.
Step 2: The reconstruction weights W_{ij}^* for each x_i are computed by minimizing the following error function

$$\psi(W) = \|x_i - \sum_{j=1}^{N} W_{ij} x_j \|^2 \tag{1}$$

subject to the constraint $\sum_{j=1} W_{ij} = 1$, and $W_{ij} = 0$, if x_j is not a neighbor of x_i.
Step 3: Using the optimal reconstruction weights W_{ij}^*, the embedding Y_i's are computed by minimizing the following error function.

$$\varphi(Y) = \sum_{i=1}^{N} \| y_i - \sum_{j=1}^{N} W_{ij}^* y_j \|^2 \tag{2}$$

where $W^* = arg\ \min_w \psi(W)$. The error function is minimized subject to the constraints $\sum_i y_i = 0$ and $\sum_i y_i y_i^T / n = I$. The embedding is given by $Y^* = arg\ \min_Y \varphi(Y)$.

The weight W_{lj} stores the contribution of x_j to the linear construction of x_l. These weights characterize the local geometric properties of the dataset around each input. The optimal weights for each input can be efficiently calculated by solving the system of linear equations $Q_\ell W_\ell = e$ for every x_ℓ where the ij^{th} entry of Q_ℓ is

$$Q_\ell(i,j) = d_{\ell i}{}^2 + d_{\ell j}{}^2 - d_{ij}{}^2. \tag{3}$$

where, d_{ij} is the distance between the ith and j^{th} items. It will be defined for both the categorical and numeric data differently, in the following sections.

The Q_ℓ matrix might sometime be singular. To overcome this problem the matrix is regularized as $Q_\ell := Q_\ell + r_\ell Tr(Q_\ell)$ where r_ℓ is a small regularization parameter. The optimal reconstruction weights can be obtained in closed form as

$$W_\ell = \frac{Q_\ell^- e}{e^T Q_\ell^- e} \tag{4}$$

where Q_ℓ^- is the generalized inverse of Q_ℓ.

In local linear embedding, it is assumed that a $(K-1)$-dimensional hyperplane passing through the K data points that constitute the K-nearest neighbors of x_ℓ. The hyperplane is represented by the affine combination of these points. When x_ℓ (assumed to be outside the hyperplane) is projected onto the hyperplane, the coefficients of the affine combination for the projection gives the reconstruction weights.

Incremental LLE

In the context of IDS, we need to project vectors of incoming new processes into lower dimensional space. For this purpose, we make use of the method proposed by Kouropteva et al. [10]. Let x_{N+1} be the vector corresponding to a new process. Let X_{N+1} be the matrix of the K nearest neighbors of x_{N+1}: $X_{N+1} = \{x_{N+1}^1, x_{N+1}^2, \ldots, x_{N+1}^K\}$ and $Y_{N+1} = \{y_{N+1}^1, y_{N+1}^2, \ldots, y_{N+1}^K\}$. By using the assumption that the manifold is locally linear, the following equation is approximately true: $Y_{N+1} = X_{N+1}Z$, where Z is an unknown linear transformation matrix of size Dd, which can be determined as $Z = (X_{N+1})^{-1}Y_{N+1}$. Because X_{N+1} is the neighborhood of x_{N+1} and LLE preserves local structures, the new projection can be found as $y_{N+1} = x_{N+1}Z$.

4   Representation of Sequences

Research on HIDS based on system call data is concerned with two types of representation of system call data, one is term frequency of each system call and the other is decision table representation based on subsequences of system call. Let $S = \{S_1, S_2, \ldots, S_D\}$ (say, $|S| = D$) be the set of system calls made by all training processes. Let P be the set of training processes. The ℓth process P_ℓ is represented as $< P_1^\ell, P_2^\ell, \ldots, P_n^\ell >$, where P_j^ℓ is the jth system call in P_ℓ.

4.1   Term Frequency

This representation draws an analogy between text categorization and intrusion detection, such that each system call is treated as a word and a set of system calls generated by a process as a document. In this approach, a process, P_ℓ, is represented by an ordered list $< c_1^\ell, c_2^\ell, \ldots, c_D^\ell >$ where, c_j^ℓ denotes the frequency of system call S_j in the process P_ℓ. For example, let $S = \{$access audit chdir close creat exit fork ioctl$\}$. Let two processes be $P_1 = <$access close ioctl access exit$>$, and $P_2 = <$ioctl audit chdir chdir access$>$. Then we can represent the two processes in terms of frequencies as, $P_1 = <2, 0, 0, 1, 0, 1, 0, 1>$ and $P_2 = <1, 1, 2, 0, 0, 0, 0, 1>$.

This representation formulates each process as a vector of D-dimension (in this example $D=7$). But, it is to be seen that, this form of representation of a process does not preserve the relative order of system calls in the sequence. We also have to know all the system calls of a process and their frequencies in order to represent it in this form. In other words, we have to wait till the termination of the process to represent it. This approach is not suitable for on-line detection as the frequency cannot be determined until after the process terminates [22].

4.2   Decision Table

In supervised classification, the posteriori knowledge is expressed by one distinguished attribute called decision attribute. A table wherein one of the attributes is decision attribute is called a *decision table*. Every other column represents an attribute that can be measured for each object. A decision table is said to be *consistent* if each unique row has only one value of decision attribute. We propose here to represent the system call data in the form of a decision table.

Forrest *et al.* [6] suggest the use of small sequences of system calls, made by a process, as the profile of the process. The study done by Lee *et al.* [11] also validates this observation. But if we analyze normal and abnormal processes, we find that not all parts of an abnormal process are responsible for intrusion. Thus intrusive part should be detectable as a subsequence of the whole abnormal sequence of the process. Thus one point of focus of this study is to determine the adequate length of such subsequences. Also as pointed out earlier, not all of the subsequences of an abnormal process are abnormal. Many of them will be identical to those occurred in normal processes.

We can extract all the subsequences from each of the processes by taking a sliding window of size D $(D \leq n)$. Thus, the ith subsequence of P_ℓ is given by,

$$< P_{\ell(i)}, P_{\ell(i+1)}, \ldots, P_{\ell(i+D-1)} >$$

Each subsequence of a normal process is labeled as normal. In case of abnormal process, as pointed out earlier, not all of the subsequences are abnormal. Thus a subsequence corresponding to an abnormal process, matching with any of the normal subsequences, is discarded; otherwise it is labeled as abnormal. It should be noted that by removing duplicate subsequences, we get a consistent decision table because no subsequence can belong to normal as well as abnormal classes.

Let P_1 and P_2 be normal and abnormal processes respectively.

P_1 = <fcntl, close, close, fcntl, close, fcntl, close, open> and
P_2 = <fcntl, close, fcntl, close, open, open>

We transform P_1 into a set of subsequences using a sliding window of length 5 ($=D$). We label all the 4 subsequences as normal. While calculating the subsequences of P_2, the first subsequence <fcntl, close, fcntl, close, open> matches with the last subsequence of P_1 and therefore it is discarded. The second subsequence <close, fcntl, close, open, open> is labeled as abnormal and added to the decision table. The final decision table is shown in Table 1. It can be seen that the decision table, thus created, is consistent.

Table 1. Representation of subsequences

Objects	A_1	A_2	A_3	A_4	A_5	Decision
1	fcntl	close	close	fcntl	close	normal
2	close	close	fcntl	close	fcntl	normal
3	close	fcntl	close	fcntl	close	normal
4	fcntl	close	fcntl	close	open	normal
5	close	fcntl	close	open	open	abnormal

5   Term Frequency Approach

We convert processes under normal execution, each of which is an ordered sequence of system calls, into vectors, as described in section 4.1. From all the normal processes, a matrix $X = [c_j^\ell]$ is formed, where c_j^ℓ denotes the frequency of S_j, the jth system call of S, in P_ℓ, the ℓth process. Here, $1 \leq j \leq D$ and $D = |S|$. As X is a matrix consisting of numerical values, the distance between two processes P_k and P_ℓ of X is defined as the Euclidean distance which is given in equation (5).

$$d_{k\ell} = \sqrt{\sum_j \left(c_j^k - c_j^\ell\right)^2} \qquad (5)$$

This equation is used in equation (3), to calculate the value of Q by this approach. We apply LLE as described in section 3 on matrix X to get a corresponding dimensionally reduced matrix Y, where Y_ℓ represents the reduced vector of vector P_ℓ in X.

In order to categorize a new process p into either normal or abnormal class, we first check if the new process p contains a new system call which does not belong to set S. In that case we flag it as abnormal, with the assumption that a system call that does not appear in the normal set is suspicious and thus the process is abnormal. Otherwise, we represent p in a vector form finding the term frequency of each of the system calls and determine the embedding of p on the manifold structure by the incremental LLE method, which gives the corresponding reduced vector Y_p. We calculate similarity between Y_p and all the processes Y_ℓ in Y using the cosine formula [18], given as,

$$CosSim(Y_p, Y_\ell) = \frac{Y_p \cdot Y_\ell}{\| Y_p \| \cdot \| Y_\ell \|} \qquad (6)$$

where $\| A \|$ refers to the norm of the vector A. If any one of $CosSim(Y_p, Y_\ell)$, $\forall \ell$, is equal to 1, then p is detected as normal. Otherwise, we find the average similarity value by taking the K highest similarity values. When the average similarity value is above some threshold (λ), process p is considered as normal, and if not, abnormal. The algorithmic representation of the proposed scheme is given in Figure 1.

Training Phase

1. Form matrix $X = [c_j^\ell]$ from a set of normal processes
2. Apply LLE on X to find the corresponding reduced dimensioned representation Y

Testing Phase

1. **For** each process p in the testing data **do**
2.   **if** p has some system calls which does not belong to S **then**
3. p is abnormal; goto step 1 for next process
4.   **endif**
5.   find Y_p
6.   **For** each process P_ℓ in the training data **do**
7.   compute $CosSim(Y_p, Y_\ell)$
8.   **if** $CosSim(Y_p, Y_\ell)$ equals 1.0 **then**
9. p is normal; goto step 1 for next process
10.   **end if**
11.   **end do**
12.   find average similarity value $AvgSim$ by taking K highest $CosSim$
13.   **if** $AvgSim < \lambda$ **then**
14. p is abnormal
15.   **else**
16. p is normal
17.   **end if**
18. **end do**

Fig. 1. Algorithmic representation of the Term Frequency based detection method

6 Decision Table Approach

We represent normal processes in the form of a decision table as described in section 4.2, extracting subsequences of length D. Each of these subsequences is labeled as normal. So, now it can be interpreted as a matrix $X = [x_{ij}]$, where x_{ij} refers to the jth system call of the ith subsequence, where $1 \leq j \leq (D+1)$, where the last column is the class attribute. Here, each row of X consists of a sequence of categorical values. So, we define the similarity between two subsequences χ_k and χ_ℓ as,

$$sim(\chi_k, \chi_\ell) = \frac{\chi_k \otimes \chi_\ell}{2D - (\chi_k \otimes \chi_\ell)} \qquad (7)$$

where, $(\chi_k \otimes \chi_\ell)$ refers to the number of attributes having same value between the two subsequences. Thus, the distance between χ_k and χ_ℓ is defined as $d_{k\ell} = 1 - sim(\chi_k, \chi_\ell)$, which is used in equation (3) to calculate Q, by this approach. It is to be noted that, we ignore the class attribute while calculating the similarity between two subsequences. For example, if we have two subsequences as $\chi_1 = $ <fcntl open open fcntl close> and $\chi_2 = $ <open open fcntl close close>, then $(\chi_1 \otimes \chi_2) = 2$, so $sim(\chi_1, \chi_2) = \frac{2}{(10-2)} = \frac{1}{4}$ and thus, $d_{12} = 1 - \frac{1}{4} = \frac{3}{4}$. Using this distance measure, we apply the LLE method on X to obtain Y, which is a dimensionally reduced *numerical representation* of X.

Given a new process p for classification, we first extract all the possible subsequences of length D from it. If all of them are present in the training pool i.e. X, then we flag the process as a normal one. Otherwise, for each subsequence $p_{(i)}$ of p which is not present in X, we find its corresponding $Y_{p(i)}$. We calculate similarity between $Y_{p(i)}$ and each of the vectors Y_ℓ in Y using equation 6. Taking the K highest similarity values we find the average similarity value for $Y_{p(i)}$. If the average similarity value of any of the subsequence is below some threshold (λ), then the subsequence is abnormal and so the whole process is flagged as abnormal. One measure advantage of this method is, we need not have to wait till the execution of the process completes and can extract and test the subsequences as the process is executing. The algorithmic form of the proposed scheme is presented in Figure 2.

Training Phase

1. Construct a decision table X from the normal processes with length of the subsequence as D
2. Apply LLE on X to find the corresponding reduced dimensioned representation Y

Testing Phase

1. **For** each process p in the testing data **do**
2.   **For** each subsequence p_i of p **do**
3.   **if** $p_i \notin X$ **then**
4.   find $Y_{p(i)}$
5.   compute $CosSim(Y_{p(i)}, Y_\ell) \; \forall Y_\ell \in Y$
6.   find average similarity value $AvgSim$ by taking K highest $CosSim$
7.   **if** $AvgSim < \lambda$ **then**
8. p is abnormal
9.   goto step 1 for next process
10.   **end if**
11.   **end if**
12.   **end do**
13. p is normal
14. **end do**

Fig. 2. Algorithmic representation of the Decision Table based detection method

7   Experimental Setup and Results

We test both our approaches upon the *BSM audit logs* data, from the well-cited DARPA'98 dataset [2], as it contains host-based process level information. A detailed procedure for the extraction of process from the audit logs can be found in [17].

On analyzing the entire set of BSM logs (list files), we locate the five days which are free of any type of attacks - Tuesday of the third week, Thursday of the fifth week and Monday, Tuesday and Wednesday of the seventh week. There are around 2412 normal sessions reported during these five days of data, from which we extract 676 processes.

For unbiased evaluation of our approach, we used ten-fold cross-validation. In this cross-validation method, we partition the data (676 normal processes) into ten disjoint sets of nearly equal size and select one partition as testing set and the remaining nine are combined to form the training set. This process is repeated 10 times, each time selecting one set as testing set and the other nine as training set, to cover all the data in a circular manner. So, each time we train with 608 processes and test with 68 processes, which gives the *false positive* rate. Thus, *false positive* is equal to the number of normal processes detected as abnormal divided by the total number of normal processes.

Table 2. List of 55 attacks used in testing data set

1.1_it_ffb_clear,   1.1_it_format_clear,   2.2_it_ipsweep,   2.5_it_ftpwrite,
2.5_it_ftpwrite_test,   3.1_it_ffb_clear,   3.3_it_ftpwrite,   3.3_it_ftpwrite_test,
3.4_it_warez, 3.5_it_warezmaster, 4.1_it_080520warezclient, 4.2_it_080511warezclient,
4.2_it_153736spy, 4.2_it_153736spy_test, 4.2_it_153812spy, 4.4_it_080514warezclient,
4.4_it_080514warezclient_test,   4.4_it_175320warezclient,   4.4_it_180326warezclient,
4.4_it_180955warezclient,   4.4_it_181945warezclient,   4.5_it_092212ffb,
4.5_it_141011loadmodule,   4.5_it_162228loadmodule,   4.5_it_174726loadmodule,
4.5_it_format,   5.1_it_141020ffb,   5.1_it_174729ffb_exec,   5.1_it_format,
5.2_it_144308eject_clear, 5.2_it_163909eject_clear, 5.3_it_eject_steal, 5.5_it_eject,
5.5_it_fdformat,   5.5_it_fdformat_chmod,   6.4_it_090647ffb,   6.4_it_093203eject,
6.4_it_095046eject,   6.4_it_100014eject,   6.4_it_122156eject,   6.4_it_144331ffb,
test.1.2_format, test.1.2_format2, test.1.3_eject, test.1.3_httptunnel, test.1.4_eject,
test.1.5_processtable,   test.2.1_111516ffb,   test.2.1_format,   test.2.2_xsnoop,
test.2.3_ps, test.2.3_ps_b, test.2.5_ftpwrite, test.2.4_eject_a, test.2.2_format1

In order to test the detection capability of our method, we incorporate 55 intrusive sessions into our testing data. Table 2 lists these attacks. A number in the beginning of the name denotes the week and day and the later part denotes the name of the session (attack). For example, the attack name 3.1_it_ffb_clear means that the attack was launched in the 3rd week, on the 1st day viz. Monday and the name of the attack is ffb (in clear mode). On the basis of our initial results, we find that the methods are unable to detect 3 attacks, out of 55, viz "2.2_it_ipsweep," "test.1.5_processtable," and "test.2.2_xsnoop." On consulting DARPA attack description, we feel that it is highly unlikely to detect these attacks by using our host based method due to the manifestation of attack information. Therefore, we take remaining 52 attacks for our final experimentation. These attack sessions consist of almost all types of attacks launched on the victim Solaris machine during seven weeks of training and two weeks of testing period and that can be detected using BSM logs. An intrusive session is said to be detected if any of the processes associated with this session is classified as abnormal. Thus *detection rate* is defined as the number of intrusive sessions detected, divided by the total number of intrusive sessions.

7.1   Term Frequency Approach

There are 50 unique system calls in the whole set of 676 normal processes (Table 3). Every run of cross validation has a different subset of 608 normal processes of training data. Let S ($|S| = s$) be the set of unique system calls in the training set. We noted that every S contains all the 50 unique system calls but in general, this may not be true. All the 608 training processes are then represented as s dimensional vectors. LLE on these vectors is applied while varying K (no. of nearest neighbours) for values 5, 10, 15 etc. and varying d (target dimension) for values 10, 20, 30 etc. We test with the remaining normal processes and 52 attacks as explained above. We get the optimal accuracy for $K = 10$ and $d = 20$. In ten runs of our method for ten-fold cross-validation, we get ten different sets of detection rates and false positive rates. We take the vertical average to obtain a combined result. The combined average result is given in Table 4 for different values of threshold and the ROC curve is shown in Figure 3. Our method attains 100% detection rate with 45.13% false positive and with substantial decrease in the false positive rate (with false positive of 29.13%) we can get a near perfect detection rate of 99.81%.

Table 3. List of 50 unique system calls

```
access, audit, auditon, chdir, chmod, chown, close, creat, execve, exit,
fchdir, fchown, fcntl, fork, fork1, getaudit, getmsg, ioctl, kill, link,
login, logout, lstat, memcntl, mkdir, mmap, munmap, nice, open, pathconf,
pipe, putmsg, readlink, rename, rmdir, setaudit, setegid, seteuid, setgid,
setgroups, setpgrp, setrlimit, setuid, stat, statvfs, su, sysinfo, unlink,
utime, vfork
```

Table 4. Detection Rate and False Positive Rate with Term Frequency method

Threshold	Detection rate	False positive rate
0.40	0.365385	0
0.45	0.367308	0.0029412
0.50	0.446154	0.0102942
0.55	0.5519231	0.022059
0.60	0.7326924	0.0368568
0.65	0.8461539	0.0649817
0.70	0.9519231	0.1063419
0.75	0.9807691	0.152206
0.80	0.9942307	0.2111212
0.85	0.9980769	0.2912684
0.90	0.9980769	0.4246325
0.91	1.0	0.451287

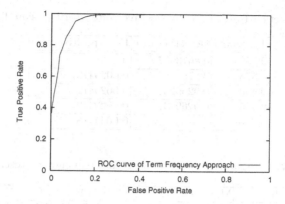

Fig. 3. Figure showing ROC curve of Term Frequency approach

Table 5. Comparative analysis for Term Frequency representation

Tag	Method	Max DR with FP=0	Min FP with DR=1	AUC
R_{0a}	BWC SVD kNN wo CV	0.37	0.048	0.9930
R_{0b}	BWC SVD kNN w CV	0.626	0.5789	0.9321
R_{1a}	LLE wo CV	0.403846	0.000378	0.9999
R_{1b}	LLE w CV	0.3653	0.4513	0.9696

Table 5 shows a comparative analysis of our result with some of the best results reported in the literature[4][18]. Most of the earlier experimental results are
carried out for distinct training set and test set and these methods did not adopt
n-fold cross-validation where the training set is split in the ratio of $n-1 : 1$ to get
test set. In either category of methods, LLE approach gives better results than the
earlier ones. For instance, the method of LLE without adoption of cross-validation
(tagged as R_{1a} in Table 5) performs better than the earlier methods by Rawat *et
al.* [18] and Lio *et al.* [13]. Similarly, from the same table it can be seen that our
method of LLE with cross-validation (tagged as R_{1b}) reports better result than Binary Weighted Cosine (BWC) method [18] with cross-validation (tagged as R_{0b}).

7.2 Decision Table Approach

Selection of value of D, the length of subsequence, is important for two reasons.
First, if D is small then it gives a compact signature which is very much practical
to check for online processes. Conversely, if it is large then it may increase the
complexity of detection. Second, small value of D increases the granularity and
may thus divide the actual signature into many parts. We take all the 608 unique
processes (training set) and build a decision table with D=10.

We take the value of K and d to be 10 and 5 respectively, and test for remaining 68 normal and 52 attack processes using the proposed Decision Table
approach. After the ten-fold cross-validation, we take a vertical average to get a

Table 6. Detection Rate and False Positive Rate with Decision Table method

Threshold	Detection rate	False positive rate
0.350	0.8673077	0
0.375	0.875	0.0029412
0.400	0.9269231	0.0029412
0.425	0.9269231	0.0029412
0.450	1	0.0044118

Table 7. Comparative analysis for Term Frequency representation

Tag	Method	Max DR with FP=0	Min FP with DR=1	AUC
R_{2a}	LLE wo CV	0.0385	0.0061	0.9981
R_{2b}	LLE w CV	0.8673	0.0044	0.9996

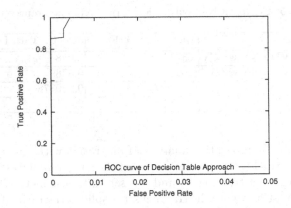

Fig. 4. Figure showing ROC curve of Decision Table approach

combined result, which is shown in Table 6 (in terms of detection rate and false positive rate) and the ROC curve is shown in Figure 4. As can be seen from Table 6, our method is able to achieve 86.73% detection rate with 0% false positive and detection rate of 100% with only a marginal false positive rate of 0.44%. Table 7 shows a comparative analysis of our result (tagged as R_{2b}) with the one reported earlier[4] (tagged as R_{2a}). This shows that our mode of experiment is able to remove biasness in the distribution and shows improved results.

7.3   Observations

By analyzing the results of both the approaches, we find that Decision table approach gives better results than the Term frequency approach. But the overhead involved in Decision table is more, as we have to check each subsequence of a process for abnormality, whereas in case of term frequency approach, we need to check for abnormality only once for a process. Also, Decision table approach is more practical in an online detection scenario as we don't have to wait for the whole process to execute, and can start the analysis as soon as we receive subsequence of length D.

8   Conclusions

In this paper, we explore the usability of LLE method in the arena of HIDS. The motivation of the present work is the requirement to have a fast and accurate HIDS. We propose two methods to achieve the aim. The first method is based on frequencies of system calls, and the second method is based on subsequences of sequences of system calls invoked by processes. The later method is useful when we want to configure IDS as reactive, for the malicious subsequence corresponding to whole sequence, can be detected before the process exits. The use of LLE enhances the overall performance of IDS mainly due to two reasons. First, it reduces the dimension, thereby making the computational efforts less. Second reason being the reduction of noise in the data. By reducing the noise, we can expect a better classification of normal and abnormal data. Our future work will be focusing on analyzing more on system call data and in particular DARPA BSM data. As a part of this, we are focusing on the properties of data for which LLE yields better results.

Acknowledgement

This research is partially supported by Council of Scientific and Industrial Research (CSIR), New Delhi under the grant no. 25(0149)06/EMR-II and the CASCADAS European project (IST-027807).

References

1. Cabrera, J.B.D., Ravichandran, B., Mehra, R.K.: Detection and classification of intrusions and faults using sequences of system calls. ACM SIGMOD Record, Special Issue: Special Section on Data Mining for Intrusion Detection and Threat Analysis 30(4), 25–34 (2001)
2. DARPA 1998 Data Set, MIT Lincoln Laboratory (1998), available at http://www.ll.mit.edu/IST/ideval/data/data_index.html
3. Dash, S.K., Reddy, K.S., Pujari, A.K.: Episode based masquerade detection. In: Jajodia, S., Mazumdar, C. (eds.) ICISS 2005. LNCS, vol. 3803, pp. 251–262. Springer, Heidelberg (2005)
4. Dash, S.K., Rawat, S., Pujari, A.K.: LLE on System Calls for Host Based Intrusion Detection. In: Proceedings of the 2006 International Conference on Computational Intelligence and Security, Guangzhou, vol. 1, pp. 609–612 (2006)
5. Forrest, S., Hofmeyr, S.A., Somayaji, A.: Computer Immunology. Communications of the ACM 40(10), 88–96 (1997)
6. Forrest, S., Hofmeyr, S.A., Somayaji, A., Longstaff, T.A.: A Sense of Self for Unix Processes. In: Proceedings of the 1996 IEEE Symposium on Research in Security and Privacy, pp. 120–128. IEEE Computer Society Press, Los Alamitos, CA (1996)

7. Ghosh, A.K., Schwartzbard, A.: A Study in Using Neural Networks for Anomaly and Misuse Detection. In: Proceedings of the 8th USENIX security Symposium, Washington, DC, USA, pp. 141–151 (August 23-26, 1999)
8. Hofmeyr, S.A., Forrest, A., Somayaji, A.: Intrusion Detection Using Sequences of System Calls. Journal of Computer Security 6, 151–180 (1998)
9. Kang, D.-K., Fuller, D., Honavar, V.: Learning Classifiers for Misuse and Anomaly Detection Using a Bag of System Calls Representation. In: Proceedings of the 2005 IEEE workshop on Information Assurance and Security, pp. 118–125 (2005)
10. Kouropteva, O., Okun, O., Pietiknen, M.: Incremental locally linear embedding. Pattern Recognition 38, 1764–1767 (2005)
11. Lee, W., Stolfo, S., Chan, P.: Learning Patterns from Unix Process Execution Traces for Intrusion Detection. In: Proceedings of the AAAI 1997 workshop on AI methods in Fraud and risk management, pp. 50–56. AAAI Press, Stanford (1997)
12. Lee, W., Stolfo Salvatore, J.: Data Mining Approaches for Intrusion Detection. In: SECURITY 1998. Proceedings of the 7th USENIX Security Symposium, pp. 79–94. Usenix Association (January 26-29, 1998)
13. Liao, Y., Vemuri, V.R.: Use of K-Nearest Neighbor Classifier for Intrusion Detection. Computers & Security 21(5), 439–448 (2002)
14. Mordohai, P., Medioni, G.: Unsupervised Dimensionality Estimation and Manifold Learning in high-dimensional Spaces by Tensor Voting. In: 19th International Joint Conference on Artificial Intelligence, Edinburgh, Scotland, pp. 798–803 (2005)
15. Mukkamala, R., Gagnon, J., Jajodia, S.: Integrating Data Mining Techniques with Intrusion detection Methods. In: Research Advances in database and Information System Security: IFIPTCII, 13th working conference on Database security, July, Kluwer Academic Publishers, USA (2000)
16. Patwari, N., Hero, A.O., Pacholski, A.: Manifold learning visualization of network traffic data. In: Proc of the 2005 ACM SIGCOMM workshop on mining network data, Philadelphia, PA, pp. 191–196 (2005)
17. Rawat, S., Gulati, V.P., Pujari, A.K.: A Fast Host-Based Intrusion Detection System Using Rough Set Theory. In: Peters, J.F., Skowron, A. (eds.) Transactions on Rough Sets IV. LNCS, vol. 3700, pp. 144–161. Springer, Heidelberg (2005)
18. Rawat, S., Gulati, V.P., Pujari, A.K., Vemuri, V.R.: Intrusion Detection Using Text Processing Techniques with a Binary-Weighted Cosine Metric. Journal of Information Assurance and Security 1, 43–50 (2006)
19. Roweis, S.T., Lawrance, K.S.: Nonlinear Dimensionality reduction by locally linear embedding. Science 290, 2323–2326 (2000)
20. Tandon, G., Chan, P.: Learning Rules from System Calls Arguments and Sequences for Anomaly Detection. In: DMSEC 2003. ICDM Workshop on Data Mining for Computer Security, Melbourne, FL, pp. 20–29 (2003)
21. Tandon, G., Chan, P.K.: On the Learning of System Call Attributes for Host-Based Anomaly Detection. International Journal on Artificial Intelligence Tools 15(6), 875–892 (2006)
22. Warrender, C., Forrest, S., Pearlmutter, B.: Detecting Intrusions Using System Calls: Alternative Data Models. In: IEEE Symposium on Security and Privacy (1999)
23. Wespi, A., Dacier, M., Debar, H.: Intrusion Detection Using Variable-Length Audit Trail Pattern. In: Debar, H., Mé, L., Wu, S.F. (eds.) RAID 2000. LNCS, vol. 1907, pp. 110–129. Springer, Heidelberg (2000)
24. Zhang, J., Li, S.Z., Wang, J.: Manifold learning and applications in recognition. In: Intelligent Multimedia Processing with Soft Computing, Springer, Heidelberg (2004)

Author Index

Vol. 4284: X. Lai, K. Chen (Eds.), Advances in Cryptology – ASIACRYPT 2006. XIV, 468 pages. 2006.

Vol. 4283: Y.Q. Shi, B. Jeon (Eds.), Digital Watermarking. XII, 474 pages. 2006.

Vol. 4266: H. Yoshiura, K. Sakurai, K. Rannenberg, Y. Murayama, S.-i. Kawamura (Eds.), Advances in Information and Computer Security. XIII, 438 pages. 2006.

Vol. 4258: G. Danezis, P. Golle (Eds.), Privacy Enhancing Technologies. VIII, 431 pages. 2006.

Vol. 4249: L. Goubin, M. Matsui (Eds.), Cryptographic Hardware and Embedded Systems - CHES 2006. XII, 462 pages. 2006.

Vol. 4237: H. Leitold, E.P. Markatos (Eds.), Communications and Multimedia Security. XII, 253 pages. 2006.

Vol. 4236: L. Breveglieri, I. Koren, D. Naccache, J.-P. Seifert (Eds.), Fault Diagnosis and Tolerance in Cryptography. XIII, 253 pages. 2006.

Vol. 4219: D. Zamboni, C. Krügel (Eds.), Recent Advances in Intrusion Detection. XII, 331 pages. 2006.

Vol. 4189: D. Gollmann, J. Meier, A. Sabelfeld (Eds.), Computer Security – ESORICS 2006. XI, 548 pages. 2006.

Vol. 4176: S.K. Katsikas, J. López, M. Backes, S. Gritzalis, B. Preneel (Eds.), Information Security. XIV, 548 pages. 2006.

Vol. 4117: C. Dwork (Ed.), Advances in Cryptology - CRYPTO 2006. XIII, 621 pages. 2006.

Vol. 4116: R. De Prisco, M. Yung (Eds.), Security and Cryptography for Networks. XI, 366 pages. 2006.

Vol. 4107: G. Di Crescenzo, A. Rubin (Eds.), Financial Cryptography and Data Security. XI, 327 pages. 2006.

Vol. 4083: S. Fischer-Hübner, S. Furnell, C. Lambrinoudakis (Eds.), Trust and Privacy in Digital Business. XIII, 243 pages. 2006.

Vol. 4064: R. Büschkes, P. Laskov (Eds.), Detection of Intrusions and Malware & Vulnerability Assessment. X, 195 pages. 2006.

Vol. 4058: L.M. Batten, R. Safavi-Naini (Eds.), Information Security and Privacy. XII, 446 pages. 2006.

Vol. 4047: M.J.B. Robshaw (Ed.), Fast Software Encryption. XI, 434 pages. 2006.

Vol. 4043: A.S. Atzeni, A. Lioy (Eds.), Public Key Infrastructure. XI, 261 pages. 2006.

Vol. 4004: S. Vaudenay (Ed.), Advances in Cryptology - EUROCRYPT 2006. XIV, 613 pages. 2006.

Vol. 3995: G. Müller (Ed.), Emerging Trends in Information and Communication Security. XX, 524 pages. 2006.

Vol. 3989: J. Zhou, M. Yung, F. Bao (Eds.), Applied Cryptography and Network Security. XIV, 488 pages. 2006.

Vol. 3969: Ø. Ytrehus (Ed.), Coding and Cryptography. XI, 443 pages. 2006.

Vol. 3958: M. Yung, Y. Dodis, A. Kiayias, T.G. Malkin (Eds.), Public Key Cryptography - PKC 2006. XIV, 543 pages. 2006.

Vol. 3957: B. Christianson, B. Crispo, J.A. Malcolm, M. Roe (Eds.), Security Protocols. IX, 325 pages. 2006.

Vol. 3956: G. Barthe, B. Grégoire, M. Huisman, J.-L. Lanet (Eds.), Construction and Analysis of Safe, Secure, and Interoperable Smart Devices. IX, 175 pages. 2006.

Vol. 3935: D.H. Won, S. Kim (Eds.), Information Security and Cryptology - ICISC 2005. XIV, 458 pages. 2006.

Vol. 3934: J.A. Clark, R.F. Paige, F.A.C. Polack, P.J. Brooke (Eds.), Security in Pervasive Computing. X, 243 pages. 2006.

Vol. 3928: J. Domingo-Ferrer, J. Posegga, D. Schreckling (Eds.), Smart Card Research and Advanced Applications. XI, 359 pages. 2006.

Vol. 3919: R. Safavi-Naini, M. Yung (Eds.), Digital Rights Management. XI, 357 pages. 2006.

Vol. 3903: K. Chen, R. Deng, X. Lai, J. Zhou (Eds.), Information Security Practice and Experience. XIV, 392 pages. 2006.

Vol. 3897: B. Preneel, S. Tavares (Eds.), Selected Areas in Cryptography. XI, 371 pages. 2006.

Vol. 3876: S. Halevi, T. Rabin (Eds.), Theory of Cryptography. XI, 617 pages. 2006.

Vol. 3866: T. Dimitrakos, F. Martinelli, P.Y.A. Ryan, S. Schneider (Eds.), Formal Aspects in Security and Trust. X, 259 pages. 2006.

Vol. 3860: D. Pointcheval (Ed.), Topics in Cryptology – CT-RSA 2006. XI, 365 pages. 2006.

Vol. 3858: A. Valdes, D. Zamboni (Eds.), Recent Advances in Intrusion Detection. X, 351 pages. 2006.

Vol. 3856: G. Danezis, D. Martin (Eds.), Privacy Enhancing Technologies. VIII, 273 pages. 2006.

Vol. 3786: J.-S. Song, T. Kwon, M. Yung (Eds.), Information Security Applications. XI, 378 pages. 2006.

Vol. 3108: H. Wang, J. Pieprzyk, V. Varadharajan (Eds.), Information Security and Privacy. XII, 494 pages. 2004.

Vol. 2951: M. Naor (Ed.), Theory of Cryptography. XI, 523 pages. 2004.

Vol. 2742: R.N. Wright (Ed.), Financial Cryptography. VIII, 321 pages. 2003.

Lecture Notes in Computer Science

Sublibrary 4: Security and Cryptology